One-Third of a
NATION
African American Perspectives

N One-Third of a NATION

African American Perspectives

Selected Essays from a 1989 Howard
University Conference on the Status and
Future of African Americans

EDITED BY

Ura Jean Oyemade Bailey

AND

Lorenzo Morris

HOWARD UNIVERSITY PRESS
Washington, D.C.

Howard University Press, Washington, DC 20059

Manufactured in the United States of America

This book is printed on acid-free paper.

10 9 8 7 6 5 4 3 2 1

Library of Congress Cataloging-in-Publication Data

One-Third of a Nation: African American Perspectives / edited by Ura
Jean Oyemade Bailey and Lorenzo Morris.
    p. cm.
  Includes bibliographical references and index.
  ISBN 0-88258-170-8 (alk. paper)
  1. African-Americans-Social conditions-1975-Congresses.
2. African-Americans-Social conditions-1975-Forecasting-Congresses.
3. United States-Race relations-Congresses. 4. United States-Race
Relations-Forecasting-Congresses. I. Bailey, Ura Jean Oyemade. Morris,
Lorenzo, 1946- .
E185.86.O54   2001
305.896′073-dc21

                                                    99-034930 CIP

DEDICATION

The Editors wish to dedicate this publication to the following individuals, all of whom served as unwavering sources of strength and encouragement throughout the project: Johnella Banks, *Chair, African American Family Life Committee*; Paula Jewell, *Co-Chair, Housing Committee*; Leroy Wells, Jr., *Chair, Budget Committee*; James A. Bayton, *Chair, Racism and Race Relations Committee*; and Edwin Gordon,* *Director, Howard University Press.*

---

*Mr. Gordon was deceased by the date of this book's publication.

CONTENTS

A *Race Relations*

B *African American Family Life*

C The Role of Organized Religion

D Education, Science, and Technology

E

Media, Communications, and Culture

TABLES AND FIGURES

FOREWORD

Dr. James E. Cheek
Chairman, Advisory Board, One-Third of a Nation Task Force
President Emeritus, Howard University

One of the major problems facing American society in the last decade of the twentieth century is the fair and equitable distribution of goods and services. This problem has major bearing upon the quality of life for all citizens living in a democratic society.

The concept of freedom is an important tenet in American life, but the harsh realities of modern life reveal that there are large numbers of individuals who, for various reasons, do not share in the bountiful distribution of goods and services that one expects to find in what history tells us is the richest nation in the world.

Twentieth century history also reveals that the question of what to do, and perhaps more significantly, how to solve the wrenching problems of education, social justice, economic deprivation, science and technology, inadequate health care, and general feelings of despair that impinge upon the lives of the private and public sectors. *There is an overriding moral imperative for Howard University to exercise leadership and the liberating force of bold stewardship.* It is in this light that we are offering task force papers on these critical areas of concern.

Howard University is a microcosm of the democratic ideal; therefore, its very existence and continued definition depend on the dynamics of diverse people and ideas. In the long run, the University serves as a crucible to formulate and bring creative and imaginative processes to bear on the problems and issues that threaten the quality of life for this and succeeding generations.

Historically, Howard has always been a catalyst for action, and since its founding in 1867, the University has exercised, with courage, compassion, and candor, initiative for change in society. It is a commitment that few universities in this nation are willing or able to make.

We must, therefore, assert and reaffirm the inherent concept of humanity. Although the past is irrevocable, the future must offer hope. It is in this hope that we place our trust. Given the rich resources of minds that are here at Howard, we accept the challenges of the present day.

For all of us who have been brought to this time and to this place, the necessity of leadership and of urgent action is involved. Our very survival calls out for a new sense of direction.

When the University stresses the relevance of knowledge, it means something very specific: an educational process that is not only enlightening, but one that leads to performance and personal fulfillment; one that emphasizes not only self-advancement but public duty.

Howard University provides us all with the setting to direct our energies, our talents, and our efforts ever more vigorously and courageously to affirm our heritage. No institution of higher learning exists apart from the vicissitudes of human affairs, and no college or university can ever hope to thrive without involvement and commitment to the liberation of the mind and of the spirit.

Our history is replete with accounts of those who, though oppressed, though physically confined, exercised the freedoms of mind and spirit. Henry David Thoreau, nineteenth century author of *Civil Disobedience*, said to his jailers, "Although you have jailed my body, my mind is still free." Frederick Douglass, ardent leader in the anti-slavery movement, wrote, "The silver trump of freedom has roused my soul to eternal wakefulness."

We must devote our energies and our efforts to strengthening our institutions, and to that end we must carry on the task which is our obligation and our responsibility. These are the challenges, and until every individual in our society possesses the idea that hopes can be fashioned into realities, we cannot and will not rest.

If Howard is to meet the unrelenting demands of its mission, it must be a catalyst for freedom. Thus, we are dedicated to the advancement of knowledge and the formation of tomorrow's leaders, who will contribute to the community, to the nation, and to the world.

PREFACE

Taft H. Broome, Jr.
Chair, Howard University Faculty Senate 1988–1992

T he call rang out from the Hudson Institute in June of 1987 in its
Workforce 2000 and again from the American Council on Education and the Education Commission of the States in May of 1988 in
their report *One-Third of a Nation*. The call rang out a vision of a
twenty-first century United States of America, whose workforce and
school-age populations would consist in one-third part of minority
groups. The call was for better readiness of these groups to assume
greater responsibilities for America's future.

The most significant response to this call came in November of 1989
from Howard University in its conference, *One-Third of a Nation:
African American Perspectives*.

More than 350 presenters were gathered together in answer to the
call. They came from academia, government, grass-roots organizations, et al. Six presidents of historically black colleges and universities
gathered together in one room. Governor Bill Clinton gave the keynote
address, and Jesse Jackson, Hon. Parren Mitchell, Hon. Bill Gray,
Hon. Mervyn Dymally, and Hon. Ron Dellums set forth great challenges to all Americans.

Faculty came from Florida A&M University and from Stanford University; from political science, theology, and engineering. They transcended the boundaries of their particular learned disciplines for the interdisciplinary pursuit of the high ground provided by the call. And they presented and debated; they planned and, thereafter, acted. These proceedings document these challenges, ideas, debates, and plans.

At no time are these proceedings more urgently needed than today because they were made before the fall of the Berlin Wall and the collapse of the Soviet Union. The urgency is to use these proceedings to invest in Americans for stewardship of the American future, rather than rely on talent ready-made abroad.

Herein lies a blueprint for the future, one grounded on all that is good in the African American experience. It is a blueprint for all that can be good in the American experience.

ACKNOWLEDGMENTS

This publication is based on the proceedings of a national conference on the status and future of African Americans, titled "One-Third of a Nation: African American Perspectives," that was convened at Howard University, November 8–12, 1989, and chaired by Ura Jean Oyemade Bailey and Lorenzo Morris.

The editors would like to extend sincere thanks to the members of the National Advisory Board to the One-Third of a Nation Task Force chaired by Dr. James E. Cheek, President Emeritus of Howard University. Board members included Ms. Yvonne Brathwaite Burke, Dr. Bernard Watson, Mrs. Barbara Proctor, Dr. Jewell Plummer Cobb, Ms. Hannah D. Atkins, Mr. William E. Phillips, Mr. Robert B. Washington, Dr. Blenda Wilson, Mr. LeBaron Taylor, Mrs. Eleanor Holmes Norton, and Ms. Linda Pickett.

Sincere thanks are also extended to the Issue Area Committee Chairs of the Task Force on One-Third of a Nation: Ralph Gomes, *Voting and Political Participation*; Wendell Hill, Jr., Gloria Nichols and Ernest Quimby, *Substance Abuse*; Walter Hill, *Immigration and Foreign Policy*; Thomas Groce and Ralph Gomes, *Employment and Labor*; Portia Shields and Paul-Albert Emoungu, *Education*; Alvis Adair and Cheryl Sanders, *Role of Religious Institutions*; Elizabeth Brabble and Raphael Thelwell, *Economic Development and Empowerment*; M. Lucius Walker, Jr., and Jesse Nicholson, *Science and Technology*; Johnella Banks and James Craigen, *African American Family Life*; Dorothy Bryan and Paula Jewell, *Housing*; Marian Gray

Secundy and Robert Murray, *Health*; Melbourne Cummings, Jannette Dates, and Jeff Donaldson, *Media, Communication, Art, and Culture*; Elias Blake, Jr., *Historically Black Colleges and Universities*; Richard P. Thornell, *Law and Equality*; and James A. Bayton, *Racism and Race Relations*.

Additional acknowledgments and a note of gratitude for their contributions, helpful suggestions, technical guidance, inspiration, and expert advice throughout this project are extended to the Operations Committee Chairs: Leroy Wells, Betty Brabble, Willie Smith, Genna Rae McNeil, Marion G. Secundy, Jeff Donaldson, Betty Bennett, Bernard Moon, Morris Hawkins, and Carol J. Smith; staff of the One-Third of a Nation Task Force; the Officers of the Senate: Taft H. Broome, Robert Murray, and Beatrice Adderley-Kelly; and Howard University faculty who served as members of the Task Force.

INTRODUCTION

Lorenzo Morris

A quarter of a century after the passage of the Voting Rights Act, more than a century since the establishment of most black colleges, and a century and a half after the earliest national conference of black leaders, no single conference of African American scholars addressing the full range of public policy issues has ever been held. Before now, no coherent national examination of the major national problems and opportunities affecting minorities had been solicited from the analytical perspectives of the academic community. No traditionally black institution had ever mustered the resources to provide an opportunity for a diverse representation of scholars and policy analysts, in fields from the physical sciences to the humanities, to come together to provide collective prescriptions for our national ills. Here was a long-avoided challenge, to which the One-Third of a Nation Task Force intended to respond. The task force was created by Howard University faculty in order to transcend the boundaries between public policy and scholarship, between black institutional research and program development, and between public officials and private-sector leadership concerned with minority issues.

In addition, the task force was created to overcome the boundaries of disciplinary lines in the examination of complex social problems so that researchers could work together more easily on problems that clearly overlap the lines between disciplines. Some interdisciplinary groups, research groups, and policy centers, from as far back as the 1940s Gunnar Myrdal project to the recent National Research Council study, have sought to do a comprehensive assessment of social and economic problems. These studies were conducted, however, with no primary concern for African American perspectives in the orientation of the research. Other politically focused organizations, including the National Urban League and the Joint Center for Political and Economic Studies, have exposed policy issues to an African American critique, but their work has been oriented more toward immediate legislative and policy issues than toward long-term analysis of diverse issues such as those involving science policy, ethics, and educational administration. As a consequence, public policy analysis and the basic research on which it should be built have not been developed with consistent African American input.

In 1989, the Howard University faculty took the extraordinary step of making a collective effort, through the University Senate, of trying to bring newer, stronger scholarly voices into the policy development process. Of course, department-wide and even school-wide research and policy-analysis programs had occurred fairly frequently at Howard, but a multidisciplinary effort covering most of the seventeen schools and colleges had not been created recently, perhaps not since Nobel laureate Ralph Bunche, then a political science professor, brought together a multidisciplinary policy group in the 1940s. Only now, with the substantial support of the University's administration, could the faculty form the special One-Third of a Nation Task Force, named to represent the scope of its members' major concerns. The One-Third of a Nation Task Force began with the goals and unresolved issues on the agenda of African American leaders and researchers as a base for determining the range of the group's policy interests. It then expanded those interests to include the shared concerns of other American minority groups so that ultimately the one-third of the national population that Hispanic, Asian, and African Americans would soon constitute came to prescribe the field of interest. The defining focus of the task force, however, remained, as the title of its major conference indicates, African American perspectives.

The opening session of the conference was inspiring though inauspicious, as scholarly programs often are. In fact, the choice for a main speaker at the opening ceremony was truly inspired, even if unrecognized at the time, because the speaker, Governor Bill Clinton of Arkansas, was soon to acquire the Country's preeminent policymaking position. The program began on a cool November morning with scarcely a hundred people assembled in Howard University's principal auditorium to launch the largest policy-oriented interdisciplinary conference in the history of black higher education. The audience steadily swelled in enthusiasm and in size as the compelling presentation of the main speaker, then the head of the National Association of Governors' task force on education, made his remarks. Of course, no one knew at the time, though some suspected, that Clinton would become president. At that moment, however, he had to address the nation's need for the effective education and inclusion of the one-third of the nation that would be critical to his election and to the future of the nation.

The idea for the conference was itself an exceptional departure from the normal course of academic interaction at Howard. It grew out of a multidisciplinary faculty retreat for which the agenda was no less global than the range of societal problems for which basic research was needed. What was particularly remarkable about this retreat was that it was a declaration of socially conscious faculty engagement and a rejection of the ivory-tower aloofness initiated by the representative faculty association. In the course of two-and-a-half very long days, an overwhelming consensus developed among engineers, social scientists, lawyers, physicians, and many others: that black colleges had a special social responsibility that scholarship in isolation could not satisfy. Howard University, it was agreed, was uniquely situated in terms of timing, location, and resources to take the lead in meeting that responsibility.

The timing of the conference seemed right because black and minority issues had slipped from public focus, while income, housing, and educational inequalities had sharply increased. A tangible but unheralded deterioration in the status of most blacks was occurring in nearly all areas. In fact, the relative successes of black professionals had effectively obscured the substantial decline in life chances for most African Americans.

The resources for the conference were adequate because the faculty and the president, James Cheek, had made special commitments of time and funding. Perhaps more important, there was a nationally enthusiastic response from leaders in all areas of politics, business, labor, education, and social services to the invitation to participate. For most leaders, it was seen as a rare chance to reach beyond the confines of their offices and to reflect on larger issues while retaining a concern for practical relevance.

One factor in Howard's uniqueness, and in the responsiveness to it of national leaders, is the University's proximity to the seat of national power. Along with that proximity comes a tradition of politically involved faculty who could easily guide any public policy analysis. Yet, the first issue chosen as a focus involved the rights and mechanics of electoral participation rather than its benefits—policy input rather than output. An agenda of issues in political participation and voting rights was developed by a small faculty group led by Ralph Gomes and Linda F. Williams. In its bipolar focus, the group was concerned, first, with the basic right to participate in government through the reform of voting rights procedures and enforcement and, second, with the understanding of the subtle constraints on and impediments to effective participation by minorities resulting from economic barriers and interest group practices.

The approach to this and other issue areas was first to assess the field, with its problems and established practices and innovative solutions. Second, the analysts were expected to consider the available policy options. Finally, they were expected to make recommendations. For these purposes, the planning committee sought to identify and invite the areas' leading analysts, practioners, and activists. The range of their analysis is best summarized in the introductions to each of the thirteen sections of this book. The following observations, by committee, reflect the policy options they explored, while the conclusions of each volume indicate their collective recommendations. Note that the discussions in these issue areas are based loosely on the preliminary reports of issue area chairs prepared in 1990.

VOTING AND POLITICAL PARTICIPATION
Chairs: Ralph Gomes and Linda F. Williams

Problems and Issues

Political participation has been studied as the product of several individual activities, including voting, campaigning, and lobbying, but the relative and collective effectiveness of it has not been adequately studied. The extensive economic inequality that underlines and reinforces all forms of unequal political participation has also been recognized, but its effects, both direct and indirect, have not been assessed. The corresponding complexities of racial and class inequality that go beyond direct discrimination have similarly been underestimated and often overlooked. As a consequence, the potential effectiveness of African American and low-income-group participation in electoral and informal politics has been substantially diminished.

While economic inequality has steadily become a more discernible part of racial inequality, continuing voting rights violations and inadequate enforcement mechanisms are also substantial problems. Particularly at times of redistricting, the absence of a clear criterion for court recognition of adequately representative black voting districts weakens black political organizing. In addition, de facto segregation impedes black political campaigns by depriving potential candidates of access to established political party leadership. Similarly, the continuing inequity of campaign finance turns questions of economic inequality into ones of racial inequality. In both cases, long-established barriers to open political competition take on added dimensions of inequality.

Policy Options

The chances for improving minority group representation in elected office and for expanding the influence of these groups' political participation depend as much on the private initiatives of the various groups as on public support. Realistic policy options, however, meaning choices available for the public sector, require legislative and administrative action. Private associations and community groups must be organized in the black community, as in other minority communities, to respond to election law reform, but reforms must be initiated and implemented at the federal level. Proposed reforms of voter registration, for example, can substantially promote black voter turnout, but only in the context of community-based mobilization. Similarly, campaign finance reform should help new black candidates, as well as increase black and low-income-group influence over all candidates, but only when additional spending controls are imposed. Whatever policy choices are made, they should recognize the need for reform of the process.

EDUCATION
Chairs: Portia Shields and Paul Emoungu

Problems and Issues

In a society of unequal groups, unequal educational experiences are, of course, understandable. Racial inequality in educational performance, except for the lingering effects of legal segregation, is therefore seen as the de facto effect of racial inequality surrounding the school system. Schools attribute their faults to the environment of disadvantaged students, poor infant care, deteriorated neighborhoods, and other ghetto conditions. Current research, however, demonstrates that schooling and its administration and pedagogy make major differences in student outcomes. Research on "effective" schools shows that these schools significantly influence black and other minority student outcomes. Often, however, the attention of educators has been distracted by an overemphasis on standardized testing, the perennial albatross of black education. The testing of students, though needed, should not be pursued in the absence of testing of the educational system and teaching methods. The relevance of teaching methods and testing to black community needs must be assured.

Both the substantive content of the curriculum and the structure of the schools should be examined for their adaptation to the targeted community. Among other things, the pedagogical potential of Afrocentric education has yet to be fully explored. Appropriate educational techniques still need to be adapted. The difficulty turning education policy into effective school reform is aggravated by persistent conflict among policymakers and educators over several major issues.

Primary among these issues is disagreement over the roles of the public and private sectors in fulfilling the national obligation to ensure universal access to education. The conflict has recently been expressed in the debate over school choice, a debate intensified by President Bush's desire to subsidize the parents' choice of private schooling with public funds. The argument was a direct outgrowth of the voucher proposals of the Reagan administration. More recent proposals tend to focus on choices among public schools, but the proposals, old and new, all harken back to the old issue of desegregation. The choice idea was instigated largely by people seeking to escape public school desegregation while retaining the benefits of public subsidy.

Accompanying that continuing issue is a more fundamental issue about racial group identity and responsibility in schooling. Specifically, who are the most appropriate teachers of African Americans and how should they be trained? First, the numbers and advancement of African Americans as teachers seem to be seriously threatened by controversial professional and merit standards. Second, the quality and effectiveness of the education these teachers provide have been steadily restricted ever since desegregation began in earnest. Third, the value of an educational process in which awareness of racial factors plays a significant part in teaching and learning has been substantially underestimated.

Policy Options

Because education policy debates have been animated by attempts to redefine the mutual relationship of the public and private sectors, reform prospectus for the future should probably take into account such possibilities for redefinition. Still, the importance of the other issues that surround these debates needs to be fully appreciated. Policy reform should, for example, fully assess the impact of private-sector education on African Americans. Similarly, the effectiveness of public schools should be the focus not only of private alternatives but also of restructuring options. For example, creative uses of testing can serve to improve schooling and the support for teachers and students. Moreover, there should be a national recognition throughout the processes of deciding education funding of the social costs of inadequate education resources. In other words, education support should be assessed in relation to the national needs that are served by the structure of schooling as well as by the educated product of the schools.

SCIENCE AND TECHNOLOGY
Chairs: Lucius Walker and Jesse Nicholson with Melvin Thompson

Problems and Issues

The once-popular saying that a "rising tide lifts all boats" is often presented as the metaphorical model to justify the pursuit of general economic prosperity as a solution to the problems of the disadvan-taged. The saying lost its popularity as the recognition spread that leaky or unstable boats, meaning the really disadvantaged, would sink in a rising tide. In contrast, there is a persistent myth that high tech-nology and advanced science benefit all Americans fairly equally. Yet, in fact, the most formidable challenge to African American efforts to bridge the gaps of racial inequality comes from unequal access to the tools, skills, and benefits of modern science. It is rather the prospect of an emerging class of the technologically illiterate that is likely to heighten race/class inequality. The underrepresentation of African Americans in all professions is probably most serious in science-related areas. What is worse, the trends in higher education in no way suggest that the situation can be reversed without major intervention.

This intervention should begin in the education system before the major fields of specialization are selected and even before college. Few African Americans enroll in advanced mathematics and science courses in high school. As a consequence, especially low performance levels on science and math placement tests put these students at a greater disadvantage in attempting to pursue science-related college majors. Even before the science majors can be chosen, poor test per-formance on the SAT and ACT examinations generally means that the range, quality, and financial support of the colleges that these students may attend is severely restricted. Yet, the poor performance can be traced, not only to misdirection but also to inner-city schools that are especially weak in the science preparation available to students.

On the college level, traditionally black institutions, which cur-rently enroll only 20 percent of all black college students, produce a disproportionately high number (a majority in some fields) of science and engineering degree recipients. Still, the number and proportion of African Americans earning doctoral degrees in science and engineer-ing has grown only very slowly, and in some fields it has declined. On the other hand, the employment opportunities for black professionals with degrees in these fields are substantial. The market for the tech-nologically skilled has been so strong that the employment opportunities and income of African Americans, once they have started their careers, closely parallels that of all other Americans.

Policy Options

An essential focus of any science and technology policy concerned with African Americans must be educational mobility and access. The school system and the college admissions and retention programs have not adequately addressed the special problems of science and engineering majors. Selective educational programs should be directed toward young African Americans who are potentially attracted to these fields. In addition to education, science-related employment opportunities should be made accessible and promoted in relation to their utility for reducing the clear underrepresentation of African Americans.

MEDIA AND COMMUNICATIONS
Chairs: Melbourne Cummings and Janette Dates

Problems and Issues

As in nearly all policy areas, whether education, electoral politics, or science and technology, the media and mass communication fields suffer from a gross underrepresentation of black professionals. Unlike these other areas, however, the blatant exclusion of African Americans from the media has been widespread and persistent. Well after the Civil Rights movement had peaked, and after the violent racial confrontations of the late 1960s had forced national recognition of racial inequality, African Americans were still only 1 percent of the country's working journalists in the early 1970s. As the 1990s arrived, only 4 percent of the nation's newspaper reporters were African American.

Perhaps more important than the underrepresentation of African Americans in the media is the substantial disregard for and disinterest in the informational and cultural demands of these consumers. What do black communities seek in terms of communications? What do their residents need and want to stay informed about? The development of an "audience model" that is responsive to the black community's interests and preferences would long ago have been generated by a nondiscriminatory media market.

On the basis of better analyses of media use patterns by African Americans, a better assessment of the behavioral impact of the media on these consumers could be made. Such assessments are particularly important for African American children, who are among the most frequent viewers of television. The recent rise in urban violence among teenagers apparently can be correlated with the glamorized portrayal of violence in the media. Moreover, popularized images of black community lifestyles on television and in the movies can readily feed the negative self-concepts and low self-esteem from which disruptive youth often suffer.

With the Reagan administration came a resurgent fascination with deregulation, which, given a lack of focused analysis, has negatively affected the treatment of minorities. The presumed greater freedom expected from deregulation has resulted in a narrower, less accessible communications industry. For example, initial cable television service arrived in minority communities slowly. Once it was put in place, the cost to low-income consumers was barely affordable. Again, the looseness of regulation has not resulted in the competitive service from which low-income consumers would benefit.

Policy Options

Substantial progress could be made through private initiative in the mass media with little or no government regulation. The development of media production guidelines that are sensitive and responsive to black audiences would be helpful and still consistent with good business. For the most part, however, some greater government regulation is needed to ensure equitable access to the mass media, including both network and cable television. Ownership and control of the industry have been so distorted by recent deregulation that a special public initiative is needed to promote the diversification of the industry. Along with other federal agencies, the Federal Communications Commission needs to reassert an orientation toward addressing identifiable public and community interests and away from giving priority to serving the industry's interests.

SUBSTANCE ABUSE PREVENTION
Chairs: Gloria Nicholson and Earnest Quimby

Problems and Issues

One of the things that the mass media regularly report from the black community is the prevalence of drug abuse. What is much less frequently reported is the depth of suffering and deprivation that poorer black neighborhoods endure as a consequence of the high levels of abuse. A subculture has grown up within these drug-infested communities and engulfed the creative spirit of the community activists in a struggle for stability and security rather than a focus on comprehensive growth and development. In many ways, the future of these communities, and especially that of the young, is being mortgaged to pay for a weakly controlled, steady stream of "controlled" substances into the black community.

The gradually aging national war on drugs has yet to generate the kind of fully funded nationwide programs or the legislation needed to implement effective programs of treatment, prevention, and correction of substance abuse. In addition, current research has been biased away from comprehensive analyses of the overall problem and evaluation of effective prevention and treatment programs. The extent and distribution of substance abuse around the country remains unclear. Rather, impressions and an emphasis on symptoms, as opposed to fundamental problems, tend to deform local and national public policy responses. In the black and Hispanic communities, in particular, public assessments of drug abuse often reflect stereotyped assumptions. There is, therefore, a special need for the development of data on the epidemiological, clinical, and sociological factors in minority community substance abuse.

Policy Options

Before there can be a clear solution, there must be a clear assessment of the problem. Through the overlapping use of local, state, and federal authority, some comprehensive sets of data on the extent of the abuse problem should be developed. To begin with, however, local and national service providers and legislators should be regularly exposed to the best research findings relevant to program implementation on substance abuse. This policy implies a special role for research and educational institutions. It also means that those institutions, including traditionally black colleges and community groups, that normally serve minority communities should be delegated special research and program implementation authority.

HEALTH
Chairs: Marian Gray Secundy and Robert Murray

Problems and Issues

Fortunately, the state of health of African Americans has improved considerably in the later part of the 20th century. Unfortunately, their health still lags behind that of white Americans, and this lag is especially wide and disadvantageous for black males. No doubt, the availability of public health assistance from Medicare and Medicaid has contributed to the gains, because 20 percent of African Americans under 65 years old have neither public nor private health insurance. Without these programs, or with major reductions in service, African Americans could lose a benefit comparable to a civil right: the right to basic health care services.

The deficiencies and racial inequities in health care are easily recognized, but forceful and effective demands for change have not been as evident outside the black community. Unless African Americans can make stronger and more effective demands for improvement, little improvement can be expected. Real shortages of black physicians, nurses, and other health care professionals have added to the difficulty of reducing the gap between white and black access to health care.

Along with the deficiencies in the health care system, a significant decline in the quality of life and the standard of living has meant a further deterioration in the state of black health. In the 1980s, the average black family saw its expendable real income erode. Poor families became relatively poorer. Private health insurance failed to expand its coverage to include the new working poor. For the urban poor, and especially poor children, the absence of private health care coverage is a common problem.

Policy Options

Although the challenge to policymakers is substantial, the problems are not difficult to understand. In the absence of private funding, some greater government intervention to ensure and provide health care access seems inevitable. That intervention will probably involve greater regulation of private associations, greater public funding of health care providers, or a combination of these two approaches. In any case, the only credible options include a greater federal role and responsibility.

Unfortunately, new public initiatives are likely to be resisted by political conservatives who view health care as one of the benefits the private sector rewards to the economically successful. Instead of linking good health care to wealth, there should be a clear national commitment to the position that it is the right of all citizens. That commitment should emphasize equity in access to services for all.

Beyond the simple expansion of access, there needs to be some reorientation. For all social groups, more emphasis on prevention and the promotion of good health is important. For low-income groups, including most African Americans, this emphasis is particularly important.

Traditionally black institutions need to take the lead in implementing these reforms. Their leadership may require the development of collaborative arrangements or coalitions of various groups or institutions in order to gain a greater benefit.

ECONOMIC DEVELOPMENT AND EMPOWERMENT
Chairs: Betty Brabble and Raphael Thelwell

Problems and Issues

A group of physicians working in one of Africa's poorest countries recently observed that good health is tied as much to wealth and education as to formal health care services. So much of a society's medical, social, and political stability is tied to its economic development that nearly all policy concerns eventually lead to the economy. For African Americans, it is no less true that poor health conditions, lack of political power, unemployment, and deteriorating neighborhoods are only as durable as the lack of economic development and empowerment.

The historical debate between Booker T. Washington and W. E. B. Du Bois over whether the economic or the formally political aspect of power is primary persists today. Current problems, however, make moot the earlier choice of whether to pursue independent black business development before or after civil rights and voting power were gained. Through regulations and program development, much of private small business is guided by public policy. Another portion of black business is influenced by government set-aside programs.

There are, of course, exceptional cases of corporate business success by independent black groups, but these successes serve to highlight the more typical cases. More prevalent are cases in which black businesses encounter discrimination in lending practices, contract competition, or related areas. Existing regulations against discrimination are not as effectively enforced as they should be.

In addition to combating discrimination in business, some black businesses need to relate to larger social changes. For example, among African Americans, as well as other Americans, women are playing increasingly pivotal roles in the economic sector. New business opportunities and access for women can also benefit the black community in general. For instance, a large percentage of female heads of households in the black community could benefit from child care services to complement their work or business-development schedules.

Policy Options

Along with other groups, African Americans in business would benefit from a more consistent coordination of monetary and fiscal policies by the federal government. Small business must be able to borrow money if stimulus programs are to have the desired effect. Ultimately, such access to investment capital will require effective monetary policy if money is to be made available. Replacing the Gramm-Rudman-Hollings bill for limiting the size of the federal deficit with more effective legislation is a reasonable goal.

In areas of social welfare as well, black businesses could benefit from policies designed to help labor and small business. An improved urban transit system, for example, would facilitate the movement of workers in labor-intensive developing businesses. Child care would also help black women in business just as national health care support would help new entrepreneurs.

EMPLOYMENT AND LABOR
Chairs: Thomas Groce and Ralph Gomes

Problems and Issues

Employment opportunities for minorities are fast becoming a problem of national economic development rather than simply one of equity. Underemployment of minorities represents the underutilization of an essential national resource for which the nation's economy suffers. As the congressional study *Workforce 2000* observes, a third of the nation's workforce will soon consist of Hispanic, Asian, and African American labor. To sustain an annual unemployment rate of 14 percent, the official black rate of unemployment, rather than 7 percent or less, would mean turning the American dream into a perpetual economic depression. Yet, African Americans have endured this condition almost without relief in the last decade.

As the nature of the demand for labor changes, moving increasingly toward technological functions that require higher levels of training and skill development, American labor confronts a major new challenge. African Americans are at a particular disadvantage in meeting the technological challenge. The risks of structural unemployment, however, are only as great as government's failure to provide for structural transition. Minority-group American labor is trapped primarily by inadequate education, lack of job training and retraining, relocation constraints, and, of course, slow economic development. Government—federal, state, and local—is uniquely positioned to provide the needed education and training. Similarly, some public sector support for labor relocation and retraining is essential to the pursuit of changing markets.

Even with government intervention for disadvantaged labor groups in general, some racially focused aspects of job discrimination against African Americans remain. While the discrimination takes a more subtle form than traditionally adjudicated under Title VII for the Civil Rights Act, the evidence of discrimination in overall income and status seems indisputable.

Policy Options

Just as much of our nation's infrastructure needs rebuilding, so can our nation's labor supply be rebuilt. The labor pool is already developing a more ethnically and racially diverse composition. Programs that help the underprepared job seekers, black and white, should be pursued as a matter of development and equity.

With regard to equity, the absence of African Americans in the upper echelons of the corporate world obviously cannot be attributed to fair competition. Rather, the logical extension of fair employment practices would suggest more of an effort to encourage minority access to managerial positions. Again, the inspiration cannot be left exclusively to the private sector, though this sector should certainly be called on for program development.

Similarly, both the public and private sectors have a stake in the adaptation, training, and relocation of labor to address technological transformation. The mutual public/private support of these programs can be cost effective.

HOUSING
Chairs: Dorothy Bryan, Jerome Smith, and Paula Jewell

Problems and Issues

Together with our nation's deteriorating infrastructure of public roads, bridges, and so on is a steadily declining housing stock. Along with the declining housing stock has come a stubbornly increasing level of unemployment that could be well served by more housing construction. Yet, the two do not come together because neither government nor private business has the capital to put into these long-term investments. Perhaps the one place where these two errant economic factors can be brought into productive harmony is in the area of housing construction and rehabilitation.

As the population has grown, the housing supply has persistently lagged behind it to the extent that only the relatively well-off among young families can afford to buy new homes. Housing affordability, meaning housing that costs less than 30 percent of household income, has declined rapidly in the last decade. The proportion of black families able to afford adequate housing dropped 10 percent in 1987 from its 1976 level of 73 percent. Young middle-income families by the year 2000 will have great difficulty purchasing a private home at market loan rates without some redirection of public policy.

Low-income families are increasingly unable to afford rents in the private sector and are unable to find places in public housing. The recent proposals for approaches to subsidized housing, which would turn public housing over to low-income families for home ownership, fail to consider realistically the basic income requirements of ownership. More than a marginal one-time subsidy is needed for poor families to buy and maintain a home. In fact, housing subsidies are needed by the lower middle class as well.

In order to limit market distortions where housing subsidies are expanded, some promotion of the housing supply needs to come from the public sector. The federal role in low-income housing dropped substantially during the Reagan administration. A return to some extent, therefore, to production incentives such as those generated under the New Deal programs is worth considering. Whatever the program, however, a visible public role in the housing market will be necessary to ensure equitable access for African Americans. As recent media disclosures of mortgage and rental discrimination should remind us, African Americans still do not have nearly the same access to housing as do most other Americans. In fact, there are really two housing markets, to paraphrase the Kerner report, one white, one black, separate and unequal.

Although the right to decent housing is not written in the national Constitution, it is inscribed in the national consciousness, in our image of ourselves. As homelessness and inadequate housing proliferate, our national sense of self, our national culture, is eroded. All groups must have open and reasonable access to private and public housing in order to satisfy the spirit of the laws expressed in the 1968 Civil Rights Act and implied long ago in the 1949 Housing Act.

Policy Options

Where housing and rent subsidies are needed, they should be provided in varying forms at the state and local levels and with an increasing federal role. They should be made available to the extent that any basic necessity can be publicly funded. Thus, the possibility of making these subsidies entitlements for low-income families should be examined. At the same time, the gaps between income and housing affordability for middle-income families could be addressed through housing mortgage subsidies.

In order to boost the supply of low-income housing, public subsidies have frequently gone to private owners and developers of rental properties. A better approach would focus assistance on the nonprofit housing associations. Still, some policy-based recognition of the special difficulties faced by black families should be added. Along with other state and federal agencies, the Department of Housing and Urban Development should ensure compliance with fair housing laws. Housing access may be more unfair now in terms of race and class than it has been for a decade.

IMMIGRATION AND FOREIGN POLICY
Chair: Walter Hill

Problems and Issues

Few people would have thought at the planning stage of the One-Third of a Nation Task Force to put immigration and U.S. foreign policy together, but the nature of scholarship brought them together almost automatically. As it happened, the faculty and researchers who, by self-selection, choose to explore the one also choose to examine the other. While the research of most faculty focused on foreign policy, with only an emergent interest in immigration, immigration still had a commanding presence. Some of the researchers were initially interested more in immigration, but that interest was nourished by a foreign policy analysis background.

In both cases, the sights and news stories of new waves of desperate immigrants escaping oppression, fleeing starvation, or simply seeking new economic opportunities were hard to ignore. Especially for African Americans, the more recent images of oppressed people in the African diaspora struggling across closed borders to uncertain and unrewarding futures brought out a sense of special responsibility. At the same time, the potential impact of these and other immigrant groups on the economic status of African Americans, who have only begun to emerge from their discriminatory treatment, has moderated the sympathy and support that might otherwise have been expected.

The high levels of immigration projected by task force analysts through the 1990s do not seem to be abating. On the contrary, the highest levels of immigration around the world in this century were reached in the last decade. The new immigrants were largely fleeing the deprivations of the developing world in Central America and Asia. In the future, this collection will be substantially augmented by Eastern Europeans seeking greater opportunity and stability.

The decline of communism in Eastern Europe, beginning with the collapse of the Berlin Wall, has also transformed U.S. foreign policy. It has brought the world out of bipolar competition and into a multilateral framework. Although the failure of communist regimes has been dramatic, the ascendance of American capitalism has not been so dramatic; in fact, it has not really happened. The United States has become the only superpower, but it is far from becoming the singular focus of international economic development. From the restrictive markets in the European Community and in Japan to the weakness of the North American trade agreements, a major new approach to foreign policy has yet to emerge.

In contrast to the economically expanding roles envisioned for Europeans as immigrants, as evolving nations, or as economic alliances, the expectations for Africans are low, at best. While U.S. foreign policy is undergoing an uncertain transition everywhere, the only uncertainty for Africa is whether it will get any serious attention at all from the United States. Yet, for African Americans the continent of Africa and its national offspring are likely to remain the primary focus of their interests in U.S. foreign policy.

Policy Options

Of the range of issues in U.S. foreign policy and immigration that need serious attention, the issues concerned with Africa may be the most critical, but they are getting little attention from government. Too little attention is focused on the post-Cold War needs of African countries seeking both to overthrow postcolonial authorization regimes and to build viable economies. The United States should be more involved in economic support as well as in support for democratization in Africa.

Some reassessment of American spending for the maintenance of its military machine at the expense of domestic concerns is obviously called for. Not only would a redirection of federal spending affect domestic spending, it might also reduce hostility toward immigration by reducing fears of domestic job loss to foreign labor. Enthusiastic American support for short-term U.S. military interventions such as the Gulf War has always been mitigated by American fears of job loss. The link between these expenditures ought to be recognized in policy development.

Whether the focus is Europe, Africa, or the Caribbean, there should be more concern for the link between migration and U.S. foreign policy. Pressures on our borders, as well as displacement in unstable societies—Haiti, for example—are in some ways the consequences of American misjudgments. A concerted effort should be made to respond to the political or economic tragedies that may compel massive migration from developing countries before the crises emerge.

As Eastern Europe evolves, Americans need to be conscious of the opportunities for trade as well as for the expansion of competition. Europe contains more skilled labor and higher levels of labor productivity than Africa and is, therefore, seen as a more acceptable source of immigrants. Europe is also likely to see the United States as a competitive economic threat. The approach to Europe and related trading partners should be tempered by greater recourse to the developing world where such recourse is economically feasible.

HISTORICALLY BLACK COLLEGES AND UNIVERSITIES
Chair: Elias Blake, Jr.

Problems and Issues

In the aftermath of the formal desegregation of American higher education, it has been increasingly suggested that black institutions may be a thing of the past. Their right and reason for existence have been brought into question. Questions have been raised in both state legislatures and federal courts about the continuing value and viability of historically black colleges and universities (HBCUs). Yet, there can be no realistic doubt that these institutions are an integral part of the black community, of higher education, and, ultimately, of the nation's future. What the future may hold for HBCUs is unfortunately dimmed by misguided policies of desegregation that mistakenly sought to strengthen white, previously segregated institutions at the expense of the historically open black institutions. Implicitly, the label of "segregated" was thus appended to the victims rather than to the beneficiaries of racial inequality.

Beginning with the *Adams* cases in the early 1970s, the path of desegregation litigation began to turn away from the expansion of access to higher education and toward a redefinition of the racially identifiable structures in which public higher education occurs. By the end of the 1980s, challenges against state subsidies for unequal black institutions began to focus less on the sources and explanations for the inequality and more on the justification for maintaining racially identifiable institutions. Echoing the call for a color-blind society, the federal courts in the *Ayers* case (later, *U.S. v. Fordice* 1992) in Mississippi began to put a federal stamp of approval on the demolition of state-supported institutions that serve African Americans. Now, the concept of racial balance in school enrollments is being propelled across the South on the wings of the anticipated savings that are expected to result from the elimination of black schools.

Of the more than one hundred historically black colleges and nearly forty four-year public institutions, the only ones that are clearly safe in the near future are those detached from public funding. The threat to public funding, though stimulated in part by budget problems, is generated primarily by a concern for keeping institutional access and control in the hands of traditional leaders of education policy. Most of these traditional leaders, like their students, are not black.

In contrast, the defense of these institutions has hinged on their continuing provision of an educational service to black students and scholars that traditionally white institutions could not provide. The survival of these institutions may call for a more affirmative or offensive posture in which the culturally distinct functions of higher education in a racially bifurcated society are recognized as an essential social value. Education should no longer be idealized as culturally and racially neutral when that ideal has served largely to obscure continuing racial bias.

Whatever the outcome for black higher education, the effect on American society is critical. Outside of the family and the church, the black college has been, it is widely argued, the only stable institution in black society. The church, black or white, is constitutionally beyond government intervention. Higher education, when it positively favors African American traditions and interests, should not be punished for the hostility of the racially biased environment that these traditions and interests have sought to overcome.

Policy Options

First, the federal courts respond in large part to community and legislative support for educational institutions. Court demands for the removal of vestiges of segregation can be satisfied without removing the established benefits of the struggle to overcome segregated conditions, namely, the liberating benefit of HBCUs. A concerted legislative approach to redefining support for these institutions is therefore needed in every Southern state legislature.

Second, approaches to racial integration need to be promoted that hinge not on naive concepts of racial balance but rather on an understanding of full participation in the comprehensive institutional framework. African American access to the best available higher education must be recognized as a national virtue undiminished by its statistical racial context. In this sense, the preservation of those institutions with proven records of successfully serving African Americans should be a goal of public policy.

Third, the political, economic, and social leadership of the black community should consider how much of the community's current status and future are tied to the survival of these institutions. What are the realistic and reliable options for responding to the leadership needs of the black community without these institutions? There are possibilities, of course, but a responsible and reliable choice cannot bypass the mainstay of the black community that these institutions are and always have been.

AFRICAN AMERICAN FAMILY LIFE
Chairs: Johnella Banks and James Craigen

Problems and Issues

As one might well expect from the myriad of problems already discussed, as well as from recognized research, the bulk of the problems for African American life come not from the family itself but from the family's adverse social and political environment. The issue is not whether the family can adapt to urban pressures but whether urban adaptations in public policy are hostile to the survival of the black family.

While there has been increasing consciousness of the negative effects of racial discrimination on an individual's chances, there has been very little consciousness of the effects of persistent institutional racism on the family. Institutional racism includes a broad range of barriers to employment, housing, education, and so on that individuals are supposed to have a fair chance of overcoming. In fact, victims of this latent discrimination are not competing equally with others because the rules of competition contain built-in biases. The strain of the victims' failures and, more important, of their successes can damage the family relationship.

For example, persistent unemployment is stressful enough for any family, but structural unemployment stimulated by institutional racism can greatly restrict family adjustment options. Real opportunities and the expectations of employment possibilities can measurably affect a family's ability to overcome short-term unemployment. Weaker families are more vulnerable to drug abuse, divorce, and unhealthy lifestyles. Strong black families overcome these obstacles more readily than weak ones but still must face other problems.

Given their incomes and the fact that the working mother is nearly the norm, child care is critical for black families. The apparent proliferation of federal and state child care legislative proposals in the 1980s greatly overstates the availability of the service. For poor working mothers, it is still too costly or inaccessible.

Fortunately, many more of the problems attributed to the black family in recent years can be remedied by better employment, housing, and education than the 1980s reaction against the war on poverty would suggest. Class inequality is by all evidence a persistent part of racial inequality. Recent attempts to analytically separate the social impact of class and race have been unrealistic in their treatment of racial factors. The family is, after all, a complex institution vulnerable to the strains of individual inequality and to the cultural and social bias of the institutional racism that surrounds it.

Policy Options

For the African American family, the options available for public pol-icy are simple; briefly put, families need to explore them all. Basically, the African American family is sound and adaptable, but the adequate conditions for stability and security are not generally available. The range of conditions that threaten social life that were discussed in other policy areas must be addressed here as well: unemployment, housing, child care, and education, to name the major ones. What needs to be learned in this area is where the strengths of the family are and how they can be developed. Failed public policy of the 1980s and before has been excused on the basis of distorted critiques of African American family life. Public reinforcement of the African American community requires a recognition of the valuable role of the family.

CROSS-CUTTING CURRENTS OF RACE AND EQUALITY

Among the many lessons of this collection of studies is the realization that racial factors generate persistent and global differences in the life chances of Americans, but these differences appear less and less in iso-lation from other forms of inequality. Most racial inequalities, like most social differences to which we readily admit, appear to be polit-ically neutral or acceptable and, therefore, beyond the range of public policy. When these racial inequalities are combined with acceptable social inequalities and are magnified by them, it is more difficult to see and assess the inequality or injustice. Still more troublesome for pub-lic policy, it is difficult to design a policy because no one expects to uproot all forms of social inequality.

Instead, the special disadvantages experienced by African Americans in every policy area have been depreciated by the popular claims that the disparities result from a sociocultural maladjustment in the black community. In fact, research shows a relative absence of concerted public policy or private leadership in any of the areas discussed in this work. Where policy has been uniformly channeled toward meeting some of the 1980s' moderate preferences, programs have consistently reflected goals backed by little policy research. The research that has been used has virtually excluded African American perspectives.

In a special effort to understand the processes by which discrimination persists and is yet unrecognized in an egalitarian society, two special roundtable sessions were established. One session, under the direction of Professor James Bayton and called "Racism and Race Relations," explored the sociopsychological characteristics of current discriminatory behavior. The research, presented in the context of public policy, influenced the tenor of the conference papers as they were selected and edited for these volumes. Because of the unfortunate death of Professor Bayton, however, this research could not be published here.

The second roundtable was the "Law and Equality" session, chaired by Professor Richard Thornell. It examined the legal and enforcement issues surrounding civil rights across the board in recent years. As in the session on racism, the panelists found that progress in civil rights had come to a standstill. In large part, the complexities of interpretation in law, as in race relations, have made the uniform application of legal policy difficult. As a consequence, each policy area contains its own host of legal issues linked to its own civil rights regulations. The issues of law and equality are therefore increasingly defined by the policy areas in which they are to be applied. Direct discrimination persists, but the law must now deal with more substantive and subtle issues in the areas of regulation and program development.

The explicit focus here is African American perspectives on public policy and private leadership. Yet, we are interested in the contributions of all researchers, analysts, and political leaders to the assessment of these perspectives. These two volumes thus seek to present a fairly comprehensive review of issues affecting African Americans and all Americans as we approach the year 2000.

Race Relations | A

1 One-Third of a Nation: "Race and Racism"

LORENZO MORRIS

In the perennial American effort to understand and define race and racism, we have worked too hard to define racism and not hard enough to understand race. We take race for granted as a fact of birth that we reconfirm every time we look in the mirror. I know that I am black and you are white, or vice versa. Race is immutable; therefore, we could *not* redefine society's racial distribution. Conversely, we assume that racism involves a complex set of evolving social relations. Understanding this complexity requires a continual re-evaluation of our attitudes and intentions. The virtuous alternative to racism is left undefined and unclear, floating ambiguously between conscious "racelessness" (the denial of race) and "racial indifference" (race neutrality).

Racism simply consists of two extremes: At one extreme, the person denies by attitude or behavior the social significance of race; at the other, the person overemphasizes its social significance and sees race as a filter for all social relations. A more reasonable approach is to avoid extremes and to adhere to the center, where the person recognizes race as a distinct social entity. The difficulty is not in determining whether a group identity is "felt" but in defining the group—the race.

RACE

In effect, the mirror lies; it lets us repeat the biases of perception acquired through sustained habituation or socialization (Omi and Winant 1986, 60; Bayton 1989). Race is a social convention reinforced by the physical

| 1

symbol we see in the mirror. It is a product of ancient, aging social agreements on which we have built years of social habits (Gould 1981, 31–39). Race is more in the heads of its American observers than in their bodies. According to James Jones (1993) and Michael Blakey (1994), race is not biologically grounded. Yet the prevailing anthropological and biological opinions have not been able to convince race-sensitive Americans because such recognition upsets everyone's sense of identity.

The biological assumption of race is linked to other social conventions that we want to preserve. The individualist ethic implies that in a free society we can control our work and much of our environment unhampered by others. Furthermore, denying the biological assumption upsets our hope for egalitarian and racially indifferent standards by which each member of society can be measured. Finally, biological claims of race reinforce our claims of success, as well as our criticism of the irresponsibility and failure of others (Jones 1988, 117).

The social conventions tied to the easy recognition of race may still be valuable; they have made sense in the past. Inequalities of class and gender have been so widely accepted that race, by contrast, has been rather conspicuous. All race consciousness worth serious attention needs to be built on other forms of inequality such as class, culture, or ethnicity. Without them, race consciousness takes on the unstable rigidity of a dogma that marginalizes it or transforms it into a nationalist symbol. If race consciousness does not serve other social purposes, it will dissipate or harden into nationalist separation. Without egalitarian concerns, race consciousness may be linked to the Klan or tied to hostile separatist uprisings.

Race has also been a symbol of community and a focus of unity among each group of whites and blacks or other minorities. As more than a symbol, race has unified disparate people with conflicting material interests around a common racial group interest. For example, the self-protective struggles of poor and undereducated white urban opponents of busing in the 1970s in places like South Boston, where upward mobility for whites in local schools was no better than for African Americans, present a case of undefined common racial interests. The commonality and unifying capacity stem largely from ambiguity, which gives rise to submerged socioeconomic interests that are difficult to articulate apart from their racial packaging. What distinguishes race consciousness from racism is the singular focus on the unequal packaging of race.

RACISM

Simply put, racism consists first in denying race and second in confusing racial inequality with other inequalities. Such inequalities may be secured by hiding behind the protective cloak of racial inequality or by being promoted as the product of differences that have been magnified as inequalities. Such inequalities normally occur because they, along with gender differences, provide the easiest venues for all contestable inequalities to appear and survive in competitive society. For sustained differences of wealth, however, race historically provides the safer venue.

To be poor and white in American Society has historically expressed both deprivation and compensation. To be poor and black has historically implied deprivation and justification. For whites, deprivation has implied potential mobility and undefined resources for achievement or failure. For blacks, deprivation has implied both acceptance and accommodation—accommodation because for nearly everyone poverty seems a natural way of life, and acceptance because the criteria for upper mobility reside in an environment of deprivation. In either case, racially identifiable deprivation has been perceived as a lot better than being "poor" because the only comparison is "rich." After all, class consciousness in any form in America is socially unacceptable.

The denial of race in American culture is inextricably linked to individualism. The almighty "me" of Adam Smith, Max Weber, and others thrives in the collective presence of other self-satisfied individuals (Weber 1976). The independent, pioneering "me" that Americans value is threatened by any sense that the advantages popularly associated with white Americans should have anything to do with being white.

Understandably, the interdependent and interactive nature of human development must be recognized at some level by all open-minded Americans. With that recognition comes an awareness that individual success or failure is affected by "the group." More precisely, there are universalistic concepts of the group, just as there are of the individual. If being black sets a person back in schooling, employment, or elsewhere and if being white puts a person ahead, such effects are "automatically" neutral for anyone in either group. If the group label is important, then all members should be equally aware of it and capable of reacting to it. If the group label is unfair, then indifference or inaction is the fault of all who fail to react to it.

CHANGING CONTEXTS OF RACE AND RACISM

The violent racists of the 1960s and before, like the stereotyped Sheriff Bull Connor or the Klansmen, had a peculiar appeal to mainstream America because they made the real centers of power and the mainstream look virtuous. Violent racists could be cast by the media as archetypes of social rejects and enemies of society because their brutal domination over southern blacks made that dominance a more prominent group characteristic. Their brutal image further released other white Americans from a sense of racial community. In other words, the frontline enforcers of segregation during civil rights protests were perceived as motley collections of rednecks who were exercising their personal expressions of racism. Racism during the civil rights movement was, of course, relatively easy to define. It could be localized on the wrong side of desegregation. Equal opportunity, it was hoped, lay hidden beneath the race-conscious covers.

In the South, the transition to segregation from slavery was mediated by the short-lived integrationist advance known as Reconstruction (Woodward 1965). Yet the Northerners' need for post-war occupation of the conquered secessionist states made race a secondary interest to their political prerogatives. For moderate Republicans, who first supported and then lost interest in the freedmen, their level of race consciousness, more than their racial prejudice, changed. In the post-war South, the devastation of war and the ensuing social and political disorientation made race one of the few components of the old social structure on which a person could count (Franklin 1969, 300–36). As Reconstruction ended after 1877, Northerners' interest in racial matters declined. Whatever the causal relationship, the denial of race heralded the institutionalization of segregation. In case after case, federal courts announced that God (indirectly) and nature had provoked the racial division, while the state and government had remained innocent of racism. In the 1896 *Plessy v. Ferguson* decision, the Supreme Court warned that race was given by the natural order. Thus racial separation was largely beyond the state's control.

From the end of Reconstruction through the 1950s and the emergence of the civil rights movement, virtue, in contrast to racism, could be ensured by playing along with the established systems of gross racial inequality. The 1960s revolution was associated with legal progress in civil rights and was much more than a normal evolution of American race consciousness. The new liberal consciousness has persisted with declining enthusiasm for several decades largely because the changing socioeconomic and political environment has made race a declining focal point of controversy and stability—as in Reconstruction.

Brown v. Board of Education marked an important evolutionary step because it assigned public guilt and political culpability for the past. The Supreme Court recognized that "the hearts and minds" of young people separated by race could be and had been "harmed" through their race-conscious treatment by southern governments (Morris 1993, 22). Admittedly, the guilty parties in segregation were powerful public authorities acting outside legitimate governmental authority. The Supreme Court rejected the systematic roots found for segregation. Race thus remains in the implied language of the courts on the periphery of legitimate political consciousness (Morris, in this volume). Race, in both *Plessy* and *Brown*, is a politically awkward and inappropriate concept.

Compensatory Race Consciousness

The phase of national politics after the civil rights movement was marked by a compensatory notion of race consciousness. The 1965 presidential order calling for affirmative action grew out of a race-conscious mode, but its implementation seemed aimed toward race indifference. President Lyndon B. Johnson alluded to images of a road race in which black competitors needed special help to compete fairly because other racers had a head start. Johnson said, "You do not take a person who, for years, has been hobbled by chains and liberate him, bring him to the starting line of a race, and then say, 'You are free to compete with all the others,' and still believe that you have been completely fair" (Johnson 1965, 3). Special help was popularly translated into "special preference." Yet, it was not racial inequality that was to be compensated in existing public or private systems as much as it was the historical influences of past discrimination. Of course, no one assigned a termination date.

As affirmative action took root, however shallow, race itself faded into the background. Furthermore, the 1970s inclusion of women and minorities set in concrete the race indifference of affirmative action programs.

Guilty Race Consciousness and Institutional Racism

By the time reverse discrimination litigation began to bury affirmative action, the question of disadvantage for any socioeconomic group had not been forcefully raised. Judging from the controversial 1990s reverse discrimination cases in Texas (*Hopwood* 1996) and New Jersey schools, African Americans have returned to the center stage of affirmative action conflict. Only this time, they are being labeled as having received an unfair special advantage because of their race.

In the 1960s, Governor George Wallace stood in front of a public school door in Alabama and swore to block all black students from entering white schools—a behavior considered regressive. With time and political pressure, Governor Wallace moved away from the doors and pursued black voters in his re-election bid—a behavior considered progressive. As for the schools and educational progress, nothing was compelled to change. The institution of education, its authorities, and even its teachers remained unscathed by the presence or absence of "official" racism. What had changed was individual behavior conducted under the color of authority. The old laws were evidence of "individual racism" because they effectively "individualized" race as a social entity, while they deprived individuals of a claim to personal achievement (Jones 1988, 127). Obviously, the segregationist rules deprived African Americans of benefits, but those rules also deprived white Americans of the ability to hold up their successes and wealth as the uncontested product of individual efforts. Only a race-neutral, often called "color-blind," policy could legitimate the broad socioeconomic inequalities not tied to law (Barnett 1976).

President Bill Clinton's 1997 Race Initiative Advisory Board indicated its goal of going beyond individual racism so it could attack more complex barriers to race relations and could shore up waning support for affirmative action. Once we agree by law and practice that discrimination is illegal, the subject is tangible because race is observable around the victim of racism.

THE CULTURAL AMBIGUITY OF RACE

We have all shared equally in elevating the complexity of racism. Racism deserves substantial social attention primarily because of the moral (normative) aspect of guilt and innocence associated with it. Color-blindness is a misnomer because the attitude is really a color obsession. In his far-reaching intellectual exploration of the color line, W. E. B. Du Bois in *The Souls of Black Folk* identified characteristics in black and white experiences that could be used to define racial characteristics (Du Bois [1903] 1994, 115–26). The problem with his efforts was that the substance is less revealing than the process.

Race-related cultural elements have been readily accepted in religious practices and music because that recognition holds no social consequence beyond those already experienced. But advocates of "ebonics," as a black language linked to education, encountered unanticipated hostility because they underestimated the breadth of social consequences for their actions. To redefine the limits of standard English meant to define more narrowly the limits of teacher mobility and mainstream education (Smitherman 1986). The 1997 California debates on the issue show that the existence and content of black language lacked the institutional and political clout to make its analysis worth pursuing (Hoover 1997, 17, 34).

Although some political groups have hastened to celebrate the passing of discrimination, the inequality of racial groups remains undeniable.

CONCLUSION

Because there is currently no consensus, all that remains for the race conscious is to be open to sociocultural significance. Such openness is uncomfortable because awareness of racial differences is normally stimulated by other uncomfortable inequalities, which, of necessity, divide white Americans and thus make everyone more sensitive to his or her standing in the social hierarchy. In sum, this society seeks to preserve multiple hierarchies of inequality in areas such as schooling, employment, or housing. At the same time, it considers moving its traditional tenants off the bottom rungs of the social ladders. One serious problem is that the bottom rungs always remain occupied. The logical interplay of equal opportunity and American individualism is that when rewards are distributed, we all end up unequal—some rich, some poor, some with, and some without. The awkward accommodation that Americans make for that inequality of outcome is even more tenuous for those who find themselves labeled with the successful group and yet located with the unsuccessful.

REFERENCES

Barnett, M. 1976. A theoretical perspective on American racial public policy. In *Public policy for the black community*, eds. M. Barnett and J. A. Hefner. New York: Alfred.

Bayton, J. 1989. Unpublished comments in the "One-third of a Nation Conference" held at Howard University, Washington, DC.

Blakey, M. 1994. Passing the buck: Naturalism and individualism as anthropological expressions of Euro-American denial. In *Race*, eds. S. Gregory and R. Sanjek. New Brunswick: Rutgers University Press.

Du Bois, W. E. B. [1903] 1994. *The souls of black folk*. New York: Dover.

Franklin, J. H. 1969. *From slavery to freedom*. 3rd ed. New York: Random House.

Gould, S. J. 1981. *The mismeasure of man*. New York: Norton.

Hoover, M. R. 1997. Ebonics: Myths and realities. *Rethinking schools*. (Fall).

Hopwood v. Texas 78 F. 3rd 932 (1996).

Johnson, L. B. 1965. "To fulfill these rights." Commencement address delivered at Howard University (June 4). Washington, DC.

Jones, J. 1988. Racism in black and white. In *Eliminating racism*, eds. P. Katz and D. Taylor. New York: Plenum.

Morris, L. 1993. Race specificity in American law and public policy. *Harvard Journal of African American Public Policy* 2:11–32.

Omi, M., and H. Winant. 1986. *Racial formation in the United States: From the 1960s to the 1980s*. New York: Routledge and Kegan Paul.

Smitherman, G. 1986. *Talkin' and testifyin'*. Detroit: Wayne State University Press.

Weber, M. 1976. *The Protestant ethic and the spirit of capitalism*. New York: Scribner.

Woodward, C. V. 1966. *The strange career of Jim Crow*. 2nd ed. New York: Oxford University Press.

2 Beyond Moral Bankruptcy: Some Economic Costs of American Racism

BILLY J. TIDWELL

The question of the costs of racism has slowly but inexorably moved toward the center of public consciousness and concern. The reference here is not simply to the recognized human hardships the phenomenon visits upon its victims. Nor is it limited to the nebulous notion of moral degeneracy. The costs also include what the society has had to pay in social instability, the impairment of its capacity to produce and progress, and constraints on its role as a purveyor of democratic principles in the developing world. And, of course, there are the economic costs—the adverse effects of racism in dollar terms.

As the twenty-first century approaches, bringing new demands and challenges, it is essential that there be more public understanding and appreciation of the past, present, and future costs of racism. It is important that policymakers conduct more hard-nosed benefit-cost analyses of the problem to assess the best interest of the general welfare. For, under present conditions, the problem of racism goes well beyond the moral imperative to "do the right thing." It has become an urgent matter of national security. Consequently, we must decide as a nation whether we can continue to bear the costs. We must decide as a nation whether it is finally time to balance the ledger of racial justice.

Two considerations are key in this regard. First, the racial demography of the nation is changing rapidly, with African Americans and other minorities comprising a growing share of the total population. Between now and the year 2000, the African American population is expected to increase by 12.8 percent, compared to a 5.2 percent growth rate for whites.[1] Corresponding changes are occurring in the composition of the civilian labor force. By the year 2000, African Americans will account for 17.4 percent of all new workers, up from 15 percent in 1988. The proportion of white new workers is projected to decline by 7.5 percent during this period.[2]

Thus, African Americans could be the critical American human resources of the future. However, they must be prepared and allowed to contribute their talents, unencumbered by the race-based constraints on development and access that have been endemic to their experience in America. The cost of racism in this respect could quite literally bring the nation to the brink of bankruptcy as a competitor in the changing global marketplace.[3]

Second, the movement toward democratization in the former Soviet Union, Eastern Europe, and other parts of the world is widely applauded as a positive development that is in the geopolitical self-interest of the United States to promote. Although the changes appear irreversible, the incipient democracies are nonetheless fragile systems whose future is very much in the balance. The degree to which this country is able to provide moral as well as material support could be decisive in some cases. In this connection, the continuing specter of racism in America, the persistence of racial conditions that contradict the nation's most fundamental democratic principles, limits its ability to exert moral influence in the international community. Racism and discrimination are severe liabilities.

These observations simply underscore the importance of coming to grips with the costs of racism and investing the nation's collective energies in more progressive directions. The price of the status quo, already too high, may go even higher unless the right kinds of commitments are made.

This chapter seeks to advance understanding of the racism problem by examining some of its economic costs. Although the focus is on this "bottom line" issue, the high degree of interplay between economic costs and the other costs mentioned previously is recognized. For context, we first provide an overview discussion of American racism in concept and practice.

AMERICAN RACISM

Whatever perspective one adopts and whatever historical period it is applied to, racism or racial discrimination against African Americans denotes one overriding condition—subordination. Generically, racial discrimination can be defined as "differential treatment by members of a dominant race which functions to deny or to restrict the choices of members of a subordinant race."[4] Under slavery, the differential treatment of African Americans was systematic and all encompassing. Slaves were regarded as chattel, and therefore did not share in the protections, rights, and privileges the Constitution conferred on all American citizens. Indeed, slavery in the United States was marked by the efficacy and completeness of the subordination process.[5] The system was driven by a single purpose, human exploitation, and was justified by an ideology of biological and spiritual superiority.

Emancipation brought very little relief to African Americans. Except for a brief period during Reconstruction, freedmen and freedwomen continued to occupy a caste-like status. Their subordinant condition was affirmed by the U.S. Supreme Court's infamous "separate but equal" decision in *Plessy v. Ferguson* (1896) and codified in an elaborate framework of segregationist "Jim Crow" laws and practices that prevailed for nearly four generations.[6] Jim Crowism was virtually as effective as slavery itself in denying to African Americans the choices and opportunities experienced by the white majority. Further, the doctrine of white supremacy was reinvigorated during this period, penetrating deeply into the value system of the larger society and sharply regulating relations between races. Also, African Americans continued to be exploited for monetary benefit—as sharecroppers, tenant-framers, and so on.

It is worth pausing here to emphasize two salient points. First, for most of their history, racial discrimination against African Americans has been a matter of official government policy. Thus, the government's role has gone well beyond merely condoning mistreatment. Government institutions created, implemented, and enforced the rules of racial oppression. This circumstance aligns the historical experience of African Americans with that of Native Americans and other racial and ethnic groups that have been the objects of such discrimination and prejudice.[7]

Second, the generation and maintenance of structured inequalities in quality of life has been a hallmark of American racism. There have always been clear standards in this society as to what constitutes individual and family well-being and what it means to be "successful." In terms of basic subsistence needs, the enjoyment of amenities, prestige, emotional and physical health, and so on, the American conception of "the good life" is universally shared. By the same token, the mechanisms for social mobility and the "pursuit of happiness" have been well defined and functional. The effect of racism, however, has been to systematically restrict the quality of life of African Americans by denying them access to these mainstream vehicles for socioeconomic advancement and otherwise limiting their rewards from personal initiative. The upshot is that African Americans have been relegated to a much lower standard of well-being in all vital areas of life than what is enjoyed by the white majority. The durability of these disparities attests to the potency of racism as a force in American life.[8]

Resuming the chronology, the legal status of African Americans was fundamentally altered in 1954 by *Brown v. Topeka Board of Education*, which overturned the "separate but equal" ruling in *Plessy v. Ferguson*. Declaring that separation was inherently unequal, the Supreme Court ushered in an era of radical restructuring of American race relations. Further court decisions, the 1964 Civil Rights Act, the 1965 Voting Rights Act, and a series of executive orders redefined the federal government's attitude toward equal opportunity and its constitutional obligation to ensure racial equality. There is no doubt that the larger spate of judicial, legislative, and executive actions that commenced in 1954 brought profound improvement in the African American condition. But have they eliminated racism? Have they eradicated racial inequality? Have they resolved the perennial American dilemma? Such questions continue to dominate public debate.

Those who believe racism has been overcome often cite the positive changes in racial attitudes that have occurred over the years. Indeed, a substantial body of survey research suggests that the prevalence of racially hostile and unaccepting sentiment among whites has declined sharply.[9] On the other hand, the marked upsurge of racially motivated violence against and by African Americans in recent years suggests that racism, in its basest form, is still very much a part of the American scene.[10]

Just as the evidence concerning racial attitudes is mixed, so too are the assessments of the socioeconomic status of African Americans. On the one hand, the long-term progress of black Americans, in both absolute terms and relative to the condition of whites, has been impressive. In terms of income level, for example, a basic measure of economic well-being, African American families averaged $21,528 in 1991, compared to $1,986 in 1947. In 1991, the ratio of black to white median family income was 0.57:1.0, up notably from 0.51:1.0 in 1947. Similarly, median earnings of African American workers climbed from $79 per week in 1947 to $348 in 1991, closing the earnings gap with white workers by more than 12 percent. In occupational mobility, only 6 percent of African American workers held positions as professionals and managers in 1940. By 1991, this figure had grown to 16.3 percent, narrowing the racial disparity by 11.4 percent.

In educational attainment, the median years of schooling for African Americans in 1940 was 5.7, compared to 8.8 years for whites. By 1991, black Americans were averaging 12.4 years, as opposed to 14.8 years for whites. Likewise, in 1940, fewer than 2 percent of black females or males had completed college, while 5 percent and 7.5 percent of their respective white counterparts were college graduates. In the four ensuing decades, the proportion of African American females completing four years of college increased to 11.6 percent; 11.4 percent of African American males were in this category. The corresponding figures for whites were 25.4 percent and 22.2 percent.[11]

Similar long-term gains have been observed for other important status indicators. On balance, the cumulative data document empirically what one might intuitively expect: African Americans are generally much better off today than they were one-half century or even one generation ago.[12]

On the other hand, the long-term progress is counterbalanced by the persistence of deep racial inequalities in key areas of individual and family well-being. Moreover, the relative advancement of African Americans has slowed and, in some cases, even reversed in recent years. In 1970, for example, the median income of black families was 61.3 percent of the median for whites. In 1991, the percentage was 56, considerably lower. In 1972, black workers were twice as likely to be hit by unemployment than their white counterparts. In 1991, the racial unemployment gap was 2.1:1. In 1980, the African American poverty rate was 2.8 times the poverty rate for whites. In 1991, the racial poverty gap was 2.9:1.

The overall wealth status of African Americans is just 23 percent of the wealth of whites. Per capita, blacks average about $9,000 in wealth or net worth, compared to $45,000 for whites. African Americans own barely 3 percent of the nation's businesses and account for just 1 percent of the United States' total gross receipts. In the health area, the racial disparity in infant mortality rates has widened during the past decade, and life expectancy among African American males has declined.[13]

As the previous data indicates, racial parity in critical areas of socioeconomic well-being remains elusive. Indeed, I have projected in another publication that, at current rates of change, parity in most instances will not be achieved for long into the future, if ever.[14] This evidence cogently demonstrates that racism is still operative in the body politic and that the effects of the historical oppression of African Americans have not been overcome. The evidence also confirms the operation of contemporary racism in much more subtle, institutional ways, as compared to the blatant exclusionary forms that existed in the past. "Modern prejudice," writes Pettigrew, "is subtle and indirect. It is a part of widely and deeply held values, and it is reinforced institutionally. Old-fashioned bigotry can still be found throughout the nation, but confusion between it and modern prejudice obscures the current phenomenon. In fact, it is its careful separation from the older, cruder types of bigotry that helps to distinguish these new patterns of racism."[15]

THE COST ISSUE

From the early days of slavery to more recent times, social analysts and commentators have propounded the cost of racism and discrimination in heavily moral terms. Gunnar Myrdal is rightfully credited as having formulated the most influential conceptualization of racism as a moral issue. In introducing his seminal study of the problem, he states:

The American Negro problem is a problem in the heart of the American. It is there that the interracial tension has its focus. It is there that the decisive struggle goes on. . . . Though our study includes economic, social and political race relations, at bottom our problem is the moral dilemma of the American. . . . The "American Dilemma" . . . is the ever-changing conflict between . . . the valuations preserved on the general plane which we shall call the "American Creed," where the American thinks, talks, and acts under the influence of high national and Christian precepts, and . . . the valuations on specific planes of individual and group living, where . . . group prejudice against particular persons or types of people . . . dominate his outlook.[16]

Thus, Myrdal's perspective highlights the departure between the actual status and treatment of African Americans and the society's avowed democratic ideals. The viewpoint conjures up related notions of "equity," "fairness," and "justice." Contemporary students of race relations have retained this focus on morality, even as they give it a pragmatic slant. A representative articulation is offered by Silverman, who admonishes that America "must accept the Negro as an equal and participating member of society because it is the only right thing, the only decent thing, to do. In the long run, the greatest threat to the United States is not political or military, but moral."[17] Even in the popular culture, the morality factor remains a commanding preoccupation, as illustrated by the public response to the Spike Lee film, *Do the Right Thing*.

Except on the most metaphysical level, it is virtually impossible to disentangle the premium on moral rectitude from more practical considerations of cost and consequence. Morality is serviceable, while immorality can seriously disserve the interests of a society and the welfare of all of its members. As Knowles and Prewitt argue in their analysis of American racism, "it adversely affects whites as well as blacks."[18] In *Beyond Black and White*, psychiatrist James Comer summarizes the concern:

The white mind has cost white people, black people and the nation dearly. It is impossible to calculate the price in dollars and cents. . . . It has meant the loss of an enormous amount of human talent. The number of black lives snuffed out by violence is beyond counting. The number of black lives crippled and maimed is even greater. The psychological and social development of America's children—white as well as black—has been stunted. As a result, the nation is not prepared for an advanced scientific and technological age.[19]

The economic effect of racism and discrimination is without doubt the overriding factor in any assessment of costs. In American society, where the free-enterprise system reigns supreme, the general welfare is defined and pursued in terms of economic interests. This observation is not intended as an indictment. Free enterprise is most compatible with our democratic precepts and, for the most part, has afforded Americans an exceptionally high standard of living. Hence, the primacy of economics is not in dispute. To the contrary, our aim is to demonstrate that racism has been a serious hindrance on economic performance and well-being. In this sense, there is little question that we can no longer afford the price.

We address two interrelated concerns—the economic price that African Americans themselves have had to pay and the price that racism has cost the general economy. The first concern is the more straightforward and obvious of the two. White Americans have clearly recognized the economic deprivations suffered by black Americans, even though there continues to be substantial disagreement regarding the extent to which the African Americans themselves are responsible for their current economic problems. The cynical sentiments are expressed most vocally in popular discussions of the so-called "black underclass." Nevertheless, white Americans have evinced through the years both a more supportive attitude toward the principle of equal opportunity and compassion for the difficulties that African Americans on the whole have experienced in realizing economic well-being.

It is necessary to stress, however, that white America generally has approached this subject from a moral standpoint, that is, from the standpoint of the "American dilemma" as originally conceived. There has been relatively little appreciation of the interface between the economic well-being of African Americans and that of the society at large. Thus, in considering the need to eradicate racism in the economic area, the question, "What's in it for me?" has not been treated as a priority issue; the operative answer being, "Very little." This view is misguided.

Our second objective, then, is to examine how the economic conditions of African Americans affect the nation's economy and, thus, the individual economic self-interest of the white majority. There is some indication that a more enlightened perspective on this topic is beginning to take hold. For instance, in 1989, *Money* magazine, the highly respected periodical on financial affairs (with a predominantly white readership), published a major article, "Race and Money." One of the most cogent assertions of the article is that, "While blacks bear the brunt of racism, the resulting inequalities cost all Americans enormously."[20] We estimate some of this cost in the second part of this analysis.

Costs to African Americans

The economic costs of racial inequality to African Americans are examined using four basic indicators of group economic status: income level, unemployment rate, occupational representation, and earnings. In each case, the condition of African Americans is compared to that of the white majority. Hence, any reference to racial equality or parity involves the relative positions of these two groups.

Income. Income is the most basic measure of economic status, and per capita income is used here to estimate the cost of racism. Table 1 shows African American and white personal income data for the years 1980–1991, adjusted for inflation. In columns a and b, we see how the two races compare in terms of actual per capita income for each year. The personal income of blacks is consistently far less than that of whites. In proportional terms, the level of black to white income ranges from a low of 56.3 percent in 1982 to a high of 59.5 in 1988. For the period as a whole, then, African Americans averaged less than 60 cents to each dollar of income received by whites.

The instructive data for our purposes are contained in columns c–e. Column c shows the actual aggregate income of African Americans for each year, while column d indicates what this amount would be under the condition of racial parity—i.e., if African Americans had the same per capita income as whites. The figures in column e represent the difference between African Americans' actual total income and their total as determined from the parity computation. This difference is the "cost" of racial inequality in income. The order of magnitude is immediately apparent. The personal income loss for African Americans

TABLE 1. Comparison of African American and White per Capita Income and Estimated Costs of Racial Inequality 1980–1991, in 1991 Dollars

Year	Afr. Amer.	(a) Per Capita Income White	(b) Ratio AA/Wh (%)	(c) Total AA Inc. (actual in billions)	(d) Total AA Inc. (with parity)	(e) Cost (est. in billions)
1991	$9,170	$15,510	59.1	$288	$481	$193
1990	9,396	15,907	59.1	290	477	187
1989	9,608	16,362	58.7	292	489	197
1988	9,522	15,999	59.5	285	469	184
1987	9,166	15,758	58.2	270	458	188
1986	8,956	15,350	58.3	259	451	192
1985	8,658	14,773	58.6	247	428	181
1984	8,228	14,340	57.4	222	410	178
1983	7,870	13,846	56.8	218	390	172
1982	7,636	11,573	56.3	208	377	169
1981	7,753	13,573	57.1	208	370	162
1980	7,950	13,625	58.3	210	366	156

Source: Based on U.S. Bureau of the Census, *Current Populations Reports*, "Money Income and Poverty Status in the United States: 1991," and National Urban League, *The State of Black America 1993*.

runs as high as $197 billion in 1989. The grand total for the 12-year period is a mind-boggling $2.2 *trillion!* This is a staggeringly large number by any standard. It is also worth noting that the size of the estimated income loss figure increased by $37 billion over the period, a growth rate of 24 percent.

Of course, the parity and cost estimates are subject to a number of caveats. For example, a more rigorous analysis would take into account the different age distributions of the black and white populations. The average age for African Americans as a group is lower, and the group is therefore more likely to include persons not yet old enough to produce income. Assuming that blacks should have the same per capita income as whites might generate inflated parity estimates. Likewise, any number of determinants may operate to sustain the personal income gap between blacks and whites. What proportion of the problem to assign to racism as opposed to more race-neutral causes is a vexing question that is not easily answered.

TABLE 2. African American and White Unemployment Rates and Unemployment Ratios, 1980–1991

Year	Afr. Amer. (%)	White (%)	Ratio AA/Wh
1991	12.4	6.5	2.2
1990	11.3	4.7	2.4
1989	11.4	4.5	2.5
1988	11.7	4.7	2.5
1987	13.0	5.3	2.4
1986	14.5	6.0	2.4
1985	15.1	6.2	2.4
1984	15.9	6.5	2.5
1983	19.5	8.4	2.3
1982	18.9	8.6	2.2
1981	15.6	6.7	2.3
1980	14.3	6.3	2.3

Source: U.S. Bureau of Labor Statistics, *Handbook of Labor Statistics,*
August 1989, and National Urban League, *The State of Black America 1993.*

While space does not permit an analysis sufficiently sophisticated to account for all variables, the raw numbers alone make it clear that racism and discrimination have acted to deny substantial personal income to African Americans. One cannot help but contemplate what such added consumption power would mean to the economic welfare of African Americans themselves and to the nation's commerce.

Unemployment rates. One of the principal constraints on African American income is their inordinately high level of unemployment. Indeed, severely disproportionate unemployment rates distinguished the economic status of African Americans throughout the 1980s and into the 1990s. The severity of the problem is detailed in Table 2, which presents overall black and white unemployment rates from 1980–1991.

As Table 2 shows, blacks were more than twice as likely as whites to be unemployed in each year. One should bear in mind that the economy experienced two major recessions in the early part of the decade, which had a devastating impact on the workforce as a whole. In particular, the respective jobless rates for 1982 and 1983 reflect the gravity of the economic downturn. Until the recession of 1990, the jobless rate among both groups had declined progressively. However, the racial unemployment gap showed little change. To the contrary, the gap was virtually as large in 1991 as it was in 1980. In good economic times and bad, then, disproportionate unemployment dominates the labor market experience of African Americans.

One gains a more direct understanding of the impact of disproportionate African American unemployment in cost terms by focusing on the actual number of jobs lost in a given year. Swinton provides such an assessment for 1988:

> Even without looking at the impact on discouragement and labor force dropout, the higher unemployment rates experienced by blacks cost blacks hundreds of thousands of jobs every year. . . . During 1988, on average, the unemployment parity gap was over 1 million jobs. Black men experienced a 379 thousand job shortage due to lack of parity in unemployment while black women suffered even more, experiencing a 425 thousand job shortfall. Black teenagers lost 182 thousand jobs due to lack of parity in unemployment.[21]

Finally, it is important to observe that the phenomenon of disproportionate African American unemployment occurs across occupations and industries without regard to educational achievement levels. For example, one study found that the racial unemployment gap among certain categories of administrators and managers was 4.5:1— for example, African Americans in these occupations were four and one-half times as likely as their white counterparts to be jobless.[22]

Occupational representation.   Not only are African Americans much more likely than whites to be unemployed, they are also much more likely to be employed in lower-status, lower-paying occupations and are correspondingly less likely to hold the more prestigious and rewarding positions in the occupational structure. Racism and discrimination in economic life continues to cost African Americans dearly in these respects, as indicated by the data in Table 3.

The first two columns in the table show what percentage of all workers in each occupational category African Americans and whites

TABLE 3. Occupational Representation of African American
Workers, 1991

Occupation	% *Afr. Amer.*	*Difference Between* *AA % for* *Occup. & %* *of Total Employed*
Mgrs. & profs.	6.3	–3.9
Exec., admin., & managerial	5.7	–4.5
Professional	6.7	–3.4
Tech., sales, admin. support	9.3	–1.0
Technicians & related support	8.9	–0.8
Sales	6.6	–4.0
Adm. support	11.4	1.2
Service	17.2	7.5
Private household	22.6	12.5
Protective service	16.7	6.6
Other service	16.7	7.3
Precision prod., craft, & repair	7.8	–2.6
Oper.'s fabricators, & laborers	15.0	4.9
Farming, forestry, fishing	6.4	–3.5

Source: Bureau of Labor Statistics, *Employment and Earnings*, January 1992, Table 22.

represent. The third column shows the degree to which African Americans are over- or underrepresented in a given category, relative to their percentage of the employed workforce, which in 1991 was 10.1 percent.

The pattern is clear: African American workers are overrepresented in the lower status occupations and underrepresented at the upper end of the occupational scale. For example, while they comprised just 10 percent of employed workers in 1991, African Americans accounted for 15 percent of all operators, fabricators, and laborers, an overrepresentation of 5 percent. Similarly, they were overrepresented by 12.5 percent among private household workers. On the other hand, African Americans accounted for only 5.7 percent of all executives, administrators, and managers and just 6.7 percent of all professional workers. Although the occupational status of African Americans has improved considerably over time, the obvious inference is that racism and discrimination continue to thwart parity.[23]

TABLE 4. Median Weekly Earnings of African American and White
Workers, by Sex 1991

	Afr. Amer.	*White*	*% AA/Wh*
Total	$348	$446	.78
Females	323	374	.86
Males	374	509	.73

Source: Bureau of Labor Statistics, *Employment and Earnings*, January 1992, Table 54.

Earnings.   The most obvious effect of the occupational disadvantages of
African Americans is found in their earnings levels. Overall, the earnings
of full-time African American workers in 1991 were just 78 percent of the
earnings of their white counterparts (see Table 4). African American
males fared much worse than did females. The percentage of black to
white earnings among males was .73, compared to .86 among females.

These earnings differentials have changed very little over the past
decade. They, too, suggest the continued operation of racial discrimination in the labor market, and the data help to clarify the economic
costs African Americans incur as we approach the twenty-first century. The earnings variable figures prominently in our analysis below
of the economic cost to the society as a whole.

Cost to the National Economy

Historically, the American economy has been the envy of the Western
world. There has seemed to be no limit to the ability of the capitalistic,
free-enterprise system to generate income, wealth, and a progressively
higher standard of living for the American people. America's stature as
a leader in economic development continues, but it has been seriously
challenged in recent decades by economies that have proved to be highly
competitive. Japan, West Germany, and South Korea are exemplary
among the countries that have made impressive progress in developing
their economies over the past forty years or so. As a result, the world
marketplace has changed dramatically. Americans have experienced the
ramifications of this development in painful ways. There is growing concern that the erosion of America's position in the global economy will
continue unless forthright actions are taken to reverse the trend.

The central issue is how to improve the nation's economic productivity and efficiency in the face of changing demands on performance. In this connection, many agree on the need to undertake progressive structural and technological initiatives, even while disagreeing concerning specific actions. At the same time, policy makers and business leaders are placing increased emphasis on the importance of removing existing constraints on economic progress. This is the context in which the contemporary role of racism and discrimination must be critically examined, and the issue of the economic costs of racism takes on far-reaching significance.

For years, economists and other social scientists have debated the question of whether and how racial discrimination militates against the nation's economic interests. The question is exceedingly complex, and the divergent scientific literature reflects this difficulty.[24] However, the consensus of opinion asserts that racism is indeed a major hindrance to the overall functioning of the economy, as here stated by Thomas D'Amico:

> Discrimination will be costly to society, since it results in a clear and potentially serious loss of efficiency. When society's rewards and penalties are distributed to its members in a manner not consonant with their relative productivities, then at least some scarce resources are bound to be overallocated to relatively unproductive members of the "favored" race . . . and underallocated to more productive members of the race being discriminated against. . . . Society's aggregate real output, therefore, will fall below its potential . . . [25]

Duffey puts the issue squarely in terms of the utilization of human resources: "Discrimination on the basis of gender or race is not only harmful to its victim, it wastes important resources. When talented people are denied access to jobs commensurate with their potential, productivity and economic competitiveness suffer."[26]

As to the economic dysfunction of discrimination against African Americans, in particular, Perlo's conclusion accords with our own judgment:

Economic discrimination [of blacks] is the nation's number one economic problem. No economic problem affecting the majority of the population can be solved or significantly eased unless the solution includes a vast improvement in the economic situation of black people and substantial reduction of the discrimination against them.[27]

The data previously cited illustrate that "vast improvement" in the condition of African Americans remains to be achieved. Most notably, African Americans continue to be disproportionately unemployed and underemployed, both of which circumstances bespeak a counterproductive underutilization of human resources. What does it cost the economy? Table 5 provides a partial but revealing answer.

Table 5 shows the ratio of black to white per capita earnings in 1989; the actual aggregate earnings of African American workers during the year; what the aggregate earnings of African American workers would have been under the condition of racial parity (i.e., if their per capita earnings were equal to that of white workers); the difference between the actual and parity aggregate earnings estimates; and the proportion of the year's overall Gross National Product (GNP) this difference represents.[28] Columns 2, 3, and 4 interest us the most.

In 1989, the aggregate earnings of African Americans were about $219 billion. If parity had prevailed, the total would have been $311.9 billion. As labor is a principal component of GNP, the absence of earnings parity costs the American economy approximately $93 billion in 1989. Put differently, racial equality would have boosted the GNP for the year by about 1.8 percent. In fact, for each year between 1980 and 1989 (data not shown), the GNP would have been close to 2 percent higher had

TABLE 5. Estimated Effect of Racism on the Economy, as Measured by Difference Between Actual African American Earnings and Earnings Under Parity 1989

% of AA to White Earnings	Total AA Earnings (actual in billions)	Total Under Parity (in billions)	Diff. Betw. Actual & Parity (in billions)	% of GNP
.70	$219.1	$311.9	$92.8	1.8

Source: Computed by author from data in U.S. Bureau of Labor Statistics, *Employment and Earnings*, January 1990. GNP data from Bureau of Economic Analysis.

there been earnings parity between the races. Thus, the total loss to the economy during this period is in the hundreds of billions of dollars.

CONCLUSIONS AND RECOMMENDATIONS

In this chapter, we sought to estimate some of the economic costs of racism in American society. Of course, such analyses are problematic. The issues are inherently elusive and terribly complex. Cause and effect relationships are difficult to conceptualize and even more difficult to determine empirically.

Despite the caveats, the upshot can be stated simply: American racism is a profoundly costly problem. Thus, the failure of this nation to come to grips with the existence of racism and discrimination should be a matter of deep concern to us all. We all pay a heavy price. To be sure, reasonable people will disagree over various cost estimates and the overall magnitude of the problem. However, there should, at the very least, be a consensus that the costs are too high and that the problem must be solved.

It is important to underscore the policy considerations set forth at the beginning of this chapter. Inexorable changes in the demography of the country, coupled with the emergence of an increasingly competitive global marketplace, have altered drastically the framework within which we must assess our needs as a nation and set our national priorities. In addition, the momentous political developments in Eastern Europe and other parts of the world, which have brought resurgent movements toward democracy, are vitally linked to our own self-interest. To this dynamic mix we also must add the nation's worsening fiscal crisis, spearheaded by a huge federal budget deficit. In the context of these exigencies, the continued presence of racism in our national life is much more than a nuisance, embarrassment, or moral outrage. It is a liability of immense proportions.

American society has therefore reached a critical point of departure that could have decisive implications for the long-term future. Whether we will pursue the right course toward strength and vitality or continue to endure the failures of the past is uncertain. What is certain is that the future is ours to control. What is certain is that action based on enlightened self-interest holds the greatest promise. What is certain is that lowering the costs of racism is a key prerequisite to progress. Basic recommendations to this end follow.

First, we must make an unqualified recommitment to ensure equal opportunity in all areas of social and economic life. This suggestion is not mere platitude. In recent years, the mobility prospects for African Americans have been seriously undermined by regressive policies on the part of the national government. Even the U.S. Supreme Court, whose earlier decisions in pivotal civil rights cases were indispensable to the promotion of racial equality, has since issued highly detrimental rulings—against minority set-asides in *Croson v. Richmond*, restricting employment contract rights as they relate to racial discrimination in the workplace in *Patterson v. McLean Credit Union*, and allowing for reopening of settled affirmative action cases in *Martin v. Wilkes*.

In its wisdom, the U.S. Congress passed the 1991 Civil Rights Act, legislation in part designed to cushion the adverse effects of these judicial decisions. In addition, this action helps to send a message to the rest of the world regarding this nation's willingness to rectify injustice, whatever its source.

Second, we must be determined to educate, train, and prepare by all means necessary the present generation of African American youth to meet the nation's changing human resource needs. This will require not only that we discard stereotypical, racist thinking about their capacity to learn and perform but also that we appropriate and deliver effectively the resources necessary to maximize their potential. There is a clear investment decision involved here. Some might argue that the investment should be in new technology that reduces further reliance on human labor. A strategy that emphasizes educating people, in this view, is not cost effective, particularly when one considers the severity of the educational disadvantages of African Americans. However, such a "write-them-off" attitude is narrow-minded and counterproductive.

That we must realize more technological improvements is beyond dispute. Our chief international competitors are moving aggressively in this direction. At the same time, these other nations have evidenced a much more progressive orientation toward the development and use of human resources. No matter how technologically advanced we become in the coming decades, our economic productivity and competitiveness will still be heavily dependent upon enhancing the nation's human capital. If African Americans are disregarded, the society could well find itself in a serious human resources shortage and ill equipped to meet the competitive challenges ahead.

Third, there must be a concentrated effort to revitalize the economically depressed urban centers where African Americans continue to be disproportionately represented. The effects of institutionalized racism are manifest most acutely in these areas, and the costs we pay for their neglect multiply in disturbing ways. The wave of violent urban unrest that swept the nation during the 1960s is a compelling case in point. From Watts, California to Detroit, Michigan to Washington, D.C., the riots in our cities were immensely costly—in human lives, economic losses, and social instability.

Regrettably, we failed to appreciate and respond to these tragic events as direct and inevitable consequences of deprivation, disregard, and the persistence of racial injustice. Consequently, the price mounted with another episode of rioting in South Central Los Angeles in April of 1992. Moreover, in this instance, the violence and destruction spread well beyond the boundaries of the African American community to more affluent areas of the city.

Even in the absence of violent discontent, we incur the substantial costs of dependency. Our urban centers offer little opportunity for African Americans to be productive, to enjoy self-sufficiency, and to contribute to the economic vitality of the community and the nation as a whole.

We are aware that the so-called "black ghettos" were produced by a complex of interacting forces and do not suggest that the effects of these developments can be easily or completely reversed. Nonetheless, it is clear that these areas need not be perpetual liabilities, veritable wastelands of human talent. They are replete with potential. In a real sense, the degree to which we tap this potential could be the most telling indicator of the society's success in lowering the costs of contemporary racism.

Given the imperatives, the 1992 election of Bill Clinton to the presidency, along with a more diverse and progressively minded group to Congress, was a welcome development. However, the initial optimism, which was widespread among both African Americans and the general population, has waned. At this writing, the new national leadership has had little success in translating the rhetoric of "change" into policy and program initiatives. The defeat of the president's economic stimulus package was a significant disappointment in this regard. Even though the proposed legislation represented merely a step in the right direction, the political consensus necessary for its passage did not materialize.

Whether the balance of the Clinton administration will be more fruitful is uncertain. However, there is no doubt that, absent serious policy redirections, the costs of racism will continue to escalate.

REFERENCES

Burkey, Richard M. 1971. *Racial discrimination and public policy in the United States*. Lexington, MA: D. C. Heath.

Comer, James P. 1972. *Beyond black and white*. New York: Quadrangle, 1972.

D'Amico, Thomas F. 1987. The conceit of labor market discrimination. *Economics of Discrimination Thirty Years Later* (AEA Paper and Proceedings) 77 (May).

Duffey, Joseph. 1988. Competitiveness and human resources. *California Management Review* (Spring).

Elkins, Stanley M. 1959. *Slavery: A problem in American institutional and intellectual life*. Chicago: University of Chicago Press.

Farley, Reynolds, and Walter R. Allen. 1987. *The color line and the quality of life in America*. New York: Russell Sage Foundation.

Jacob, John E. 1989. Change, challenge, and choice: African Americans and workforce 2000. Statement submitted to the House Committee on Education and Labor, June, Washington, DC.

Jaynes, Gerald David, and Robin M. Williams, Jr., eds. 1989. *A common destiny: Blacks and American society*. Washington, DC: National Academy Press.

Johnston, William B., and Arnold H. Packer. 1987. *Workforce 2000: Work and workers for the 21st century*. Indianapolis, IN: Hudson Institute.

Jones, Dionne J. 1988. *Racially motivated violence: An empirical study of a growing social problem*. Washington, DC: National Urban League Research Department.

Knowles, Louis L., and Kenneth Prewitt, eds. 1969. *Institutional racism in America*. Englewood Cliffs, NJ: Prentice-Hall.

Myrdal, Gunnar. 1944. *An American dilemma.* New York: Harper.

1988 Commission on the Cities, the. 1988. Race and poverty in the United States—and what should be done. In *Quiet riots: Race and poverty in the United States,* ed. Fred R. Harris and Roger W. Wilkins, New York: Pantheon, 1988.

Perlo, Victor. 1975. *Economics of racism U.S.A.: Roots of black inequality.* New York: International.

Pettigrew, Thomas F: 1985. New patterns of racism: The different worlds of 1984 and 1964. *Rutger's Law Review* 37 (Summer).

Silberman, Charles E. 1964. *Crisis in black and white.* New York: Vintage.

Smith, James P., and Finis R. Welch. 1986. *Closing the gap: Forty years of economic progress for blacks.* Santa Monica, CA: Rand.

Stampp, Kenneth, M. 1956. *The peculiar institution: Slavery in the ante-bellum south.* New York: Vintage.

Steinfield, Melvin 1970. *Cracks in the melting pot: Racism and discrimination in American history.* New York: Macmillan.

Swinton, David H. 1989. Economic status of black Americans. In *The state of black America 1989,* ed. Janet Dewart. New York: National Urban League.

Tidwell, Billy J. 1987. Racial discrimination and inequality. In *Encyclopedia of social work,* vol. 2. Silver Spring, MD: National Association of Social Workers.

———. 1987. Topsy turvy: Unemployment among black administrators and managers. *The Forum* (National Forum for Black Public Administrators) 3 (February).

———. 1988. *Black employment in the private sector: A twenty-year assessment.* Washington, DC: National Urban League Research Department.

———. 1989. *Stalling out: The relative progress of African Americans.* Washington, DC: National Urban League Research Department.

———, ed. 1993. *The state of black America 1993.* New York: National Urban League.

Updegrave, Walter L. 1989. Race and money. *Money* (December).

U.S. Bureau of the Census. 1989. Projections of the population of the United States, by age, sex, and race: 1988 to 2080. In *Current population reports.* Washington, DC: U.S. Government Printing Office.

————. 1992. *Statistical abstract of the United States: 1992*. 112th ed. Washington, DC: U.S. Government Printing Office.

U.S. Bureau of Labor Statistics. 1989. Outlook 2000. *Monthly Labor Review* 112 (November).

Weaver, Frederick Stirton. 1978. Cui bono? and the economic function of racism. *Review of Black Political Economy* 8 (Spring).

Woodward, C. Vann. 1966. *The strange career of Jim Crow*. New York: Oxford University Press.

NOTES

1. U.S. Bureau of the Census, "Projections of the Population on the United States, by Age, Sex, and Race: 1988 to 2080," *Current Population Reports* (Washington, DC: U.S. Government Printing Office, January 1989).

2. U.S. Bureau of Labor Statistics, "Outlook 2000," *Monthly Labor Review* 112 (November 1989).

3. For relevant arguments, see William B. Johnston and Arnold H. Packer, *Workforce 2000: Work and Workers for the 21st Century* (Indianapolis, IN: Hudson Institute, 1987). See also John E. Jacob, "Change, Challenge, and Choice: African Americans and Workforce 2000," statement submitted to the House Committee on Education and Labor, Washington, DC, June 1989.

4. Richard M. Burkey, *Racial Discrimination and Public Policy in the United States* (Lexington, MA: D.C. Health, 1971), 9.

5. Stanley M. Elkins, *Slavery: A Problem in American Institutional and Intellectual Life* (Chicago: University of Chicago Press, 1959), Kenneth M. Stampp, *The Peculiar Institution: Slavery in the Ante-Bellum South* (New York: Vintage, 1956).

6. See, for example, C. Vann Woodward, *The Strange Career of Jim Crow* (New York: Oxford University Press, 1966).

7. See Billy J. Tidwell, "Racial Discrimination and Inequality," *Encyclopedia of Social Work*, vol. 2 (Silver Spring, MD: National Association of Social Workers, 1987), 448–55. See also Melvin Steinfield, *Cracks in the Melting Pot: Racism and Discrimination in American History* (New York: Macmillan, 1970).

8. Gunnar Myrdal, *An American Dilemma* (New York: Harper, 1944); Gerald David Jaynes and Robin M. Williams Jr., eds., *A Com-*

mon Destiny: Blacks and American Society (Washington, DC: National Academy Press, 1989); Billy J. Tidwell, *Stalling Out: The Relative Progress of African Americans* (Washington, DC: National Urban League Research Department, 1989).

9. Thomas F. Pettigrew, "New Patterns of Racism: The Different Worlds of 1984 and 1964," *Rutgers Law Review* 37 (Summer 1985): 686.

10. Dionne J. Jones, *Racially Motivated Violence: An Empirical Study of a Growing Social Problem* (Washington, DC: National Urban League Research Department, 1988).

11. U.S. Bureau of the Census, *Statistical Abstract of the United States: 1992,* 112th ed. (Washington, DC: U.S. Government Printing Office, 1992); Jaynes and Williams, Jr., eds., *A Common Destiny.* See also Reynolds Farley and Walter R. Allen, *The Color Line and the Quality of Life in America* (New York: Russell Sage Foundation, 1987).

12. Ibid. See also James P. Smith and Finis R. Welch, *Closing the Gap: Forty Years of Economic Progress for Blacks* (Santa Monica, CA: Rand, 1986).

13. Jaynes and Williams, Jr., eds., *A Common Destiny*; Tidwell, *Stalling Out.* See also Billy J. Tidwell, ed., *The State of Black America 1993* (New York: National Urban League, 1993) and the 1988 Commission on the Cities, "Race and Poverty in the United States— and What Should Be Done," in *Quiet Riots: Race and Poverty in the United States,* ed. Fred R. Harris and Roger W. Wilkins (New York: Pantheon, 1988), 172–84.

14. Tidwell, *Stalling Out.*

15. Pettigrew, "New Patterns of Racism," 692.

16. Myrdal, *An American Dilemma,* xxi.

17. Charles E. Silberman, *Crisis in Black and White* (New York: Vintage, 1964), 16.

18. Louis L. Knowles and Kenneth Prewitt, eds., *Institutional Racism in America* (Englewood Cliffs, NJ: Prentice-Hall, 1969), 127.

19. James P. Comer, *Beyond Black and White* (New York: Quadrangle, 1972), 119–20.

20. Walter L. Updegrave, "Race and Money," *Money* (December 1989): 154.

21. David H. Swinton, "Economic Status of Black Americans," in

The State of Black America 1989, ed. Janet Dewart (New York: National Urban League, 1989), 31–32.

22. Billy J. Tidwell, "Topsy Turvy: Unemployment Among Black Administrators and Managers," *The Forum* (National Forum for Black Public Administrators) 3 (February 1987): 1–3.

23. Billy J. Tidwell, *Black Employment in the Private Sector: A Twenty-Year Assessment* (Washington, DC: National Urban League Research Department, 1988).

24. For a relevant discussion, see Frederick Stirton Weaver, "Cui Bono? and the Economic Function of Racism," *Review of Black Political Economy* 8 (Spring 1978): 302–13.

25. Thomas F. D'Amico, "The Conceit of Labor Market Discrimination," *Economics of Discrimination Thirty Years Later* (AEA Papers and Proceedings) 77 (May 1987): 310.

26. Joseph Duffey, "Competitiveness and Human Resources," *California Management Review* (Spring 1988): 98.

27. Victor Perlo, *Economics of Racism U.S.A.: Roots of Black Inequality* (New York: International, 1975), 3.

28. Limiting the base to those in the workforce avoids the problem of including transfer income in the estimate. Such income, of course, does not contribute to the GNP.

3 | The Language of Race in Public Policy

LORENZO MORRIS

The celebration of a major social and political victory in the wake of protracted and intense struggle often leads to euphoric exaggerations of what has been achieved. A national sign of relief after hard-fought political battles may lead to misconceptions about the degree of political transformation any victory is capable of precipitating. The successful passage of the Civil Rights movement from protest to "legitimacy" and from disruption to institutionalization under the law gave rise to much rejoicing that may have obscured the persistent failures lying just beneath the surface of law and adjudication. The 1960s passion for change and the enthusiasm for the progress made in race relations have left a legacy of misconceptions about the status of these relations in American law and policy. The tangible hallmarks of progress, substantial as they may be, distort and disguise the scarcely altered continuity of the legal and political structure for dealing with racial problems.

The tangible policy products of the legal and political processes have changed dramatically, and it was the prospect of this change that initiated the long sigh of relief that began in 1954 with *Brown v. Topeka Board of Education*. Had the expectations surrounding *Brown* been limited to the promise of delegitimating racial segregation, the celebration might not have been premature. Yet, popular expectations, as well as the claims of political leadership, went far beyond legal reform to the widely heralded assertion of fundamental transformation in societal perceptions of values on race. All that had actually changed, however, was the consistency and conformity of the application of law to racial discrimination, along with public awareness of civil rights inconsistencies. In a fundamental sense, old legal and public policy standards on race had been preserved. Accordingly, little groundwork has been laid for forthcoming changes in the legal status of racial inequality before the law and the treatment of racial issues in American public policy.

In terms of the guiding principles of American public policy on race, the law, including civil rights law, merely defines the parameters within which public choices are to be made, and the methods by which they may be implemented. The recentness of most civil rights laws encourages the perception of these laws as part of a continuing policymaking evolution when, in fact, most modern civil rights legislation embodies the fundamental preferences of a bygone period in American politics. In other words, what legislators in the 1960s felt compelled to translate into law, and what judges felt they needed to affirm in their decisions, were established policies that were merely undergoing adaptation or refinement. A change of legislative or judicial "policy" was thus initiated primarily in an effort to reaffirm old law in the face of new societal pressures.

The visible evolution of American civil rights from the nineteenth century to the present is widely interpreted as an uneven but relentless movement toward an increasingly race-conscious exercise of public authority. Government responsibility for the equitable treatment of black Americans is frequently understood to flow historically from the identification and attempted rectification of the injustices imposed on blacks in the past. Yet, given persistent pressures, it is rather the failure to define the injustices, or at least the failure to examine their racial content, that gives rise to new legislation.

The history of black American political protest has generally been defined by the development of protests around goals of equity and benefits for black Americans as a whole. The focus on race in the initiation stage of a political movement is usually so strong that the public expression of goals generates a fearful popular response. By the time the goals are translated into law and public policy, however, the focus on race has been completely diluted. By contrast, equity, albeit interracial, has been given a new meaning. The elimination of a race-conscious focus for public policy and law—and not its articulation, it shall be argued—has been the overall by-product of the presumed historical progress toward civil rights protection. As black Americans have increasingly turned national attention toward their particular interests, national public authority has redefined those interests as radically indifferent, national interests. Such redefinition has not occurred, however, without a real transformation of the interests and their outcomes.

First, this transformation will be explored through a look at the concept of race in twentieth-century judicial interpretation. Rather than demonstrating a liberating evolution of race relations, legal concepts of race show an overlooked continuity and consistency that emerged from the nineteenth-century endorsement of segregation to the 1960s rejection of it.

Second, that continuity, it will be argued, is broken only by the evolution of the federal government's responsibility for mediating or remediating the social disruption that the uniformed intervention of lesser public authorities may have caused. Government is seen as engaged in short-term corrections rather than enduring adjustment.

Third, these adjustments are fundamentally oriented toward reducing government involvement in racial issues. Race was seen by the courts in the nineteenth century as beyond the purview of government regulation; it is seen in the twentieth century as something that should be beyond government's reach completely.

Fourth, the prevailing approach to race as a subject unsuitable for public responsibility serves to deform the public approaches to compensation and disadvantage. The policies that started out with a strongly race-conscious focus and an egalitarian base were diluted to the affirmative action policies we know today. The dilution of the policies flows logically from the assertion of the traditional approach to disadvantage. In this approach, all compensatable disadvantages must be recognizable as disadvantages that everyone can feel and theoretically experience.

Fifth, the language of legislation and policy regulation has developed around the wholly interracial and universalistic ideal that the only real measure of inequality is one that includes material assets—that is to say, a form of inequality open to all and tolerated by everyone as long as it is consistent with competition.

Finally, the protestors may express the protests that give rise to policy intervention in race-specific terms, but legislative process will inevitably denude the policy of any meaningful racial content.

BACKGROUND OF RACE SPECIFICITY

As for the legal principles guiding public policy on racial issues, *Brown*, with its consequences for desegregation, appears to have broken dramatically from the fundamental guidelines of prior civil rights law. There was so much rejoicing over *Brown*'s overturning the segregationist precedent established by *Plessy v. Ferguson* (1896) that what *Brown* preserved and even reinforced in *Plessy* has been virtually overlooked. In its fundamental guidelines for the treatment and definition of racial issues, *Brown*, it will be argued here, substantially confirms *Plessy*. The Supreme Court preserved the parameters and concepts of race before the law expressed in *Plessy*, but changed the focus to allow greater freedom for government in the implementation of Constitutional law.

The question of race facing American society may always have been whether blacks and whites should live in racially segregated, desegregated, or integrated patterns. But that was not the question before the courts in the 1950s, nor in the preceding century. The primary question for adjudication was, rather, what role government should play in the interracial relationship as it evolved under societal impulses. That American society should or should not be desegregated through the force of government intervention was at issue only insofar as other governmental responsibilities compelled such intervention. These other responsibilities included, significantly, the government's prior responsibility for having created official segregation and sustained quasi-official segregation.

Of course, the social climate had substantially changed between 1896 and 1954. In 1896, "the commingling of the races," in *Plessy*'s terms, was viewed as a violation of the natural, if not divine, order of human nature. By 1954, it was seen as the ineluctable goal of social evolution. Yet in both periods government's active role in creatively changing the status of race relations was never affirmed as a value in itself. Rather, in 1954, government accepted its responsibility for undoing its own previous intervention in race relations and for addressing the "sociopsychological harm" its prior suborning of segregation had helped (though not necessarily intentionally) to create. Justice Earl Warren's appeal to the virtues of a "color-blind" society was an affirmation that society was changing, and had already changed, from the "color-conscious" society of *Plessy*. His opinion did not, however, affirm government's authority to do more than eliminate the color-consciousness it had itself consciously institutionalized.

The Court's recourse to the equal protection clause of the Fourteenth Amendment of the U.S. Constitution gave the impression that equal protection under the law meant eradicating all distinctions based on race when, in fact, only those distinctions founded in segregationist law were explicitly entailed. One could easily encapsulate the conceptual difference here by concluding that racial *segregation* and *discrimination* were deemed unconstitutional in 1954, while racial *separation* was not. Such a conclusion is, however, fairly meaningless for the time period and probably today as well, because racial separation was historically inconceivable without the reinforcement of law. No reputable jurist would have tried to speculate before the courts whether a hypothetical structure of race relations was separationist or integrationist. In fact, such speculation might well have been deemed juridically inappropriate, as racial separation and integration per se were beyond the reach of law.

As a consequence, desegregation began to take form through the courts within the very narrow confines of removing the legal barriers, while leaving open the ambiguous issues of racial interaction as though they were on the periphery. What could or should be done about the vestiges of segregation could scarcely be clarified without also clarifying the field of race relations *without* regard to segregation. In other words, what was beyond the barrier to desegregation was also beyond the range of conceptualization in the courts.

In effect, the Supreme Court ruled that segregation and discrimination were illegal because they involved "authoritative" subjugation. In the absence of authority, therefore, racial prejudice, implying personal, sociopsychological, or ethnocentric disempathy, was beyond legal redress. The distance between these conditions may well involve the sociopsychological harm of which the Court spoke, but the cause of the harm, not the harm itself, was the subject of adjudication, Yet, by inculpating government behavior in a harmful relationship, the Court cast a strong suspicion of unconstitutionality over all unequal racial relations. As far as the actual content or substance of these relations were concerned, the Court delegated authority to the school system, as a private entity, and retained the authority to judge the equity of the school's behavior. Accordingly, the Court concluded its 1955 booster declaration in *Brown II* with a show of faith in the school's ability to define race relations:

> School authorities have the primary responsibility for elucidating, assessing, and solving these [desegregation] problems; courts will have to consider whether the action of school authorities constituted good faith implementation of the governing constitutional principles. . . .
>
> Traditionally, equity has been characterized by a practical flexibility in shaping the remedies and by a facility for adjusting and reconciling public and private needs. . . . [1]

The idea that quasi-private school authorities have primary responsibility for "shaping" the public interest in interracial equity suggests at a minimum that public authorities are liberated from the need to promulgate specific equity criteria. Instead, the action of these authorities was perceived in *Brown* as primarily, if not exclusively, limited to policy implementation. The policy in this instance was presumed to be "equity," while race and race relations were problems that needed to be forced into conformity with traditional, and by implication nonracial, models of equity.

The problem for the Court was, and remains, that it cannot arrive at an operational definition of race relations that improves on the one in *Plessy*. In fact, it cannot produce a concept of race, as a politically relevant phenomenon, but rather must presume that race is essentially a genetic or physiological entity. The logic of this presupposition is that race relations are apolitical and socially irrelevant when they are good and socially and politically relevant only when they are bad.

In this regard, *Brown* confirms the *Plessy* conclusion that law and the Fourteenth Amendment could not have as their objective "to abolish distinction based upon color."[1] Now, almost one hundred years later, government accepts no responsibility for such distinctions. In its reference to the negative effects of "commingling of the two races," *Plessy* indicates that the boundary condition for any political action (distinction) on race is simple (physical) interracial contact. *Brown,* on the other hand, admits to a customary connection between race and sociopsychological factors in its reference to "the hearts and minds" of schoolchildren. The admission that feelings may normally accompany racial identification, however, does not involve a conceptual or principled statement about racial distinctions. It simply refers to the environmental conditions, meaning social and economic circumstances, under which race relations may occur.

The public policy legacy of this physiological concept of race is evident in the numerous laws (particularly state laws) and policies dealing with "racial balance." Like physical objects, race relations have been submitted to a weights and measures system like that used to distribute material goods. For example, the Massachusetts Racial Imbalance Law of 1965 affirms the quantifiability of the policy outcomes to be sought from improved race relations by stating that " . . . racial imbalance shall be deemed to exist when the percent of non-white students in any public school is in excess of fifty percent of the total number of students in such school."[2]

This law, like *Plessy,* reduces race relations to fractions or degrees of physical contact. *Plessy,* the plaintiff, was referred to as "one-eighth negro"—a fraction with more influence than size, but a fraction nonetheless. Race, therefore, was seen as an individual characteristic. The Imbalance Law treats race relations as judgeable through numerical standards. In so doing, it focuses on the school building, meaning another social institution, but not on the school's relevance to these relations. Yet, the policy treatment, as well as the targets of the treatments (the racial groups) are still treated as a collection of individuals. The concept remains perfectly individualistic, and the process surrounding it implies that each individual, and not the school or the society, is solely responsible for the racial distinction he or she brings to the school. The courts consequently have sought primarily to deal with the distribution of the distinction and frequency of its concentration on the supposition that race relations would somehow be favorably affected by its redistribution. Yet, the quality and content of race relations has, as we shall see, generally escaped judicial attention.

As a guiding principle for American public policy, therefore, *Brown* bequeathed conflicting messages to policymakers. Its reformist message was clearly that government must undo the "racism" it had helped to propagate throughout society. It was unclear, however, what that racism might involve beyond segregation. As a result, the conflictive legacy of *Plessy,* as sublimated in the *Brown* decision, was to become a serious problem for public policy. The subliminal legacy has two distinct components. First, race is simply physical at base; it is regrettably social but not, in essence, political. Second, the ideal race relations are those that are free of government intervention.

It took about a generation, but this legacy finally resurfaced in the judicial process in the landmark case, *Regents of the University of California v. Bakke* (1978).[3] In *Bakke,* the Court asked the regents if their school had been guilty of prior segregation and/or discrimination. Not surprisingly, the school authorities responded, "No." The Court effectively said "That's just fine, then you can leave race in its proper place—a place beyond your reach." The Court added, however, that the school could involve race (i.e., the social factor) as long as it did not do so in the name of public or governmental authority. Race-consciousness was, therefore, to be grounded either in public compensation for past sins of discrimination or in private initiative for private or social purposes.

The prescriptions for public policy provided by the Court are threefold. First, ignore race itself to the extent that race is purely physical in nature. Second, redress the social inequities involving race where they have governmental implications, but ignore these inequities where they are apolitical. Third, remain indifferent to all inequality that may emerge without government intervention. Subsequently, conflict has emerged most strongly over (a) the meaning of the relationship and (b) the interpenetration of racial differentiation and social inequities. For social inequities in education, employment, and housing, policymakers, like litigators, have argued that inequality among blacks and whites is as acceptable, if not good, for blacks as it is for poor and wealthy whites. They have disagreed over the extent of racial bias for which government might be held accountable and on which it might have a corrective impact. This disagreement has more to do with the power and potential of government than with its moral obligations. Most often, therefore, the results of litigation have been clearer where, to elicit direct public action, the reach of the social aspect is defined by past discriminatory experience. Without a clear, race-specific record in litigation, policy prescriptions have directed real implementation and real value choices to the private sector, while leaving government's role ambiguous. Here, for example, there is clear consistency between the *Bakke* and *Weber* (1979) cases. *Bakke* seemed to restrict race-consciousness and to limit affirmative action, while *Weber* seemed to promote both of them. Yet, these cases share the common ground of attributing race-specific action and real policy implementation to the private sector. Higher education, almost as much as private industry, though publicly financed in the *Bakke* instance, has traditionally retained independent and privileged authority in the areas of admissions and scholarship evaluation. The Court's recurrent reference to established and acceptable university practices in admissions helped to affirm that standard.

The ambiguities remaining for policymakers concern both race and the social inequality historically and judicially linked to it. Understandably, policymakers and legislators have focused on resolving the latter ambiguity, that of race-related social inequality. With a more philosophical bent than normally condoned in American political culture, they might have sought to return to the primary question, race itself, to understand the linkage. Instead, they followed the path of a pragmatic culture and sought to find and act on inequality without assessing its roots. Unfortunately, the primary focus on socially recognizable inequality is deceptive (at least as the Court has presented it). It is deceptive because such inequality can only be recognized through its nonracial parameters. In general terms, a situation is deemed inequitable between members of dominant and nondominant societies in a culture (in this case, between white and black Americans) because members of the dominant society (in this case, mostly whites) have experienced such a situation as inequitable among themselves.

In America, such a deceptive focus leads to policy based on faulty logic, first, because the policymaker assumes that any inequality to be addressed exists without regard to race. Second, and more profound, the standards for equality must be found among existing unequal relationships in white society. Third, the guidelines or criteria for rectifying an admitted racial inequality must not upset the customary relationships among whites. Ultimately, the logic is flawed because the unconscious subject or focal point for judging inequality in policy implementation for blacks becomes whites rather than blacks.

In practice, the question of how a process such as admissions or employment is unfair to blacks is subliminally restructured to become: "How might this process be unfair to whites?" In its original form, the legislator or policymaker must then explain the concept of unfairness in universal language, meaning that the measure should be one that whites can accept on their own experience. After all, the goal of the modern courts has been to treat blacks like everyone else. If the explanation is bifurcated, allowing for the possibility that blacks are so special or unique that no explanation across the races can uniformly apply to both, then all public policy comes to a halt. Instantly, the issue is treated as one of private action, beyond the public sphere, because it is race-specific. Race-specificity has been effectively defined by *Brown* as beyond the range of public action, except as compensation for previous race-specificity. Therefore, a judicially recognized point of inequality between blacks and whites must ultimately be defined in terms of an inequality among whites only, except in cases of compensation.

Still, the notion of race-specific compensation leaves open a broad parameter of public action. It raises the primary ambiguity, the physical concept of race, to the status of a public policy dilemma. The dilemma has been superficially confronted through statistical measures of racial parity and "equality" of results, as with school enrollment data. In large part, however, it has been evaded by once again refocusing policymaking on whites rather than blacks. Theoretically, compensatory practices would address the "sociopsychological harm" that blacks have experienced. In practice, however, it is easier and more politically manageable to address the presumed *instruments* of harm. Accordingly, for example, where educational discrimination has harmed blacks one can focus either on the harm or on the discriminatory structures. For schools, the courts and policymakers have focused on the administration of schools and its redistribution of students rather than on the substantive educational harm and corresponding pedagogical remedies. The practical policy impact is thus to look first at what education administration is among whites and then to seek to bring blacks into that same form of administration.

The object of education policy, then, whether it is busing or special admissions, is to prevent blacks from having a race-specific education. At first glance, this might appear to be a race-neutral approach, but is so only if one assumes that behind the long-segregated white school doors nothing specifically white was done. In fact, such a presupposition is consistent with race as a physical concept. Moreover, it is conducive to measuring disadvantages for blacks as their degree of distance from the institutional environment of whites. As we shall see shortly, affirmative action programs are frequently just such an affirmation of the virtues of traditionally white institutions and practices. We first look at the race-related concepts in these traditions.

CONSTITUTIONAL LAW AND RACE SPECIFICITY

A perusal of federal laws on racial issues will show either that blacks as a racial group have not been a subject of a legal issue or that blacks constitute such a sensitive issue that any reference to them is virtually taboo. At least 90 percent of all legislative references to black American status or issues fail to mention blacks directly in their legal prescriptions. At most, a direct reference may occur as an example of a problem but not as a primary component of the problem. Even more scarce in terms of legal prescriptions (no exceptions are evident), and more clearly taboo, is direct reference to "whites." It is as if the American individualistic tradition prohibits direct legislative statements for or about a racial group, even though the intent of the legislation's initiators may be clearly race-specific. There is, perhaps, a tradition of self-deception here, a special kind of "moral dilemma," in Gunnar Myrdal's terms.[4]

In some sense, racially specific language may be difficult to reconcile with the broad constitutional applications often anticipated in civil rights. Law and regulation work most effectively when their objects are defined by legal or illegal *behavior* (e.g., discriminatory housing sales) rather than by the description of the regulations' normal *subjects*. Whatever the legal writing constraints on identifying blacks directly, there exists an equally proscriptive political constraint, involving our cultural predilection to attribute legislative authority, sanction, and/or benefits only to individuals who, by definition, are individually and uniformly responsible before the law.

This cultural predilection shows itself in the nation's origin, in the Declaration of Independence linking "life, liberty and the pursuit of happiness." Only individuals can hold and exercise liberty, and only individuals may pursue happiness as it was then understood. That understanding was indisputably translated by John Locke, who argued for life, liberty, and "property."[5] In a capitalist society, only individuals (or private collections of them) can hold property for capitalistic purposes.

The conceptual constraint this cultural norm poses for racial awareness is evident in the Constitution's indirect contemporary references to the status of African Americans. The most prominent of these is the "three-fifths" compromise, which permits electoral representation of slaveholders on a numerical basis by counting slaves owned as three-fifths of a person. An understandable but unfortunate misinterpretation of the clause is that it is often thought to "define" each black individual as three-fifths of a person. On the contrary, the clause is only marginally relevant to blacks in its intent, though significant in its effect:

> Representatives and direct taxes shall be appointed among the several states which may be included within this union, according to their respective numbers, which shall be determined by adding to the whole number of free persons, including those bound to service for a term of years, and excluding Indians not taxed, three-fifths of all other persons. [6]

Although relevant to blacks, the clause primarily defines inegalitarian relationships among whites in the electoral structure. In fact, its principle relevance to blacks depends on the proposition of inequality among whites in the representative process. Namely, some forms of property determine a voter's importance in the selection of representatives. Here, the critical distinction between whites as property holders and the poor is clarified by the reference to indentured servants. There can be no doubt that being white has a Constitutional value in itself.

Of course, the prior conflicts between North and South may have necessitated a special deference to plantation property values in order to stabilize the union. What that historical link says about race and the state should not be overlooked. At minimum, it indicates that the sublimation of racial identification was consistent with other national political and economic compromises. The ability to specify black and white was contingent on the nation's ability to confront the divisive concepts of property rights among whites. For better or worse, that confrontation was postponed until the Civil War.

Along with that confrontation came a fleeting consciousness of race and political structure. Race and racism, however, once more escaped explication in the law. The Reconstruction amendments to the Constitution, the Thirteenth, Fourteenth, and Fifteenth amendments, recognized the complicitous role of American law in controlling racial inequality. Yet, the law was presented as the cure, the savior of an ill-conceived social system that was not being reined in by its rational force.

The greater race-consciousness emerged with the end of Reconstruction, the Compromise of 1877, and the reinstitutionalization of legally supported racism. In this compromise, the North came to terms with the South on ending its military occupation and on electing the next president.[7] More significantly, they came to terms on the role of race in national politics. Henceforth, racial issues were to be excluded from interparty politics. By excluding specifically black concerns and black party officials from Northern support, both parties effectively labelled racial issues as too ideologically disruptive to conform to the developing two-party system—a system heavily dependent on fundamental ideological consensus.

The early voting rights successes against the most blatant discriminatory practices illustrate a desire to escape from race consciousness. The fight against the "grandfather clause," manifested in *Guinn v. United States* (1915), appears to show commitment to African Americans who had been denied the franchise on the bogus criterion that their grandfather had not voted (during slavery).[8] Given the host of existing and developing discriminatory tactics at the time, the rejection of the clause may be more directly attributable to the blatancy of its racial component than to the quality of its racial bias. The poll tax and the literacy test, for example, persisted with legal protection for another fifty years.

What was blatantly racial about this clause may be called individual racism. *Individual racism* explicitly specifies a racial group for adverse treatment. The grandfather clause did that and more: It not only singled out blacks, it singled out whites. It specified being white in almost explicit terms as a basis for the right to vote. It was this latter race-consciousness—the consciousness of being white—that was particularly repulsive to a judicial system accustomed to universalistic concepts. The denial of rights to blacks would thus have to hinge on some "individualistic" failure or deficiency of blacks and not on the narrow race-conscious privilege of whites, in part because it insulted whites.

To institutionalize racism, it was necessary to deinstitutionalize race. To make racism legally and politically viable, race itself became a legal and political nonentity. In a related manner, Derek Bell observes of the Fourteenth Amendment's equal protection clause that protection of rights is individualistic: "The guarantees of the Fourteenth Amendment extend to all persons. . . . The guarantee of equal protection cannot mean one thing when applied to one individual and something else when applied to a person of a different color."[9]

Accordingly, the assumption of individual equality of rights among whites may well have required that any racially directed denial of rights be couched in individualistic dogma. In particular, equal protection of the laws was conceived as applying only to individuals (and incorporations of individuals) and not to racial groups.

THE PHYSICAL AND SOCIAL CHARACTER OF RACE

The great contribution of the *Brown* case to the legal analysis of race was its groundbreaking recognition that racial inequality was socially and politically determined. By using sociopsychological data in the articulation of its ruling, the Court effectively recognized that equal protection had relevance beyond the individual. In this and subsequent civil rights cases, such as *Hobson v. Hanson* (1967), the courts recognized that the pursuit of equity through public action required recognizing the social and racial network in which people live.[10] In so doing, it made an important adjustment to the individualistic ethic by admitting that individuals did not have to be individually oppressed for inequality to exist. The courts did not, however, admit that government could be responsible for this holistic, nonindividual repression.

An outstanding example of this failure to consider governmental accountability is the Court's interpretation of Kenneth Clark's data in the "black dolls" experiment, cited in *Brown*. The experimental findings showed that black elementary school girls, like white ones, had a preference for white dolls. The conclusion was that such a preference by blacks indicates a negative self-image, presumably promoted by segregation. The kind of legal redress that the Court deemed appropriate indicates more of a social than political conception of race relations. Schools were told to desegregate, but the implementation of that order was to be as private and remote from federal governance as possible. No public accounting for the psychological remediation of these or any little black girls was ever planned. Although the states controlled the desegregation policy, implementation was effectively nonpublic or quasi-private. A more public and politically accountable interpretation of the findings would have called for race-conscious redistribution of educational authority for community control. Obviously, such a decision would have raised questions about equal protection but would still have been more consistent with the historical government role in education, which has been focused on the administration and financing of education and not on its substance or pedagogy. In fact, the unwillingness of the federal government to follow its school desegregation orders to the point of educational impact may have led to the crisis over busing in the 1970s and to the turn against busing in the 1980s. Perhaps, more to the point of showing the privatization standard in the Court's approach, it produced no procedures for determining how or whether the self-esteem of those black girls or any others would be affected by its desegregation order.

The same issue emerged in a vastly transformed political context at the end of 1990, when a U.S. Department of Education official, Michael Williams, asserted that "minority-only" scholarships would be deemed in violation of the law by the department. In seeking to mitigate the hailstorm of protest that ensued, President Bush had the department reinterpret its declaration to permit "privately funded" minority scholarships. Because the justification for the original order was the presumption of (reverse) discrimination, apparently private discrimination was not considered a governmental responsibility. Right or wrong in its legal interpretation, the Bush administration evidently saw nothing in civil rights law that required governmental responsibility for racial inequality per se. Before the Williams order, no public effort was made to assure that progress toward racial equality with whites for blacks was being made by this administration. Under the order, the whole question of racial inequality was removed a step further from public scrutiny. The only remaining public obligation for scholarship claimed by the administration involved the assurance of "merit" standards with some deference to financial need. Merit, like financial status, of course, has long been approached as an individual attribute in our individualistic tradition.

A brief example will illustrate the artificial distinction made between merit-based and race-specific policies. In *Bakke* (1978), the claim of reverse discrimination was upheld, in large part because Allan Bakke had received higher standardized test and school-generated scores than had minority students in the University of California–Davis medical school special admissions program. Almost forgotten in the ensuing public debate was the fact that both parties to the case had stipulated before the California Supreme Court that Bakke's merit was not disputed. In other words, an essential conflict between race and merit could be assumed to exist and yet be beyond governmental concern. If, for example, there had been demonstrable cultural bias in the testing or other scores, the courts would have had to ignore it. Race and merit were to be treated as politically external and, in this case, competing quasi-social and physical entities. Only the consciousness or awareness of race in school policy was subject to adjudication. That active consciousness would have to be assuaged by the guilt of prior discrimination or justified by some social and educational interest. Race-consciousness in this case replaced discrimination as the link of race to normal social and political function.

If race and merit were to be treated as socially and politically determined qualities, then they could obviously overlap. No longer could the cross-racial neutrality of tests generated without regard to blacks be taken for granted. Merit, individualistically treated through the early stipulation before the court, became the social goal. The affirmation of that goal—really a private standard—became the object of judicial intervention. Race-consciousness would thus be judged as consistent or inconsistent with that goal. Race-consciousness, not racial inequality, became the politically relevant aspect of race relations. Unfortunately, there was no judgment on merit consciousness.

In effect, the application of the equal protection clause was directed toward maintaining the artificial dichotomy between race and merit, artificial because it was never examined by the litigants. Instead, the social neutrality of race was presupposed. Among other things, the sanctity of merit standards from race relations could only be questioned by risking the overall sanctity of merit. If admissions standards for blacks lose their objective image, then the question of inequality in judgments among whites is immediate. Only a race-specific standard for public policy that takes into account broad areas of social distribution would not also disrupt public policy for whites.

COMPENSATION AND DISADVANTAGE

When affirmative action was first formally proposed by President Lyndon Johnson in 1968 (Executive Order 11246), the potential for a race-specific interpretation was there in the suggested adherence to goals for racial inclusion. Instead, the media emphasis on compensation for past discrimination became more prominent, except where goals were the focus of attack. The focus of compensatory racial policy inevitably turns to prevailing standards among white Americans. Of course, for such standards no one wants to be race specific. That would require specifying in historical form the characteristics and acquisitions of society attributable to its exploitation of blacks. To pursue this line of analysis would, in turn, provide grounds for socially disruptive claims on much acquired individual property among whites. Again, the constitutionally sanctioned integrity of private property over group rights for blacks has never been repudiated. Only individual rights have standing before the courts. Accordingly, the dilemma of group identity and claims for black individuals remains unresolved.

A society without popular myths is a society on the verge of civil war, or so it seems with our myths about race relations. One of the more popular myths, which clings on in the political arena without a shred of intellectual backing, concerns historical compensation. It is encapsulated in the statement that "we and our property have nothing to do with the racism and exploitation of our grandparents." Yet, less than three normal lifetimes ago, this was a slave society. Only 35 years ago, segregation was the law of the land. Quite obviously, employment conditions such as old-boy networks and apprenticeships would not be old if they did not go that far back. And yet, these are the defining characteristics of institutional racism.[11]

A realistic function of political power is that white beneficiaries of historical inequality cannot be held responsible for the full material amount of their benefit. As a consequence, the courts have turned to looking at "disparate treatment" instead of compensation. More precisely, the courts were once willing to consider as evidence of continuing discrimination cases showing that employers' practices had a "disparate impact" on blacks. The Supreme Court's rejection of employee testing that shows a statistically large bias against blacks in terms of results (*Griggs v. Duke Power Co.* [1971]) was a step toward legitimating the racial group as politically and legally recognizable.[12] The focus on impact, however, proved to demand too much of a focus on African Americans. Consequently, the courts' recourse to disparate treatment was more consistent with society's aversion to race specificity. The race focus is still present, but now the primary subjects are whites. It is a focus that looks at blacks only to ask how they may not be treated like whites.

Of course, other social factors work against judicial reliance on impact standards as illustrated in the voting rights cases where the issue was "intent" versus statistically demonstrable impact. In *Bolden* (1980) the plaintiff wanted at-large elections declared in violation of the Voting Rights Act. The system of at-large elections for city council, it was argued, effectively prevented blacks from winning elected office.[13] Evidently, the Supreme Court felt that the individual prejudices of white voters against black candidates were perfectly consistent with equal protection, as long as they were not implemented or mobilized by public authority. To be found in violation, therefore, one must show that the voting procedure was primarily and originally intended by public authorities to discriminate. The fact that many such procedures have their origin in the post-Reconstruction backlash against blacks has yet to have its full judicial recognition.

Intent standards, like disparate treatment standards, return whites to center stage, if unconsciously. Ironically, intent standards should owe something to the precedent-setting use of sociopsychological data in *Brown*. Still, such data, along with most evidence of intent, are virtually impossible to mount before the courts in the absence of name-calling, Klan-like bigotry.

Disparate treatment places the normal treatment of whites in the position of an ideal standard. If the admissions standard or employment practice is fair to whites, as individuals, then it is presumed to be fair to blacks. If, for example, the employment test does not draw on any group characteristic of white applicants (for example, asking an applicant to recite the pledge of the White Citizen's Council), then it is deemed legitimate for blacks as well. Hence, it is assumed that a test that discriminates among whites is good for blacks and whites.

One of the problems here for blacks is that minor inequities among whites may turn into gross inequities for blacks and still go unnoticed. There is really no way to tell, because the primary standard or yard-stick of bias remains within white society. Accordingly, the recent Supreme Court ruling in *Wards Cove v. Antonio* (1989) requires plaintiffs against discriminatory practices to prove that the practices were directed against them as an outside group.[14] In other words, blacks are required to give evidence of how whites perceive themselves as an inclusive racial group in order to prove that they are being exclusive. This naively assumes that white racism depends on white race self-consciousness, something that is often, but by no means always, true.

LEGISLATIVE LANGUAGE AND RACE

As the preceding observations on the courts' interpretation of race as a subject of law suggest, race has unclear standing in American jurisprudence. In the host of federal and state civil and voting rights laws, blacks are mentioned primarily as examples of the range of enforcement subjects. Most frequently, race is a negative example, as in the statement, "...without regard to race, creed, or national origin." Occasionally, it becomes the measure of effective policy implementation. Where racial parity is sought and where affirmative action goals or quotas are used, race has an ambiguous standing. In these cases, for instance school busing, racial group distribution appears to be the primary object of the legislation when, in fact, it is not. The legislation is always concerned with rights and the equitable protection of them. To ensure that education policy, for example, complies with nonracial equal protection, a race-focused parameter is applied by law. Similarly, with affirmative action goals and quotas, the real object of policy is the compensation for, or the removal of, racial bias from the public policy sector.

Race-focused interests have themselves been the primary object of legislation, but those interests are then distilled or disguised to emphasize their most universal component. For example, Title III of the Higher Education Act of 1965 was clearly intended by its authors to channel federal subsidies to traditionally black colleges and universities. Yet Title III was named the "Developing Institutions" act to give the impression to the uninformed that any new struggling college would be eligible for such subsidies. In fact, since the end of the 1970s, the vast majority of benefiting institutions have been traditionally white.[15] The disguise was a concession to anti-race-conscious political sentiment rather than to legal constraints. Virtually all the Congressional supporters knew what the act intended; they simply did not want to commit themselves to it in principle.[16] The colors of their real sentiments were later shown when the benefits were redirected to two-year white colleges and the new four-year colleges.

In this regard, William Julius Wilson, an apostle of the thesis that "racial differences are dissolving into class differences," makes a questionable assumption by arguing that social welfare policies are always "race-neutral" when he states that, "After all, Americans across racial and class lines continue to be concerned about unemployment and job security, declining real wages, escalating medical costs, the sharp decline in the quality of public education[, and] crime and drug trafficking in their neighborhoods."[17]

Nothing in American law and public policy is, or ever has been, so race specific that it is not also in the interest of white Americans. In the rare cases where race-specific intentions have penetrated public authority, the language of the law, (for example, the Fourteenth Amendment), has been manipulated to include white American interests. Where policies have been developed around a black political issue, the goals and structures of program implementation respond to white American interests.[18] Affirmative action has not been judicially sustained where whites as a group are disadvantaged, but only where whites appear to have "too much" advantage. Full employment policies, for example, could well exist without regard to blacks, although blacks are clearly in need of such policies. Conversely, if blacks were the originators and the primary focus of full employment policies, the language and structure of the resulting programs would inevitably be as race neutral as possible. Historically, one can never expect race-focused black politics to result in race-specific legislation. Just as the equal protection clause is indebted to black politics, many social welfare programs have their origins in race-conscious initiatives.

THE NEUTRALIZING TENDENCY OF POLICY FORMULATION

Prominent among the surviving, though barely so, race-focused programs are minority set-asides. Clearly affirmed by the Supreme Court in 1980 as a form of compensation, they are now the constant target of hostile political and economic conservatives.[19] Almost immediately, these programs were expanded to include a variety of minority groups and women for whom the same kind of past discrimination would not be claimed. The speed with which other groups were included suggests the shortness of the lifespan of race focus in the public arena. More important, these set-asides structured black participation as peripheral to a white-dominated economic center. More precisely, they provide for the satellite dependence of small minority contractors on more successful white contractors in the principal roles.

In *Richmond v. Croson* (1989), the Supreme Court's rejection of set-asides as reverse discrimination demonstrates the elasticity of race specificity (to the extent it is present).[20] The evidence in this case showed that blacks and other minorities continued to be grossly underrepresented in city contracting in Richmond, Virginia, but their underrepresentation was no longer the central issue. Rather, the white plaintiff argued that he was victimized because he had followed the rules, while the set-aside contractor had had every chance and failed to meet the initial requirements. These requirements were set up to meet the city's contractual needs as guided by its assessment of the marketplace. In essence, therefore, set-asides were expected to help minorities accommodate the marketplace. In the end, which interest was primary? The success of the reverse discrimination claim indicates that the white-dominated economic center was the ideal to which blacks were expected, with help, to adjust. If, as conceived by Congressman Parren Mitchell, it was the black business that counted most in the policy's implementation, it became just business.

The retreat from race specificity would be largely complete if it were not for continued public subsidy of traditionally black colleges and universities. Where, for example, set-aside programs have survived, they have done so only by diversifying their focus to include women and/or Hispanics. Even here, the subsidies are justified as historical compensation rather than as race-specific policy. Yet, they are commonly thought of in the latter frame of reference.

The long series of court cases initiated in 1973 by the NAACP Legal Defense Fund against Southern state dual systems, the *Adams* cases, have not been able to confront the central issue: Should government policies be race specific? Rather, they have argued, in effect, that society is race conscious and divided and that government must take cognizance of these conditions while pursuing racial equality. Of course, the pursuit of racial equality without clear race specificity leads to a narrow approach to desegregation. Public colleges in the South, both black and white, were accordingly subjected to a series of desegregation orders under the guidance of the Fifth District Court. By 1987, when the litigation was temporarily terminated, most public black institutions still existed, but all were moving, or claiming to be moving, toward desegregation.

Ironically, none of the black colleges had ever been guilty of segregating.[21] Segregation, like discrimination, requires that those responsible have authority to exclude. Authority within these colleges applied almost exclusively to their educational and administrative content. Authority to exclude people on any nonacademic basis was always lodged with the white-controlled state boards. Thus, the reform of behavior intended had more to do with white officials than black educators. Yet, the greatest tangible impact was on these black educators, whose schools were threatened with possible extinction.

The survival of black institutions should have brought to the surface of education policy and the legal arena the question of racial *separation* without *segregation*. After all, these black schools and their students cling firmly to their independence. Still, the question has never been more than peripheral to debate in policymaking and judicial arenas. Instead, the states initiated institutional programs to redistribute students by race in response to the court. Only a recourse to upholding educational traditions and respecting the special socioeconomic needs of students has preserved the black public institutions.

Given the judicial interpretations of equal protection since 1954, it is clear that the courts cannot endorse the public creation of racially separate institutions. Nor can any institutions be publicly subsidized where the subsidy serves, in the context of racial separation, to sustain a racial disadvantage. Still, a question remains about mutually acceptable and privately subsidized separation where substantive access to resources, such as schooling, is equally available interracially.

This question may be as much concerned with conceptualization as with policy. What is racially separate depends on the definition of *race*. Schools may select their programs, their scholarly orientation, and social support systems to appeal to students with specific interests. In the private sector, traditionally black schools do just that. The impression, then, that they are racially exclusive is less probable because of the "social" interests that the schools exist to propagate. The "physical" characteristic of the students in this case appears to be more coincidental. The tendency of the legal arena to treat race in purely physiological terms generates a greater ambiguity about separation.

If one returns to *Brown's* reference to protecting "the hearts and minds" of students, the possibility surfaces of getting beyond the physiological. It emerges from the kind of race specificity in the sentiment expressed by the Supreme Court. This perspective, though not consistent, identifies race as an ephemeral social entity. In this concept, the physical substratum is strong enough to elicit a physical and even numerical interpretation of desegregation wherever equal protection is affirmed. Yet, the response to "simple" racial separation should be guided by a concern for its sociopsychological and cultural significance to race relations.

In this perspective, a black college may be a vestige of segregation as a physical entity but a bulwark against it as a social and cultural entity. Accordingly, one would have to weigh the value of both aspects before attempting to destroy or transform these institutions. Concomitantly, one could no longer feel that physical desegregation serves the spirit of *Brown,* where a separate black cultural or social creation had emerged out of the segregated conditions.

Second, the social perspective on race also focuses directly on African Americans. The vast majority of desegregation cases, it has been argued, have really focused on whites in terms of primary concepts. In contrast, the popular reaction to the *Adams* litigation has elevated blacks to the position of a social and cultural entity with a life and desire for "liberties" of its own. Equally important, the desire to preserve black institutions has begun to raise consciousness of race as a legitimate political entity. In other words, society is not only composed of black and white individuals subject to governmental redistribution. It is also composed of social-racial groups that determine the character and life-chances of their constituent individuals. Government cannot independently act on all collections of individuals because race (among other social factors) makes the individual politically inaccessible, if not insignificant, when race is the subject of policy.

In some historical sense, the legitimate individual attributes have been effectively defined in American law and politics as "white" or, rather, as the commonly recognized attributes of individuals in the dominant society. Since the three-fifths compromise, the sanctity of the individual as a property holder and political actor has been tied to the denial of the racial and social foundations of that property. When political demands involving voting rights and civil rights have succeeded in court, it has been largely through the insinuation of numbers of black individuals into patterns of behavior primarily characteristic of white Americans. The rise of the black middle class is as much a result of the constraints of civil rights as it is a product of its success. Some critics want to blame middle-class blacks as well as civil rights leaders for not paying enough attention to the needs of the mass of black Americans. While they could easily deserve some blame, the specific social objectives, meaning patterns of upward mobility, available to civil rights leaders were circumscribed by established social and political patterns in white society. Even where blacks are concerned, public policy should always be expected to resist disruption to white society. Admitting a few more into an individualistic and unequal system is far less disruptive than demanding that a subset of equality among blacks be created. After all, that demand would require race-consciousness, and true race-consciousness means race specificity.

CONCLUSION

The majority of men resent and always have resented the idea of equality with most of their fellow men. This has had physical, economic and cultural reasons . . . especially I presume the cultural and spiritual desire to be one's self without interference from others; to enjoy the anarchy of the spirit which is inevitably the goal of all consciousness.[22]

Embodied in the ideal self-concept of the true individualist is an unconfined and unattached, if not anarchic, ego, which abhors self-categorization and group identification. Prime among the group pressures to be resented is the pressure to concede to racial identification. The truly naive individualist resents any other race with which regular interaction compels self-doubts and reflection on personal independence or social interdependence. The typical American individual resents the race-consciousness of all others because it compels a consciousness of his or her own racial confines. Close encounters with racial differences force awareness of the social interdependence entailed in one's own racial identity. In brief, many white Americans, as individuals, resent and always have resented black race-consciousness because it forces them to admit that they are white; that their attainments are tied to their race and not just to themselves.

American public policy and lawmakers have always been concerned with race, but have always been afraid to address it directly. Beginning with the political sensitivity surrounding the constitutional issue of white people's (slave) property, no one could confront it directly without destabilizing the fragile union between North and South. In the end, the differing nature of property between North and South drew attention to group differences among whites and to the social, rather than private, basis of property.

The resistance to affirmative action has as much in common with these early concerns for property rights and social stability as it does with the 1960s civil rights reaction. Concessions to modern civil rights demands were conceptually fairly easy to make, first, because they conform to the ideas of individualism and nonracial universalism. Second, of course, the structure and control of property was left untouched. In this regard, the major political difference between the constitutional issue and affirmative action debates is that the menace of instability is more visibly interracial in the latter case.

Whatever their factual basis, claims of reverse discrimination are to some degree heightened by the sense that other individual attainments were not really personal but social (and also racial). Resistance to race-conscious policies is an early expression of fear that greater inequalities (or differentiation) among whites are forthcoming. In a sense, it is a fear of being white; it is a desire to be a better self-creation than others who were also "created" white.

Whenever a public agency has been challenged on the racial content of its policies, its response has tended to be race specific, but the direction of that specificity has been disguised. When the issue of special treatment or discriminatory treatment of blacks has emerged, officials have sought a universal standard for comparison. If the redress proposed involves a simple civil rights extension or retrenchment from affirmative action, then the resolution has an individualistic character. Behind the standard guiding decisions has always been a fairly uncritical acceptance of the characteristic patterns of behavior in white society. While concerned with the black community, the unconscious focus of race-specific politics has been the white community.

Ultimately, the resistance to race specificity in American law and public policy is grounded in an unwillingness to expose patterns of distribution to public scrutiny detached from traditional values. It is an unwillingness to confront, all in one sweep, the diverse ground rules on which American inequalities in attainment and wealth are justified. In sum, it is a fear of confronting the intricacies of white inequality.

REFERENCES

Barnett, Marguerite, and James Hefner. 1976. *Public policy for the black community.* New York: Alfred.

Bell, Derek. 1968. *Civil rights: Leading cases.* Boston: Little, Brown.

Bell, Derrick A. 1973. *Race, racism and American law.* Boston: Little, Brown.

Blakey, William A. 1994. An agenda for excellence and equity in black colleges and universities: Prospects and relations. (In this volume.)

Davidson, Chandler. 1984. An overview. *Minority vote dilution.* Washington, DC: Howard University Press.

Dorsen, Norman. 1969. *Discrimination and civil rights.* Boston: Little, Brown.

Du Bois, William E. B. 1968. *The dusk of dawn.* New York: Harcourt, Brace & World.

Franklin, John Hope. 1969. *From slavery to freedom.* 3d ed. New York: Vintage.

Jones, Mack. 1987. The voting rights act . . . In *Readings in American political issues,* ed. Franklin D. Jones and Michael Adams. Dubuque, IA: Kendall Hunt.

Moore, John A., and Myron Roberts. 1985. *The pursuit of happiness.* 3d ed. New York: Macmillan.

Morris, Lorenzo. 1979. *Elusive quality: The status of black Americans in U.S. higher education.* Washington, DC: Howard University Press.

Morris, Lorenzo, ed. 1990. *The social and political implications of the 1984 Jesse Jackson presidential campaign.* New York: Praeger.

Myrdal, Gunnar. 1944. *An American dilemma.* New York: Harper.

Sculnick, Michael W. 1989. Key court cases. *Employment Relations Today* (Autumn).

Tollett, Kenneth S. 1982. *Black colleges as instruments of affirmative action.* Washington, DC: Howard University Institute for the Study of Educational Policy.

Tussman, Joseph, ed. 1963. *The Supreme Court on racial discrimination.* New York: Oxford University Press.

U.S. Commission of Civil Rights. 1968. *Political participation.* Washington, DC: U.S. Government Printing Office.

Wilson, William Julius. 1990. Race-neutral programs and the Democratic Coalition. *The American Prospect* 1 (spring): 79.

NOTES

1. *Brown v. Board of Education of Topeka, Kansas,* 349 U.S. 294 (1955). See Joseph Tussman, ed., *The Supreme Court on Racial Discrimination* (New York: Oxford University Press, 1963), 45.

2. Massachusetts General Laws, Ch. 71 (1965) No. 37D. See Norman Dorsen, *Discrimination and Civil Rights* (Boston: Little, Brown, (1969).

3. *Regents of the University of California v. Bakke,* 438 U.S. 265 (1978).

4. Gunnar Myrdal, *An American Dilemma* (New York: Harper & Row, 1944).

5. John A. Moore and Myron Roberts, *The Pursuit of Happiness* 3d ed. (New York: Macmillan, 1985), 47.

6. U.S. Constitution, Article I, Section 2.

7. John Hope Franklin, *From Slavery to Freedom,* 3d ed. (New York: Vintage, 1969), 324–32. See also Lorenzo Morris, ed., *The Social and Political Implications of the 1984 Jesse Jackson Presidential Campaign* (New York: Praeger, 1990), chap. 4.

8. *Guinn v. United States,* 238 U.S. 347 (1915). See U.S. Commission on Civil Rights, *Political Participation* (Washington, DC: U.S. Government Printing Office, 1968), 6.

9. Derek Bell, *Civil Rights Leading Cases* (Boston: Little, Brown, (1980), 433.

10. Cases examining the racial impact of homogeneous grouping (tracking) have suggested that individual attainment cannot be fully measured without substantial reference to the social context at several levels. In *Hobson v. Hansen,* 269 F. Supp. 401 (D.D.C. 1967), Judge J. Skelley Wright concluded: "Racially and socially homogeneous schools damage the minds and spirit of all children who attend them."

11. Marguerite Barnett and James Hefner, *Public Policy for the Black Community* (New York: Alfred, 1976), 7.

12. *Griggs v. Duke Power Co.,* 401 U.S. 424 (1971). Derrick A. Bell, *Race, Racism and American Law* (Boston: Little, Brown, 1973), 759.

13. Chandler Davidson, "An Overview," *Minority Vote Dilution* (Washington, DC: Howard University Press, 1984), 17–18.

14. *Wards Cove v. Antonio,* 109 S. Ct. 2115 (1989). Michael W. Sculnick, "Key Court Cases," *Employment Relations Today* (Autumn 1989): 238.

15. William A. Blakey, "An Agenda for Excellence and Equity in Black Colleges and Universities: Prospects and Relations," (in this volume).

16. Lorenzo Morris, *Elusive Equality: The Status of Black Americans in U.S. Higher Education* (Washington, DC: Howard University Press, 1979), 194–95.

17. William Julius Wilson, "Race-Neutral Programs and the Democratic Coalition," *The American Prospect* 1 (Spring 1990): 79.

18. Mack Jones argues that structures for enforcing civil and voting rights often serve to modify but otherwise fundamentally reinforce

white dominance. See Mack Jones, "The Voting Rights Act . . . ," in Franklin D. Jones and Michael Adams, *Readings in American Political Issues* (Dubuque, IA: Kendall Hunt, 1987).

19. See for example, *Fullilove et al. v. Klutznick et al.*, 448 U.S. 448 (1980).

20. *Richmond v. Croson*, 109 S. Ct. 706 (1989).

21. Kenneth S. Tollett, *Black Colleges as Instruments of Affirmative Action* (Washington, DC: Howard University Institute for the Study of Educational Policy, 1982), 41, 54.

22. William E. B. Du Bois, *The Dusk of Dawn* (New York: Harcourt, Brace & World, 1968), 134.

African American Family Life | B

4 | Overview and Recommendations

Annie Brown, Ura Jean Oyemade Bailey, and James E. Craigen

Families in general and African American families in particular face an uncertain future at the dawn of the twenty-first century. Twelve years of a national government captive to partisan interests that sought to reverse decades of social policy efforts to address inequities in society, and the post-industrial restructuring of the U.S. economy, have had a devastating effect on American society. For African American families who have experienced a history of discrimination and economic marginality, these governmental actions and technological changes have had an even more pervasive and negative impact. The dynamics of racism have historically rendered African Americans as a group vulnerable to the slightest changes in the socioeconomic and political landscape of America. Often the last hired, even in times of prosperity, they are often the first fired in times of recession and economic retrenchment.

The viability and strength of the family, considered the basic institution of society, is closely tied to its interaction with the broader system of societal institutions, particularly the economic system. The historic struggle of the African American family has been the challenge to meet the needs of its members in an often hostile and nonsupportive climate of economic and social discrimination. The real story has been the resiliency and adaptability of this unit against all odds. Nevertheless, it would be foolish to dismiss the real pressures and challenges that threaten the future of African American families in an American society in transition.

The papers selected as chapters for this section address issues related to the current status of the African American family, and also provide a framework for more accurately examining its strengths and weaknesses in relation to future challenges. These chapters also address the paradoxical aspects of research and policy in relation to the African American family. The evidence of an emerging middle class at the same time that an increasing number of African American children are living in poverty presents a challenge for both researchers and policymakers. The authors systematically explore the current status of African American families in relation to health, mental health, child care, and the difficulties posed for social policy research. The central focus of concern is the future viability of the African American family and the development of policy that could more effectively assist it in meeting the needs of its members.

Dr. Lawrence Gary, in "Challenges Facing African American Families at the Dawn of a New Century," identifies several challenges facing the African American family in its struggle to remain viable. He focuses on two somewhat related issues: (a) providing for the continued biological functioning of each family member and (b) reducing the psychological damage of stressful life events.

Dr. Gary acknowledges the basic tasks of the family in providing the necessities of food, clothing, and shelter, but focuses on health behavior as important to survival: People must be healthy to reproduce successfully, which is part of the maintenance of biological functioning. In relating the importance of health to survival, Dr. Gary uses data from the National Center for Health Statistics to highlight the disparity in the life expectancy of black and white Americans. African Americans are disproportionately represented on negative indicators of health status such as accidental deaths, homicides, substance abuse, and AIDS. But health behavior is often a response to stress. The African American family is confronted with an array of problems, including racism, poverty, divorce, child abuse, unempolyment, and alcoholism, that place the family unit under considerable stress. Research has shown that too many stressful life events (pleasant and unpleasant) contribute to the development of physical and psychological disorders. The vulnerability of the African American family renders it susceptible to societal pressures with fewer resources to combat them.

Dr. Gary provides findings from a study of 50 African American families in the Washington, D.C., area who were identified by community groups for their perceived strength and stability. Ten characteristics and attributes were identified in varying combinations in those families considered strong. Dr. Gary concludes that these attributes could provide the impetus for strategies for program development to benefit a large number of families.

Dr. Robert Hill, in "Race, Class, and Culture: Common Pitfalls in Research on African American Families," takes issues with researchers who point to the declining significance of race as a determinant of the economic status of African American families in American society. Hill contends that this view of race is misleading because it focuses more on the internal "culture of poverty" defects than on external barriers such as racism, classism, and sexism as determinants of the life chances for African Americans. Further, Hill believes that the misuse of the concepts of race, class, and culture by mainstream social scientists and policymakers impedes the development of meaningful public policy for combating problems associated with racism, poverty, unemployment, and family instability.

According to Hill, it is the failure to distinguish between concepts such as discrimination and prejudice, and to separate individual racism from institutional racism, that leads to fallacious research. This lack of clarity raises serious questions about the validity of much of the data used to inform policymakers on issues related to African Americans, and at times presents a decidedly distorted optimistic view of the state of race relations in America.

Dr. Walter Allen, in "Whatever Tomorrow Brings: African American Families and Government Social Policy," examines the relationship between U.S. government social policy and the status of African American families and their children. His paper in many ways synthesizes the ideas presented in the other papers on the role and status of the African American family. Like Hill, he points out the weaknesses in much of the research methodology informing government social policy affecting African American family life, noting that in the final analysis, decisions about the utility of social programs affecting African Americans are debated and then decided largely in terms of other factors, such as cost, publicity value, political value, and political expediency.

Like Gary, Allen highlights the strengths of the African American family and its contributions to the maintenance of positive mental health in African American communities. Yet, he cautions against losing sight of the reality, that large numbers of black people and black families find themselves in precarious and deteriorating positions, progressively less able to nurture, protect, and provide for their children. What is needed for African American families are the kinds of structural supports in society that will help mitigate the effects of institutionalized racism.

Dr. Valora Washington contributes to the discussion of the African American family in the twenty-first century by examining the status of its most vulnerable members—the children. Although her paper is specifically entitled "Child Care Policies and Young African American Children," the fate of children is inextricably bound to the ability of their families to provide for, nurture, and protect them. Given the status of African American families in this country, African American children face challenges to their growth and survival because of racism, regardless of social class.

Dr. Washington explores a number of legislative initiatives aimed at providing and improving the quality of child care, noting that, unlike many European countries, where child care is universal, in the United States child care policies are often tied to welfare reform. In addition to pointing out that such legislation leaves out a number of poor children who do not receive AFDC benefits, Dr. Washington cautions against policy directed solely toward economic deprivation to the exclusion of race and racism. Such initiatives can obscure the special needs of African American children.

Other papers presented at this conference also targeted issues of concern to African American families. All resonated with a sense of urgency that stressed the need to respond to the plight facing African American communities. The call was not just for more programs, but rather for policy development based on sound research methodology. This means that researchers and policymakers will need to clarify the meaning of such concepts as class, race, and culture.

SUMMARY AND RECOMMENDATIONS

The status of African American families cannot be divorced from the socioeconomic and political climate of American society. In a time of declining national resources and a shifting world order, addressing the issues of African American families can not be left to political expediency. We must make an intentional effort to develop a national family policy that is sensitive to the needs of those most vulnerable families. In the area of social policy, Dr. Allen suggests that the most helpful action policymakers could undertake would be "a review of extant legislation, programs, and procedures to assess the intended and unintended consequences for black families."

The contributors all share in the idea that African American families should play a part in the development of policies that affect their lives; that real change will occur only through the empowerment of all people; and that empowerment must be based on the strengths that exist within African American families and communities. It is not that African American families need to change their values to become integrated into American society, but rather that American society needs to redefine its values in relation to racism, discrimination, and cultural diversity. Only then will meaningful social science research be conducted that will generate the data needed to develop family policies that will benefit all families, yet will also consider the special needs of African American families.

5 | Challenges Facing African American Families at the Dawn of a New Century

LAWRENCE E. GARY

A s the primary socializing agent, the family shapes the personalities, attributes, values, and behavior repertoires of its individual members. While the family is expected to provide a great deal to individuals, it cannot carry out its tasks without certain resources and supports. In other words, it does not exist in a vacuum. It is part of a larger system where it must interact with other institutions.[1] The family is a very important institution for the survival of a people. Of critical concern to African American communities in particular and to the American society as a whole is the viability of African American families. From a historical perspective, a number of social forces have made it difficult for African American families to function effectively in American society.[2] As we approach the year 2000, it is critical that we give appropriate attention to increasing our understanding of how well African American families are functioning.

In this chapter, we will identify several challenges facing African American families in general at the dawn of a new century, and will closely examine two of them. We will conclude with a discussion of the attributes of strong African American families. These objectives will be achieved by selectively reviewing the literature on families in general and African American families in particular, and by reporting on a research project titled *Stable Black Families*.[3]

THE CONCEPT OF FAMILY

What is a family? The answer to this question is no longer obvious, for the definition of family has changed over time. In their classic work, *The Family: From Institution to Companionship*, Burgess, Lock, and Thomas define *family* as "a group of persons united by ties of marriage, blood, or adoption; constituting a single household; interacting and communicating with each other in their respective social roles (husband and wife, mother and father, son and daughter, brother and sister); and creating and maintaining a common culture."[4]

This is a rather restricted definition, which emphasizes well-defined roles and legal and genetic ties of family members. The U.S. Bureau of the Census defines a family as two or more persons related by birth, marriage, or adoption who reside in the same household.[5] This definition also is too restrictive in that it focuses on the nuclear family and not on larger kin groups. Also, it does not consider psychological bonds essential in family dynamics.

The traditional concept of a family as a married couple with children or as a group of adult kin has been challenged by emerging family forms such as the single-parent family, the egalitarian marriage, the dual worker marriage, the childless marriage, gay couples, the serial family, the composite family, and the commune family.[6] The definition of the family has also been expanded by some courts and governments. For example, in July 1989, the New York Court of Appeals ruled that a long-term gay couple may be considered a family under the state's rent control regulation. In other words, the court added gay couples to the legal definition of a family.[7] San Francisco, California; Madison, Wisconsin; and West Hollywood, California, are other places that have legitimized gay couples as family units by expanding their rights as domestic couples. We must also note that various individuals and groups have vigorously opposed extending certain rights to gay domestic partners.[8]

Nontraditional families are present in many communities, and especially in African American communities.[9] Census reports reflect dramatic changes in the family forms of our society. Over the past generation, there has been a significant increase in single-parent families. For example, in 1970, 32 percent of black children under the age of 18 years old lived in single-parent families, but in 1990, the per-

TABLE 1. Percentage of Children Living in Various Family Groupings
According to Race, 1970–1990

Race and Group	1970 Percent	1980 Percent	1985 Percent	1990 Percent
All races				
Two parents	85	77	74	73
One parent	22	20	24	25
Mother only	11	19	3	22
Father only	2	2	2	25
Neither parent	3	3	2	2
TOTAL	100	100	100	100
White				
Two parents	90	83	80	79
One parent	9	15	18	19
Mother only	8	14	16	16
Father only	1	1	2	3
Neither parent	1	2	2	2
TOTAL	100	100	100	100
Black				
Two parents	59	42	40	38
One parent	32	46	54	55
Mother only	30	44	51	51
Father only	2	2	3	4
Neither parent	9	12	6	7
TOTAL	100	100	100	100

Source: U.S. Bureau of the Census, *Statistical Abstract of the United States: 1993*, 113th
ed. (Washington, DC: Government Printing Office, 1993), 64.

centage was 55. For the white population in 1970, 9 percent of children under 18 years old lived in single-parent families, but in 1990,
the percentage was 19. Table 1 shows the percent of children under 18
years old by presence of parents according to race.

As a result of these and other changes (people marrying much later,
more getting divorced, more children being born out of wedlock, and
others), the public is beginning to recognize these new forms as families. In a survey by the Massachusetts Mutual Life Insurance Company
of 1,200 randomly selected adults, the respondents were asked to define the word *family*. By a margin of three to one, the subjects defined
it as "a group of people who live and care for each other" over the traditional definition of "related by blood or marriage."[10] These data
suggest that American people are changing old perceptions much

faster than are the courts, the policymakers, and indeed the social scientists Wilson and Tolson describe this change as follows:

> The meaning of the concept of family has become an issue in the family research because of the changing norms of American family life. Several researchers have observed that while the nuclear family appears to be a central component of the American concept of family, it is becoming increasingly inconsistent with the actual family experiences of many individuals who do not live in a household consisting of mother, father, and children.[11]

Defining *family* from the perspective of the nuclear family model is not adequate as we approach a new century. It is necessary, given current family norms, to move beyond treating other family forms as either incomplete or deviant variations of the nuclear family. Census data show that fewer than 26 percent of the nation's households fit the traditional concept of a family in 1990.[12] These different family forms have implications for the role of the family as a socializing unit. Research is needed to document how these forms function in our society. As we redefine the concept of family, we must be aware of the policy ramifications of what kinds of families will be considered normal or deviant. Some family researchers have already identified and accepted the existence of diverse family structures and forms in the African American community.[13] Wilson and Tolson concluded that, "interestingly, the normative structure of the black family has always reflected diverse forms of familial organization and embeddedness in extended family networks and may become the prototype of that survival."[14]

SURVIVAL CHALLENGES FOR AFRICAN AMERICAN FAMILIES

In reviewing the literature on African American families, several social scientists have identified challenges confronting this institution.[15] It can be argued that certain minimum conditions must be met for a group to survive in an industrial society.[16] These functional requisites for survival are implemented through the major institutions of the society. The family is viewed as a key institution in this process.

   All of society's institutions must work together to meet the major challenges facing African American families. They must provide for the continued biological functioning of each family member (eliminating threats to physical health and coping, e.g., by decreasing the incidence and prevalence of substance abuse and morbidity and lowering mortality rates; ensuring the proper disposal of toxic industrial wastes; increasing study of transplants and genetic markers; and improving access to medical services and technology). They must also provide for the adequate reproduction of new family members. (Who is qualified to have children? What are the normative systems that regulate child bearing? Why the recent documented decline in the sperm count of African American men in the United States? What factors contribute to teenage pregnancies? What should be done about pregnant drug abusers?) These institutions, in concert, must ensure the adequate socialization of each family member, especially the children. Who is teaching African American children survival skills? What socialization skills are needed for an information society? Who is the cultural broker or cultural bearer in African American families? How does one raise strong children? What are the attributes of successful African American children? Existing systems must allow for equitable and efficient production, distribution, and consumption of goods and services accounting for and utilizing such factors as assets and income of black households, small business regulations and affirmative action policies, unemployment and underemployment, wage discrepancies between black and white workers, tension at the workplace, and a high tendency to spend rather than save additional income. Ways must be found to maintain order within the family and with outside groups (e.g., effectively dealing with such disruptive issues as homicides, racial attacks, domestic violence, family rules, and power issues within families). The surrounding society must support family-oriented efforts to reduce the psychological damage of stressful life events (e.g., daily hassles, racial discrimination, family life cycle, normative changes from outside the family, and normative changes inside the family). Individuals, families, and all social institutions must sincerely work to improve interpersonal relationships between men and women (taking into account factors such as the rising divorce rate, spousal abuse, characteristics of the pool of individuals available for and interested in marriage, dating behavior, ratio of women to men in social and professional situations, and functions of male–female relationships). All must act to develop and project positive social images. (What are the images of African American families in the media? Who are the cultural heroes in African American communities? What African American values and principles are reflected on such programs as *The Cosby Show*?) The family as an institution must have broad social support to develop empowerment strategies for the family unit as well as for each family member (e.g., developing self-reliance and techniques of self-help, and understanding such ideas as internal versus external locus of control and power and how to use it). Finally, but perhaps most importantly, all individuals and institutions together must maintain the motivation to survive (defining and reinforcing the spiritual framework, the purpose and meaning of life, the various functions of the African American church, and encouraging cultural enhancement). In this chapter, we will discuss only two of the above issues: the need to provide for the continued biological functioning of each family member and the need to reduce the psychological damage of stressful life events.

BIOLOGICAL FUNCTIONING OF FAMILY MEMBERS

One of the primary challenges facing African American families is to provide for the continued biological functioning of each of its members. In other words, the family must be concerned with providing for the basic necessities of food, clothing, shelter, and so forth that are so important to maintaining the health status of the family and community. The health behavior of a people is very much related to survival—people must be relatively healthy to reproduce successfully, and reproduction is a part of the maintenance of biological functioning.[17]

According to the National Center for Health Statistics, the health status of African Americans is not good compared to that of white Americans. A growing gap in the life expectancies of blacks and whites has emerged. From 1984 to 1990, the life expectancy of whites rose from 75.3 to 76.1 years, while for blacks, it declined form 69.5 to 69.1 years.[18] It is believed that this disparity in the life expectancy of blacks and whites is due to accidental deaths, homicides, substance

TABLE 2. Percentage of Persons 18 Years and Older Who Currently Smoke Cigarettes, According to Sex, Race, and Age: United States, 1991

Age	White Male	Black Male	White Female	Black Female
18 years and older, age-adjusted	27.0	34.7	24.2	23.1
18–24 years	25.1	15.0	25.1	11.8
25–34 years	32.1	39.4	28.4	32.4
35–44 years	32.1	44.4	27.0	35.3
45–64 years	28.0	42.0	25.3	23.4
65 years and older	14.2	24.3	12.1	9.6

Source: National Center for Health Statistics, *Health, United States*, 1992, (Hyattsville, MD: Public Health Service, 1993), 102.

abuse, and AIDS. For example, although African Americans represent 12 percent of the population in the United States, they represent 26 percent of adult and 53 percent of child AIDS cases.[19] Also, while cigarette smoking has declined in recent years, blacks, except those between the ages of 18 and 24, are more likely to be cigarette smokers than are whites (see Table 2). Smoking has a very negative impact on the family, as well as on the individual, from a health perspective. Data show that cigarette smoking causes lung cancer and emphysema; children of smokers are more prone to have respiratory illnesses and asthma than are children of nonsmokers, and infants of parents who smoke are more likely to die of Sudden Infant Death Syndrome than are infants whose parents do not smoke. Alcohol abuse also has an adverse impact on African American families and their health.[20]

In recent years, both the alcohol and cigarette industries have increased their advertising targeted to the African American community as a means of expanding their sales.[21] These promotional strategies are designed to get African Americans to drink, to smoke, and to spend their money on these products. However, scant funds are being allocated to remind them about the adverse health consequences of smoking and drinking.[22]

The family can play an important role in promoting healthy lifestyles. In 1985, *American Health* commissioned the Gallup organization to survey how families helped their members to live healthy lives. Focusing on health behavior, the researchers were interested in who helps individuals change their behavior in a number of ways, including quitting smoking, exercising more, reducing alcohol consumption, controlling job stress, losing weight, and eating better. The research question was whether the doctor or the family (including de facto members such as a boyfriend or girlfriend) helped the respondent to change in the relevant behavior areas. In all areas, respondents said the family played a more significant role in health promotion than did the doctor. For cutting down on alcohol consumption, the family was twice as likely as the doctor to be helpful. When respondents were asked who helped the most, the husband or wife, the research showed that the wife was more helpful than the husband.[23] This and other research clearly points to the need to design programs that will stimulate families to work together to reduce the incidence of substance abuse and addiction and to promote healthy lifestyles in general.

IMPACT OF STRESS ON THE FAMILY

During its life cycle, the typical African American family may be confronted with many problems, including poverty, divorce, child abuse, alcoholism, and racism.[24] These and other problems place the family unit under considerable stress. We live in a stress-ridden society, one in which survival itself means experiencing varying degrees of stress.

The notion of *stress* implies excessive exposure to environmental forces that can harm a person's well-being. There are many definitions and uses of the concept of stress. Some social scientists have defined stress as environmental events that make demands on the person, while others have defined it as the individual's response to events.[25] Stress is defined in the *Modern Dictionary of Sociology* as "any unpleasant and disturbing emotional experience due to frustration. . . . Stress often results from an alteration or interference with an individual's usual pattern of behavior."[26]

Some scholars assume that too many stressful life events (pleasant and unpleasant) will increase the probability of one's susceptibility to illness.[27] Research has shown that stressful life events (e.g., the death of a spouse, divorce, residential moves, arrests, in-law problems, financial problems, and so on) contribute to the development of physical and psychological disorders, including heart disease, cancer, chronic asthma, and mental illness.[28]

In examining the link between stress and health, researchers have developed a variety of scales to measure stress, including the Schedule of Recent Experiences, the Life Experience Survey, Daily Hassles, the Social Readjustment Rating Scale, and the PIER Life Events Scale. From a psychometric perspective, these instruments have a number of methodological and conceptual problems that have implications for policy, planning, and clinical practice and the interpretation of results.[29] For example, normative data have not been systematically presented for some of these scales. The researchers have used different operational definitions of stress, which creates problems of comparability. Also, the selection of specific events for inclusion in the life events inventories has been somewhat arbitrary, with an emphasis on stressful and infrequently occurring events. Moreover, the field of stressful life events research has given little attention to cultural or ethnic issues.[30] Some researchers do not seem to understand that certain events, such as the marriage or death of a close family member, have different meanings and significance for members of different ethnic groups. For example, Rosenberg and Dohrenwend concluded that questionnaires, such as the Holmes and Rahe Social Readjustment Rating Scale, that used a marriage item with a preassigned value to assist the respondents in rating other life events may not be appropriate for all ethnic groups.[31] In comparing African and Hispanic Americans with middle-class whites, Komaroff, Masuda, and Holmes found some similarities among the three groups, but the two minority groups were more similar to each other than they were to the white middle-class group.[32] According to Pine, Padilla, and Maldonado:

> Ethnic or cultural influences exist that affect the cognitive appraisal of the stressfulness of life events. However, because information is limited, it may be premature to base any conclusions on existing data. Research that focuses on the relationship between life events and disorders needs to consider whether ethnic or cultural factors are involved. The first step in this direction is to explore possible differences among ethnic groups on a traditional life-events measure in order to identify which, if any, items are perceived differently by any of the groups.[33]

TABLE 3. Death Rates per 100,000 for All Causes According to Sex, Race, and Age, United States, 1990

	Race and Sex			
Age	White Male	Black Male	White Female	Black Female
All ages, age-adjusted	644.3	1,061.3	369.9	581.6
Under 1 year	896.1	2,112.4	690.0	1,735.5
1–4 years	45.9	85.8	36.1	67.6
5–14 years	26.4	41.2	17.9	27.5
15–24 years	131.3	252.2	45.9	68.7
25–34 years	176.1	430.8	61.5	159.5
35–44 years	268.2	699.6	117.4	298.6
45–54 years	548.7	1,261.0	309.3	639.4
55–64 years	1,467.2	2,618.4	822.7	1,452.6
65–74 years	3,397.7	4,946.1	1,923.5	2,865.7
75–84 years	7,844.9	9,129.5	4,839.1	5,688.3
85 years and older	18,268.3	16,954.9	14,400.6	13,309.5

Source: National Center for Health Statistics, *Health, United States, 1992*, (Hyattsville, MD: Public Health Service, 1993), 62, 63.

When one looks at items such as the death of family members, divorce, imprisonment or arrest, and job loss on the Holmes and Rahe scale, it is clear that African Americans are exposed to a large number of stressful life events. Data show that death as a stressor is much more prevalent in the African American community than it is in the white community.[34] For example, as shown in Table 3, in 1990 the age-adjusted death rate per 100,000 for white males was 644.3; it was 1,061.3 for black males. During the same period, the age-adjusted death rate per 100,000 for white women was 369.9; it was 581.6 for black women (see Table 3). At every age level, except 85 years and over, blacks have a higher death rate than do whites. Death from homicide is a major stressor for African Americans, especially males. As Table 4 shows, in 1981 the age-adjusted homicide rate per 100,000 for black males was 68.7; it was 8.9 for white males. In other words, black males were almost eight times more likely to be murdered than were white males. Black females were almost five times more likely to be homicide victims than were white females. The death of a parent, child, father, or mother is a stressor in part because it causes other family

TABLE 4. Death Rate per 100,000 for Homicide and Legal Intervention, According to Sex, Race, and Age, United States, 1990

| | Sex and Race | | | | | |
| | Male | | | Female | | |
Age	Black	White	Differential	Black	White	Differential
Under 1 year	21.4	6.4	3.34	22.8	5.1	4.47
1–4 years	7.6	1.8	4.22	7.2	1.4	5.14
5–14 years	5.1	1.1	4.64	3.6	0.8	4.5
15–24 years	138.3	15.4	8.98	18.9	4.0	4.73
25–34 years	125.4	15.1	8.31	25.3	4.3	5.88
35–44 years	82.3	11.4	7.22	15.6	3.2	4.88
All ages, age-adjusted	68.7	8.9	7.72	13.0	2.8	4.64
All ages, crude	69.2	9.0	7.69	13.5	2.8	4.82

Source: National Center for Health Statistics, *Health, United States, 1992*, (Hyattsville, MD: Public Health Service, 1993), 76, 77.

members to redefine their roles and learn how to survive without the missing person.[35] The grieving process, which can lead to a period of emotional turmoil, is also a stressful result of such a death. The family has the expenses of burying the deceased, as well. Given certain cultural norms, a burial can cause major financial problems for a family.

Thus, African Americans must develop functional strategies for reducing the incidence and prevalence of stressful life events, especially those related to health behavior, because of their impact on the family. Strong families learn how to cope with stressors, and data suggest that family structure and interaction affect the level of health and health behavior of family members.[36] More research attention needs to be devoted to understanding how strong African American families cope with stressors in our society.

ATTRIBUTES OF STRONG AFRICAN AMERICAN FAMILIES

In the past, African American family research has been dominated by a perspective that emphasized pathology.[37] The African American family was often presented as being weak, dysfunctional, deficient, and deviant. Words or concepts such as *competent, successful,* or *healthy* were seldom used to describe or examine family functioning in the African American community. However, in recent years, social scientists are beginning to accept the reality that there are some strong, stable families.[38] According to Wilson and Tolson, "the most significant trend of black family research is the shift from a deficit to a strength view, which has occurred as a result of the change in the socio-political status of American blacks. This change not only influenced the way blacks perceived themselves; it influenced the way they were perceived by others as well."[39]

Family researchers have attempted to measure family strengths in several ways. Some researchers prefer to observe their subjects directly, while others rely on questionnaires, self-reports, and inventories. Some researchers collect data directly from the subjects. The variables of family life cycles and family crises are also given differing importance depending on the biases and value judgments of the researchers. Several research models, such as Olson et al.'s circumplex model of marital and family systems, the McMaster model of family functioning, and the Beavers-Timberlawn model, have been utilized in assessing family strengths, and each makes certain assumptions about what constitutes healthy functioning within the family.[40]

In studying the attributes of strong families, some researchers have emphasized resources such as adaptability and integration, and others have focused on qualities that contribute to successful marriage and family relationships.[41] Some typical attributes of strong families identified by family researchers are love and understanding, a balance of independence and interdependence, clear generational boundaries, role flexibility, an ability to foster the growth and development of family members, altruism, spirituality, shared power, and positivism. In *Secrets of Strong Families,* Stinnett and DeFrain identify six qualities that seem to contribute significantly to the strength and happiness of families: (a) family members showing appreciation toward each other; (b) possessing the ability to deal with a crisis in a positive manner; (c) spending time together; (d) having a high degree of commitment to the family; (e) having good communication patterns; and (f) possessing a high degree of religious orientation.[42]

In contrast to Stinnett and DeFrain, who directly surveyed families, Curran sent questionnaires to professionals who worked with families and asked them to identify traits that they thought were characteristic of strong families. Based on her study, a healthy family communicates, listens to, affirms, and supports its members. Such a family teaches members respect for each other, develops a sense of trust, and has a sense of fair play and humor. Members of a healthy family exhibit a sense of shared responsibility, are taught a sense of right and wrong, and have a strong sense of family in which rituals and traditions abound. A healthy family has a balance of interaction among its members, has a shared religious core, respects the privacy of its members, and values service to others. In addition, a strong bond fosters family table time and conversation and shared leisure time. Finally, a healthy family admits to and seeks help with problems.[43]

Billingsley and Hill are, perhaps, the forerunners in emphasizing family strengths in the analysis of African American families.[44] In this regard, Billingsley uses the construct of "opportunity screens" as the key to the survival and stability of strong, families. These opportunity screens, or attributes, of strong African American families include a set of family values, a religious conviction and behavior, educational aspiration and achievement, economic security and property ownership, kinship bonds or ties, and community involvement. Analyzing and interpreting census data, Hill identifies as strengths found in African American families a strong kinship bond, a strong work orientation, an adaptability of family roles, a strong achievement orientation, and a strong religious orientation. Both Billingsley's and Hill's research have made significant contributions to our understanding of African American family stability and strengths, but they do not provide adequate empirical evidence to support their respective propositions.

Other researchers have been able to document empirically that the family strengths identified by Billingsley and Hill are indeed present in many African American families.[45] Based on these investigations, the following traits are important or crucial in any definition or characterization of African American family strengths: (a) a strong economic base (stable employment, property ownership, a strong work orientation); (b) achievement orientation (educational aspiration and expectation, educational attainment); (c) the adaptability of roles (role flexibility, shared responsibility); (d) a strong kinship bond (a high degree of commitment, mutual obligations); (e) coping capabilities (an ability to deal with crises in a positive manner, helping networks, exchanges); and (f) love (an ability to affirm one another, to respect others, to appreciate each other).

These traits may not be found in all strong families to the same extent, intensity, and duration. Moreover, it is assumed that the age of the family head, the kind of family structure, marital history and behavior, socioeconomic status, the family of origin's behavior, family size, social transactions (formal and informal), psychological attributes of family members, and other factors affect family strength and stability. A discussion of these factors is beyond the scope of this paper.

In our study of stable African American families, my colleagues and I attempted to identify attributes of such strong families.[46] The study was based on five assumptions. First, there is a need to examine the behavior of strong, healthy families, rather than focusing on weak and unhealthy ones. We believed that such a study could provide the data necessary for creating meaningful family development programs. Second, both men and women in family settings need to be studied. In the past, family researchers have focused primarily on mothers and their children in their analyses of African American families.[47] Such research acquired a tendency to collect information from the mother and her children regarding how the father functions in the family. In fact, we know more about the African American man's absence from his family than we know about his presence in the family. Third, researchers need to focus on how stable African American families solve problems, not just the extent of problems within these units. Families are not perfect. All families have problems, and those who succeed in solving them may serve as models for others. Fourth, data from non-institutional sources are the key to developing programs for African American families. In the past, too many family researchers have relied on secondary data sources (such as the U.S. Census Bureau, the U.S. Department of Labor, state welfare and health departments, etc.) for their analyses of African American families. Fifth, a sociocultural frame of reference should be used to study African American people. With such a model, researchers will not have to assume a uniform black or white community and will not need to use a comparative research paradigm, where the question is always: How do black families differ from white families? The research question might instead be how families differ within the context of the African American community. For example, do religious black families behave differently from nonreligious black families? A sociocultural approach to African American family life will allow researchers to look at a range of internal and external variables that affect family behavior.

Our study used 50 families who lived in Washington, D.C. (26 headed by a husband–wife structure and 24 headed by females) as participants. They were nominated by community groups because of their perceived strength and stability. To participate, the family had to have been together for at least five years and to have a minor child present in the home. Once the nominations were received from the organizations, individual interviews with husbands and wives and the female householders were scheduled by telephone. Seventy-six individual interviews—26 with husband–wife pairs (one interview with each spouse) and 24 with single-family (female) householders—were conducted. Staff members and other experienced interviewers administered the questionnaire. Each interview averaged two hours in length.

Based on a detailed analysis of these interviews, we were able to identify attributes and characteristics of strong, stable African American families. The importance of each attribute and the combination of attributes varied somewhat from one stable family to another, but in general, these families possessed the following:

1. *A strong economic base* (as reflected in a relatively high and/or stable family income, employment, home ownership, a strong work orientation)
2. *A strong achievement orientation* (high educational attainment and expectations, goal directed, etc.)
3. *An adaptability of family roles* (having role flexibility, sharing responsibility, communicating with each other)
4. *A high degree of religious or spiritual orientation* (as evidenced by church membership, church attendance, a sense of right and wrong, teaching moral values, a shared religious core)
5. *A strong kinship bond* (a high degree of commitment to the family, a feeling of mutual obligation, kin interaction and support)
6. *A sense of racial pride* (telling children about African American history, discussing racism in one's family, telling children what it is like to be African American, preference for being so identified)
7. *Display of love and acceptance* (the ability to affirm one another and to respect, appreciate, and trust each other)

8. *Resourcefulness* (possessing personal talents and skills, self-reliance, self-sufficiency, independence, the ability to cope with crises)
9. *Community involvement* (service to others, membership and active involvement in community organizations)
10. *Family unity* (possessing a sense of cohesiveness, family pride, family togetherness, and commitment; that is, the family comes first)

Our findings were similar to those of others researchers who were interested in family strengths. Our research confirmed the five family strengths identified by Hill and most of the attributes discussed by Billingsley. However, we did find differences. For example, in contrast to Billingsely and Hill, three additional attributes emerged from our data: a sense of racial pride, a display of love and acceptance, and resourcefulness. The latter attribute is somewhat different from Hill's concept of the role adaptability of family members. In our study, *resourcefulness* was defined in terms of family members' possessing personal talents and skills that were important for coping with problems, thus leading to an emphasis on self-reliance and independence.

CONCLUSION

As we approach the twenty-first century, African American families are confronted with many challenges, including the need to provide for the continued biological functioning of each family member and for the adequate reproduction of new family members, in part by arranging for the production, distribution, and consumption of goods and services. African American families must provide for the adequate socialization of each family member, while maintaining order within the family and with outside groups and reducing the psychological damage of stressful life events. Individuals, families, and society as a whole must improve interpersonal relationships between men and women. We must project positive social images. We must develop empowerment strategies for the family as well as for each family member, and, most importantly, African American families must maintain the motivation for survival.

In addition, the traditional concept of a family as a married couple with children or a group of adult kin must be broadened to include other family configurations. Politicians, policymakers, and social scientists must understand that these nontraditional family forms are now prevalent in our society and that they are a significant percentage of the population. As a result, social policies must reflect diverse family structures and forms. Billingsley identifies 12 different types of African American families.[48] Given this reality, it is possible for each of these family types to be strong and viable. In their study of well-functioning, two-parent, working-class families, Lewis and Looney state, "Perhaps more than any other issue, this study points out the need to explore further the heterogeneity of families at a particular socioeconomic level. This study demonstrates that the concept of working-class, two-parent, black families is such a broad description that tells us very little."[49] In other words, there are different types of families at various socioeconomic levels. There are also different types of families at various ideological and political levels. We have to develop programs that affirm this diversity in family types.

Professionals who plan to develop family programs to assist dysfunctional families in becoming functional need to have some idea or model toward which they should work. They need to know the defining characteristic of a "normal, healthy, African American family" in this society. The research reported in this chapter, together with other studies, should help us to identify these attributes empirically. Moreover, one can begin to define a strong family as one possessing certain qualities that help it to cope effectively with the difficulties and challenges of life. A strong family does not succumb to problems, but surmounts them.

In recent years, several practice models have been developed in response to the need for information for working with ethnic families, especially African American families. Books such as *Family Therapy with Ethnic Minorities* (1987), *Black Families in Therapy: A Multi-System Approach* (1989), *Ethnic-Sensitive Social Work Practices* (1981), *Social Work Practice and People of Color: A Process-Stage Approach* (1986), and *Understanding Race, Ethnicity and Power: The Key to Efficacy in Clinical Practice* (1989), have provided important insight into how to help African American families to cope in a complex and often hostile environment.[50] An underlying theme in each of these books is the notion that the concept of empowerment is the key to helping families. In *Black Empowerment: Social Work in*

Oppressed Communities, Solomon defines *empowerment* as "a process whereby persons who belong to a stigmatized social category throughout their lives can be assisted to develop and increase skills in the exercise of interpersonal influence and the performance of valued social roles." She believes that empowerment should not be viewed as a goal, but should also be viewed as a process of intervention in working with African American clients. It is important for African American families to be taught that they should be in control of their lives. Social workers, psychologists, ministers, and teachers should not become the substitute parent for young people. It is important to keep in mind, at the dawn of a new decade and a new century, that families, and people in general, are motivated to change by emphasizing their strengths rather than their weaknesses. Thus, it is important for professionals to devote more time and attention to identifying attributes of strong African American families, and to developing strategies for translating these attributes into family programs that can benefit a large number of families.

REFERENCES

Allen, Walter, R. 1978. The search for applicable theories of black family life. *Journal of Marriage and Family Life* 40 (February): 117–129.

Bakeman, Roger, Eugene McCray, Judith R. Lumb, Rudolph E. Jackson, and Patricia N. Whitley. 1987. The incidence of AIDS among blacks and Hispanics. *Journal of the National Medical Association* 79 (September): 921–928.

Baldwin, Dorothy. 1991. *Understanding male sexual health.* New York: Hippocrene Books. 76.

Berry, Mary F., and John W. Blassingame. 1982. *Long memory: The black experience in America.* New York: Oxford University Press.

Billingsley, Andrew. 1968. *Black families in white America.* Englewood Cliffs, NJ: Prentice-Hall.

———. 1988. The impact of technology on Afro-American families. *Family Relations* 37 (October): 420–425.

Boyd-Franklin, Nancy. 1989. *Black families in therapy: A multi-system approach.* New York: Guilford.

Brenner, M. Harvey. 1973. *Mental illness and the economy.* Cambridge, MA: Harvard University Press.

Burgess, Ernest W., Harvey J. Locke, and Mary M. Thomas. 1963. *The family: From institution to companionship.* 3rd ed. New York: American Book Company.

Burr, Wesley. 1973. *Theory construction and the sociology of the family.* New York: John Wiley & Sons.

Cetron, Marvin, and Owen Davies. 1989. *American renaissance: Our life at the turn of the 21st century.* New York: St. Martin's.

Devore, Wynetta, and Elfreide G. Schlesinger. 1981. *Ethnic-sensitive social work.* St. Louis, MO: C.V. Mosby.

Dohrenwend, Barbara S., and Bruce P. Dohrenwend. 1981. *Life events and life stress.* New York: Neal Watson.

Dorus, Walter, and Edward Senay. 1980. Depression, demographic dimensions, and drug abuse. *American Journal of Psychiatry* 37 (June): 699–704.

Engram, Eleanor. 1982. *Science, myth and reality: The black family in one-half century of research.* Westport, CT: Greenwood.

Epstein, Norman B., Duane S. Bishop, and S. Levin. 1978. The McMaster model of family functioning. *Journal of Marriage and Family Counseling* 6: 19–31.

Fine, Mark, Andrew I. Schwebel, and Linda James-Myers. 1987. Family stability in black families: Values underlying three different perspectives. *Journal of Comparative Family Studies* 18 (Spring): 1–23.

Fleming, R., A. Baum, and J. E. Singer. 1984. Toward an integrated approach to the study of stress. *Journal of Personality and Social Psychology* 46 (April): 939–949.

Footlick, J. K. 1990. What happened to the family? *Newsweek* (special issue, Winter–Spring): 14–20.

Gary, Lawrence, ed. 1981. *Black men.* Beverly Hills, CA.

———. 1985. Correlates of depressive symptoms among a select sample of black men. *American Journal of Public Health* 75 (October): 1220–1222.

Gary, Lawrence E., Lula A. Beatty, Greta L. Berry, and Mary D. Price. 1983. *Stable black families: Final report.* Washington, DC: Howard University, Institute for Urban Affairs and Research.

Gurin, Joel. 1985. From "me" to "we": The U.S. generation. *American Health* 4 (October): 40–41.

Hill, Robert. 1972. *The strengths of black families*. New York: Emerson Hall.

Ho, Man Kung. 1987. *Family therapy with ethnic minorities*. Newbury, CA: Sage.

Holmes, Thomas H., and R. H. Rahe. 1967. The social readjustment rating scale. *Journal of Psychosomatic Research* 11: 213–218.

Jaynes, Gerald D., and Robin M. Williams, Jr., eds. 1989. *A common destiny: Blacks and American society*. Washington, DC: National Academy Press.

Jewell, K. Sue. 1988. *Survival of the black family: The institutional impact of U.S. social policy*. New York: Praeger.

Komaroff, Anthony L., Minow Masuda, and Thomas H. Holmes. 1968. The social readjustment scale: A comparative study of Negro, Mexican, and white Americans. *Journal of Psychosomatic Research* 12: 121–128.

Leslie, Gerald R., and Sheila K. Korman. 1985. *The family in social context*. 6th ed. New York: Oxford University Press.

Lewis, Jerry M., W. R. Beavers, John T. Gossett, and Virginia A. Phillips. 1976. *No single thread: Psychological health in family systems*. New York: Brunner/Mazel.

Lewis, Jerry M., and John G. Looney. 1983. *The long struggle: Well-functioning working-class black families*. New York: Brunner/Mazel.

Lum, Doman. 1986. *Social work practice and people of color: A process stage approach*. Monterey, CA: Brooks/Cole.

Martin, Elmer P., and Jo Anne M. Martin. 1978. *The black extended family*. Chicago: University of Chicago Press.

McAdoo, Harriet P. 1978. Factors related to stability in upwardly mobile black families. *Journal of Marriage and the Family* 40 (November): 762–778.

McCubbin, Hamilton I., and Barbara M. Dahl. 1985. *Marriage and family: Individual and life cycles*. New York: John Wiley & Sons.

Mindel, Charles H., Robert W. Habenstein. 1981. *Ethnic families in America: Patterns and variations*. 2nd ed. New York: Elsevier.

National Center for Health Statistics. 1993. *Health United States, 1992*. DHHS pub. no. (PHS) Hyattsville, MD: Public Health Service.

Olson, David H., Hamilton I. McCubbin, Howard Barnes, Andrea

Larsen, Marla Muxen, and Marc Wilson. *Families: What makes them work.* Beverly Hills, CA: Sage.

Otto, Herbert A. 1963. Criteria for assessing family strengths. *Family Process* 2 (September): 329–337.

Pinderhughes, Elaine. 1989. *Understanding race, ethnicity, and power: The key to efficacy in clinical practice.* New York: Free Press.

Pine, Charles, Amado M. Padilla, and Margarita Maldonado. 1985. Ethnicity and life events: Cognitive appraisals and experience. *Journal of Clinical Psychology* 41 (July): 460–465.

Pottock, Otto. 1957. Design of a model of healthy family relationships as a basis for evaluation research. *Social Service Review* 31 (December): 369–376.

Pratt, Lois. 1976. *Family structure and effective health behavior: The energized family.* Boston: Houghton Mifflin.

Rabkin, Judith G. and Delmer L. Struening. 1976. Life events, stress and illness. *Science* 194 (3 December): 1013–1020.

Rosenberg, Emily J., and Barbara S. Dohrenwend. 1975. Effects of experiences and ethnicity on ratings of life events as stressors. *Journal of Health and Social Behavior* 16 (March): 127–129.

Royse, David D., and Gladys T. Turner. 1980. Strengths of black families: A community perspective. *Social Work* 25 (September): 407–409.

Seligmann, J. 1990. Variations of a family. *Newsweek* (special issue, Winter–Spring): 38–46.

Soloman, Barbara B. 1976. *Black empowerment: Social work in oppressed communities:* New York: Columbia University Press.

Stack, Carol B. 1974. *All our kin.* New York: Harper & Row.

Staples, Robert, ed. 1986. *The black family: Essays and studies.* 3d ed. Belmont, CA: Wadsworth.

———. 1987. Social structure and black family life: An analysis of current trends. *Journal of Black Studies* 17 (March): 267–286.

Staples, Robert, and Alfredo Mirande. 1980. Racial and cultural variations among American families: A decennial review of the literature on minority families. *Journal of Marriage and the Family* 42 (November): 887–903.

Stinnett, Nick, and John DeFrain. 1985. *Secrets of strong families.* Boston: Little, Brown.

Strong, Bryan, and Christine DeVault. 1989. *The marriage and family experience.* 4th ed. St. Paul, MN: West.

Taylor, Robert J., Bogart S. Leashore, and Susan Toliver. 1988. Assessment of the provider role as perceived by black males, *Family Relations* 37 (October): 426.

Theodorson, George A., and Achilles G. Theodorson. 1969. *Modern dictionary of sociology.* New York: Thomas Y. Crowell.

Tuckson, Reed V. 1989. Race, sex, economics and tobacco advertising. *Journal of the National Medical Association* 81 (November): 1119–1124.

U.S. Bureau of the Census. 1993. *Statistical Abstract of the United States: 1993.* (113th ed.) sec. P-23, no.162. Washington, DC: U.S. Government Printing Office.

Watts, Thomas D., and Roosevelt Wright, eds. 1983. *Black alcoholism: Toward a comprehensive understanding.* Springfield, IL: Charles C. Thomas.

Wilson, Melvin, and Timothy Tolson. 1986. A social interactional analysis of two and three generational black families. In *In praise of fifty years: The Groves conference on the conservation of marriage and family,* eds. Paul W. Dail and Ruth H. Jewson, Lake Mills, IA: Graphic.

NOTES

1. Gerald R. Leslie and Sheila K. Korman. *The Family in Social Context,* 6th ed. (New York: Oxford University Press, 1985); Charles H. Mindel and Robert W. Habenstein, *Ethnic Families in America: Patterns and Variations,* 2nd ed. (New York: Elsevier, 1981).

2. Mary F. Berry and John W. Blassingame, *Long Memory: The Black Experience in America* (New York: Oxford University Press, 1982); Andrew Billingsley, *Black Families in White America* (Englewood Chiffs, NJ: Prentice-Hall, 1968); Eleanor Engram, *Science, Myth and Reality: The Black Family in One-Half Century of Research* (Westport, CT: Greenwood, 1982).

3. Lawrence E. Gary, Lula A. Beatty, Greta L. Berry, and Mary D. Price, *Stable Black Families: Final Report* (Washington, DC: Howard University, Institute for Urban Affairs and Research, 1983).

4. Ernest W. Burgess, Harvey J. Locke, and Mary M. Thomas, *The*

Family: From Institution to Companionship, 3rd ed. (New York: American Book Company, 1963), 2.

5. George A. Theodorson and Achilles G. Theodorson, *Modern Dictionary of Sociology* (New York: Thomas Y. Crowell, 1969), 146.

6. J. K. Footlick, "What Happened to the Family?" *Newsweek* (special issue, Winter–Spring, 1990): 14–20; Leslie and Korman, *The Family in Social Context,* 30–45; Bryan Strong and Christine DeVault, *The Marriage and Family Experience,* 4th ed. (St. Paul, MN: West, 1989).

7. J. Seligmann, "Variations of a family," *Newsweek* (special issue, Winter–Spring, 1990): 38–46; Marianne Yen, "Court Adds Gay Couples to Definition of Family," *The Washington Post,* (7 July 1989, p. A3.)

8. Mike Causey, "Redefining the Family," *The Washington Post* December 1989. p. D2; Seligman, "Variations of a Family," 38–46; and Yen, "Court Adds Gay Couples," p. A3.

9. Phillip S. Gutis, "What is a Family? Traditional Limits Are Being Redrawn," *New York Times,* 31 August 1989, pp. C1, C6.

10. Michelle Locke, "An American View of Values," *The Washington Post,* 31 October 1989, p. C5.

11. Melvin Wilson and Timothy Tolson, "A Social Interactional Analysis of Two and Three Generational Black Families," in *In Praise of Fifty Years: The Groves Conference on the Conservation of Marriage and Family,* eds. Paula W. Dail and Ruth H. Jewson (Lake Mills, IA: Graphic, 1986), 43.

12. U.S. Bureau of the Census, *Statistical Abstract of the United States: 1993,* 113th ed. (Washington, DC: Government Printing Office, 1993), 59.

13. Billingsley, *Black Families in White America* 15–21; Robert Staples, ed., *The Black Family: Essays and Studies,* 3rd ed. (Belmont, CA: Wadsworth, 1986); Robert Staples and Alfredo Mirande, "Racial and Cultural Variations Among American Families: A Decennial Review of the Literature on Minority Families," *Journal of Marriage and the Family* 42 (November 1980): 887–903.

14. Wilson and Tolson, "A Social Interactional Analysis," 44.

15. Andrew Billingsley, "The Impact of Technology on Afro-American Families," *Family Relations* 37 (October 1988): 420–25; Marvin Cetron and Owen Davies, *American Renaissance: Our life at the Turn*

of the 21st Century (New York: St. Martin's, 1989); Gerald D. Jaynes and Robin M. Williams, Jr., eds., *A Common Destiny: Blacks and American Society* (Washington, DC: National Academy Press, 1989); K. Sue Jewell, *Survival of the Black Family: The Institutional Import of U.S. Social Policy* (New York: Praeger, 1988); Robert Staples, "Social Structure and Black Family Life: An Analysis of Current Trends," *Journal of Black Studies* 17 (March 1987): 267–86.

16. Leslie and Korman, *The Family in Social Context*, 6, 7.

17. Leslie and Korman, *The Family in Social Context*, 7. See note 15. Also see Dorothy Baldwin, "Understanding Male Sexual Health," (New York: Hippocrene Books, 1991), 76.

18. National Center for Health Statistics, *Health, United States, 1992*, (Hyattsville, MD: Public Health Services, 1993), 44.

19. Roger Bakeman, Eugene McCray, Judith R. Lumb, Rudolph E. Jackson, and Patricia N. Whitley, "The Incidence of AIDS Among Blacks and Hispanics," *Journal of the National Medical Association* 79 (September 1987): 921–28. For data on cigarette smoking, see note 18.

20. Thomas D. Watts and Roosevelt Wright (eds.), *Black Alcoholism: Toward A Comprehensive Understanding* (Springfield, IL: Charles C. Thomas, 1983).

21. Reed V. Tuckson, "Race, Sex, Economics, and Tobacco Advertising," *Journal of the National Medical Association* 81 (November 1989): 119–1124; Watts and Wright, *Black Alcoholism*.

22. Tuckson, *"Race, Sex, Economics, and Tobacco Advertising."* pp. 1119–1120.

23. Joel Gurin, *"From 'Me' to 'We': The U.S. Generation,"* *American Health* 4 (October 1985): 40–41.

24. Billingsley, "The Impact of Technology"; Lawrence E. Gary, ed., *Black Men* (Beverly Hills, CA: Sage, 1981); Jaynes and Williams, *A Common Destiny*.

25. R. Fleming, A. Baum, and J. E. Singer, "Toward an Integrated Approach to the Study of Stress," *Journal of Personality and Social Psychology* 46 (April 1984): 939.

26. Theodorson and Theodorson, *Modern Dictionary of Sociology*, 422.

27. Thomas H. Holmes and R. H. Rahe, "The Social Readjustment Rating Scale," *Journal of Psychosomatic Research* 11 (1967): 213–18.

28. M. Harvey Brenner, *Mental Illness and the Economy* (Cambridge, MA: Harvard University Press, 1973); Walter Dorus and Edward Senay, "Depression, Demographic Dimensions, and Drug Abuse," *American Journal of Psychiatry* 137 (June 1980): 699–704; Barbara S. Dohrenwend and Bruce P. Dohrenwend, eds., *Life Events and Life Stress* (New York: Neal Watson, 1981); Lawrence E. Gary, "Correlates of Depressive Symptoms Among A Select Sample of Black Men," *American Journal of Public Health* 75 (October 1985): 1220–22; Judith G. Rabkin and Delmer L. Struening, "Life Events, Stress and Illness," *Science* 194 (3 December 1976): 1013–20.

29. Rabkin and Struening, "Life Events, Stress and Illness."

30. Charles Pine, Amado M. Padilla, and Margarita Maldonado, "Ethnicity and Life Events: Cognitive Appraisals and Experience," *Journal of Clinical Psychology* 41 (July 1985): 460–65.

31. Emily J. Rosenberg and Barbara S. Dohrenwend, "Effects of Experiences and Ethnicity on Ratings of Life Events as Stressors," *Journal of Health and Social Behavior* 16 (March 1975): 127–29.

32. Anthony L. Komaroff, Minow Masuda, and Thomas H. Holmes, "The Social Readjustment Scale: A Comparative Study of Negro, Mexican and White Americans," *Journal of Psychosomatic Research* 12 (1968): 121–28.

33. Pine, Padilla, and Maldonado, "Ethnicity and Life Events," 460.

34. National Center for Health Statistics, *Health, United States,* (Hyattsville, MD: Public Health Service, 1993), 62, 63.

35. Hamilton I. McCubbin and Barbara B. Dahl, *Marriage and Family: Individuals', and Life Cycles* (New York: John Wiley & Sons, 1985).

36. McCubbin and Dahl, *Marriage and Family;* Lois Patt, *Family Structure and Effective Health Behavior: The Energized Family* (Boston: Houghton-Mifflin, 1976).

37. Walter R. Allen, "The Search for Applicable Theories of Black Family Life," *Journal of Marriage and Family Life* 40 (February 1978): 117–29; Billingsley, *Black Families in White America;* Engram, *Science, Myth and Reality: The Black Family.*

38. Allen, "The Search For Applicable Theories,"; Mark Fine, Andrew I. Schwebel, and Linda James-Myers, "Family Stability in Black Families: Values Underlying Three Different Perspectives," *Journal of*

Comparative Family Studies 18 (Spring 1987): 1–23; Robert Hill, *The Strengths of Black Families* (New York: Emerson Hall, 1972).

39. Wilson and Tolson, "A Social Interactional Analysis," 43.

40. David H. Olson, Hamilton I. McCubbin, Howard Barnes, Andrea Larsen, Marla Muxen, and Marc Wilson, *Families: What Makes Them Work* (Beverly Hills, CA: Sage, 1983); Norman B. Epstein, Duane S. Bishop, and S. Levin, "The McMaster Model of Family Functioning," *Journal of Marriage and Family Counseling* 6 (1978): 19–31; Jerry M. Lewis, W. Robert Beavers, John T. Gossett, and Virginia A. Phillips, *No Single Thread: Psychological Health in Family Systems* (New York: Brunner/Mazel, 1976).

41. Wesley Burr, *Theory Construction and the Sociology of the Family* (New York: John Wiley & Sons, 1973); Herbert A. Otto, "Criteria For Assessing Family Strength," *Family Process* 2 (September 1963): 329–37; Otto Pottock, "Design of a Model of Healthy Family Relationships as a Basis for Evaluation Research," *Social Service Review* 31 (December 1957): 369–76.

42. Nick Stinnett and John DeFrain, *Secrets of Strong Families* (Boston: Little, Brown, 1985).

43. Delores Curran, Traits of a Healthy Family, (Minneapolis, MN: Winston Press, 1983).

44. Billingsley, *Black Families in White America,* 97, 98; Hill, *Strengths of Black Families, 5.*

45. Jerry M. Lewis and John G. Looney, *The Long Struggle: Well Functioning Working-Class Black Families* (New York: Brunner/Mazel, 1983); Elmer P. Martin and Jo Anne M. Martin, *The Black Extended Family* (Chicago: University of Chicago Press, 1978); Harriette P. McAdoo, "Factors Related to Stability in Upwardly Mobile Black Families," *Journal of Marriage and the Family* 40 (November 1978): 762–78; David D. Royse and Gladys T. Turner, "Strengths of Black Families: A Community Perspective," *Social Work* 25 (September 1980): 407–9; Carol B. Stack, *All Our Kin* (New York: Harper & Row, 1974).

46. Gary et al., *Stable Black Families.*

47. Robert J. Taylor, Bogart S. Leashore, and Susan Toliver, "An Assessment of the Provider Role as Perceived by Black Males," *Family Relations* 37 (October 1988), 426.

48. Billingsley, *Black Families in White America,* 17.

49. Lewis and Looney, *The Long Struggle,* 151.

50. Man Kung Ho, *Family Therapy with Ethnic Minorities* (Newbury, CA: Sage, 1987); Nancy Boyd-Franklin, *Black Families in Therapy: A Multi-System Approach* (New York: Guilford, 1989); Wynetta Devore and Elfreide G. Schlesinger, *Ethnic-Sensitive Social Work Practice* (St. Louis, MO: C. V. Mosby, 1981); Doman Lum, *Social Work Practice and People of Color: A Process Stage Approach* (Monterey, CA: Brooks/Cole, 1986); Elaine Pinderhughes, *Understanding Race, Ethnicity, and Power: The Key to Efficacy in Clinical Practice* (New York: Free Press, 1989).

51. Barbara B. Soloman, *Black Empowerment: Social Work in Oppressed Communities* (New York: Columbia University Press, 1976), 6.

6 Race, Class, and Culture: Common Pitfalls in Research on African American Families

ROBERT B. HILL

M any analysts are puzzled by the "paradox" (Peterson 1991) of rising rates of unemployment, poverty, and single-parent families among blacks occurring at the same time that there is said to have been a "declining significance of race" (Wilson 1978). The conventional explanation given is the "polarization" thesis (Wilson 1978)—that the life chances of "middle-class" blacks are now determined more by class than by race, while the worsening conditions among the black "underclass" are due more to internal "underclass culture" (Auletta 1983; Murray 1984) defects than to external barriers such as racism, classism, and sexism.

I contend that the notions of polarization and declining racism prevent proper understanding of the contemporary institutional mechanisms for perpetuating the subordination of minorities by misusing three concepts: race, class, and culture. More significantly, the abuse of these key concepts by mainstream social scientists and policy analysts impedes the development of meaningful public policies for combating racism, poverty, unemployment, and family instability by diverting attention from the actual social forces responsible for racial and economic inequality.

For example, if external forces or policies are not significant determinants of the social ills in inner cities, the major policies needed are those that focus on the internal deficiencies of "underclass" blacks. Similarly, if the only subgroup in the African American community that is in crisis is the nonworking poor, there is no need to develop policies for enhancing the social and economic well-being of the black working-poor, near-poor or middle-class. I will describe in this chapter how the concepts of race, class, and culture are distorted by conventional social scientists.

CONTEMPORARY FORMS OF RACISM

A major deficiency of the thesis of declining racism is its failure to distinguish prejudice from discrimination, and individual from institutional racism.

Prejudiced Attitudes

Widespread disagreement about the significance of contemporary racism is caused in part by failure to distinguish between its two basic components: prejudice and discrimination. Although often used interchangeably, these terms differ substantively from each other. *Prejudice* involves negative or unfavorable attitudes or beliefs, while *discrimination* involves negative or hostile behavior.

To what extent has prejudice declined in America? According to most opinion polls and surveys, there has been a sharp decline in hostile attitudes toward racial minorities in recent years. For example, nationally representative surveys conducted by Louis Harris and Associates revealed that the proportion of whites opposed to school busing fell from 85 percent to 57 percent between 1963 and 1988. Similarly, over the same 25-year period, the proportion of whites who felt that blacks were moving "too fast" to achieve racial equality dropped from 64 percent to 23 percent (National Conference of Christians and Jews 1978; NAACP Legal Defense and Educational Fund 1989).

Analysts caution against misconstruing these poll trends as reflecting a sharp increase in racial tolerance (Jackman 1973; McConahay, Hardee, and Batts 1981). In fact, proponents of "modern" or "symbolic" racism contend that racial prejudice is still pervasive in America (McConahay and Hough 1976). They argue that socially undesirable beliefs have been replaced by intense hostility to racial "symbols," such as busing, affirmative action, quotas, open housing, welfare, and immigration, which can be justified on nonracial grounds (Kinder and Sears 1981, 414–16). Such contemporary racism is difficult to measure by conventional opinion polls, as it is often disguised or unconscious (Sighall and Page 1971).

The continuing significance of racism is also said to be manifested in the widespread discrepancy between high support for broad principles of racial equality and low support for specific policies to implement those principles (Jaynes and Williams 1989: Hacker 1992). For example, Schuman, Steeb, and Bobo (1985, 74, 88) made an analysis of a nationally representative survey, which revealed that, while nine out of ten whites agreed that black and white children should be able to attend the same schools, only 15 percent were in favor of black and white children being bused from one school district to another. The researchers (Schuman, Steeb, and Bobo 1985, 74, 88) also found that, while 71 percent of whites disagreed with actions by whites to keep blacks out of their neighborhoods, only half (49 percent) of them felt that white homeowners should not be able to discriminate against blacks who are interested in buying homes.

Discriminatory Behavior

A decline in prejudiced attitudes does not necessarily indicate a corresponding drop in discriminatory behavior. Numerous studies reveal sharp discrepancies between attitudes and actions in the area of race relations (Wicker 1969). Unfortunately, because pollsters and most other survey researchers of racism concentrate almost solely on intolerant attitudes, national trend data on intolerant behavior are virtually nonexistent (Hill 1984).

In his pioneering work, *The Nature of Prejudice*, Allport (1954) identifies five forms of intolerant behavior: antilocution, avoidance, discrimination, physical attack, and extermination. *Antilocution* refers to antagonism that is expressed in words about members of other racial or ethnic groups. It is frequently manifested in racial epithets, such as "nigger," "wop," or "spick," or in stereotypical statements made privately or publicly.

Avoidance refers to actions that involve withdrawing—or staying away—from members of minority groups. *Discrimination* is defined by Allport as actual differential mistreatment of minorities in public and private settings in such areas as employment, housing, health, education, politics, criminal justice, social services, and recreation. Segregation is an institutionalized form of discrimination.

Physical attack refers to acts of violence against minorities, such as assaults on individuals during race riots, cross burnings on lawns, harassment of black families in predominantly white neighborhoods, racially motivated assaults by students or mobs, and desecration of Jewish synagogues. *Extermination* refers to mass actions of genocide against minorities, such as pogroms and massacres.

Most survey researchers do not use the various forms of intolerant behavior identified by Allport in their studies of prejudice and discrimination. The only form that opinion polls have some data on is avoidance—and that has been mostly hypothetical! For example, based on the nationally representative NORC General Social Survey of 1982 (Davis and Smith 1982), questions such as the following are usually asked: "How strongly would you object if a member of your family wanted to bring a black friend home to dinner?" (Davis and Smith 1982, 101); or "If you were driving through the neighborhoods in a city, would you go out of your way to avoid going through a black section?" (Davis and Smith 1982, 186).

Thus, most of what we know about intolerant behavior based on such surveys is hypothetical. We know very little about the extent to which hypothetical actions would be manifested in real-life situations. This is why more creative social scientists (LaPiere 1934; McConahay and Hough 1976) have assessed intolerant behavior based on systematic observation of actual actions rather than on hypothetical responses to survey and opinion poll questionnaires.

In fact, the sharp declines in prejudiced attitudes reflected in opinion polls are strongly contradicted by a recent surge (Tidwell 1993; Jones 1990–91) in racial hostility as manifested in (a) racial strife on numerous college and university campuses, (b) attacks against blacks living in or passing through predominantly white neighborhoods (as well as the reverse behavior), and (c) racial slurs by prominent public and private officials. Many analysts (Petersen 1991; Sniderman and Piazza 1993; Cummings 1983) find it difficult to explain these racial antagonisms—at a time of the "declining" significance of race—and are uninformed as to the kinds of strategies that would be most effective in reducing racial strife.

Another important contributor to this quandary is the failure of social scientists to build on Merton's (1948) classic typology of prejudice and discrimination. Merton (1948, 192–193) cautioned against the conventional wisdom that these patterns occurred conjointly and only existed in two forms: either the presence of prejudice and discrimination or the absence of both. He observed that two additional types are possible: (a) prejudice without discrimination and (b) discrimination without prejudice.

Prejudice without discrimination refers to "fair-weather illiberals," (Merton 1948: 196–97) prejudiced individuals who are unable to translate their intolerant attitudes into intolerant behavior because of external constraints (such as affirmative action laws, residence in a very liberal community, or the absence of minorities in their communities). Discrimination without prejudice refers to "fair-weather liberals," (Merton 1948: 195–96) nonprejudiced individuals who manifest intolerant behavior because of external constraints (such as residence in a prejudiced community or close association with prejudiced friends) or whose actions have racially discriminatory consequences of which they are *unaware*.

Thus, social scientists have a responsibility to inform policymakers and the public at large that both prejudiced and nonprejudiced individuals may discriminate or may not, depending on the particular circumstances. In short, the manifestation of prejudiced attitudes and discriminatory actions is not solely determined by the "good" or "bad" intentions or motives of individuals.

Institutional Racism

If social science data did demonstrate overwhelmingly that both prejudice and discrimination have declined markedly, it would not necessarily follow that racism has declined in America. For it is possible that while racism may have dropped sharply among individuals, racism among American institutions may have risen or remained the same. Thus, it is imperative that social scientists study the various forms and consequences of institutionalized racism.

Institutional racism is comprised of two components: institutionalized prejudice and institutionalized discrimination. Institutional prejudice (or *cultural racism* [Jones 1972, 35]) refers to norms, values, beliefs, or customs of the dominant society that are deemed superior to those of racial and ethnic minorities (Jones 1972). The stereotypical portrayal of African American families by the media as "pathological" (Arax 1983, 1) and "overdependent on welfare" (Cummings 1983, 1; Gibbs 1994, 26) is an example of prejudice propagated by institutions. Institutional discrimination refers to those laws, regulations, policies, and informal practices of organizations or institutions that result in differential adverse treatment or subordination of racial and ethnic minorities. As Carmichael and Hamilton (1967) observe, institutional prejudice and discrimination can be either unintentional or intentional.

Intentional institutional discrimination may be overt or covert. Overt discrimination is the deliberate mistreatment of minorities by organizations or institutions based on *explicit* racial or ethnic criteria. Examples include slavery, the passage of the Black Codes after emancipation, and the imposition of de jure segregation in the North and the South. Covert intentional discrimination involves the deliberate mistreatment of minorities by organizations or institutions based on nonracial criteria that are strongly correlated with race. Covert discrimination is also known as *patterned evasion*, the deliberate use of proxies for race to deny equal opportunities to racial minorities. Grandfather clauses, literacy tests, and poll taxes are early examples of patterned evasion in the field of voting rights.

Recent examples of intentional institutional discrimination (Hill et al., 1993, 43; Feagin 1978, 15–17) are (a) public and private urban renewal that displaces poor and working-class African American families from their homes and communities in order to construct housing for middle-income and upper-income whites; (b) *redlining*, a procedure that involves the refusal of banks, insurance companies, and other corporate institutions to grant home mortgage loans, commercial credit, and insurance for fire, property, and automobiles to families living in targeted neighborhoods; and (c) zoning that is designed to prevent black families from living in white communities by prohibiting low-income and multifamily dwellings.

Structural Discrimination

Another major impediment to the development of viable policies for reducing racial inequality is the failure of social scientists to systematically investigate the role of "structural" or "unintentional" institutional discrimination (Hill 1988). According to Downs (1970, 76):

> Racism can occur even if the people causing it have no intention of subordinating others because of color, or are totally unaware of doing so. Admittedly, this implication is sure to be extremely controversial. Most Americans believe racism is bad. But how can anyone be "guilty" of doing something bad when he does not realize he is doing it? Racism can be a matter of result rather than intention because many institutional structures in America that most whites do not recognize as subordinating others because of color actually injure minority group members far more than deliberate racism.

Unintentional institutional discrimination is defined as the consequences of societal forces or policies that have disparate adverse effects on racial and ethnic minorities, although not designed to be discriminatory (Friedman 1975; Feagin 1978). Society-wide trends such as recessions, inflationary spirals, the closing of plants in inner cities, automation, the shift from manufacturing to high tech and service industries, and so on, have had unintended discriminatory effects on African American and other low-income workers and families. Such structural discrimination is a major contributor to persistently high rates of "structural unemployment" (Glasgow 1981, 71–72) in the African American community. Hare (1988, 83) describes structurally discriminatory processes in the field of education:

> This writer further argues in what he terms a "class-plus" analysis, with classism as the engine and racism as the caboose, that black Americans have simply been chosen to absorb an unfair share of an unfair burden in a structurally unfair system.
>
> [O]ur structural determinism approach assumes that the character of the social system is preponderant as the determiner of the hierarchical arrangement of people within it, over either their biological or cultural dispositions. It is further argued that, in addition to the inherent intergenerational inequality caused by inheritance, the educational system through its unequal skill-giving, grading, routing, and credentialing procedures, plays a critical role in legitimating structural inequality in the American social system. . . . The structural argument . . . charges

that the social system needs people to replenish its ranks at all levels of skills and credentials, and that in producing such differences the schools respond to structural needs rather than innate differences.

However, because the differential adverse effects of many society-wide forces or public policies on African Americans have been unintentional, most social scientists do not perceive them as forms of institutionalized racism and discrimination. Yet, social forces or policies that have racially discriminatory effects are "discriminatory" by result, if not by intent or design. Whether high unemployment in the black community is perpetuated by periodic recessions or deliberate discriminatory hiring practices, the consequences are the same for black workers and their families. Social scientists must make it clear that nonracial proxies with the same adverse consequences as explicit racial criteria are functionally equivalent in their effects.

In fact, social scientists lag significantly behind the legal profession in assessing various strategies for combating structural or "unintentional" discrimination. For example, in the area of voting rights, the courts (Hill et al. 1993; Calmore 1989) have made it clear that all forms of electoral procedures (such as at-large elections, runoff primaries, and multimember districts) that have disparate adverse effects on minorities are "discriminatory" and unconstitutional, even if they were not designed to have such impact.

Moreover, the U.S. Congress overwhelmingly inserted the "effects" standard in its renewal of the Voting Rights Act in 1982 to ensure that consequences and not intent would be the overriding criterion for determining the constitutionality of particular electoral procedures. Similarly, in *Griggs v. Duke Power Co.* (1971), the U.S. Supreme Court declared unconstitutional an employment test that had a disproportionate effect on racial minorities, although the test was not originally designed to have this impact. Furthermore, important legal strides (Calmore 1989) have been taken to combat housing policies with racially discriminatory consequences that may not have been intended.

Some civil rights groups (NAACP Legal Defense and Educational Fund 1989) refuse to acknowledge the phenomenon of structural or "unintentional" discrimination, because they think that it would relieve both racists *and* liberals of any moral or legal obligation to take remediative action. This would not necessarily result if these leaders understood that a new litmus test could be developed for identifying contemporary racists. The presumption of unintentionality for structurally discriminatory policies attempts to avoid prejudging the intentions of decision makers when such motives may be ambiguous or not easily discernible, and to focus on the discriminatory effects of such policies—regardless of intentions.

The actual intentions of policymakers would be assessed by a new test: the extent to which they are willing to eliminate, modify, or cushion the disparate adverse effects of societal trends and policies *after* they have been made aware of their inequitable consequences. For those decision makers who refuse to alter those inequities, it may then be reasonably inferred that those "unintended" effects were actually "intended." In short, those recalcitrants may now be reclassified as "intentional discriminators" or "racists." Far from letting racists off the hook, civil rights leaders would have a new weapon in their arsenal to combat all forms of intentional and unintentional discrimination. Social scientists could assist such efforts by conducting more systematic studies of the various manifestations of structural or "unintentional" discrimination.

THE ABUSE OF THE CLASS CONCEPT

Class is another popularly misused concept in studies of individuals differentiated by ethnic and income group. Conventional usage of this concept suffers from six deficiencies: (a) ambiguous criteria for defining membership in a different class strata; (b) use of shifting criteria for defining membership in the same class stratum; (c) use of class criteria that are not validated independently; (d) failure to use measures of vertical mobility in analyses of class strata; (e) treating atypical abstractions of class strata as if they were typical in reality, and (f) excluding the African American working class by undue concentration on "underclass" and "middle-class" strata. These shortcomings impede effective targeting of public and private policies to individuals and families in clearly specified socioeconomic strata.

Ambiguous Class Criteria

One of the most frequent abuses of the class concept, by social scientists as well as by the media, is the failure to provide explicit criteria for membership in different class strata. Numerous references (Wilson 1978; Wilson 1987; Murray 1984; Auletta 1983; Moynihan 1987; Jaynes and Williams 1989) are made to the "middle class," "lower class," and "underclass" without clearly defining these terms or specifying the size and composition of those class strata. Analysts such as Wilson (1987, 8), who make frequent use of the term *underclass*, tend to define it as a subgroup of the poor who are characterized by *long-term* unemployment, poverty, and welfare dependency:

> Included in this group are individuals who lack training and skills and either experience long-term unemployment or are not members of the labor force, individuals who are engaged in street crime and other forms of aberrant behavior, and families that experience long-term spells of poverty and/or welfare dependency. These are the populations to which I refer when I speak of the *underclass*.

Yet, contrary to his own definition, none of the data that Wilson presents to depict the prevalence of the "underclass" in the African American community refer to *long-term* attributes. Instead, he employs cross-sectional data on *current* joblessness, poverty, and welfare recipiency and never disaggregates, among African Americans, the long-term from the short-term jobless, poor, and welfare recipients. By including both subgroups in his statistics, the "underclass" is made to appear much larger than it actually is. Furthermore, the cross-sectional data are misused as if they were longitudinal data on poor African Americans in inner cities.

Shifting Class Criteria

Another frequent abuse of the class concept is the use of shifting criteria for defining membership in specific class strata. For example, many analyses (Wilson 1978; Landry 1987) of "middle-class" African Americans are based on data applying to all persons in white-collar jobs, or all persons with a college education, or all two-parent families, or all families with incomes above a national median, or all suburban families.

These diffent criteria weaken rather than strengthen any claims about a distinct middle class because the size and composition of its members vary markedly depending on the criteria used. Some of these data purporting to depict the middle class contain individuals and families also in fact part of Wilson's "underclass." Sizable numbers of African Americans in white-collar jobs, with college educations, in two-parent families, and living in suburban areas are long-term poor or jobless (Landry 1987; Billingsley 1993; Hill et al. 1993). Such analyses provide fragmented and misleading descriptions of different socioeconomic strata because of the failure to use *one* consistent set of criteria throughout the research.

Use of Unvalidated Criteria

Many social scientists (McAdoo 1978; Pinckney 1984; Landry 1987, Jencks 1991; Billingsley 1993) do use consistent classifications of class strata throughout their studies. These classifications are usually derived from widely used indexes of social class that were developed during the 1940s. Most systematic measures of social class today are composite, that is, they comprise two or more of the "objective" criteria of education, occupation, or income. Based on these criteria, individuals and families are rank ordered and subdivided into socioeconomic strata (SES), such as (a) high SES, moderate SES, and low SES; or (b) upper class, middle class, working class, and lower class (or underclass).

The major advantages of using past socioeconomic indexes are that the size and composition of members of various strata do not change at different stages of the study because only one classification is used, and that they facilitate comparing findings with those of prior studies. Although the reliability of findings about social class is enhanced by replicating popular composite indexes, the validity of these results has yet to be demonstrated because of several shortcomings.

First, the number and type of criteria comprising these indexes are used without any theoretical or empirical justification. Most researchers on class strata invariably fail to ask, for example, why three criteria are needed rather than one, two, or four, or why certain criteria (e.g., education, occupation, or income) are more appropriate than others (e.g., residence, leisure activities, or self-reported class).

Second, composite class indexes are often arbitrarily defined as independent variables without any validation of their predictive or explanatory power for the specific issues under study. The same criterion or index is used regardless of wide variation in key dependent variables. Most class analysts fail to determine which combinations of criteria (e.g., education and occupation, education and income, occupation and income, etc.) are more appropriate for which kinds of outcomes (e.g., fertility, maritial stability, poverty, health, crime, socialization, etc.). Unfortunately, most class criteria (such as occupation or education) are selected on the basis of convenience rather than for their theoretical relevance.

Third, procedures for scoring and weighting each criterion in composite class indexes are often adopted without demonstrating the criterion's applicability for all groups under study. Most class analysts fail to ask whether certain criteria should be weighted differently for different groups, such as for minorities or women. For example, persistent job discrimination against highly educated African Americans has made occupation a less reliable predictor of class rank for them than is education. Yet, most researchers conform to the traditional practice of assigning greater weight to occupation over education for all individuals, regardless of racial or ethnic group. Similarly, because most occupational indexes in the past have been derived largely from a job structure occupied primarily by white males, these indexes have much less validity for rank ordering the occupations of women in general and minorities in particular. McAdoo (1983) is one of the few scholars today to modify "classic" socioeconomic indexes to increase their relevance for African Americans by applying greater weight to education over occupation.

Absence of Vertical Mobility

One of the most persistent weaknesses of sociological analyses of class among African Americans is the virtual absence of any systematic assessment of vertical mobility. This is most evident in the lack of any analyses of *downward* mobility among the "middle class" and *upward* mobility among the poor or "underclass." For example, Wilson's (1978, 1987) studies of "middle class" and "underclass" African Americans tend to be static and tautological.

Rather than acknowledging that the large increases in the population of "middle-class" African Americans since the 1960s were mainly due to upward mobility of individuals from working-class and "underclass" families, Wilson (1987) contends that those who made the greatest strides were from already advantaged families (i.e., college educated or middle income). Studies by Landry (1978) and McAdoo (1978) of the growth of the black middle class strongly contradict such contentions. Similarly, Wilson (1987) argues that the "stable working class" made similar advances (such as moving to the suburbs) as middle-class African Americans. Thus, working-class individuals and families who move to the suburbs are tautologically defined as "stable." Who then, are the "unstable" working class, and how do they differ from the "underclass"? There is no room in Wilson's analyses for "underclass" families becoming "working class" and "working class" families becoming "middle class."

Wilson's analyses also do not allow for downward mobility among the middle class. Yet, numerous studies (Danziger and Weinberg 1986; Farley and Allen 1987; Jaynes and Williams 1989; Hill et al. 1993) of middle-income Americans have revealed that their living standards markedly eroded during the 1970s and 1980s due to four back-to-back recessions, record-level inflation, and other social forces. Consequently, contrary to popular belief, the number of female-headed families rose more sharply among the middle class than among the poor—among both blacks and whites. For example, the number of single parents rose ten times faster among college-educated than grade-school educated black and white women during the 1970s. There is strong evidence (Landry 1987; Farley and Allen 1987; Jencks 1991; Billingsley 1993) that sizable numbers of (white and black) women currently heading poor families were formerly in middle-income, two-parent families. Static class analyses obfuscate adequate understanding of the factors responsible for upward and downward mobility among all class strata in the African American community.

Reifying Abstractions

One of the most frequent flaws in studies of class stratification of minorities and low-income groups is the reifying of class prototypes. *Reification* is the fallacy of treating conceptual abstractions as if they existed in reality. Many commentators fail to realize that the number and composition of class categories, such as upper class, middle class, and lower class, are arbitrary extractions of reality that differ according to the objectives of the analysts. For example, Marx and Engels (1932) found it expedient to use only two class strata (bourgeoisie and proletariat), while Warner and Lunt (1942) found it useful to employ six social classes (upper-upper, lower-upper, upper-middle, lower-middle, upper-lower, and lower-lower) in several of their community studies.

Myrdal (1944, 2:1130) identified the fallacy of reification in his criticism of the Warner school for treating abstract prototypes as if they were real:

> In such an approach it is of importance to keep clear at the outset that our class concepts have no other reality than as a conceptual framework. . . . We must choose our class lines arbitrarily to answer certain specific questions. . . .
>
> The authors of the Warner group . . . often give the reader the impression that they believe that there are in reality clearly demarcated social classes [and] each of these classes has its distinctive patterns of familial, recreational and general social behavior. . . .
>
> Because of this misconception . . . which is sometimes called reification . . . these authors become tempted to give us a somewhat oversimplified idea about social stratification in the Negro community . . . what they are actually presenting is an ideal-typical—and, therefore, overtypical—description based on much detailed observation which is all organized under the conceptual scheme applied. By unduly insisting upon the realism of this analysis, however, they come to imply a rigidity in the class structure which is not really there.

Wilson's analysis of the "truly disadvantaged" (1987, 8) provides several instances of the fallacy of reification. For example, he asserts, "Today's ghetto neighborhoods are populated almost exclusively by the most disadvantaged segments of the black urban community, that heterogeneous grouping of families and individuals who are outside the mainstream of the American occupational system."

Yet, the data that Wilson uses to describe the neighborhoods of the "most disadvantaged" segments of African Americans are based on poverty area statistics from the 1970 and 1980 Censuses. Although Wilson depicts inner-city neighborhoods as consisting "almost exclusively" of poor and welfare families, poverty area data from the 1980 Census reveal that two out of three (66%) of African American families living in poverty areas are not poor and four out of five (81%) are not on welfare. Thus, Wilson makes unwarranted generalizations from atypical prototypes of poor and welfare families to characterize the majority of African American residents of poverty areas. It is important to note that because of intense criticism by several scholars (Jencks 1991; Gans 1992) of Wilson's misuse of the "underclass" concept, Wilson (1991) has agreed to no longer use this terminology.

In his work, *Losing Ground*, Murray (1984, 129–32) provides numerous examples of reification because he conveys the impression that the prototype of the welfare family is "typical" of the majority of black families. Yet, data from the 1992 Current Population Survey reveal that welfare families comprise only 18 percent of all black families (U.S. Bureau of the Census 1992a, 89), and poor, female-headed families in poverty areas account for only 14 percent of all black families (U.S. Bureau of the Census 1992b, 63). On the other hand, Murray (1993, 14) should be credited for placing national attention on the increasing growth of the "white underclass."

Reification is manifested most often in descriptions of the "underclass" in which African American individuals are depicted as simultaneously in a family headed by a female *and* lacking a strong work ethic *and* with a negative self-concept *and* on welfare for many generations *and* chronically poor. Not only is this prototype representative of only a tiny fraction of African Americans but, more importantly, no psychological and social data are provided to reveal the number that *simultaneously* have *all five* attributes. Such analysts fail to realize that the primary function of operational definitions, classifications, and prototypes is to abstract reality, not to mirror it. When analysts believe that their operational constructs reflect reality, their reification impedes the development of effective strategies for understanding and combating forces responsible for racial inequality.

Exclusion of the Working Class

A final example of the abuse of the class concept is the virtual exclusion of the "working class" among African Americans by concentrating almost totally on two strata—"underclass" and "middle class." Although

Wilson (1978; 1987) uses the term "stable working class" frequently in his studies, it is invariably linked with "middle-class" African Americans. Thus, he does not provide separate and distinct analyses of the black working class. Moreover, by referring only to the "stable" working class, he implies that *all* working-class African Americans are "stable."

This exclusion of working-class blacks conveys the inaccurate impression that the African American community is comprised of only two classes—"middle class" and "underclass." More importantly, by excluding the working class, analysts such as Wilson are forced to rely on static explanations to account for the surge in the size of the "underclass." Their inclusion would help to account, in part, for this surge by focusing on downward mobility among segments of the African American working class. One policy implication of focusing on the (unstable) working class is to develop strategies to stem the growth of the "underclass" by reducing downward mobility among the working class.

THE ABUSE OF THE CULTURE CONCEPT

The concept of *culture* is also widely distorted in many analyses of African Americans and low-income groups. One fundamental problem is the widespread use of this term as synonymous with other concepts, such as *society*, *class*, and *poverty*. This intermingling of substantively distinct concepts is manifested in the following deficiencies: (a) the popular denial of any African cultural patterns among African Americans; (b) the popular acceptance of a "culture of poverty" among African Americans; (c) failure to distinguish class adaptations from cultural continuities; and (d) failure to distinguish cultural attributes from cultural correlates.

Denial of African Culture

Historically, there has been a continuing debate between two schools of thought: Frazier's (1939) perspective, which holds that blacks in America have no distinctive culture of their own because 250 years of slavery virtually destroyed all vestiges of African culture, and Herskovits's ([1941] 1958) perspective, which holds that African culture continues to influence American blacks. Herskovits (p. 145) argues strongly against the view that American blacks have no African cultural legacies:

> . . . . a caution is in order concerning the degree of purity assumed to exist in the African traits to be reviewed. . . . Negroes in the United States are not Africans, but they are the descendants of Africans. There is no more theoretical support for an hypothesis that they have retained nothing of the culture of their African forebears, than for supposing that they have remained completely African in their behavior.

Contemporary scholars (Blassingame 1972; Gutman 1976; Waxman 1986; Sudarkasa 1988; Mintz and Price 1992; Miller 1993; Billingsley 1993) have provided support for Herskovits's position by identifying Africanisms in many aspects of American life, such as the extended family, child-rearing patterns, religion, language, music, art, rituals, nutrition, and health practices. Nevertheless, it is the Frazierian perspective that is widely accepted by American social scientists today. It is reflected in such assertions, as by Glazer and Moynihan (1963, 53), that "the Negro is only an American and nothing else. He has no values or culture to protect."

Acceptance of Culture of Poverty

The alleged absence of a distinctive culture among African Americans contributes to popular explanations of black styles of life defined almost solely in terms of class or socioeconomic position. Thus, the values and behavioral patterns of middle-class blacks are said to reflect those of middle-class whites, while the values and behaviors of poor blacks are said to be manifestations of an "underclass culture" or "culture of poverty." Although the "culture of poverty" term was coined by Oscar Lewis (1959) based on his studies of the rural poor in Mexico and Puerto Rico, it has been adopted wholly by contemporary proponents of "underclass culture" among inner-city minorities.

According to this thesis, the economic deprivation of the "underclass" is self-perpetuated by an array of negative and "self-destructive" lifestyles (such as families headed by females, welfare dependence, lack of work ethic, and negative self-concept) that are handed down from generation to generation. In short, poverty is intergenerationally transmitted as a cultural "way of life," rather than as a result of contemporary forces, such as racism, classism, social policies, and other societal forces. Thus, the "culture of poverty" notion leads to the "blaming the victim" syndrome. Furthermore, the fixation of the poverty culture notion on *only* the *negative* attributes of the poor is at sharp variance with the anthropological concept of culture, which focuses on positive traits as well.

Confusing Class and Cultural Lifestyles

A basic flaw in the culture of poverty thesis is its failure to distinguish clearly between situational adaptations, reactions to contemporary socioeconomic circumstances, and historical adaptations—the distinctive cultural patterns transmitted intergenerationally through socialization. It is the latter that Valentine (1968) refers to when he states that the concept of "culture" has been used by most anthropologists to refer to positive "formulas for living" that help groups to survive and advance, regardless of the contemporary circumstances. Slaughter and Mc-Worter (1985, 16) also underscore the importance of this distinction:

> In an otherwise informative volume, Martin and Martin's (1978) study of extended black families continues to espouse the idea that blacks lost their African heritage through slavery. The black extended family was viewed, not as a construction within the context of the African-American experience, but as a self-help or survival unit generated by an ahistoric group of people living in a rural or agricultural setting.
>
> The distinction we make is important. If the black extended family is an American adaptation of a long-standing African tradition, then clear cultural links to the diaspora are implied and can be expected to continue. This would occur because of a people's thrust for cultural continuity, even in a changed geographical setting (i.e., urban by comparison to rural). If it is merely a self-help or survival unit, then the black extended family will wane in scope and influence in accordance with any societal change which heralds significant social and economic improvements for black people.

To keep the concepts of class adaptations and cultural continuities distinct, it may be useful to view such conditions as high levels of unemployment, underemployment, low wages, lack of education, crowded living quarters, and female-headed families as situational class adaptations or symptoms of being poor rather than as patterns transmitted through socialization. On the other hand, it may be useful to view such patterns as extended family networks, informal adoption, flexible family roles, achievement orientation, religious orientation, and high valuation of children and the elderly as cultural continuities transmitted from generation to generation.

Based on these working definitions, the major distinction between class-related and cultural lifestyles is that the former are responses to external contemporary forces due to membership in specific socioeconomic strata, while the latter are responses to historical forces through values, attitudes, and traditions acquired through socialization in particular racial, ethnic, or religious groups. This distinction facilitates developing public policies more effectively targeted to altering negative class adaptations or lifestyles.

Confusing Attributes and Correlates

Another common weakness of most studies of cultural or class patterns is the failure to distinguish between attributes and correlates. *Attributes* refer to the *intrinsic* traits of class or cultural lifestyles, while *correlates* refer to their *extrinsic* characteristics. Attributes are constant, as they are integral to the definition of an adaptation or lifestyle, while correlates are variable, part of the hypothesis (or outcomes) to be investigated.

Whether a characteristic is part of a definition or a hypothesis depends on the specific purpose of the inquiry. Traits operationally defined as attributes in one study may be defined as correlates in another. The only restriction is that they be defined consistently throughout the same study. For example, one analyst may define *welfare recipiency* as an attribute (or constant) of the "underclass." Accordingly, all members of the "underclass" in that study would have to be on welfare. Another analyst may define the same term as a correlate (or variable) of the "underclass." This would mean that not all members of the "underclass" in the second study would be on welfare, only that this strata would have a (presumably) higher proportion of welfare recipients than higher class strata. Similarly, one researcher may define extended family household as a cultural attribute, while another may define it as a cultural correlate.

De-emphasis of Positive Cultural Traits

A major deficiency of conventional studies of the African American community is their failure to examine the role of positive cultural patterns or "strengths" (Hill 1971; Slaughter and McWorter 1985; Coontz 1992; Billingsley 1993; Miller 1993). Instead, conventional studies tend to concentrate almost totally on negative class attributes and correlates of black individuals and families. While such concentration is essential for examining the severity of social problems, it does not necessarily suggest the appropriate remedial strategies.

Focusing on positive cultural or coping patterns may contribute to the identification of more effective policies. Such a focus would attempt to strengthen black families by developing policies that build on and reinforce their cultural strengths. For example, various studies (Freeman and Holtzer 1986; Staples and Johnson 1993; Billingsley 1993) have shown that poor blacks with strong religious orientation are more likely to experience upward mobility than those with weak religious orientation. Yet, to date, few policy researchers have focused on the significance of religion in black family functioning.

SUMMARY

This chapter has described various ways that the concepts of race, class, and culture are misused in conventional studies of African American populations and of low-income groups in general. The major shortcomings in the current usage of *race* are failure to distinguish prejudice from discrimination, failure to distinguish institutional from individual racism, and failure to distinguish unintentional from intentional discrimination. The *class* concept is often misused by failing to provide specific operational definitions for the various class strata, using shifting class criteria or unvalidated criteria, the absence of data reflecting vertical mobility, reifying atypical abstractions, and excluding the black working class. The concept of *culture* is most often misused by denying African cultural legacies among black Americans, accepting popular notions of the "culture of poverty," confusing class-related lifestyles with cultural lifestyles, confusing cultural attributes with cultural correlates, and deemphasizing the role of positive cultural traits or "strengths" in the functioning of black families and communities. We contend that researchers who conduct studies that evidence increased sensitivity to these pitfalls of definition will significantly aid the development of effective public policies for blacks in particular and low-income groups in general.

REFERENCES

Allport, Gordon. 1954. *The nature of prejudice*. Reading, MA: Addison-Wesley.

Arax, M. 1983. The black family. *The Baltimore Evening Sun*, December 5–9, pp. 1, 5.

Auletta, Ken. 1983. *The underclass*. New York: Vintage Books.

Billingsley, Andrew. 1992. *Climbing Jacob's ladder: The enduring legacy of African-American families*. New York: Simon & Schuster.

Blassingame, John W. 1972. *The slave community*. New York: Oxford University Press.

Calmore, John O. 1989. To make wrong right: The necessary and proper aspirations of fair housing. In *The state of black America, 1989*, ed. Janet Dewart. New York: National Urban League.

Carmichael, Stokely, and Charles Hamilton. 1967. *Black power*. New York: Vintage.

Cheatham, Harold E., and James B. Stewart, eds. 1990. *Black families*. New Brunswick, NJ: Transaction.

Coontz, Stephanie. 1992. *The way we never were: American families and the nostalgia trap*. New York: Basic Books.

Cummings, J. 1983. Breakup of the black family imperils gains of decades. *New York Times*, November 20, pp. 1, 56.

Danziger, Sheldon, and Daniel H. Weinberg, eds. 1986. *Fighting poverty: What works and what doesn't*. Cambridge, MA: Harvard University Press.

Davis, James A., and Tom W. Smith. 1982. *General social surveys, 1972–1982; cumulative codebook*. Chicago: National Opinion Research Center.

Downs, Anthony. 1970. Racism in America and how to combat it. In *Urban problems and prospects*, A. Downs. Chicago: Markham.

Farley, Reynolds, and Walter R. Allen. 1987. *The color line and the quality of life in America.* New York: Russell Sage Foundation.

Feagin, Joe R. 1978. *Racial and ethnic relations.* Englewood Cliffs, NJ: Prentice-Hall.

Frazier, E. Franklin. 1939. *The Negro family in the United States.* rev. ed. Chicago: University of Chicago Press.

Freeman, Richard B., and Harry J. Holzer, eds. 1986. *The black youth employment crisis.* Chicago: University of Chicago Press.

Friedman, Robert. 1975. Institutional racism: How to discriminate without really trying. In *Racial discrimination in the United States,* ed. T. Pettigrew. New York: Harper & Row.

Gans, Herbert J. 1992. Fighting the biases embedded in social concepts of the poor. *Poverty and Race* (May): 1–2.

Gibbs, Nancy. 1994. The vicious cycle. *Time,* June 20. pp. 25–33.

Glasgow, Douglas G. 1981. *The black underclass.* New York: Vintage.

Glazer, Nathan, and Daniel P. Moynihan. 1963. *Beyond the melting pot.* Cambridge, MA: MIT Press.

Gutman, Herbert G. 1976. *The black family in slavery and freedom: 1750–1925.* New York: Vintage.

Hacker, Andrew. 1992. *Two nations.* New York: Ballantine Books.

Hare, Bruce R. 1988. Black youth at risk. In *The state of black America: 1988.* New York: National Urban League.

Herskovits, Melville J. [1941] 1958. *The myth of the Negro past.* Reprint. Boston: Beacon.

Hill, Robert B. 1971. *The strengths of black families.* New York: Emerson Hall.

———. 1984. The polls and ethnic minorities. *Annals,* 472 (March): 155–66.

———. 1988. Structural discrimination: The unintended consequences of institutional processes. In *Surveying Social Life: Papers in Honor of Herbert Hyman,* ed. Hubert J. O'Gorman. Middletown, CT: Wesleyan University Press.

Hill, Robert, et al. 1993. *Research on the African-American family: A holistic perspective.* Westport, CT: Auburn House.

Jackman, Mary R. 1973. Education and prejudice or education and response set? *American Sociological Review* 38 (3): 327–39.

Jaynes, Gerald D., and Robin Williams, eds. 1989. *A common des-*

tiny: Blacks and American society. Washington, DC: National Academy Press.

Jencks, Christopher. 1991. Is the American underclass growing? In *The urban underclass,* ed. Christopher Jencks and Paul E. Peterson. Washington, DC: Brookings Institution.

Jencks, Christopher, and Paul E. Peterson, eds. 1991. *The urban underclass.* Washington, DC: Brookings Institution.

Jones, Dionne. 1990–91. Racism in America. *The Urban League Review* 14 (Winter): 3–7.

Jones, James M. 1972. *Prejudice and racism.* Reading, MA: Addison-Wesley.

Katz, Michael B. 1993. *The underclass debate: Views from history.* Princeton, NJ: Princeton University Press.

Kinder, D. R., and David O. Sears. 1981. Prejudice and politics: Symbolic racism versus racial threats to the good life. *Journal of Personality and Social Psychology* 40 (3): 414–31.

Landry, Bart. 1978. Growth of the black middle class in the 1960's. *Urban League Review* 3 (Winter): 68–82.

———. 1987. *The new black middle class.* Berkeley, CA: University of California Press.

LaPiere, Robert T. 1934. Attitudes versus actions. *Social Forces* 13:230–37.

Lewis, Oscar. 1959. *Five families.* New York: Basic Books.

Martin, Elmer P., and Joanne M. Martin. 1978. *The black extended family.* Chicago: University of Chicago Press.

Marx, Karl, and Frederich Engels. 1932. *Manifesto of the Communist party.* New York: International.

McAdoo, Harriette P. 1978. Factors related to stability in upwardly mobile black families. *Journal of Marriage and the Family* 40 (November): 767–78.

———. 1983. Extended family support of single black mothers: Final report. Washington, DC: U.S. National Institute of Mental Health.

McAdoo, Harriette, ed. 1988. *Black families.* Beverly Hills, CA: Sage.

McConahay, John B., B. B. Hardee, and V. Batts. 1981. Has racism declined in America? *Journal of Conflict Resolution* 25 (4): 563–79.

McConahay, John B., and J. S. Hough, Jr. 1976. Symbolic racism. *Journal of Social Issues* 32 (2): 23–45.

Merton, Robert K. 1948. Discrimination and the American creed. In *Discrimination and the national welfare*, ed. R. M. MacIver. New York: Harper. Reprinted in R. K. Merton. 1976. *Sociological ambivalence and other essays*. New York: The Free Press.

Miller, Andrew. 1993. Social science, social policy, and the heritage of African American families. In *The underclass debate*, ed. Michael Katz. Princeton: Princeton University Press.

Mintz, Sidney, and Richard Price. 1992. *The birth of African American culture*. Boston: Beacon Press.

Moynihan, Daniel, 1987. *Family and nation*. New York: Harcourt Brace Jovanovich.

Murray, Charles. 1984. *Losing ground: American social policy*. 1950–1980. New York: Basic Books.

Murray, Charles. 1993. "The coming white underclass." *Wall Street Journal*, October 29, pp. A–14.

Myrdal, Gunnar. 1994. *An American dilemma*. 2 vols. New York: Harper.

NAACP Legal Defense and Educational Fund. 1989. *The unfinished agenda on race in America*. New York: NAACP Legal Defense and Educational Fund.

National Conference for Christians and Jews. 1978. *A study of attitudes toward racial and religious minorities and toward women*. New York: National Conference for Christians and Jews.

Peterson, Paul E. 1991. The urban underclass and the poverty paradox. In *The urban underclass*, ed. Christopher Jencks and Paul E. Peterson. Washington, DC: Brookings Institution.

Pinckney, Alphonso. 1984. *The myth of black progress*. Cambridge, MA: Cambridge University Press.

Roper Center. 1982. *A guide to Roper Center resources for the study of American race relations*. Storrs, CT: University of Connecticut.

Schuman, Howard, Charlotte Steeb, and Lawrence Bobo. 1985. *Racial attitudes in America*. Cambridge, MA: Harvard University Press.

Shimkin, Dimitri, Edith M. Shimkin, and Dennis A. Frate, eds. 1978. *The extended family in black societies*. The Hague: Mouton.

Sighall, H., and R. Page. 1971. Current stereotypes: A little fading, a little faking. *Journal of Personality & Social Psychology* 18 (2): 247–55.

Slaughter, Diana T., and Gerald A. McWorter. 1985. Social origins and early features of the scientific study of black American families and children. In *Beginnings: The social and affective development of black children*, ed. Margaret B. Spencer, G. Brookins, and Walter Allen. Hillsdale, NJ: Lawrence Erlbaum Associates.

Smith, Tom, and Paul B. Sheatsley. 1984. American attitudes toward race relations. *Public Opinion Quarterly*, 7: 15–53.

Sniderman, Paul M., and Thomas Piazza. 1993. *The scar of race*. Cambridge, MA: Harvard University Press.

Staples, Robert, and Leanor B. Johnson. 1993. *Black families at the crossroads*. San Francisco: Jossey-Bass.

Sudarkasa, Niara. 1988. Interpreting the African heritage in Afro-American family organization. In *Black families*, ed. Harriette McAdoo. Beverly Hills, CA: Sage.

Tidwell, Billy J., ed. 1993. *The state of black America, 1993*. New York: National Urban League. (See esp., Chronology of Events: 1992.)

U.S. Bureau of the Census. 1992a. Money income of households, families, and persons in the United States: 1991. *Current population reports*, ser. P-60, no. 180. Washington, DC.

U.S. Bureau of the Census. 1992b. Poverty in the United States: 1991. *Current population reports*, ser. P-60, no. 181. Washington, DC.

Valentine, Charles A. 1968. *Culture and poverty*. Chicago: University of Chicago Press.

Warner, W. Lloyd, and Paul S. Lunt. 1942. *The status of a modern community*. New Haven, CT: Yale University Press.

Waxman, Chaim I. 1986. *The stigma of poverty*. New York: Pergamon Press.

Wicker, Allan W. 1969. Attitudes versus actions. *Journal of Social Issues* 25: 41–78.

Wilson, William J. 1978. *The declining significance of race*. Chicago: University of Chicago Press.

———. 1987. *The truly disadvantaged: The inner city, the underclass and public policy*. Chicago: University of Chicago Press.

Wilson, William J. 1991. Public policy research and the truly disadvantaged. In *The urban underclass*, ed. Christopher Jencks and Paul E. Peterson. Washington, DC: Brookings Institution.

7 | Whatever Tomorrow Brings: African American Families and Government Social Policy

WALTER R. ALLEN

"Sometimes I feel like a motherless child / Sometimes I feel like a motherless child / A long, long way from home."

(From a Negro Spiritual)

Since coming to this country, African Americans have lived an existence fraught with hardship and uncertainty, yet in tribute to their character, this existence has been marked by determination and accomplishment. Historically, our relationship with the U.S. government has been paradoxical, to say the least. At one point, this government provided the legal basis for and military enforcement of our slavery. Later, the government declared our emancipation, while at the same time sanctioning institutional arrangements calculated to insure our continued social, economic, and political subjugation. Most recently, the government waged a "holy war" on those social, economic, and political inequities that had come to symbolize the African American experience in this country—only to retreat from the battle just as significant gains were being won. In this chapter, we examine the vexing relationships between U.S. government social policy and the status of African American families and their children.

In less than a decade, the dawn of a new century will break over this country—381 years after the first

African arrived. It is appropriate, therefore, that on the doorstep of this new era, we examine the current situation of African Americans, how they are faring and what the future seems to promise. Some findings from recent research give cause for celebration: We see evidence that many of the barriers once preventing the full realization of African American potential have been cast aside. We are shown evidence of an emerging middle class, increased educational access for our young, and the opening of occupational opportunities in previously exclusive areas. This is the good news from the current research record, providing evidence of progress, prosperity, and promise. Unfortunately, the bad news is also abundantly conveyed in the research record. We are told of the worsening situation with regard to families headed by females. Over one-half of our children now grow up in homes mired in poverty and its attendant difficulties by virtue of the society's economic and social welfare practices, which consign African American, single, female heads of household (and by definition their children) to lives dimmed by economic deprivation and social degradation. We are reminded of the incredible number of African American males snatched from productive roles in the community through imprisonment, premature death by homicide, retreat into drugs, and chronic unemployment. In the midst of these statistical indicators, we find cause for great concern, if not alarm, over the very future of African American family life.

A concern over the future of African American families and their children is the central motivating theme of this paper. We begin by acknowledging the critical importance of government social policy as a potential determinant of whether this future is positive or negative. In this connection, we examine how government social policy effects African American family life. Next, we explore the contributions of African American families to the maintenance of positive mental health in African American communities, where these families have demonstrated over the years a remarkable ability to engender and cultivate positive mental health among members often exposed to the most negative and horrendous of circumstances. Their ability to produce sane, productive individuals in the midst of circumstances that would seem to guarantee insanity and destructive behavior is taken here as in jeopardy, and is systematically explored. Lastly, we elevate the various social policy, theoretical, and research issues examined to a call for new values, and examine the place of values in scientific ideology, public policy, and professional roles. We close with suggestions for how changes in these values might assist in the creation of positive futures for African American families.

THE HISTORY OF FAMILY POLICY IN THE UNITED STATES

Due to fundamental changes in the structure of our society, family and individual dependence on government has become more pronounced than ever in history. The forces of urbanization, industrialization, and economic restructuring have created an immensely complex, impersonal, and insecure environment. Consequently, individual and nuclear family needs for supportive relationships have intensified as societal pressures have become more abundant and increasingly difficult to manage. Yet the effectiveness of extended family networks in the provision of such supportive services has declined due to changing family structure, norms, and geographic patterns. Government and proxy public institutions are thus increasingly called upon to fill the void left by these receding extended family and support networks.

Awareness that vital system maintenance functions were becoming difficult for extended families to perform, and the perceived consequence of this fact, combined to prompt many concerned people to call for the creation of a national family policy. In the context of this chapter, *family policy* refers to a consensus on a core set of family goals, toward which the government deliberately shapes policies, actions, and programs. Although many, if not all, governmental policy decisions at the national level influence families, the task of bringing about the adoption of a conscious, planned national family policy has proven difficult. Several historical traditions and conditions in this country represent obstacles for the development of a well-articulated national family policy (Hill 1993; Chilman 1973; Schorr 1962; Sussman 1971). Among the more important are the following:

1. *The national commitment to individualism.* From the very beginning, our society has been inclined to deal with individuals rather than families. Families have been viewed as secondary in importance to individuals, representing vehicles for the satisfaction of individual needs. This distinction has been preserved in the formal

organization of federal government activities, where one finds agencies working on the problems of retired, young, aged, poor, female, and handicapped individuals, but nowhere does there exist a single agency concerned with the family unit in its entirety.

2. *The mechanics of the free enterprise system.* As long as family goals are in concert with the goals of private industry and business, the system functions to ensure their well-being. In instances where these interests conflict, however, families suffer because they, unlike industry or business, are without the protection of professional, full-time advocates. Families lack the resources to ensure that their interests are effectively represented. Consequently, family goals are often subordinated to the more organized, better funded, corporate interests in the society.

3. *The mechanics of the democratic system.* By its very nature, the political process in the United States is antagonistic to monolithic statements of family goals. Such statements are bound to run counter to the variety of cultural, religious, and economic family variants reflected in this society. The basic tenet of democracy is to allow the majority to prevail. (In practice, this is often the group with the most power.) For this reason, we see at the national level policies that reflect the expectations of white, Protestant, middle-class families.

4. *The national ethic of noninterference in families.* Unlike any other groups or associations, families in our society are invested with unique privileges of privacy. The historical division of church and state in our culture has granted the family a special immunity from interference by the government (interpersonal and family relationships have been broadly defined as falling within the realm of the church). Families also derive this "sacred" quality, to an extent, from our national ethic advocating and protecting private property. As numerous authors have pointed out, family relationships have often been perceived, after a fashion, as property relationships. Historically, laws granted husbands de facto ownership rights over wives, while parents were accorded the same privileges with regard to their children. Government efforts to intervene in families are thus doubly hampered. Such intervention is seen as interference with rights of privacy (such as the right to religious choice) and self-determination of personal "property" (Laing 1971; Ball 1972).

5. *The limitations in family research and theory.* As a relatively young area of scientific inquiry, family studies is characterized by conceptual and methodological problems that hamper the development of solid evidence on which to base national policy. The status of basic research, which informs policy research, in family studies is somewhat rudimentary. Researchers in this area fail to share consensus over what constitutes the most appropriate conceptual and methodological perspectives in the analysis of family phenomena. By the same token, little agreement exists over the most useful data or data-collection strategies. Indeed researchers commonly disagree over the interpretation or implications of the "facts." We find, therefore, that the development of national family policies has also been retarded by the historic scarcity of systematic, dependable, empirical data to guide decisions (Klein et al. 1969).

Despite these several problems, numerous pieces of family legislation have been enacted over the history of this society. In cases where efforts to enact family policies have been successful, the policymaking machinery has functioned in a more or less predictable fashion. Proposed family policies have been most often favorably received when they conformed to one or a combination of the following standards (Schorr 1962):

1. *Standard of Congruence.* Family policy legislation fares best when it can be shown to be *congruent* with the perceived needs of individuals. The greater the degree of consistency between family and individual necessities, the more likely any legislation focused on family is to be enacted.
2. *Standard of Coincidence.* Family legislation also occurs frequently as a coincidental outcome of other planned social policy legislation. Often other societal problems and/or issues of concern prompt the development of laws and regulations which happen, by coincidence, to contain provisions relevant to family welfare.
3. *Standard of Correction.* In the rare instances where family legislation develops explicitly, it is generally intended to correct a narrowly defined problem in American family systems. The focus of such "crisis-oriented" legislation tends to be solely on the facet(s) of family life deemed to require emergency intervention.

The development of national family policies in the United States, then, has faced numerous problems. Social norms and principles of operation have combined to militate against the emergence of cogent, coordinated government programs regarding families. Where explicit governmental family policies and programs exist, these generally fail to be systematic and thorough responses to family needs. Rather, such programs have been compromised by limited information on families and legislative expediency. Predictably, problems associated with national family policy, such as those cited above, are amplified many times over when we talk about African American family policy at the national level. The historically unique social, economic, and political position of African Americans in this society further complicates the already difficult equation linking government and family.

AFRICAN AMERICAN FAMILIES AND NATIONAL SOCIAL POLICY: THEORETICAL AND SUBSTANTIVE ISSUES

The development and implementation of governmental policies for African American families provide a special case of the problems of family social policy discussed above. Complex social-historical factors combine to indelibly stamp black families in this culture with unique circumstances that distinguish them, and any governmental attempt to deal with their problems, from white families. We illustrate this point with a brief review of the literature on African American families. Basic research informs and directs policy research that serves as the general basis for policy decisions. In the United States, as elsewhere, implementation of social policy programs and strategies is normally justified on the basis of academic research.

The theoretical frameworks, data, and interpretations from academic research eventually feed into the policymaking machinery to provide a foundation for informed decision making. While the percolation effect, whereby research models and findings are translated over time into concrete social programs, may be direct and immediate, more often than not this translation is indirect and delayed. The result of such translation delay is the implementation of social programs whose intellectual traditions are unclear. We see the utility of social programs debated and decided largely in terms of secondary features (cost, publicity value, political expediency, etc.). Little or no attention is paid to the basic issues of how valid the underlying premises of the programs are and what level of empirical support exists for such positions. It thus becomes imperative for us to understand the way in which African American families are treated in U.S. scholarship, for this very treatment predicts their treatment in U.S. social policy.

THEORY AND METHOD IN THE STUDY OF AFRICAN AMERICAN FAMILIES

While the majority of theoretical weaknesses characterizing African American family studies are symptomatic of deficits in the area of family studies as a whole, there are unique theoretical problems (Hill 1993). In part, these problems arise from fundamental ideological differences between researchers. The competing ideologies may be represented as three distinct theoretical perspectives: (a) the "cultural-equivalent" perspective, (b) the "cultural-deviant" perspective, and (c) the "cultural-variant" perspective (Allen 1985).

The *cultural equivalent* perspective of African American family life is exemplified by researchers who fail to acknowledge that black families constitute distinct cultural forms, fundamentally different from white families. In their attempts to deemphasize or negate the unique characteristics of black families and to highlight characteristics they share with white families, these researches succeed in creating caricatures—black families are depicted by darkly tinted facsimiles of white families. Thus Bernard (1966, 141) speaks of "culturally white" black families; Frazier ([1939] 1964, 190) refers to one group of black families as "Black Puritans"; and Scanzoni (1971, 324) suggests that black and white family differences are reducible to social class differences. By failing to recognize the uniqueness of the African American family experience, the cultural equivalent perspective does these families a grave injustice. The perspective makes the implicit value judgment that black families constitute legitimate forms only insofar as their structures and processes replicate those of white, middle-class families.

The *cultural-deviant* perspective of African American families does not ignore their distinctive qualities. Instead, researchers who employ this perspective acknowledge the unique traits of the family and then penalize it for being different. Such research attributes differences between black and white families to weaknesses in the black family. To this extent, the cultural-deviant perspective makes explicit the normative judgments left implicit by the cultural-equivalent perspective. Adopting white, middle-class families as the "healthy" norm, researchers label deviating black families as pathological forms. Qualities that distinguish black from white families are taken as indexes of dysfunction. Therefore, the more at odds a black family is with the white, middle-class family model, the more pathological in orientation that family is judged to be. Moynihan (1965, 5) exemplifies this perspective in his widely quoted conclusion that "at the heart of the deterioration of the fabric of Negro society is the deterioration of the Negro family," while Frazier ([1939] 1964, 404–5) speaks of "wide-spread disorganization" in black family patterns. Similarly, Rainwater (1970, 155–87) characterizes black males as ineffectual, irresponsible mates and parents, and Schulz (1969, 67–69) concludes that black families are matriarchies. The combined writings of "deviance" perspectivists are injurious to the image of African American families because they lend questionable support to common myths portraying these families (and by inference all African Americans) as basically pathological in nature.

The *cultural-variant* perspective views the black family as a form distinct from the white family. Unlike the cultural-deviant perspective, however, the cultural-variant perspective does not automatically interpret distinctive qualities in black family life as signs of pathology. Rather, this perspective acknowledges that black and white families operate under different situational constraints and in response to different cultural imperatives. As a consequence, their structures, processes, and functions differ in many respects. The variant perspective recognizes and makes "cultural-relative" evaluations of differences between black and white families. Billingsley, for example, views the African American family as an "ethnic subsystem" of the larger society. Developing the notion of adaptive functioning, he views the black family as amazingly adept at fulfilling the "bio-psycho-social" needs of its members in spite of extreme hardship. He argues that black families strategically adopt forms that facilitate the efficient performance of assigned functions (Billingsley 1968, 22–33). This idea is also reflected in Stack's (1974, 124–26) reference to the culturally adaptive functions of economic "exchange" relationship among urban black families; Rodman's (1971, 197) interpretation of what are normally referred to as "problems" in lower-class black families, such as illegitimacy, female-headed households, as adaptive "solutions"; and Ladner's (1971, 44–66) description of changing female adolescent socialization patterns in black families as responses to shifting environmental conditions. The cultural-variant perspective of African American family life recognizes that while family functions are universal, cultural values and situational constraints vary; thus different structural adaptations are often required. Because theory is intricately linked with method of study and the two are mutually determinative, we now turn to the consideration of salient methodological issues.

Experience suggests that one's research methodology can only be as good as one's theory, for theory provides the procedural guidelines for research. In this sense, good theory construction (problem formulation) represents the first step in the methodological sequence. Inadequate problem conceptualization and poor theory construction have historically plagued the area of African American family studies. For the most part, researchers have been bound in their approaches by largely ethnocentric and inflexible models (Billingsley 1993; Tatum 1992). For this reason, it is not sufficient to deal solely with issues of data collection and analysis; attention must also be directed to the founding assumptions from which the central research hypotheses of a study are derived. The question, therefore, transcends issues of survey research versus experimental research, descriptive versus causal analyses, or nonparametric versus parametric statistics, and becomes one largely of *perspective*. Is the researcher's perspective sufficiently flexible to allow the application of new, more appropriate research models and analytic techniques should they prove necessary or desirable?

Within the last few years, researchers have begun to make substantial advances in the development of alternative research models for the study of African American families. Perhaps the most dramatic alternative models are attributable to researchers employing ethnographic or participant-observation approaches. Working from the premise that subjects are best understood when the researcher shares their day-to-day experiences, these researchers study African American families in natural settings. Their findings have generated a rich volume of "fresh" hypotheses concerning family support systems (Taylor 1986), African American female roles (Ladner 1971), and extended family ties (Zollar 1985). Progress toward the development of alternative research models has been made on other methodological fronts as well. Cherlin (1992) and Farley and Allen (1989) use census data to propose alternative interpretations of African American family behavior at the aggregate level, while Jackson et al. (1981) and McLanahan (1985) rely on secondary analysis of survey data to refute longstanding assumptions about the instability of African American family structure. Alternative interpretations of early African American family patterns have also been proposed by anthropologists (Mullings 1986; Sudar Kasa 1981), by a group of quantitative social-historians (Jones 1985; Gutman 1975) and by case studies (Scott 1991; Willie 1985).

OMISSIONS IN AFRICAN AMERICAN FAMILY STUDIES AND THEIR CONSEQUENCES FOR SOCIAL POLICY

Billingsley (1970, 128) identifies four areas of social science scholarship that have been presented with both the opportunity and the necessity to describe, analyze, and explain the character of African American family life in this country. Of these four areas, "Studies of social welfare problems and programs" (1970, 128) are most important to us here, for it is studies of this genre that inform social policy in our society. In this area of concern, he notes little systematic attention to the roles, structures, or cultural foundations of African American families (1970, 140). Instead, they tend to be either overlooked or, where they are addressed, portrayed in a distorted light. It becomes readily apparent that many of the "informed" social policy decisions that affect African American families have not been at all well informed. Guided by research that labeled these families as pathological, that employed inapplicable models of family life, and that applied inappropriate methodological and statistical techniques, policymakers formulated policies inimical to the welfare of the very families they were supposedly intended to help. Ultimately, we must indict American scholarship and its treatment of African American families, for it has been more of a hindrance than an aid to the process of formulating enlightened social policy.

The consequences that the academic community's shortcomings hold for social policies aimed at these families are detrimental on two levels. On one level, the general population, which ultimately passes judgment on government policy decisions through public opinion and the vote, continues to be ignorant about African American family life. Consequently, misguided views of African Americans and their families persist and fuel national resistance to the implementation of necessary social programs. On another level, policymakers themselves are impaired by faulty research conclusions that contribute to the enactment of inadequate, ill-conceived social programs. Concerned, sincere legislators and government officials are left without the knowledge essential to any successful attempt to systematically and programmatically address the needs of African American families. In sum, the record of U.S. academics, as it pertains to social policy formulation about African American families, has been at best spotty and at worst destructive.

AFRICAN AMERICAN FAMILIES: PROTECTORS OF THE REALM

Of all the functions performed by family systems in contemporary society, perhaps the most important is that of protectorate. Families serve as buffering mechanisms, intervening between their members and the larger society. In their roles as advocates, stabilizers, and defenders of individuals who are confronted with societal forces that are at times overwhelming, families certainly make real and tangible contributions to the maintenance of personal mental health. Some family sociologists even go so far as to suggest that institutional division of labor in society has evolved to a point where families now exist primarily for purposes of emotional gratification. They argue that the majority of other traditional family functions have long since been assumed by other social institutions. While I shy away from such a drastic conclusion, I am thoroughly convinced of the primary role played by families (or their less formal—though equally real—substitutes) in the maintenance of stable personalities. For this reason, I believe that understanding of family variations in "coping" styles, skills, and patterns is essential if we are to fully grasp the range of alternative models for preventative and corrective action in the arena of mental health.

African American families present, in my opinion, prototypes of effective family systems in their performance of these mental health maintenance functions. In spite of historic deprivation, discrimination, and the many other problems they face, African American families have continually produced creative, productive, stable individuals. They have successfully nurtured and maintained their members through centuries of societal indifference, if not outright hostility, toward their welfare. Paradoxically, African American families have received very little credit for their admirable work in this sphere. Negativism and oversight in research approaches continue to retard recognition of the skill and dedication with which African American families marshal limited resources to maintain positive mental health in their communities.

Limited research experience contributes to our lack of information about African American family coping styles and skills. However, Hill (1971) identifies five important types of family coping behavior relevant to the maintenance of physical well-being and positive mental health:

1. *Role flexibility.* Due to historic necessity, African American families have displayed amazing flexibility in family member role definitions, responsibilities, and performances. Children commonly assist with the care and socialization of younger siblings; children and wives are expected to share economic responsibilities with the husband-father; sex-role expectations are less stereotypic, and alternative family arrangements or configurations are more prevalent than among families in the wider society. Such flexibility in individual roles is an obvious asset in dealing with and adjusting to the pressures or strains of modern living.

2. *Close-knit kinship systems.* African American families tend, as a rule, to be well integrated into larger kin-friend networks. Researchers have shown such relationships to represent invaluable ways of supplementing material, emotional, and social resources. Coping is enhanced because the family finds itself with a larger pool of resources upon which to draw.

3. *Culture-specific norms.* African American communities are char-

acterized in a majority of cases by bicultural norms. Individuals draw upon "mainstream" and "subcultural" values as the situation dictates for prescriptions of what constitutes appropriate behaviors. Coping benefits because alternative cultural values allow African Americans to "stretch" conventional norms to fit the imperatives of the situation (Ladner 1971; Nobles 1978).

4. *Parallel institutions.* Institutions in the black community that parallel those in the white community also contribute substantially to personal adjustment. Individuals denied access to organizations and institutions in the wider society often find satisfying alternatives in their black community-based counterparts (e.g., black businesses and fraternal orders, leadership roles in black institutions, etc.). In addition, certain African American institutions—most notably the church—have traditionally represented invaluable sources of individual support and comfort in the struggle for adjustment to the rigors of life.

5. *Race and personal identity/pride.* Identification with the race has also been shown to yield positive benefits for African Americans. A stronger sense of purpose, greater security in self, better management of frustration, and more strongly developed self-identities are a few of the commonly cited outgrowths of such racial pride and identification.

These identified coping assets have obvious relevance to public mental health. I suspect that future research will reveal many others. Certainly, attention should be paid to identifying the inherent strengths of African American families. Mental health delivery systems may then be organized to complement these already existing mental health maintenance functions (Allen and Stukes 1982). We propose that government mental health delivery systems be integrated with indigenous mental health maintenance networks in order to achieve maximal coverage of African American community mental health needs. For, as English (1983, 14) notes, "Theory suggests that when used in some combination or sequential pattern, the effectiveness of family, extended-kin resources, indigenous community-based care-givers and bureaucratic mental health services is maximized." A key issue in all of this involves the need to first secure adequate input from the intended target population. The *subjects* must be consulted about their mental health needs and traditional service avenues with an eye toward achieving an effective interface between indigenous mental health maintenance activities and government-sponsored mental health delivery systems.

While it is important to accentuate the strengths of African American families in the maintenance of positive mental health, we should not lose sight of reality. Large numbers of African American individuals and families find themselves in precarious and deteriorating positions. The increasingly severe economic situation in the United States finds African Americans losing many of the gains of the 1960s. In fact, the economic stability of sizeable numbers of black families is worse now, relative to white families—than at any other time during the past 25 years. Current census statistics on black/white occupational classifications and annual incomes attest to this fact. Because black families—like all families in post-industrial societies—rely heavily on societal institutions for the creation and maintenance of environments conducive to their positive development, we must recognize the limits of mere coping. A sincere commitment by the public and private sectors to the improvement of the African American community's economic status is a necessary condition for fostering physical well-being and positive mental health. African American individuals receive significant emotional support in the loving, caring environments of their families. What they, and those families, need most are additional structural supports from society in the form of jobs, effective schools, adequate incomes, quality housing, and equal opportunity. Until such structural supports are widely available, it will be difficult to maintain positive well-being and mental health in African American communities. For, as common sense tells us, emotional support—no matter how plentiful—cannot solve all personal difficulties in a society that values economics above all else.

CONCLUSION

Government policies have been shown to often work at cross purposes with the welfare of African American families. However, some value has come from this examination of national family policy and its consequences. We have found social policies directed at African American families to be characterized by many of the same deficiencies that exist in the area of family social policy generally. Among those deficiencies are numbered a host of historical traditions and practices in this country that, when taken as a whole, prevent the development of a well-articulated, national family policy. In addition, we have discovered African American family social policy to be characterized by a unique set of problems that have collectively hampered the creation and implementation of well-conceived, effective programs. These problems are attributable in large part to outmoded research traditions that continue to yield faulty interpretations of the character of African American family life in this country. Predictably, the social policies and programs based on such shaky conceptual and empirical foundations fall short of stated goals. Such social programs tend only to substitute one set of problems for another. In a manner analogous to social programs that shift drug addict dependencies from heroin to methadone, African American families have been shifted from one category of social problems to another by well-intentioned legislation. Unfortunately, rarely do resultant government policies or programs provide for a complete "kicking of the habit." How are we to move beyond temporary, ineffective, and contradictory responses in governmental social policies and programs?

Proposals to redirect government social policy with respect to African American families are best stated in terms to two areas of concern: academic/policy research and legislative processes. Of the two fronts, the former is perhaps a more appropriate concern here, given its influence over the latter. As noted before, policymakers rely on input from academic and policy research to guide their decision making. Academic research on African American families remains in dire need of substantial refinement in theory and methods. For it is only through such refinement that social and behavioral scientists will begin to generate a store of dependable knowledge about the nature of African American family life, which can then serve as a basis for informed decision making by policymakers. Policy-related research also needs to be drastically upgraded. Researchers interested in having an impact on governmental decision making must begin to design their research and write up results in such a way as to insure that study findings will come to the attention of the government policymaking machinery. In addition, social policy researchers must develop alternative methods for the evaluation of government legislation and program implementation in order to better assess how these affect African American families.

The goals outlined here for improvement of policy and academic research can only be accomplished by commitments on the parts of private and public agents to fund the training of specialists in this area of concern. Through a combination of postdoctoral training programs, establishment of family policy research programs, and the founding of family institutes, a larger pool of professionals who understand the complex links between government family policy and African American family life can be created. While this educational effort could very well occur in conjunction with other ongoing training projects aimed at developing strategies and techniques for family policy impact analysis, it would be wise to consider other alternatives. Foremost among these is the establishment and funding of predominantly African American controlled and staffed academic research centers. For, as numerous authors point out, many of the deficits observed in this research are directly attributable to the absence of an African American perspective (Billingsley 1993; Hill 1993).

On the matter of legislative processes, the most helpful action policymakers could undertake would be to begin a review of extant legislation, programs, and procedures to assess the intended and unintended consequences for African American families. Where those consequences are negative, these policymakers should be prepared to take corrective action against punitive regulations, legislation, and practices. Legislators have been shown to rely heaviest on general data in decision making, the very type of data most susceptible to distortion. Policymakers, therefore, must develop systematic procedures to allow input into the decision making process from scholars as well as from the affected families.

I must pause, for emphasis, on the point of family input into social policy decision making. All too often, these families' "voices" go unheeded. The process of controlling, redefining, and judging their lives moves forward relentlessly, without their input. They are treated as objects, disemboweled, disempowered, dismissed. The notion is that the "experts" know best. The fact is that they do not. African American families must be made full partners in the formulation and implementation of social policy that affects their existence.

If the higher goals sought by national family policy advocates are to be achieved, if government is ever to begin formulating sensible family policy, then we as a nation must become more self-conscious of social policies and programs in the area of family. It is particularly important that the nation re-examine the consequences of social policy based on the assumption of a white, middle-class, conjugal nuclear family model. For the overwhelming majority of American families do not fit this pattern (such as many African American, Hispanic, single-parent families or families in poverty). Our need as a nation for formalized, comprehensive family policy is dire. Resources are available to develop an encompassing national family policy, sensitive to the needs of all families; what we lack at this point is a commitment to this goal.

This country is currently at a crossroads, brought on by the insistent pressures of economic stagnation, spiraling inflation, shrinking resources, and an increasingly conservative political climate. The dilemas facing the country are such as to require detailed examination of our established way of life. The historic assumptions of unbridled material growth, infinite individual possibilities, and the absence of social limits—fundamental elements of our cultural ethos—have now run head-on into the realities of limits imposed by contemporary national and world circumstances. These circumstances require that we question the future viability of a system based in part in the belief that developed nations, a minority of the world's population, are entitled to control and consume the overwhelming majority of the world's resources. Challenges to the persistence of such inequities on the world scene will, undoubtedly, become both more frequent and strident as the voices of the Third World achieve a higher pitch, wider impact, and unified economic and political clout. We shall see more agitations for changes in the world order like the recent oil embargo, the North–South Conference in Mexico, the United Nations Conference on the International Control of Information Flow, and the conflicts between UNESCO and the United States. These examples represent, at root, challenges to the presumed rights of 10 percent of the world's population to control 90 percent of the world's natural, economic, political, and information resources.

The task confronting the United States as it enters the twenty-first century will be to develop new standards of the appropriate, to generate new values. Where will such redirection of values come from if not from the educated elite, those who teach the next generation and head its key institutions? For it must be recognized, in all fairness, that many of the justifications for the status quo are generated by the society's intelligentsia—its universities, major corporations, lawyers, doctors, and professors. The relevance of this point to the shifting world order derives from the critical role played by the United States in the maintenance of the current world order and the striking parallels between how African Americans (an exploited, internal "other") are treated, as compared with the treatment accorded exploited "others" on the world scene. The suggestion is, therefore, that until this society redirects its relationships with, and definitions of, African Americans—that is, until this society learns and institutes new values—it will be unable to redefine its posture towards a largely nonwhite Third World.

"Lord, I don't want you to move my mountain/Just give me the strength to climb."

(From a Negro Spiritual)

REFERENCES

Allen, Walter. 1978. Black family research in the United States: A review, assessment and extension. *Journal of Comparative Family Studies* 9 (Summer): 167–89.

Bernard, Jessie. *Marriage and family among Negroes*. Englewood Cliffs, NJ: Prentice-Hall.

Billingsley, Andrew. 1968. *Black families in white America*. Englewood Cliffs, NJ: Prentice-Hall.

———. 1970. Black families and white social science. *Journal of Social Issues* 23 (Summer): 127–42.

Chilman, C. S. 1973. Public social policy and families in the 1970's. *Social Casework* 54: 575–85.

English, Richard. 1983. *The challenge of mental health: Minorities and their world views*. Austin: School of Social Work, University of Texas.

Frazier, E. Franklin. [1939] 1964. *The Negro family in the United States*. Chicago: University of Chicago Press.

Gutman, Herbert. 1975. *The black family in slavery and freedom, 1750–1925*. New York: Pantheon.

Hill, Robert. 1971. *The strengths of black families*. New York: Emerson Hall.

Ladner, Joyce. 1971. *Tommorrow's tomorrow*. Garden City, NY: Doubleday.

Moynihan, Daniel P. 1965. *The Negro family: The case for national action*. Washington, DC: U.S. Department of Labor.

Rainwater, Lee. 1970. *Behind ghetto walls: Black families in a federal slum*. Chicago: Aldine.

Rodman, Hyman. 1971. *Lower class families*. New York: Oxford University Press.

Scanzoni, John. 1971. *The black family in modern society*. Boston: Allyn & Bacon.

Schorr, A. L. 1962. Family policy in the United States. *International Sociological Science Journal* 452–67.

Schultz, David. 1969. *Coming up black*. Englewood Cliffs, NJ: Prentice-Hall.

Stack, Carol. 1974. *All our kin*. New York: Harper & Row.

8 Child Care Policies and Young African American Children

VALORA WASHINGTON

C hild care in the United States has always been a "system" largely unregulated and unsupported by federal and state funds. Prior to 1990, the United States had no comprehensive child care policy. Yet, federal funding for day care services comes from a variety of sources, usually as a component of another program (Stephan 1985). By 1989, before most states implemented the Family Support Act (FSA), federal funding streams for child care assistance included the Social Services Block Grant, the Dependent Care Planning and Development Grant, funds under titles 11A and B on the Job Training Partnership Act, the Education for the Handicapped Act, and the Child Development Associate Scholarship Fund (National Governors' Association 1990).

In the past decade, federal legislation has been passed that attempts to provide child care and improve its quality. For example, the Family Support Act (FSA) in 1988, created a federal child care entitlement for poor families who participate in education, training, or work activities; the act also provides for one year of transitional child care for families leaving welfare. In 1990, the U.S. Congress passed historic legislation that included a freestanding federal child care program, which enabled the states to address child care affordability, availability, and quality. Child advocates hoped that these governmental initiatives would help the United States move toward more universal, free care, as is the case for almost all European countries (Kammerman 1989).

CHILDREN IN POVERTY

Unlike most European countries, child care policies in the United States have generally focused on the poor. Indeed, the enormous numbers of young children under age six in poverty (approximately five million) has fueled the momentum for welfare reform, of which child care is a major component (Reischauer 1989).

Childhood poverty is devastating for all children, but on the whole, its effects differ within various communities in our country. In 1987, the poor included 48 percent of young African American children, 42 percent of young Hispanic children, 29 percent of young children from other minority groups, and 13 percent of white children. The poverty rate for black children rose from 41 to 48 percent between 1975 and 1987; in contrast, the poverty rate for white children under age six declined from 14 to 13 percent (National Center for Children in Poverty [NCCP]).

Our national child care policies are closely tied to welfare reform. This fact is of concern for several reasons:

Large numbers of poor children do not receive public assistance. Of the 20 percent of all children who were poor in 1985, only slightly over half were receiving Aid to Families with Dependent Children (AFDC) benefits (U.S. House of Representatives 1985). Only 24 percent of young children in married-couple poor families received AFDC benefits (NCCP 1990). Consequently, child care initiatives tied to welfare reform may not benefit these families. In 1987, only 28 percent of poor children under age six lived in families that relied solely on income from public assistance. Some 37 percent lived in families who relied solely on earnings from employment (NCCP 1990).

Many poor children do not remain on welfare throughout their childhoods. It is important to recognize the tremendous variability in poor populations (Furstenberg, Brooks-Gunn, and Morgan 1987). Children born outside of marriage who grow up with single mothers are likely to be poor for most or all of their childhoods (NCCP 1990). Yet research by Bane and Ellwood (1983) showed that 50 percent of those on AFDC use the system for short-term assistance in times of crises, usually brought on by divorce or unemployment. An additional 25 percent of individuals remain on AFDC for two to seven years. The remaining 25 percent stay on welfare for over 10 years, and it is this subgroup that accounts for 60 percent of the costs of the system. Most important, this subgroup has been identified as having an overrepresentation of young unmarried women with children under three years of age.

Children who move "on" and "off" welfare—but who depend on federal and state initiatives for child care—may experience unstable or discontinuous child care arrangements.

Policies that focus on economic deprivation, to the exclusion of race and racism, can obscure the special needs of minority-group children. African American children and families, perhaps more than any other group, are particularly affected by public policy. From conception to adolescence, black children face harsh challenges to their growth and survival because of race and regardless of social class (McAdoo and McAdoo 1985; Children's Defense Fund 1985; and Washington and LaPoint 1988). Chief among the problems is persistent poverty (Slaughter 1988).

Maxwell (1985), suggests that black children born in poverty stay in poverty for an average of ten years. Thus, it is apparent that new child care initiatives will affect black children and families disproportionally, based on their overrepresentation in the welfare system.

Yet, oblivious to racial issues, a poverty-centered approach to public policy development fails to consider that African Americans have a peculiar history in the United States that might provide insight into the causes, consequences, and cures of their impoverishment (Washington 1984). This ahistorical perspective also ignores the demographic character of the children most likely to be served under the policy (for example, see Children's Defense Fund 1985).

Race must be recognized as an important variable. For example, in general, children under age six living with single mothers are much more likely to be poor. Proportionally, many more poor black children than poor white children under age six live in mother-only families. Yet, minority children under age six are more likely to be poor than are white children, whether they live with one or two parents (NCCP 1990). In the context of these racial differences, public policies that focus solely on poverty may be inadequate.

CHILD CARE POLICIES AND AFRICAN AMERICAN FAMILIES

It is clearly evident that the debate about child care initiatives will have important implications for black families precisely *because* black children and families have been overrepresented in public programs. Therefore, our nation's "desire" to "help" runs head on against the racial sensitivities that have characterized our national life (Washington 1984, 1988). In fact, the real needs and interests of black children are often ignored or obscured because of policy dilemmas.

Some policy decisions are based on faulty logic: (a) If government assistance follows family "failure," and (b) if large numbers of families and children from a particular cultural background seem to need such assistance, then (c) something must be "wrong" with these families—with their culture, with their language, with their lifestyle, or other attributes, and (d) therefore, to help them, they first need to learn how to achieve the norm of family self-sufficiency—to emulate is the accepted tradition.

Most child care efforts have, in the course of their development, "acknowledged" family and cultural deviance. Although child development specialists today are more likely to acknowledge the strengths of diversity, questions remain: How can we respect "their" culture and "their" lifestyles, when these cultures and lifestyles appear to be associated with "the problem"? If we acknowledge societal barriers for these families (and, indeed, for *all* families), would we encourage dependency? If the government helps too much, would we promote instability in the social order? How much help, and what types of help, are "too much"? How do child care initiatives fit into this debate?

The answers to these questions can have different effects by race in a child care "system" targeted to the poor rather than to all children. This dilemma was vividly illustrated in the late 1960s, when welfare families got different amounts of money depending on whether they were black or white. AFDC benefits have also been cut off for children when their mother had more than a certain number of "illegitimate" children (Washington 1985).

CONCLUSION

Because current child care initiatives are occurring in the context of welfare reform, the proportion of African American preschool children who live in poverty is of direct concern. The focus of new legislation and its implementation strategies may make it possible for the parents to achieve economic self-sufficiency while sacrificing the quality of direct services to children in a developmental context—services African American children need.

For example, despite recent legislation, many child advocates believe that state governments are not living up to their commitments to meet the child care needs of poor families. For example, a Children's Defense Fund (1992) survey of the fifty states' child care policies under FSA documents that parental choice is stymied by inadequate health and safety protections for FSA child care and unrealistically low payments for care.

We must acknowledge the weak and deteriorating nature of our nation's child care "system." Cadden (1993) estimates that at least 40 percent of all care, 75 percent of family child care, in our nation is entirely unregulated and does not need to meet even minimal standards of health and safety; and she notes that there is no state that serves all of its children who are eligible for child care assistance. In 1988, the National Child Care Staffing Study (Whitebrook, Howes, and Phillips 1989) revealed that the average wage of teaching staff in child care centers dropped 25 percent in real earnings for this work force since the mid 1970s; not surprisingly, the typical child care center in this study lost over 40 percent of its teaching staff in the prior year. These facts are crucial because, as the study notes, the most important predictor of child care quality, among adult work environmental variables, is staff wages.

It is clear that high quality child care is less accessible to low-income working parents than to others (NCCP 1990). As African American children are overrepresented among the poor, it follows that they are similarly overrepresented in poor child care arrangements. Yet, high-quality care for these children is particularly important to their well-being and healthy development. The welfare-dependency cycle is strengthened because the lack of access to affordable child care is also a major obstacle to labor force participation by poor and welfare-dependent mothers: Lack of affordable child care is a *cause* of welfare dependency and child poverty (Polit and O'Hara 1990). Further, child care that does not have a strong early childhood education component is not enough to prepare most poor and minority children for school, yet poor children are less likely to participate in pre-kindergarten education programs than are nonpoor children (NCCP 1990). Clearly, current policies and programs do not adequately reflect what we already know about how to improve the quality of life for poor African American children.

We agree with the National Center for Children in Poverty (1990) that efforts to expand child care subsidies and to develop the quality and availability of child care resources at the community level are critical both for reducing poverty and for promoting child development. In this regard, we are pleased that President Clinton has promised expansion and "full funding" of Project Head Start. Communities, businesses, states, and the federal government must all work together to improve the availability, affordability, and quality of child care services for African American children.

Yet, despite our enthusiasm, we must bear in mind the lingering, unresolved, yet critical issues that must be clarified as the "mold" on which new or proposed policies are being set. Specifically, we must decide as a nation whether it is possible to offer a universal system of child care. The resolution of this issue, while beneficial for African American children, has broad implications. For example, it has been clearly demonstrated that changes in services for special-needs children have traditionally served as a legislative wedge for the eventual provision of services to *all* children (Gallagher 1989).

Further, research on African Americans has served an important role in advancing both policy and knowledge for all children (Gallagher 1989). Another example is in the provision of preschool services—an idea that was initiated to benefit the poor. All of America's children and families are the ultimate winners of the incremental process to expand the boundaries of public child care policy.

REFERENCES

Bane, M. J., and D. T. Ellwood. 1983. *The dynamics of dependence: The routes to self-sufficiency.* Cambridge, MA: Urban Systems Research.

Cadden, Vivian. 1993. The 10 best states for child care. *Working Mother* (February): 51–58.

Children's Defense Fund. 1985. *Black and white children in America: Key facts.* Washington, DC.

Children's Defense Fund. 1992. *Child care under the Family Support Act: Early lessons from the state.* Washington, DC.

Furstenberg, F. F., Jr., J. Brooks-Gunn, and S. P. Morgan. 1987. *Adolescent mothers in later life.* New York: Cambridge University Press.

Gallagher, James, J. 1989. The impact of policies for handicapped children on future early education policy. *Phi Delta Kappan* (October): 121–124.

Kammerman, S. B. 1989. An international overview of preschool programs. *Phi Delta Kappan* (October): 135–37.

Maxwell, Joan Paddock. 1985. *No easy answers: Persistent poverty in the metropolitan Washington area.* Washington, DC: Greater Washington Research Center, December.

McAdoo, Harriette Pipes, and John L. McAdoo eds. 1985. *Black children: Social, educational, and parental environments.* Beverly Hills, CA: Sage.

National Center for Children in Poverty. 1990. *Five million children: A statistical profile of our poorest young citizens.* New York.

National Governors' Association 1990. *Taking care: State developments in child care.* Washington, DC.

Polit, D. and J. O'Hara. 1990. Support services. In *Welfare Policy for the 1990s,* ed. P. Cottingham and D. T. Ellwood. Cambridge, MA: Harvard University Press.

Reischauer, R. D. 1989. The welfare reform legislation: Directions for the future. In *Welfare policy for the 1990s,* ed. P. H. Cottingham & D. T. Ellwood. Cambridge, MA: Harvard University Press.

Slaughter, Diana, ed. 1988. *Black children and poverty: A developmental perspective.* San Francisco: Jossey-Bass.

Stephan, Sharon. 1985. *The federal role in child day care*. Congressional Research Service. The Library of Congress, Washington, DC.

U. S. House of Representatives. 1987. *U.S. children and their families: Current conditions and recent trends, 1987*. Washington, DC: U.S. Government Printing Office.

Washington, Valora. 1984. Social and personal ecology surrounding public policy for young children: An American dilemma. In *Ecological perspectives on the development of the young child,* ed. D. Gullo and D. Caven. Springfield, IL: Charles Thomas.

Washington, Valora. 1985. Social policy, cultural diversity, and the obscurity of black children. *Journal of Educational Equity and Leadership* 5(4): 320–35.

Washington, Valora. 1988. *Black children and American institutions: An ecological review and resource guide*. New York: Garland.

Washington, Valora, and Velma LaPoint. 1988. Historical and contemporary linkages between black child development and social policy. In *Black children and poverty: A developmental perspective*. San Francisco: Jossey-Bass.

Whitebook, M., C. Howes, and D. Phillips. 1989. *Who cares? Child care teachers and the quality of care in America*. Final report of the National Child Care Staffing Study. Oakland, CA: Child Care Employee Project.

The Role of Organized Religion

C

9 | *Overview and Recommendations*

CLARENCE G. NEWSOME

Since its emergence during the latter part of the eighteenth century, the institutional black church has been at the forefront of the African American community's struggle for sociopolitical and economic well-being. In fact, the black church was born of the need in the African American community to organize for successful living in what has historically been a hostile social environment, one in which people of African descent have largely been denied equal rights and the privileges of full citizenship for reasons related to race.

During the first half of the nineteenth century, the black church was at the vanguard in protesting the evil of chattel slavery and working for its demise. The Abolitionist movement would hardly have been successful apart from the unequivocal involvement of the black church, which offered not only sustained moral and financial support, but visionary leadership as well. The black church never wavered in its opposition to slavery; its financial contribution to the cause of manumission was limited, but consistently beyond its means; and its leadership, through such people as Henry Highland Garnet and Harriet Tubman, was without equal in aggressively linking the freedom of African Americans to the freedom of all Americans.

Following emancipation, the black church became the primary means for promoting literacy among the black masses. It was also central to the effort in the black community to gain the franchise and to get African Americans elected to public office, particularly in such states as Louisiana, Mississippi, and North and South Carolina.

The same case can be made in behalf of the groundwork it helped to lay for economic development. While the educational, political, and economic needs of African Americans always exceeded the achievements, the role the black church played was nonetheless marked and distinctive during both the Reconstruction and post-Reconstruction eras.

Historians are more critical of the role the black church played in pushing for laws to outlaw lynching and segregation during the first five decades of the twentieth century. Even so, there is general agreement that it was never far from the battlefront, having spawned a number of organizations and having nurtured much of the leadership that pressed the issue of social justice in Congress and in the nation's courts. By the mid-1960s, the black church was clearly front-line and center in the Civil Rights movement. Since then it has reassumed a rather prominent role in the struggle for full inclusion and participation in the mainstream of American life. Reminiscent of its posture during the nineteenth century, through its many denominations and local congregations it has moved increasingly in the direction of mobilizing its spiritual and material resources to ameliorate, albeit with uneven success, the myriad problems besetting African Americans.

With the twenty-first century at hand, questions abound as to the ways in which the black church (as well as other forms of organized religion, such as the Nation of Islam) can make a critical difference in the welfare and well-being of the race. What can organized religion do to ensure a brighter future for today's youth? What role should it play in the political arena? What will be the best contribution of an Islamic ministry to black self-determination? Does the history of the black church portend some viable economic strategies? Beyond economic empowerment, how can the black church fully capitalize on the talents, energy, and commitment of its considerable female membership? What can it do to involve larger numbers of males in its work? In sum, what should be the essence of the black church's contribution to the race and to the nation during the twenty-first century?

In an attempt to address these and other questions, the presentations made during the religion symposium covered a range of specific issues and concerns. In "Role of Religious Institutions: A Social Psychological Model," Diane R. Brown focused on the religiousness of African Americans under thirty years old by gender, age level, and formal educational attainment. Regardless of age level or educational attainment, the religiousness of females, she argued, tends to be higher than males. This is to say that females tend to measure higher in their conscious and open expression of religious beliefs, moral posture, and participation in organized religion, e.g., the church. In one category, the frequency of prayers, "young" black males tend to measure appreciably higher than their counterparts. Yet, in most all other categories females exceed males, especially when it comes to church involvement. In part, what this suggests is the need to give more attention to the socialization of young black males into organized religion so that greater numbers of them can be cultivated as future leaders.

In "Ministry to Youth: Spreading the Good News in Troubled Times," Barbara J. Musgrove called attention to the need for the black church to become even more committed to the nurturing of African American youth. She contended that, over the past decade or so, the development of African American females and males has been adversely affected the by "three problem areas confronting all young people: . . . decreased emphasis (publicly) placed on the importance of childhood, the youth-at-risk syndrome, and the failures of the child welfare system." As she convincingly stated, "The fact that childhood is hurried for most children today means that . . . young people are denied a period of innocence, exploration, and leisure," which in turn leaves little opportunity for moral and intellectual growth. Complicating this pernicious pattern are other factors placing African American youth at high risk: the increase in single parent families; the drug epidemic; and the AIDS crisis. Moreover, "budget cuts and changes in eligibility requirements have made it increasingly difficult for minority families to receive public welfare services for their children." Against this bleak backdrop, African American religious institutions are challenged to systematically develop programs that are designed to meet the needs of youth. Such programs should be spiritually centered, inclusive, and based on sound data. They should largely be concerned with parent education, child adoption, and political action.

With political action clearly in view, Peter J. Paris presented "The Prophetic and Political Quest for Liberalism and Justice." Within the context of discussing the significance of voluntary organizations in democratic societies for promoting social change, Paris underscored a longstanding theme but had a slightly different twist. In his view, the black church can make a marked contribution to the well-being of the race during the coming century if, in light of its past involvement in the political sphere, it makes a decided "shift from the para-political activity of protest to that of political organization per se." More than support voter registration drives and voter education projects, more than raising funds for political campaigns and endorsing candidates for public office, the black church must position itself to become the spearhead of all political activity in the African American community. In a way that harkens back to the antebellum black church, Paris boldly asserted that "It must now become the loci for intensive political activity by deploying its institutional resources to the task of electing church leaders to public office." Provocatively, if not controversially, he argued that "black churches alone comprise the leadership potential" needed today for the "consolidation of the civil rights gains in more substantive public policy."

Paris stopped short of suggesting that the black church be transformed into a de facto political party. In fact, he emphasized that it should only become more organized politically as an extension of its theological and moral posture. From his vantage point, a political rationale should be predicated upon theological and moral justification. Theologically speaking, "The gospel of liberation and justice, long proclaimed by the black churches, implies institutionalization lest it be cast aside as an abstract, formal platitude devoid of historical appearance." It implies that they organize to elect black church leaders, lay and clergy, female and male, to "seats of power in order to contribute to the task of constructing a good and just society . . . ."

Along moral lines, the black church has an obligation consistent with "the purpose of the good state," namely "that of enabling the good of all its citizens, i.e., the promotion of justice for all." In as much as "the purpose of good politics is ethical in nature," African American churches and church leadership on the order of that provided by Martin Luther King, Jr., are challenged "to help citizens to internalize the purpose of the state by becoming just persons themselves." The black church is challenged to help members and non-members alike to achieve the purpose of the state by recognizing that "power (to paraphrase King) at its best is love implementing the demands of justice, and that justice at its best is power correcting everything that stands against love."

Power as love and justice inextricably links theological and moral rationale to political justification. Rooted in local organizational structures, African American churches by definition are vested with power by constituencies which do so in the interest of their total well-being, temporal and nontemporal. For this reason, Paris stressed, these churches "must maintain the trust of their people and be sensitive to their needs and willing to be public advocates for their relief." This requires deliberate political organization.

In contrast to Paris's position, Abdul Alim Muhammad, speaking to the theme, "Towards an Islamic Ministry Appropriate for the 21st Century," posited that advances along political and economic lines in the years ahead will largely be due to the growing influence of Islam in the West and especially in the African American community. From its position as an emerging religious tradition outside the American mainstream, it can play a pivotal role in leading the African American community and the nation in resolving "the ethical and moral dilemmas inherent in the American system." Its "outsider" status affords it an angle of vision on American society that makes possible a rigorous critique of injustice and hypocrisy regardless of their source. Such critique will enable the African American masses to become militant and more organized in the interest of becoming more self-sufficient by winning in the years ahead territorial concessions and reparations due the race for decades of denial.

It is the opinion of many that the black church, still the locus of the majority of African Americans involved with organized religion, is not better appreciated as a fulcrum for future social change and betterment because its history remains largely unknown, even to its membership. For this reason, Lawrence N. Jones's paper, titled, "The African American Churches: In History and Context," is the first chapter in this section. Set against the relief of a society in constant change since its beginning, Jones depicts the African American church as a major institution shaping the character of American society throughout the centuries. Inasmuch as it is not responsible for causing the plethora of problems confronting the African American community, he argues, it cannot be expected to be the means for resolving them all. Its resources have never been, and probably will never be, that vast. Nonetheless, African American churches can positively impact American society in the coming century provided they can develop more strategies and muster the will to aggregate their funds akin to the approaches taken by the Concord Baptist Church of Christ in Brooklyn, New York; the Second Episcopal District of the African Methodist Episcopal Church, Washington, D.C.; and the Congress of National Black Churches, headquartered in Washington.

For scholars such as Cheryl Townsend Gilkes, author of the second chapter, "Ministry of Women: Hearing and Empowering 'Poor' Black Women," the greatest resource the black church has enjoyed over the years has been the commitment of black women to its manifold mission. Ironically, they have never been really free themselves to promote the mission of the African American church, to the detriment of both the race and the nation. The constraints placed upon African American women, even within the ranks of their own race and religious institution, has contributed to an impoverishment of both churches and women. The failure of the churches to free up as inexhaustible a resource as that represented by the talents, abilities, and energy of their female members is the same as not having it available at all. Solutions to many current and future problems, Gilkes contends, will be forthcoming provided that the African American church affords women increased opportunities for economic, political, cultural, and ecclesiastical empowerment.

Perhaps it can be said that from Robert M. Franklin's standpoint, the black church is impoverished not only for the reason that it has denied women equal access to opportunity, but also because it has done little to reclaim the "souls" of countless African American men. In "Reclaiming the Souls of Black Men Folk: The Mission of African American Religious Institutions," the third chapter, Franklin argues that "the crisis that faces black men is fundamentally spiritual." This key factor is something the black church has failed to grasp. By comparison, the ability of the Black Muslims to address programmatically the spiritual needs of African American men is a major reason why these men are attracted to the Nation of Islam. Defining spirituality as a holistic reality, an integration of the various dimensions of human existence to a level that transcends the limitations of any particular dimension, Franklin identifies some of the reasons that the black church has failed to appeal to large numbers of men, including the dysfunctionality of much of Christian teaching in street culture, the effeminate ambience of much church life, and the absence of a strong prophetic voice. But despite their poor track record in recent years, Franklin concludes that black churches can substantially aid the cause of racial uplift by helping African American men to overcome, among other things, "rabid individualism" and poor self-esteem. Doing so would enable the church to "facilitate intrafamilial reconciliation" while teaching interpersonal and marketable work skills, all of which speak to the welfare of the African American man's soul.

The fourth and final chapter in this section, my own "The Black Church as Resource for the Twenty-First Century," in many respects encompasses the major themes of the three papers with which it is conjoined, and is thereby an appropriate conclusion. In this chapter, I identify the way in which the black church may indeed be recognized as a single reality, and on this basis make a case for its value as a resource for the twenty-first century. The black church is a metaphor for a shared religious worldview in which belief in the God of Christianity gives rise to an unequivocal commitment to racial equality and the principles of democracy by way of a tripartite emphasis on prophetic social consciousness, morality, and spiritual empowerment. I argue that the African American church will be able to help ameliorate a number of the problems confronting the race, provided that it refrains against all the countervailing forces of a postmodern world, from abandoning its historic threefold stance. I argue that such a posture holds promise precisely because of its pragmatic potential. For example, by means of sincerely and conscientiously promoting spiritual empowerment, consistent with the way in which it is espoused in black church circles, African American clergy can empower greater numbers of laypeople to assume positions of leadership in the church, which in turn can lead to better short-term and long-term planning, more efficient use of human and material resources, and more effective programming to address social crises. Stronger and more strategic networks transcending gender, age, and class will emerge within and between local congregations and denominations as an army of believers mobilize not only with the hope but with the confidence that working together is a valid alternative for any race struggling to do more than survive—rather, to thrive—in the new world order ahead.

In a recently published landmark study on the black church, entitled *The Black Church in the African American Experience,* C. Eric Lincoln and Lawrence H. Mamiya offer these words under the heading, "A Concluding Unscientific Postscript: Policy Recommendations for the Black Church":

> Black churches are not perfect institutions, but with all their limitations they represent the institutionalized staying power of a human community that has been under siege for close to four hundred years. Black personalities, movements, and ideologies have waxed and waned over the years, and will continue to do so, but black churches have remained a firm anchor stabilizing the black experience and giving it meaning through the uncertain eras of change and counterchange.

It was in the certainty that the black church will forever remain an anchor, and that organized religion will in one form or another forever remain a force in the life of the black community, that the participants in the religion symposium engaged some of the most important and pressing issues of our time with an eye toward the future. Following are some of the policy recommendations that emerged from their presentations and the ensuing discussions:

- Make a more concerted effort to socialize black youth, particularly black males, into the life of the church.
- Develop more God-centered, inclusive, data-based programs in the areas of parent education, child adoption, and political action.
- Transform the church into a political organization with an emphasis on electing church leadership to public office.
- Agitate for territorial concessions and reparations.
- Aggregate funds in the interest of gaining leverage to influence the shaping of public policy.
- Empower black women economically, politically, culturally, and ecclesiastically.
- Enable black men to overcome the disabling effects of rabid individualism, develop positive self-images and personal responsibility, facilitate intrafamilial reconciliation while teaching interpersonal skills, and teach marketable work skills.

- Empower laypeople to assume and create positions of leadership in the interest of developing more effective networks within and between local congregations and denominations to address the many problems confronting the black community.
- Produce a greater number of formally trained clergy to provide higher-quality leadership.

10 | The African American Churches: In History and Context

LAWRENCE N. JONES

Historians have come to see that it is impossible to write about the religious history of a people if it is refracted exclusively through their religious institutions. This being so, the understanding of the African American churches as institutions will be insufficiently grounded unless one attends to their founding, their history, the religious faith that caused them to be founded and sustained, and the social, political, economic, educational, and cultural context of the people involved in this process.

Identifiable African American churches have existed from the time of the American Revolution. It is impossible to know precisely how many African American churches are in existence at the present time. An educated estimate is that there are at least 65,000 identifiable congregations whose membership rolls contain/record approximately 23,700,000 names.[1] By some estimates, about seven billion dollars pass through the treasuries of these churches annually, and they are unquestionably the largest real estate owners in African American communities. Churches are virtually the only institutions in these communities that their populations own, control, program, manage, govern, and sustain. Because of their aggregate wealth in real estate and in funds, many individuals believe that African American churches can be of decisive importance in the effort to correct the perilous plight of that one-third of the nation that is African American.

THE AFRICAN CONTEXT

Though Africans may have visited the north American continent before 1619, the 20 "negars" who landed at Jamestown in that year were the first trickling of a mighty company that by 1865, at the end of the Civil War, would number approximately 4,500,000 persons. Slaves were imported from many regions of Africa, from many tribes. They spoke a variety of languages and were drawn from a variety of cultures. Despite the diversity, it is possible to speak of certain cultural patterns with family resemblances, worldviews, religious frameworks, and sense of identity as decisively different from that of their enslavers and masters. Africans tended to see existence holistically and did not separate the sacred and the secular, the living and the dead, the spirit(s) and the material in the way that many Europeans did.[2] The world was filled with spirits, all related to a supreme spirit. Spirits were good and evil and could be placated or assuaged by employing the proper ritual or intermediaries. Ancestors, though long dead, played a vital role in protecting or delivering one from the powers of evil spirits. In addition, the priest exercised a powerful role in the divination of spirits and in the exorcism of their curses or plagues. Depending upon the particular tribe, the chiefs and/or priests were the tribe's surrogates in the human community of the spirits. They were endowed with enormous power and were its mediators to the rest of the community.[3] Thus, human governance and divine sovereignty were unified in a single person. The African cosmology was holistic and inclusive.

Indigenous African religion was the cultural expression of the people developed through the long centuries of their history. While its rituals and forms varied from place to place, its cosmologies were informed by many shared assumptions. The slaves who came to America had been exposed only superficially to Christianity.[4] No missionaries accompanied the slave catchers, but as the trading settlements grew, some slaves were exposed to the religion of their captors. Though the slaves were not religious as Europeans understood the term, they were profoundly spiritual in everything they thought, every activity in which they engaged, and every aspect of their living and dying.

The Africans who were brought to America were not Christian.[5] There exist slave narratives in which the narrator identifies him or herself as believing in Allah. This is not surprising; there has been regular commercial intercourse between the Arab/Muslim North Africa and sub-Saharan black Africa from the time of Mohammed. Certainly by 1100 A.D. the conquest, Arabization, and Muslim prosyletization were well begun among the people along the principal trans-Sahara trade routes.

For Africans being introduced to slavery, the most traumatic initial experience was that of being deprived of their cultural identity. That identity, dependent upon the community to which one belonged, was the first casualty after capture in the life of the slave. Concurrently, they were introduced into a culture whose cosmology and worldview were radically different from their own. This loss of identity, the loss of one's genealogy, status, and name, coupled with the equally sudden loss of communication through language, was a psychological blow of enormous proportions. In place of an identity conferred within a cosmic context, slaves now had to find their identity principally in relationship to their owners. To be a slave was to be robbed of one's ancestors and deprived of their protection and intercessory powers in the spirit world. Slaves were deprived of significant others, who were conduits of the powers of the spirits and who exercised authority granted over them. In this sense, slaves had no recognized ancestry and therefore had no status in the community of which they became enforced and alien members. At the same time, the moral and ethical guidelines by which they had ordered their lives were rendered null and void. In the slave order, the boundaries of life were imposed by the slave master, not defined, as in their homeland, by the family or tribal grouping into which they had been born. In the African context, life's problems, dilemmas, sufferings, and hopes could be explored and dealt with via the mediation of persons who were in touch with the spirit world. Such was not the case in slavery, where the master was the supreme authority—an authority rooted in the right of ownership and confirmed by the larger society.

In sub-Saharan Africa, an individual's moral prerogatives were defined and enforced by the tribe and existed always in relationship to the well-being of all of its members. There was no "rugged individualism" in the sense of individual rights as Europeans had defined them in documents such as the *Magna Carta*, the *Bill of Rights*, the *Declaration of Independence*, and the *Constitution of the United States*.[6]

It would be erroneous to conclude that slaves suffered irreversible emotional and psychological trauma as a result of their displacement, or that they lost their consciousness of that cosmology with its moral, norms, values, social organization, and spirits. Though the community that supported and mediated that worldview was no longer accessible, slaves remembered, and that memory has lived in varying degrees in their ancestors to the present times. Scholars who have debated the degree to which Africanisms survived in the new world frequently have concentrated on the rituals and forms of African culture but have given insufficient attention to the worldview, the myths, and the beliefs that do not depend upon a specific culture as such for their survival and influence. It is not the purpose of this chapter to enter into this debate; it suffices to say that a careful reading of the ways in which African Americans carry out their private devotions and participate in formal worship will reveal that the memory of Africa broods over and is visible in both of these areas of activity.

AFRICANS IN AMERICA 1619–1860

The settlers who came to America and were Christians (and most who were not) brought with them European ideals and customs. Among the protocols in the communities from which they came was the ecclesiastical and royal demand that Christians should evangelize, civilize, and prosyletize among the "heathens," that is, among all those who did not acknowledge that Jesus Christ was the Son of God and savior of souls. It was also commonly accepted that one could not keep a Christian in bondage.

After it was determined that Africans should be *slaves in durante vitae* by both the colonial governments and the Church of England, Christians faced a critical problem in that the religious duty to convert the Africans placed their wealth in chattel property in jeopardy. This problem was "solved" for most believing slaveholders in 1727 when the Bishop of London decreed that the conversion of slaves would not change their civil status as slaves in any way.[7] New England had the largest of European settlers who came consciously seeking to escape religious persecution. New England was also the area in which slavery was the least economically viable. Most of the slaves in the region were employed in small industries, in farming, and as house servants. Those who were in bondage in Christian households were exposed to whatever family worship prevailed, and some of them were taken to church along with other members of the household. Typically, they were seated in galleries, crow's nests, or on special pews that frequently were painted black. Careful effort was made to provide "religious instruction" for some slaves, but not necessarily to convert them to Christianity. This spurious piety was designed to ensure that slaves could not qualify to participate in the political process in the New England towns and in the false expectation that religious instruction would make them more accepting of their servitude. Statistically, most slaves in New England were ignorant of the Christian faith when the nineteenth century dawned.[8]

In the North, the exposure of Africans to the Christian faith was more "miss than hit," especially prior to 1800. The emergence of self-conscious religious structures did not begin in earnest in this region until the Peace of Paris had been agreed to and all revolutionary activity involved in the severance of political ties with England had been completed. Even so, a number of congregations trace their origins to the period of the American Revolution.[9]

In the heavily populated agricultural regions and cities of the south, the exposure of slaves to Christianity was largely dependant upon the attitudes of the masters and mistresses. Periodically, plantations were visited by itinerant preachers or aggressive local preachers, some of whom were Africans, who sought to provide religious instruction for the slaves or to bring them the "true" gospel. The dominant religion being shared in this region, as in all of America, was "evangelical" Christianity, that is, a belief in the atoning death of Jesus, the certainty of judgment, a view of God as supreme judge, and confidence in the literal truth of the Bible as the "Word of God." Many Christian slaves and freedpersons were suspicious and critical of "white religion." This had the effect of causing a sizable number of them to turn deaf ears to the preaching and to seek their own, sometimes clandestine, meetings in which to worship God. This is the origin of the "invisible institution."[10]

Several northern black Baptist, Presbyterian, and Methodist congregations originated during the Revolutionary period. They were located mainly in urban centers, where freedpersons and escaped slaves lived in relative security, or in the border states and territories of the near west. Baptist policy permitted the organization of churches wherever the will existed among the people and wherever persons were available to assume positions of pastoral or lay leadership. In sheer numerical terms, prior to the Civil War, there were more black Baptists than members of any other denomination in the United States and its territories. Insofar as corporate denominations were concerned, the African Methodist Episcopal (A.M.E.) Church was unquestionably the most influential. Under the leadership of its indomitable Daniel Payne, this church established Wilberforce University (Ohio) in 1863, the first institution of higher education supported and administered by African Americans.

As the population of freedpersons and escaped slaves grew in the urban North (though they invariably lived in isolated portions of Northern urban centers), and as they were free to dispose of their labor and time, they soon began to associate in a variety of social groupings. For the first time, they were free to meet and speak together without being scrutinized by their employers or masters, as in the South. Among the first of these social organizations were the benevolent societies, which undertook to ensure the decent burial of their members, the provision of sick benefits, the welfare of widows and orphans, and the education of the young. These organizations were the roots from which several churches grew.[11]

The organization of local congregations began shortly after the end of the American Revolution. It is important to remember that the Revolution resulted in not only the severing of political ties with Europe, but also the uncoupling of religious linkages. For all churches with episcopal or synodical structures of governance, except the Catholic Church, the end of the war resulted in the establishment of American denominations.

Africans, like Europeans, organized separate congregations for different reasons. An examination of the character and personalities of the founders of different congregations makes it clear that they would have been frustrated by being prohibited from exercising their gifts for leadership in the churches of which they were members. Moreover, these men and women were vitally concerned about the general welfare and moral tone in the African community, and they could observe that these matters were of only passing interest to the existing religious establishment. Thus, these pioneering individuals organized congregations that were not only communities of faith but also self-help societies. These founders of congregations were true believers in every sense and were distressed that the redemptive power of the gospel was being short-circuited by the racial attitudes and practices of white Christians. Hence, they undertook to provide spaces in which the "true gospel" could be proclaimed.[12]

These African church organizers had no institutional models to follow save those of the churches of which they were attendees or members. This was not a major difficulty for Baptist gatherings, for historically, full discretionary power in all temporal and spiritual matters was vested in the local congregation. Believers who belonged to the Methodist church, with its episcopal and connectional polity, faced a different problem. Initially, Methodist Africans did not intend to become absolutely separate; they wished to establish separate congregations within the larger church. The African Methodist Episcopal Church, Bethel, established in 1794, remained a member of the Philadelphia Methodist Society until 1816. The African Methodist Episcopal Church, Zion, established in 1796, remained a member of the New York Methodist Society until 1821. When these two African Methodist bodies severed all ecclesiastical and legal ties with the Methodist Church, they adopted the hymnbooks, the discipline, the church order, and the order of service of that body. This is also true of the congregation that became the mother church of the African Methodist Union Protestant Church in Wilmington, Delaware. The critical difference between the African and the white churches lay in the distinctive religious experience of the Africans, in the more passionate, participatory, and free style of worship, and in a particular understanding of the gospel that related it to all of their life situations.

When the Civil War began, the African American churches could be encouraged by their promising achievements. They had survived tenuous beginnings and experienced numerical growth that was sometimes poorly administered but nevertheless reassuring. Schools had been established for adults and juveniles, and sabbath schools served the dual function of teaching reading and writing with the Bible as a textbook. The churches had erected or adapted new structures for their congregations. They had evangelized slaves and freedpersons alike. They had also established and were sustaining fraternal relations with white church bodies and with a variety of nominally intraracial ecumenical groups. In this early period, as in the present, churches were the most substantial institutions and the largest owners of real estate in African American communities.

Though these bodies of slaves and freedpersons existed under several denominational labels, the influence of African Christians was exerted primarily by individuals rather than by organized groups. Reliable estimates are that fully one-half of the African American leadership in pre-Civil War days were clergy persons. Without question, the paramount sociopolitical issue for all, slaves and free alike, was how an end could be brought to the slave system and how the injustices visited upon African Americans could be redressed. In the North, the question of access to the rights inherent in United States citizenship claimed particular attention, including the right of access to the ballot box, to public education, to equal justice before the law, and to service in places of public accommodation and transportation. The issue of the right to work was also of concern.

Despite the vigorous efforts of black Christians and some white churchmen, along with the spate of organizational activity when Fort Sumter was fired upon, the vast majority of blacks were not Christian in any formal sense. During the War, the African churches and their leaders wholeheartedly supported the Union cause and cooperated in the raising of troops. Later, they joined in pressuring President Lincoln to issue the Emancipation Proclamation. During and immediately following the War, with the blessing and permission of President Lincoln, both major African Methodist bodies sent missionaries into the South to preach the gospel, to organize churches, and to establish schools.

FROM EMANCIPATION TO CIVIL RIGHTS: 1865–1954

The end of the Civil War was a watershed for African American religious bodies and individuals. Churches sought to accommodate the tens of thousands of former slaves who had left white religious institutions and sought refuge in institutions which they could control and in which the interference of whites was minimal. They confronted the major tasks of organizing congregations, of building church houses, and of providing clergy leadership for these emergent congregations. This was the religious dimension of their work. They sought also to alleviate the social, political, and educational deficiencies in their communities. In this effort, either self-consciously as members of the church or as citizens who were Christians, they labored on behalf of the general welfare. The principal form that this effort took was the provision, initially, of elementary and secondary schools. African Christians also participated in the establishment of banks through their encouragement of thrift and housed and often sponsored moral uplift, literacy, and dramatic societies.[13] The religious bodies' most important function, however, was the assimilation of large numbers of freedpersons into a free and ordered society. Their church tutored them on how to live as free individuals; sought to undergird their moral decisions; encouraged property ownership, education, thrift, integrity in human relationships, and right conduct; and encouraged them concerning the possibility of transcending the circumstances in which they were born. They were copartners by extension in the founding of national organizations such as the NAACP, the Urban League, and those lodges that looked to the uplift of African Americans.

From the standpoint of ecclesiastical organizations, no event was of more importance in the postwar decades than the gathering of the majority of African Baptists, the largest denominational grouping, under one roof. The congregational polity of the Baptist bodies historically has made it extremely difficult for them to achieve unification. The Provident Baptist Association and the Wood River Association, founded in the late 1830s, began this process when they merged in 1853 to form the Western Colored Baptist Association, which included some, but not all, of the churches in Ohio, Illinois, Kentucky, Missouri, Indiana, Michigan, and Connecticut. Thirteen years earlier, in 1840, the American Baptist Missionary Convention had been established among the churches in New England and the Middle Atlantic States.[14]

In the interim, between these early beginnings and 1895, when the National Baptist Convention was incorporated, several associations were organized mainly to advance the causes of foreign missions and education. In 1897, a large segment of Virginia Baptists seceded from the National Baptist Convention to form the Lott Carey Missionary Convention. Still another schism occurred in 1915, when a sizeable group led by R. H. Boyd seceded to form the National Baptist Convention, Unincorporated, the second largest Baptist body in America. A third secession from the N.B.C. took place in 1961, when the

Progressive National Baptist Convention was organized. The National Baptist Convention in America, Unincorporated, itself experienced a schism in 1988 when a group of its member churches seceded to form the National Missionary Baptist Convention of America.

During the period 1890–1920, there occurred the largest in-country migration of persons that the nation ever witnessed, the movement of blacks from the farms to the cities of the South and North. The movement north became a floodtide around World War I, then leveled out for more than a decade. After World War II, movement shifted to the West. Once again the churches confronted the task of assimilating the newcomers into established congregations, or of establishing relationships with new congregations that sprang up in house churches or storefronts. Similarly, early in the century there was an efflorescence of congregations in the cities, which came to be known colloquially as "pentecostals or holy rollers."[15] These churches brought new forms of religious expression to the community, and their members generally were recent transplants from the South. Their decorum in worship was often offensive to long-established northern African American believers who were members of more traditional churches. But regardless of the forms of religious expression, the church was in the foreground, helping people adjust to life in the city, helping with employment, and teaching people who had limited skills ways of coping in an urban industrial society.

Some churches modified their structures so that the newcomers would have a genuine experience of community and participation. At the same time, the church began to be the focus for much political activity in large urban centers, sharing the stage with embryonic political organizations. Much of the leadership and many of the "foot soldiers" in the nascent Civil Rights movement were provided by individuals rooted and grounded in the faith of the African American churches.

IT'S A DIFFERENT WORLD

World War II, another decisive turning point, inaugurated the emergence of an ever-changing dynamic context to which the church, as the singular viable institution in the community, had to respond. Wedded to what was happening in the world of industry and commerce were dramatic changes in the legal status of African Americans as a result of Supreme Court decisions, beginning with *Brown v. Topeka Board of Education* (1954). The accelerating Civil Rights movement of the 1950s, 1960s, and early 1970s created a new context that the churches had helped form, but which also presented them with overwhelming and apparently intractable problems.

The changes taking place in American life and culture defined the new context within which the churches were to enact their perennial mission. Intimations of the range, depth, and scope of the changes are provided by the following overview sketch:

1. Urbanization brought anonymity to the individual and depersonalization in most interpersonal relationships.
2. Styles of architecture designed to accommodate ever-increasing populations contributed to this process.
3. The neighborhoods, with their socializing dimensions, disappeared. The church as a parish was no longer a reality—church buildings accommodated commuter congregations.
4. Public transportation and automobiles contributed further to the breaking up of community and the isolation of individuals into family units with limited participation in the communities in which they were housed.
5. In business relationships, one moved from the "handshake" as a guarantee of fairness and quality to the "warranty of maintenance contract," with the seller serving only as a link in a distribution chain.

The growth of the suburbs and concurrent flight from the cities was another element in the pattern, as individuals abandoned their neighborhoods and left the inner city to those least able to sustain its quality of life. The dispersal of industry, service institutions, offices, and residences to the suburbs also eroded the inner cities as viable places to live.[16]

Another reality confronting the churches was and is the abandonment of traditional informal agreements concerning standards of conduct. African American religion has long been rooted in the major tenets of evangelical religion, in which standards of common decency and morality are major criteria of what it is to be Christian. These have disappeared to a large degree and have brought a new sense of personal freedom, if not license, to the community that was the normal constituency of the churches. In theological terms, this eroded any sense of sin or of human culpability before any transcendent power. This is spoken of as the *secularization of culture*, with a consequent erosion of families, sexual morality, and respect for property. The proliferation of the "throw-away culture" has lent a sense of impermanence to life and to things formerly thought to identify a better quality of consciousness and morality. In a quiet way, it has destroyed the role of the church as a place of gathering—it has enlarged the neighborhood to local, national, and international dimensions and provided new bases upon which judgements are made concerning the quality of life within the compass of one's own geographic area.

The religious culture in America has changed society since World War II, and especially since the Korean and Vietnam wars. Religious pluralism has grown within American society, and it is expressed primarily in the presence of diverse ethnic religious minorities. The growth in the United States of Buddhism, Islam, and Hinduism exemplifies this change.[17] Moreover, the "rediscovery" of Africa and rising pan-Africanism have given rise to a proliferation of African or African-derived religions. The influx of Afro-Cubans and persons from Latin and Central America and from the Caribbean has given rise to religious beliefs such as Santeria, Candomble, Voudon, and Rastafarianism, which have broken the "Protestant-Catholic" Christian hegemony of the African American community.

In addition to the move a way from a homogeneous African American religious culture, there has been an erosion of quality of life in the total culture, which is exacerbated in the nation's inner cities. This erosion is manifested in the proliferating distribution and use of drugs; in the escalation of violence and fear as regular aspects of urban life, and increasingly as aspects of life everywhere; in the destruction of the traditional family, as seen in rising divorce rates and greater numbers of single-parent families; in the devastating impact of AIDS and its above-average incidence in African American communities; in the declining quality of education and concomitant confusion over what education should be like; and in the increasing emphasis on material possessions and the implicit encouragement of greed and lust for power that this emphasis precipitates.

Accompanying a broadening global consciousness had been a rapid redefinition of the rights and privileges to which all persons should have access. We are living on top of a wave of rising expectations giving rise to increased frustrations as persons perceive themselves to be the victims of powerful and wealthy others. It is clear that the gap between rich and poor has widened, and that most of the poor are members of nonwhite ethnic groups. In a time of escalating costs for food, services, housing education, medical care, services, furnishings, and transportation, the effects have been corrosive to life in African American and other communities.

Obviously, these changes are not restricted in their impact to non-white communities, but their immediate and long-range consequences are most devastatingly experienced by such groups, and despite former President Bush's promise of a "kinder and gentler America," the end is not in sight, and the grounds for hope from the perspective of many persons is nonexistent. Yet, the mission of the churches has not changed—only the context in which that mission is to be prosecuted.

TO SERVE THE PRESENT AGE

Against this backdrop of a society in radical and dynamic change in virtually every dimension of its life, it is appropriate that these implications for the African American church be examined. Though the prevalent image of the church is that it is exclusively a religious community, it also is an economic community by virtue of its ownership of property, its receipt and disbursement of funds, its function as a consumer of goods and services, and its frequent involvement in construction and in the dispersal of funds to programs and personnel around the world. As indicated earlier, there are about 65,000 congregations handling an estimated seven billion dollars annually. It is important to recognize that this is only a "guesstimate"; no one really knows how much money churches collect and disburse each year. It assumes that the average budget of all churches is at least $100,000. This amount may seem huge, but when it is divided into single church units and when expenditures for mortgages, salaries, maintenance, and assessments are taken into account, it is clear that there are no large surpluses or endowments being created. Church budgets, like the national budget, include large allocations to debt service.

A primary problem for the African American churches has been how to aggregate their funds so that they can be used to lever banking institutions and other forms of financial institutions to initiate policies favorable to African American communities. Some churches, such as the Concord Baptist Church of Christ in Brooklyn, New York, have begun the creation of self-help endowments for the purpose of underwriting projects in its community. The A.M.E. Conference (the Second Episcopal District in Washington and environs) has recently begun a $1,000,000 economic development fund. Historically, African American churches have encouraged thrift, and numerous churches have federal credit unions in which their members participate. A significant number of churches have assets totaling $1,000,000 in their credit unions. In addition, churches have been involved in housing for middle- and lower-income persons as well as for senior citizens. Frequently, a church may be the only agency in the community capable of accepting government funds for such purposes.

In 1978, the Congress of National Black Churches was organized with headquarters in Washington, DC, for the purpose of empowering its member churches (A.M.E., A.M.E. Zion, Christian Methodist, Church of God in Christ, and the three national Baptist bodies) to undertake common enterprises on behalf of its members and their communities.

This has resulted in the creation of a national casualty insurance program with the Aetna Life Insurance Company and a joint banking venture with some churches in the Washington metropolitan area. In addition, the congress had acted as a program agency and sponsor for the receipt of federal and foundation funds addressing the problems of drugs, parenting, and the strengthening of African American families. In addition, individual denominations and churches have received funds for projects designed to enhance the life of the community, including assisting teenage parents, drug rehabilitation, and health care. African American churches, from their earliest existence, have housed secular agencies, such as day care centers and, more recently, Head Start programs. They have also been the locus for community gatherings and meetings, as witnessed during the height of the Civil Rights movement. In numerous cities, African American churches have formed partnerships to sponsor and build housing and to work in cooperation with local education authorities to improve the quality of life in their communities. Several of these projects have been interfaith and interracial and have been undertaken with the support of the Industrial Areas Foundation. There are large projects of this type in Baltimore, Maryland, and East Brooklyn, New York.

It may justifiably be asked why African American churches have not made a significant impact in the economic sector. This lack of impact has several causes: (a) After churches meet their financial obligations, there are only modest amounts of cash available; (b) Church leadership is not experienced in the management of funds and is hesitant to commit the constituency's money to speculative purposes; (c) Church leaders do not trust the persons to whom they would have to commit funds. Options exist that could generate capital, including cooperative buying and banking programs, negotiated group contracts, and bank deposit programs, which by combining funds could exercise influence upon banking policy and the like. One final aspect of the problem, though more elusive in character, also needs to be recognized: The churches in America are voluntary associations. Their members contribute, attend, participate, and otherwise support their missions by individual personal decision. This means that the clergy have not only to recruit a flock, they must nurture it, lead it, and retain it. This activity frequently undercuts other kinds of constructive initiatives in the churches. It is a relatively easy task to collect money to build or rehabilitate buildings; it is much more difficult to educate and lead persons to commit their funds to risky economic development, no matter how laudable the undertaking.

The economic character of churches relates to an equally important aspect of church life: its political reality. Every voluntary agency involves a great deal of politics. The black church in particular has been political from its inception. It provided the only arena in which its clergy and members could express leadership, exercise power and patronage, and influence thought and action. Clergy were among the earliest politicians seeking public office from after the Civil War to the end of Reconstruction. Because "preachers" oftentimes were the only literate persons in their communities, they were natural candidates for public office, but this was a short-lived circumstance.[18] Frequently, when one discusses African American involvement in politics, it is not consciously noted that broad-scale involvement really is not quite three decades old insofar as the South is concerned, and that blacks have not been a decisive political factor in the North until within this same period. To be sure, in some urban areas, church congregations were courted by politicians because they had the mass base. Adam Clayton Powell, and Jesse Jackson in more recent times, are examples of such political figures. Three members in the present U.S. Congress are clergy: Fauntory, Flake, and Lewis. None of these were elected by their churches, but the churches provided the base from which they appealed to the electorate. During Lyndon Johnson's presidency, a wit spoke of the Office of Equal Employment Opportunity as the office of Clergy Employment Opportunity, but that is no longer true. Moreover, it is no longer demonstrable that religious considerations play a decisive role in political decisions that church members make. Issues having to do with matters incident to race can command virtually unanimous majorities among all African Americans. This is no less true for church folks. Individual clergy may be persons of substantial political influence, but individual churches are not usually decisive elements in electoral politics.

Despite their declining significance in the political arena, it is still the case that in urban areas candidates regularly visit African American churches as elections approach. In point of fact, where else are African Americans assembled in a manner that allows political candidates to have access without effort?

It is in the social arena that African American churches are today frequently looked to for leadership. We have already noted that they have sponsored and provided housing for numerous projects and programs devoted to these ends. Churches often run afterschool tutorial programs, workshops designed to teach parenting skills, parochial schools, programs for senior citizens, cooperative programs with the Red Cross, and programs for young persons and for single adults. Churches also hold forums on urban infrastructure, rising levels of prison populations, the budget deficit, the savings and loan crisis, aging nuclear facilities and their attendant waste, the pollution and destruction of the environment, the aging transportation system and the industrial complex, the trade deficit, and the exportation of employment to poorer countries while great numbers in this society live at or below the poverty level.

This, a partial list, is enough to show that we, as a nation, have many problems. It is not enough to look only to voluntary institutions to remedy what the national government has failed to do. There are many things that African American churches can do and are doing to improve the quality of life in their communities. Promising initiatives are already in place. But it should not be anybody's conclusion that African American churches, individually or collectively, constitute a dormant wealth of resources that can be exploited to remedy problems that they did not create and cannot solve. All of our institutions must work together to identify and solve America's weighty troubles.

SUGGESTED READINGS
General Works

Ahlstrom, Sidney E. 1972. *A religious history of the American people.* New Haven, CT: Yale University Press.

Davis, David Brion. 1967. *The problem of slavery in western culture.* Ithaca, NY: Cornell University Press.

Franklin, John H. 1967. *From slavery to freedom.* New York: Knopf.

Idown, W. B. 1973. *African traditional religion: A definition.* Maryknoll, NY: Orbis.

Johnson, Harry A., ed. 1978. *Negotiating the mainstream.* Chicago: American Library Association.

Lincoln, C. Eric. 1974. *The black experience in religion.* Garden City, NY: Doubleday/Anchor.

Mays, Benjamin E., and Joseph W. Nicholson. 1933. *The Negro's church.* New York: Institute of Social and Religious Research.

Nelsen, Hart M., and Anne K. Nelsen. 1975. *Black church in the sixties.* Lexington, KY: University of Kentucky Press.

Reimers, David M. 1965. *White Protestantism and the Negro.* New York: Oxford University Press.

Sernett, Milton C. 1975. *Black religion and American evangelicalism.* Metuchen, NJ: Scarecrow.

Williams, Ethel, and Clifton E. Brown. 1977. *The Howard University bibliography of African and Afro-American religious studies.* Wilmington, DE: Scholarly Resources.

Wilmore, Gayraud. 1973. *Black religion and black radicalism.* Garden City, NY: Doubleday/Anchor.

Denominational Histories

Boyd, Richard H. 1922. *A story of the National Baptist Publishing Board.* Nashville: National Baptist Plant.

Bradley, David H., Sr. 1956. *A history of the A.M.E. Zion Church, 1796–1872.* Nashville: Parthenon.

Bragg, George F. 1922. *History of the Afro-American group of the Episcopal Church.* Baltimore: Church Advocate.

Brawley, James P. 1974. *Two centuries of Methodist concern: Bondage, freedom and education of black people.* New York: Vantage.

Foley, Albert S. 1955. *God's men of color: The colored priests of the United States: 1854–1954.* New York: Central Seminary Press.

Freeman, Edward D. 1953. *The epoch of Negro Baptists and foreign mission boards.* Kansas City, KS: Central Seminary Press.

Gillard, John T. 1929. *The Catholic Church and the American Negro.* Baltimore: St. Joseph's Society.

Hood, James W. 1895. *One hundred years of the African Methodist Episcopal Zion Church.* New York: A.M.E. Zion.

Jackson, Joseph H. 1980. *A story of Christian activism: The history of the National Baptist Convention, U.S.A., Inc.* Nashville: Townsend.

Lakey, Othal H. 1985. *The history of the CME Church.* Memphis: CME.

Murray, Andrew E. 1966. *Presbyterians and the Negro—A history.*

Payne, Daniel A. 1891. *A history of the African Methodist Episcopal Church, 1816–1856.* Nashville: A.M.E. Sunday School Union.

Phillips, Charles H. 1925. *History of the Colored Methodist Episcopal Church in America.* Jackson, TN: CME.

Singleton, George A. 1922. *The romance of African Methodism.* New York: Exposition.

Walls, William J. 1974. *The African Methodist Episcopal Zion Church.* Charlotte, NC: A.M.E.Z.

REFERENCES

Ajaji, J. F. Ade, and Espie, Ian. 1965. *A thousand years of West African history.* Ibadan, Nigeria: Ibadan University Press.

Du Bois, W. E. B. 1961. *The souls of black folk.* Greenwich, CT: Fawcett.

Fitts, Leroy. 1985. *A history of black Baptists.* Nashville: Broadman.

Foner, Eric. 1993. *Freedom's lawmakers: A directory of black office-holders during reconstruction.* New York: Oxford University Press.

Freedman, S. G. 1993. *Upon this rock: The miracles of a black church.* New York: Harper.

Fyfe, Christopher. 1965. Peoples of the windward coast A.D. 1000–1800. In *A thousand years of west African history,* ed. J. F. Ade Ajayi and Ian Espie. Ibadan, Nigeria: Ibadan University Press.

Green, Lorenzo J. 1968. *The Negro in colonial New England.* New York: Atheneum.

Gregory, Chester W. 1986. *The history of the United Holy Church in America, Inc.* Baltimore: Gateway.

Jones, Lawrence N. 1977. The early black societies and churches: Matrix of community mission, 1778–1830. In *The Black Church: A community resource,* ed. Diana J. Jones and William H. Matthews. Washington, DC: Howard University Institute of Urban Affairs and Research.

————. 1991. The organized church: The historic significance and changing role in contemporary African experience. In *Directory of African American religious bodies,* ed. Wardell J. Payne. Washington, DC: Howard University Press.

Jordon, Winthrop. 1968. *White over black: American attitudes toward the Negro, 1550–1812.* Chapel Hill, NC: University of North Carolina Press.

Lincoln, C. Eric. 1961. *The Black Muslims in America.* Boston: Beacon.

————. 1984. *Race, religion, and the continuing American dilemma.* New York: Hill and Wang.

Lincoln, C. Eric, and Lawrence H. Mamiya. 1990. *The Black Church in the African American experience.* Durham, NC: Duke University Press.

Paris, Arthur E. 1982. *Black Pentacostalism: Southern religion in an urban world.* Amherst, MA: University of Massachusetts Press.

Rabboteau, Albert. 1978. *Slave religion: The invisible institution in the antebellum south.* New York: Oxford University Press

Ross, German. 1969. *History and formative years of the Church of God in Christ.* Memphis, TN: Church of God in Christ.

Simpson, George E. 1978. *Black religions in the new world.* New York: Columbia University Press.

Sobel, Mechal. 1979. *Trabelin' on: The Slave journey to an Afro-Baptist faith.* Westport, CT: Greenwood.

Tanner, Benjamin T. 1867. *An apology for African Methodism.* Baltimore, n.p.

Williams, Peter W. 1990. *America's religions: Traditions and cultures.* New York: Macmillan.

Woodson, Carter G. 1921. *A history of the Negro church.* Washington, DC: Associated Publishers.

NOTES

1. C. Eric Lincoln and Lawrence Mamiya, *The Black Church in the African American Experience* (Durham, NC: Duke University Press, 1990), 407. This is the most recent and most comprehensively researched study of the black church and the African American religious experience yet published.

2. Mechal Sobel, *Trabelin' On: The Slave Journey to an Afro-Baptist Faith* (Westport, CT: Greenwood, 1979), 3–17. The first chapter of this study contains a detailed discussion of the West African sacred cosmos, including a thorough discussion of recent scholarship relative to this chapter.

3. W. E. B. Du Bois, "The Faith of the Fathers," in *The Souls of Black Folk* (Greenwich, CT: Fawcett, 1961), 142–43.

4. Lawrence N. Jones, "The Organized Church: The Historic Significance and Changing Role in Contemporary African Experience," in *Directory of African American Religious Bodies,* ed. Wardell J. Payne (Washington, DC: Howard University Press, 1991), 1.

5. Christianity in Africa was restricted mainly to the coastal areas around the forts during the period of the slave trade; it penetrated the interior, from which most slaves were collected for export, only superficially. See Christofer Fyfe, "Peoples of the Windward Coast A.D. 1000–1800," in J. F. Ade Ajayi and Ian Espie, eds., *A Thousand Years of West African History* (Ibadan, Nigeria: Ibadan University Press, 1965), 225–26. See also in the same volume, A. C. Ryder, "Portuguese and Dutch in the West African before 1800."

6. Sobel, *Trabelin' On,* 3–21.

7. Winthrop Jordon, *White Over Black: American Attitudes Toward the Negro, 1550–1812* (Chapel Hill, NC: University of North Carolina Press, 1968), 191.

8. Lorenzo J. Green, *The Negro in Colonial New England* (New York: Atheneum, 1968), 268.

9. Carter G. Woodson, *The Negro Church* (Washington, DC: Associated Publishers, 1921), 35.

10. Albert J. Raboteau, *Slave Religion: The Invisible Institution in the Antebellum South* (New York: Oxford University Press, 1978).

11. Lawrence N. Jones, "The Early Black Societies and Churches: Matrix of Community Mission, 1778–1830," in *The Black Church: A Community Resource,* Diana J. Jones and William H. Matthews, eds. (Washington, DC: Howard University, Institute of Urban Affairs and Research, 1977), 1–17.

12. "A Minute to be Handed to the Abolition Society for the convention, Philadelphia, November 3, 1794," Quoted in Benjamin T. Tanner, *An Apology for African Methodism,* (Baltimore, n.p., 1867), 144–45.

13. Du Bois, "Of the Faith of Fathers," 140–51.

14. Leroy Fitts, *A History of Black Baptists* (Nashville: Broadman, 1985), 64–106.

15. German Ross, *History and Formative Years of the Church of God in Christ* (Memphis, TN: Church of God in Christ, 1969). The organized black pentecostal churches in America trace their origins to the pioneering work of William J. Seymour and the Azusa Street Revival in Los Angeles early in the twentieth century. The Church of God in Christ is the largest black pentecostal body. See also Arthur E. Paris, *Black Pentecostalism: Southern Religion in an Urban World* (Amherst, MA: University of Massachusetts Press, 1982) and Chester W. Gregory, *The History of the United Holy Church of America, Inc., 1886–1986* (Baltimore: Gateway, 1986).

16. C. Eric Lincoln, *Race, Religion, and the Continuing American Dilemma* (New York: Hill and Wang, 1984). Lincoln provides a careful discussion of the changes affecting black America and the nation in general and delineates their implications for African American religion. A recent book by S. G. Freedman, *Upon This Rock: The Miracles of a Black Church* (New York: Harper, 1993) is a study of St. Paul's Baptist Church in Brooklyn, New York, and of its pastor,

the Reverend Johnny Youngblood. This book provides an intimate look into the life of one preacher and the way in which he and his people have sought to deal with some aspects of urban reality and to capitalize on its vitality.

17. C. Eric Lincoln, *The Black Muslims in America* (Boston: Beacon, 1961). This is the seminal discussion of the movement begun by William D. Fard and continued by the Honorable Elijah Mohammed. See also Peter W. Williams, *America's Religions: Traditions and Cultures* (New York: Macmillan, 1990) and George E. Simpson, *Black Religions in the New World* (New York: Columbia University Press 1978).

18. Eric Foner, *Freedom's Lawmakers: A Directory of Black Officeholders During Reconstruction* (New York: Oxford University Press, 1993). Foner identifies 237 preachers who held public office, including 55 Baptists, 35 Methodists, 7 AMEZs, 5 Presbyterians, 3 Congregationalists, 2 Episcopalians, and 77 whose denominations are unknown.

11 Ministry to Women: Hearing and Empowering "Poor" Black Women

CHERYL TOWNSEND GILKES[*]

A frican American women have had a significant impact on United States culture and society. On occasion, their heroic responses to oppression have become visible enough to impress upon others the value of their perspective. In 1866, during the Combahee River expedition, Harriet Tubman became the first woman ever to lead United States soldiers in battle. Allegedly, one editor, writing to praise her exploits, exclaimed, "The desperation of a poor black woman has power to shake a nation that so long was deaf to her cries." In one of the most critical and pivotal theological conversations of the late twentieth century, novelist Alice Walker's (1992 [1982]: 187) Celie, responding to Shug's attempt to blunt her impending heresies and blasphemies, shouts, "Let' im hear me, I say. If he [God] ever listened to poor colored women the world would be a different place, I can tell you." Celie's and Shug's revision of their thoughts about God takes place during a lifetime of abuse and humiliation. They develop a love and admiration for each other as they rebel against their victimization by those closest to them. The perspectives of the novelist and the editor both tell a vital truth about the standpoint, perspective, or point of view of African

[*]The author gratefully acknowledges the support of Colby College, the Episcopal Divinity School, and the W. E. B. Du Bois Institute for Afro-American Research at Harvard University for their support in the preparation of the final manuscript of this chapter.

American women in the United States—that, in a racist and sexist world, "poor" African American women might possibly have a more realistic view of that world. Indeed, Celie's revelation points to something many activist women, especially African American churchwomen of the late nineteenth and early twentieth centuries, have long suspected: that the wisdom that comes from the responses of African American women to their sufferings, if taken seriously by God and society, has the power to transform the world. Yet in spite of Celie, Shug, Harriet Tubman, and so many others, the popular images of black women continue to signify their continued subordination, denigration, and silencing in this society.

There are many images of African American women in the popular culture of the United States. There is one image, associated with the highly profiled, talented, and famous, such as Lena Horne and Oprah Winfrey, which exalts the successful black woman as a symbol of strength, vitality, and liberation. Another image, associated with the covers of *Newsweek* and *Time*, is the image of the impoverished welfare mother, the resident of public housing projects, the teenage mother, and the neglectful, crack-addicted mother, usually rolled up into one monstrous body. Between these extremes of historically charged contemporary images exists a reality of diverse experiences for African American women. That diverse reality has been a significant engine in religion and movements for social change.

Indeed, the creative persistence of analysts and artists has given us new terms and phrases—such as "multiple jeopardy" and "multiple consciousness" (King 1988) and "womanist" (Walker 1983)—to use as we try to organize black women's experience into a theoretical or practical portrayal. The ability of African American women's experience to defy portrayal in conventional terms is related to certain distinctive realities. African American women have been the victims of the longest, most sustained cultural assault experienced by any racial-ethnic-gender group. They have been victimized by institutionalized racism as practiced in the United States in its tridimensional expression: economic exploitation, political exclusion, and cultural humiliation. The cultural humiliation of African American women has been intensified by the moral evaluations attached to their economic and political roles. The cultural assaults mounted against the African American community as a whole have burdened the institutions in which women take part. These institutional pressures are compounded by cultural assaults aimed directly at their "woman" experiences. These externally imposed crises are intensified by the cultural ambivalence African Americans themselves express toward the contributions of women when racism elicits explicitly sexist forms of self-hatred.

Among the crises facing African Americans today, and one that will follow us into the twenty-first century, is the situation of poor women in our communities. Folk wisdom recognizes the importance of "the mothers" to the survival and health of the community and to the perpetuation of worthwhile dimensions of African American culture. Christian ministry is defined ultimately by its service to, with, and on behalf of "the least of these." In the context of the African American community, women constitute "the least of these" and the peculiarities of their situation have profound consequences for the entire community. William Julius Wilson pointed to the depth of the crisis more than a decade ago:

> The problem for black female-headed families is not so much the absence of fathers, but that in an overwhelming majority of cases they are impoverished. Indeed, the poverty stricken nature of the underclass is symbolized by the female-headed family pattern. The main problem, to repeat, is that the lower-class black family is experiencing severe economic problems and the growing percentage of female-headed families is one of the symptoms, not the cause of that condition. In this connection, a program of economic reform, if it is to be meaningful, has to be directed not solely at improving the economic opportunities of poor black men, but also of improving the job prospects of poor black women. It would even be wise to include in this reform program the creation of publicly financed day care centers so that women can realistically pursue such opportunities when they arise (Wilson 1980, 161).

Wilson's distress was echoed by such earlier sociologists as E. Franklin Frazier, Kelley Miller, W. E. B. Du Bois, and Oliver Cromwell Cox, when they expressed similar concerns about urban black women. At no time in the African American experience have women not been among "the least of these." As the primary caretakers of children and as the first to feel the effects of economic crisis, the deprivation of black women often *is* the deprivation of the entire community.[1]

The terms *ministry* and *women* are currently charged with great meaning as African American churches face the challenges of the twenty-first century. The current attention to women in the ordained ministries of Christian churches has been part of a larger critique of culture that insists upon the inclusion of women at all levels of public leadership. At the same time, populist emphases in women's history remind us that the activities of women at all levels of churches also constitute "ministry." The discussion of "ministry to women" must be sensitive to both dimensions of concern. By *ministry*, we mean not only that associated with pastoral vocations, but also the broad range of Christian service within and beyond church walls that is aimed at spiritual, physical, and social regeneration and transformation.

Any discussion of ministry or service to women must be historical in nature. In the African American experience, women have been central to the emergence and development of religious traditions, congregations, and denominations. During slavery, women were key to the crystallization of religious and family institutions as sources of survival and of resistance to slavery's dehumanizing effects. Women reinforced the importance of religion among themselves through autonomous women's rituals, prayer groups, and leadership structures (White 1985). Their voices, the voices of "the least of these," were irrevocably woven into the traditions and organizations that became central to the community's response to changing social institutions and to economic and political challenges. Historically, any change in the socioeconomic status and political organization and participation of black women has meant a transformation of the organizational fabric of Black Churches. While a comprehensive and exhaustive understanding of this is not possible in the space available, in this chapter we review and note highlights pointing to the women's traditions that today are resources for reformulating the meaning and practice of "ministry" to meet the new and diverse problems black women face.

These selected historical highlights of African American women's experiences suggest the importance of the interrelationships among black women, their churches, and their families. Such an exploration also sketches the way black women's concerns and consciousness have operated as social forces to shape institutions and communal responses to social problems. Not only has the changing socioeconomic status of black women shaped their demands on the churches and the churches' responses to them, but recent changes in the economy have affected black women's needs for ministry as well as the content of those ministries. As contemporary churches and communities explore ways to respond to crises affecting black women, it is important to explore the responses of the past that shaped the traditions that exist in the present, and which may provide what Bernice Johnson Reagon (1983, 363) calls, "the key to turning the century with our principles and ideals intact."

We will review the ways in which major historical changes have affected African American women and their relationships to their churches. Focusing on the aforementioned tridimensional reality of institutionalized racism, we will then discuss ways to address the empowerment of African American women. We will conclude by noting how the distribution of opportunities for women in professional ministry creates a contradiction for talented African American women who feel called to address the problems of the masses in the African American community through the offices of ordained Christian ministry. Effective ministry to African American women as they confront crises and, by extension, to their families and communities, will depend on a massive reorganization of attitudes about women, about women in ministry, and about the meaning of ministry in black Christian churches.

"POOR" BLACK WOMEN

James Cone and others have pointed to the tripartite reality of institutional racism in the United States: economic exploitation, political exclusion, and cultural humiliation. The African American response to that racism has manifested itself in part in an adaptive self-hatred that accepts models defined by the dominant society as normative for the black community. Existence in this society has involved a twofold struggle. One part consists of constantly challenging the dominant society; the other is an internal contest over roles, values, and strategies for survival as well as for social change. Women have been central to both sides of this struggle. Indeed, it has been argued that the legal and cultural statuses of African women and their descendants have been central to the peculiarities of slavery and its aftermath in the United States (Giddings 1984, 35; Cooper 1892, 31). Among women, there exists a "multiple consciousness" in response to this "multiple jeopardy" that has been ever-present in the history of African American women in the United States.

In spite of the centrality of women's reality and roles and in spite of the legendary "sheroes,"[2] such as Harriet Tubman, Sojourner Truth, Ellen Craft, Milla Granson, and others who emerged from slavery, African American churches have not consistently empowered the voices of women. Perhaps it was in the slave churches that their voices were heeded most attentively. Although white society recognized and empowered the black male preacher, even when he was a bondsman, it mostly ignored the women. Accounts of the slave community indicate that enslaved men and women did not ignore women. White (1985, 119–41) points to several instances where powerful women arose as spiritual leaders who were able to exercise authority over the community. Webber (1978) argues that slave communities exhibited a real lack of sexism in their allocation of leadership, authority, and respect.

The church's voice during slavery was a clear and unwaveringly prophetic one. It was a voice that insisted simultaneously on the overthrow of slavery and the humanity of enslaved women and men. Occasionally, that voice was found in the themes that undergird the slave revolts, most notably Nat Turner's. Webber points to the centrality of women in constructing, maintaining, and transmitting a worldview whose cultural themes emphasized solidarity and religious faith: "Even women preachers appear often enough though admittedly less frequently than male preachers, to suggest that there was no community prohibition against their filling this crucial role" (1978, 149). Biographies of nineteenth-century evangelists (Andrews 1986) and in Toni Morrison's 1987 novel, *Beloved,* in the person of Baby Suggs, remind us that the voice of the preaching woman has been a significant force for psychic survival. Yet, it was all too often ignored and hindered from attaining authority after Emancipation.

The suppression of women's voices within African American churches coincides with what Wilmore (1983) calls, "the deradicalization of the Black Church" as the prophetic voices of people like Henry M. Turner and Harriet Tubman died out. Around the beginning of the twentieth century, women lost ground in their access to platforms and pulpits. Churches were urged to "regularize," and regularized churches had male pastors in the pulpits. Some churches accommodated the religious zeal of women, allowing them to lead worship and pray "from the floor" as missionaries and evangelists. According to Evelyn Brooks Barnett Higgenbotham (1993), a "feminist theology" emerged among Baptist women between 1885 and 1900 as they contested the masculinism that threatened them with silence and marginality. Apparently, the work of these women as equals, first within the American National Baptist Convention and later within the National Baptist Convention, was delegitimized. Once they were, in the words of Nannie Helen Burroughs (Higgenbotham 1993), "hindered from helping," these women formed the Women's Auxiliary Convention of the National Baptist Convention, from which they wielded tremendous influence within the church and the community at large. A number of women found places for their voices in the Holiness movement of the late nineteenth century, and in the Pentecostal movement of the early twentieth century. Baptist and African Methodist women were recruited and "converted," became the pioneer educators of these new churches, and were also powerful evangelists and revivalists who "dug out" or founded urban churches as women and their work moved to the cities.

As their suppression within their churches progressed and the church became less prophetic and more priestly in its response to political realities, African American Christian women created other avenues for their "ministry." One of these was a women's movement that culminated in the formation of the National Association of Colored Women. It is important *not* to view this club movement of the late nineteenth and early twentieth centuries primarily as secular. It is more accurately viewed as a movement of prophetic Christian women who fulfilled their calling in their responses to social issues and in their demands for social change. The club movement's motto, "Lifting as We Climb," reflected their sense of shared suffering and mission. These women rejected the notion of competitive American individualism in favor of a corporate mobility designed to liberate. Throughout the papers of these movements, one repeatedly finds Christian themes. Often the women's church work and community work overlapped significantly. Mary McLeod Bethune, for instance, was a graduate of Moody Bible Institute and an experienced street preacher. When she was denied a missionary post in Africa, she claimed her Africa to be right next door and founded what is now Bethune-Cookman College. Other black women's narratives, such as that of Mamie Garvin Fields (1983), describe similar missionary motives. Such leaders as Mary Church Terrell traveled the country exhorting church women to act on behalf of their communities. Others expressed a biblical hermeneutic that undergirded their worldviews and actions. In her novel *Iola Leroy or the Shadows Uplifted,* Frances Ellen Watkins Harper (1987 [1893]) points to the church as a place to reconstitute the African American community and to formulate strategies and ethics for social change.

These women were part of a leadership class of "preachers and teachers." In addition to being heroic educators, writings such as Lucie Campbell's hymn, "Something Within," hint that these "teachers" were also carriers of the gospel. "If anything characterizes the role of black women in religion in America, it is the successful extension of their individual sense of regeneration, release, redemption, and spiritual liberation to a collective ethos of struggle for and with the entire black community" (Dodson and Gilkes 1986, 81). Historically, African American women have argued for a collective approach to the community's suffering. Their advocacy has focused on the experience of men and children, sometimes giving their own specific concerns less emphasis than they deserve. Yet every dimension of the black women's experience cries out for a specific response from the church, which needs to hear and empower the voices of "poor" black women.[3]

Novelist Alice Walker (1983, xi–xii) has offered the term *womanist,* along with a definition that organizes and interprets the heroic historical experience of African American women with reference to their femaleness, their relationship to community, their strategies for change, and their cultural emphases. What Walker has identified as a holistic and universalist commitment to the community's survival, Collins (1989) has described as a "recurrent humanist vision" among black women activists and writers. Both Walker and Collins illuminate a consciousness that emerges from suffering and recognizes the suffering of others. Given the pivotal place of African American women in the racial-ethnic, class, and gender hierarchies of American culture, a ministry that concentrates on their empowerment should benefit the entire community.

ECONOMIC EMPOWERMENT

African American women's work history is linked inextricably with their religious history. Their roles as workers defined their history and status in the United States. Many of their responses to that history have been dependent on their religious opportunities and spiritual resources. As enslaved and free women, their work has been inseparable from the well-being of the entire African American community. As wage earners, they have been the poorest, least protected, and most insurgent group of workers. Slave or free, these vulnerable women have been among the staunchest supporters and most enterprising participants in the religious life of their communities.

As enslaved women, they were subjected to the same violence and exploitative working conditions as men. Angela Davis (1981, 5) points out that the work roles of enslaved women set the foundations for a "new standard of womanhood" and established a different relationship between black women and the labor force. As a result:

> Proportionately, more Black women have always worked outside their homes than have their white sisters. The enormous space that work occupies in Black women's lives today follows a pattern established during the very earliest days of slavery. As slaves, cumpulsory labor overshadowed every other aspect of women's existence. It would seem, therefore, that the starting point for any exploration of Black women's lives under slavery would be an appraisal of their role as workers.

Their combined role as workers and mothers was pivotal to the formation of African American consciousness. Men were often the chroniclers of exploitations specific to women. One such memoirist described his mother's impact by simply saying, "My mother was *much* of a woman" (Jones 1985).

These working women were also expected to reproduce the African labor force in America. As the demand for slave labor rose, the system depended more and more on natural increase and unparalleled legal repression to maintain itself. White (1985) points out that force, fraud, and other inducements were used to make enslaved women the most fertile population in the world (at that time). Central to their situation was a need for more humane conditions for mothering. These concerns provided the basis for an extensive network of mutual aid among women that was, she argues, the base upon which the legendary strength of slave women rested. By helping each other, they were able to cope with work and motherhood in ways that became surrounded by folklore. The network's mutual aid included prayer meetings and religious leaders who healed, prayed, exhorted, and prophesied, displaying remarkable amounts of influence and authority within slave communities.

At the end of slavery, people sought liberation from the sexual and material oppression of the rural South. Women were eager to work for themselves and their families. To do this, they educated their daughters as well as their sons. The educational ethic among freed women and men contributed institutions and policies that benefited the entire South. On occasion, black southerners in some areas had higher school attendance rates than their white neighbors. Part of the community's educational strategy was to free women from the sexual exploitation that came with agricultural and domestic work. Educated daughters, they hoped, would not have to work in "the white man's kitchen." Even with this work ethic, black women disappeared from the fields immediately after slavery. Their former owners accused them of "playing the lady." Some have argued, however, that fear of sexual exploitation prompted this disappearance (Painter 1977; Jones 1984).

Some of the most poignant descriptions of the work orientation of African American women are found with reference to their religious and educational orientations. Women worked and saved and ran farms to educate husbands called to the ministry (Sterling 1984). Women also found enterprising ways to earn extra money to educate children in church-related schools and to support the missionaries who taught them. White female employers complained about the precedence church activities sometimes took over their own needs (Jones 1984). The investments of "Negro washerwomen," according to Woodson (1930), were the foundations of the great black insurance companies in the South. The economic enterprise of African American women, when successful, as in the cases of Maggie Lena Walker, Madame C. J. Walker, and Mary Ellen ("Mammy") Pleasants, benefited the entire community (Giddings 1984). Pleasants, a Catholic, financially supported the founding of several black Protestant congregations in California. Woodson states that the least educated and hardest-working women were the ones most eager to invest in religiously suffused mutual aid associations, community uplift projects, and new small businesses.

Black women's work in the South moved to the cities before the demand for male rural labor declined. This transformation was a significant force in urbanization. Women outnumbered men in the cities. These migrant women, and eventually their families, became the nuclei around which new urban congregations formed. Many of these new late nineteenth- and early twentieth-century churches were part of the Holiness and Pentecostal movements. Many congregations were founded by the women who then sent "home" for male pastors. At the same time that sociologists, such as E. Franklin Frazier (1939), decried the cities as places of "destruction," women were transforming the organizational and cultural matrix of the African American church. The urbanization of women's work not only produced new churches but also new music, contributing to another cultural transformation in which women's voices are significant: the emergence of gospel music. Urban churches represented a substantial economic investment on the part of women. That investment was so prominent that, according to Branch (1988), Montgomery Improvement Association founder E. D. Nixon defined the civic responsibilities of Montgomery's pastors in terms of what they "owed" the "washerwomen." For Nixon, it was obvious that the religious leadership derived its salaries and prestige from working women. The centrality of churchwomen to the Montgomery Bus Boycott movement and to the Civil Rights movement overall is a story that is only beginning to be told (Robinson 1897).

In spite of their hard work and sustained participation in the labor force, black women remain poorly remunerated and, in the aggregate, fall behind white men, black men, and white women. Only college-educated black women, a disproportionately small group, approach or surpass white women's income levels. This seeming anomaly is a consequence of black women's continuous labor force participation and the disincentive to remain in the force that married, college-educated white women experience because of the economic opportunities available to their husbands (King 1988). Currently, according to Rothenberg (1988), the poverty rate of all *working* black mothers (13 percent) *equals* the poverty rate of white men who are *not* in the labor force. Elderly black women represent one of the poorest groups. And, it is elderly African American women who are responsible for the organizational integrity of black religious organizations.

African American churches need to be in the forefront of movements and strategies to uplift African Americans economically. African American women and their communities stand to benefit from advocacy for economic justice more than any other group of women. Assuming the role of advocate for economic justice for African American women is essential to the ministry of churches. Recently, some churches have confused the roles of evangelism and prophecy. In their zeal to attract men, these churches ignore their mission to call social institutions to account for their failures to people. The most glaring economic failure (of many) in this society is the historical failure to secure economic justice for black women. Nannie Helen Burroughs and other churchwomen in the club movement recognized this contradiction and saw the call to secure economic justice as an essential task for creating an ideal society for everyone. This task still awaits the full energies of the church.

POLITICAL EMPOWERMENT

It is in the area of political empowerment that the institutional discrimination of African American churches most directly excludes women. "Get to the ministers!" is still an American political ethic, according to Charles V. Hamilton (1972), when most white politicians are seeking the "black vote." In urban politics, ministers are most likely to be approached when officials are seeking to represent the "voice" of the black community on civic boards and in appointed political offices. The refusal of African American churches, particularly Baptist churches, to include women in ordained and authoritative leadership directly excludes women from participating in decision making that affects the communities in which they comprise the majority population.

Today, women do not accept such exclusion. The traditions of women's community work have provided alternative pathways to public leadership. Sometimes the path involves a highly public secular career in human services or electoral politics. While black women as congresswomen, mayors, state representatives, agency heads, city or town council members, and Republican and Democratic party workers, make a substantial contribution to the political empowerment of black communities, they are often isolated from the male religious enclaves that are accorded special privileges of access to white political powers. Because black churches remain the most important site for working- and middle-class people who vote and otherwise participate in traditional politics, women's exclusion from church leadership dilutes their influence in other public spaces.

Historically, African American women have insisted upon participating in the political destiny of black people. The nineteenth and twentieth centuries are full of examples of such participation. One of black America's earliest political writers and the first woman of any race to speak publicly and leave existing manuscripts, Maria Stewart, offered incisive political-theological perspectives on the plight of black people (Richardson 1987). Sojourner Truth once challenged Frederick Douglass by asking, "Is God dead, Frederick?" Her challenge reminded Douglass and their listeners that, regardless of how hostile the society, African Americans were not totally alone in their struggle. She also underscored the significance black people attach to biblical-theological frameworks of social justice. Mary McLeod Bethune's missionary zeal moved her from higher education to the political arena during the Depression. She became, as convener of President Franklin Roosevelt's black cabinet, head of the National Youth Administration, and president of the National Council of Negro Women, the most powerful black leader since Booker T. Washington.

The activities of African American women during the Civil Rights movement, although extensive and crucial, have not been adequately documented or assessed. However, two women, Ella Baker and Fannie Lou Hamer, both exude a common spirituality in spite of their radically different social origins. Ella Baker, the daughter of a minister, became a traveling prophet for the National Association for the Advancement of Colored People (NAACP) as a field secretary before becoming the executive director of the Southern Christian Leadership Conference (SCLC) and the organizer of the Student Nonviolent Coordinating Committee (SNCC). Her speaking schedule, as portrayed in a film biography (Grant 1986), provides documentation of the extensive network of churches open to organizers from the NAACP. Hamer was explicitly theological in her calls for participation in the Civil Rights movement. The same energy and assertiveness that made her an effective song leader in her church made her an effective public speaker and advocate for black people's political empowerment (Mills 1993). White women feminists point to such women as Hamer as catalysts for their own assertiveness and political growth (King 1987).

These specific examples highlight the models of political participation that women often provide for the community. Although churchwomen can be as hierarchical and authoritarian as any other human beings, they are more willing to "mother" others toward developing effective political participation and leadership skills. My own research on urban community workers uncovered networks and other organized settings in which women who became empowered actively recruited and trained others for similar kinds of participation and leadership. One may argue that women are more willing to do this because they have been so often forced to do this, but my observation of women's organizations leads me to conclude that black women enjoy exercising power by guiding others in its exercise. Both church mothers and community mothers utilize this model of influence in their organizations (Gilkes 1985; 1986).

If the church follows through in its advocacy for women's political empowerment, as in economics, such empowerment would be another source of benefit for the entire community. W. E. B. Du Bois recognized this during his campaigns for women's suffrage from the pages of *The Crisis*. We now know that African American women vote in patterns that contradict their actual socioeconomic position in society, in spite of their structural and social alienation. The enhanced empowerment of African American women holds prophetic possibilities for the entire community. Including women in the institutional life of the church so as to enhance their access to public power would enable the church to benefit from their skills and talents in a way that others outside the church and outside the black community already do. Many activist women who do not attend church regularly explain their absence in terms of the discrimination they perceive. The inclusion of women would also represent a significant affirmation to women and a balance for the demands that the dominant culture often places on the male role—demands that enhance the individual career sometimes at the expense of the community's collective interests.

CULTURAL EMPOWERMENT

The attainment of economic and political justice are really matters of "simple justice." Addressing the cultural humiliation of African American women is a challenge to the church that involves what is perhaps the most complex, most significant, and least understood emergency, one with devastating consequences for self-esteem. *Cultural humiliation* referes to the way in which African American images, traditions, values, and symbols are devalued and regarded as deviant by the dominant (white) society. Some have argued that the low self-esteem of African American women and girls contributes to the behaviors that choke off their most significant opportunities. Where the patriarchal dimensions of the society provide a few opportunities for black men that support a positive self-esteem, that same patriarchal ethic exacerbates the alienation of African American women.

African American women, by choice and by chance, violate nearly every dimension of American gender norms. Schur (1984) has pointed to the importance of "gender norms" in defining the position of women in our society. These include meeting certain standards of beauty, a model of marriage and motherhood that enforces economic dependence, and social deference. Violation of these norms brings about the exclusion and punishment of women in a variety of ways. Schur describes the failure to meet society's beauty norms as "visual deviance." African American women, in terms of their color alone, stand out from and against the culture's idolatry of whiteness. Not only are they assaulted from outside their communities, but African American women who are too dark face an outrageous complex of attitudes and behaviors from within their own communities. Often the behavior of men and their stated preferences for lighter or white women reflect black men's own self-hatred, but in spite of the changes brought about by the Black Power movement, Walker (1983, 290) is still able to lament, "If the present looks like the past, what does the future look like?"

Ironically, black churches are often pastored by men who are the most fiercely committed to the dominant culture's notions of beauty and do not see these notions as white, male, and exclusionary. Those notions are affirmed and reaffirmed from the pulpit to the door, often in quite subtle ways. The prettiest and lightest little girls in the church are often encouraged in ways that allow them to discover that their visual status is a resource for success; they are socialized to be "cute" and to grow up to be beautiful. In contrast, the darker and plumper girls are encouraged to be serious, develop leadership skills, and, above all, do well in school. Some black women have called this the "pretty-ugly" syndrome in black culture.[4] Although poets and black feminists have vocalized this issue, churches have been strangely silent on the "pretty-ugly" ethic that abounds in our communities. Both strategies hurt! Many "pretty" black women are intellectually underdeveloped in a community that offers relatively little protection to its female children. Unless they are specially protected by middle-class organizations, such girls/women are subjected to inordinate amounts of sexual aggression. Wallace (1979) tries to point to this phenomenon in *Black Macho and the Myth of the Superwoman,* complaining that the "prettiest" little girls in ghettoes or inner cities seemed to be the most likely candidates for teenage pregnancy. At the same time, many "dark" black women are excluded from feeling good about themselves by the withholding of those acts of ceremonial deference within their own communities that "honor" their womanhood.

Issues of beauty represent just one of the rocky areas of a complex and dangerous course that African American women must negotiate in American culture. Issues of body image, sexuality, white and black cultural definitions of work and family roles, and the way in which black women's deviation from dominant cultural definitions reflects on the total community all combine to place an inordinate amount of pressure on black women. The "Mammy" image, particularly, as expressed in literature, movies, and television, is an assault on black women's work roles. The highly publicized attempt of a crack-addicted mother in St. Louis, Missouri, to sell her infant for twenty dollars worth of crack cocaine may be a singular but dramatic indicator of the damage wrought through cultural humiliation. As Giddings (1984) has noted, in the history of the community, black women have been materially worse off and at the same time exhibited far less social pathology.

The church must take seriously its prophetic role in regard to women's self-esteem. Drug abuse, violence, and teenage pregnancy are all related to issues of low self-esteem. In many ways, both subtle and overt, the vast majority of females in the African American community are assaulted by stereotypes and ideologies that humiliate them (and, incidentally, humiliate by reflection those who use them in their dealings with black women). Although I personally find the sexism and patriarchy of Islam objectionable, particularly in its African American varieties, Islam is currently the only corporate religious voice that states categorically and loudly that American standards of beauty and fashion "shame" and humiliate African American women. Without reverting to a more restrictive view of gender roles, African American churches must address the cultural humiliation of women.

Andolsen (1986) identifies four major areas where white feminists and black feminists disagree. Besides work, rape, and male-female solidarity, the issue of beauty and the racial privilege associated with it stands out as a source of tension. She notes that while the images of black males in the media have changed and become more diverse, the images of black women have not. The "Mammy" and the "Jezebel" still dominate the culturally acceptable images of black women. Actresses who refuse to participate in roles that reinforce stereotypes and culturally demean simply do not work as often and do not reap the economic rewards of those who do. How often do we see Ruby Dee, Esther Rolle, and Cicely Tyson in large-budget motion pictures? How often do we see African American actresses featured in nonstereotypical roles?

Refashioning social meanings and cultural definitions is an essential task for changing society. It is also one of the most controversial and difficult, as the political correctness backlash of the 1990s demonstrates. Critiques of culture depend, for their thoroughness and prophetic insight, on the standpoints or points of view of their authors. If the church thoroughly carries through its challenge to the cultural humiliation of women, the Afro-Christian critique of culture should be the most penetrating and the most prophetic. The production of a humane cultural experience for all African American women depends upon such a radical cultural critique. The church must work to produce that humane experience. The uplift of the downtrodden involves an aggressive campaign to redefine those aspects of culture that demean and exclude and humiliate. Such a prophetic stance involves the call to black women, issued in Alice Walker's (1983) definition of a *womanist*, to be self-loving "regardless."

CONTEMPORARY ISSUES AND SPIRITUAL EMPOWERMENT

If confusion over mission and identity are of any importance in the ability of any group of people to resist oppression, the last decades of the twentieth century may be the worst for African Americans. In spite of the misery and suffering of slavery and the wholesale terror and assault that characterized the Jim Crow era, a unity of purpose and a sense of shared suffering helped mediate the conflicts between women and men. Within the current context of social fragmentation, underclass isolation, and theological diversity, the economic and political issues confronting women are compounded by confusion and conflict over scripturally prescribed roles for women and misperceptions about the actual status of African American women in society. Many male pastors and other spokespersons believe falsely that African American women are doing better than the men in their communities. This is an unfortunate distortion of the situation of a small proportion of professional women. The cultural context of the United States has consistently assaulted and punished the economic roles of black women and, through various public policies, engineered blame for the disadvantage of black men in the direction of black women.

The distorted images of African American women's professional and economic success provide further fuel to many men's belief that the ministry is still the only place where African American men have access to influence and authority. As a result, resistance to women's ordination is still quite fierce among many African American ministers. Currently, the largest black denomination, the National Baptist Convention, U.S.A., Inc. (NBC), does not recognize the ordination of women at a level of national policy. Although the NBC leaves the issue of ordination to the local churches and their associations, the overwhelming sentiment expressed by delegates has rejected efforts of leaders to encourage the acceptance of women's ordination. Contrary to the Baptist legacy of congregational autonomy and freedom of conscience, local and regional Baptist associations will go to great lengths to restrain churches and pastors from ordaining women. At times the struggle to maintain denominational power and public prominence seems to overshadow the response of these organizations to the current emergencies of public life. The black Methodist denominations—African Methodist Episcopal, African Methodist Episcopal Zion, and Christian Methodist Episcopal churches—all ordain women. However, they have elected no women bishops. Several pentecostal denominations, including the largest, the Church of God in Christ, do not officially ordain women, while other denominations do. The picture for women in the ordained ministry *within the historically African American denominations* is not good.

Ironically, there are two contradictions at work among black professionals and white churches. Other black professional men, particularly in male-dominated professions such as medicine and law, have had no problem affirming the leadership of black women, electing them to the presidencies of the National Medical Association and the National Bar Association, as well as to the presidencies of other professional, clinical, and academic associations. Most mainstream white Protestant denominations, with the exception of the Southern Baptist Convention, do affirm white and black women in professional ministry. Episcopalians, United Methodists, Congregationalists, Presbyterians, and Disciples of Christ ordain women without significant conflict. Episcopalians and United Methodists have elected black women bishops, and Presbyterians have elected a black woman as moderator or presiding officer. Ironically, the denominations most associated with upper- and middle-class whites in the United States have provided the greatest access to ecclesiastical authority for black women. These churches are also more flexible in their approach to biblical interpretation. The churches with the greatest mass appeal in black communities facing the greatest crises have thrown up the greatest barriers to women's empowerment in their national bodies and local congregations.

Churches in black communities are more female than their white counterparts. The more "mass" the church, the more female has been the congregation. Regardless of this skewing, Hoover (1979) gives an overall figure of 75 percent to describe women's participation. This figure masks a range that reaches past 90 percent in some congregations of the Sanctified Church (Dodson and Gilkes 1986). The full empowerment of the church to speak to the needs of all African American people cannot be accomplished without the full empowerment of women at every level.

CONCLUSION

This chapter cannot answer all of our questions about the church's mission regarding African American women. One aim has been to identify key ideas or themes that will make it possible not only to serve the needs of African American women in a changing society, but also to contribute to the solution of national problems from a strong, viable, and flexible religious tradition. I believe, in precisely the ways in which the black Christian club women—ministers truly—of the late nineteenth and early twentieth centuries believed when they adopted the motto "Lifting as We Climb," that to struggle and push from the bottom of our communities will mean that the whole community will rise. Listening to and empowering "poor colored women"—whether economically, politically, or culturally "poor"—is essential to the material and spiritual redemption of African American communities.

Our communities sit literally on the edge of cultural, political, and economic destruction. Significant segments of the African American community are experiencing a relentless economic genocide.[5] Our central challenge is this: If the "black church" or the "African American religious experience" or the "Afro-Christian tradition" (whatever we may wish to call it) is as strong as our sagas, legends, and sermons insist that it is, then the church must, in its best historical tradition, respond to this crisis with an internal ministry that addresses the needs of those who are suffering and projects an uncompromising prophetic force outward that demands and effects significant social, economic, political, and cultural change. In an 1886 speech before the colored clergy of the Protestant Episcopal Church in Washington, D.C., Anna Julia Cooper (1892, 32) insisted that:

> "*I am my Sister's keeper!*" should be the hearty response of every man and woman of the race, and this conviction should purify and exalt the narrow, selfish, and petty personal aims of life into a noble and sacred purpose.

We still have not answered Cooper's challenge to become, as a community, as a nation, and most importantly, as a church, our "sister's keeper." The echo of that call to ministry still stands unanswered. Harriet Tubman, Alice Walker's "Celie," and Anna Julia Cooper all challenge us to heed the voices of "poor" colored women. It may not be an overstatement to say that the community's response to the historical roles of black women, particularly active/activist black Christian women within and outside of their churches, may be the key to the moral and historical contributions of the entire black community to the twenty-first century.

REFERENCES

Andrews, William L., ed. 1986. Sisters of the spirit: Three black women's autobiographies of the nineteenth century. Bloomington, IN: Indiana State University Press.

Andolsen, Barbara. 1986. *Daughters of Jefferson, daughters of bootblacks: Racism and American feminism.* Macon, GA: Mercer University Press.

Branch, Taylor. 1988. *Parting the waters: America in the King years, 1954–63.* New York: Simon and Schuster.

Collins, Patricia Hill. 1989. "The social construction of black feminist thought." *Signs: Journal of Women in Culture and Society* 14 (4).

Cooper, Anna Julia. 1892. *A voice from the south by a black woman of the south.* Xenia, Ohio: Aldine.

Davis, Angela. 1981. Women, race, and class. New York: Random House.

Dodson, Jualyne, and Cheryl Townsend Gilkes. 1986. Something within: Social change and collective endurance in the sacred world of black Christian women. In *Women and Religion in America*, ed. Rosemary Radford Ruether and Rosemary Keller, vol. 3. San Francisco: Harper & Row.

Fields, Mamie Garvin, with Karen Fields. 1983. *Lemon Swamp and other places: A Carolina memoir.* New York: Free Press.

Frazier, E. Franklin. 1939. The Negro family in the United States. Chicago: University of Chicago Press.

Giddings, Paula. 1984. *When and where I enter . . . : The impact of black women on race and sex in America.* New York: William Morrow.

Gilkes, Cheryl Townsend. 1985. 'Together and in harness': Women's traditions in the sanctified Church. *Signs: Journal of Women in Culture and Society* 11(4): 80–130.

———. 1986. The roles of church and community mothers: Ambivalent American sexism of fragmented African familyhood? *Journal of Feminist Studies in Religion* 2 (Spring): 41–59.

Grant, Joanne, producer. 1986. "Fundi: The story of Ella Baker." New York: Icanus Films.

Hamilton, Charles V. 1972. *The black preacher in America*. New York: William Morrow.

Harper, Frances Ellen Watkins. 1987. Tola Leroy or the shadows uplifted. Boston: Beacon Press (originally published 1893).

Higgenbotham, Evelyn Brooks Barnett. 1978. Nannie Helen Burroughs and the education of black women. In *The Afro-American woman: Struggles and images*, eds. Sharon Harley and Rosalyn Terborg-Penn. Port Washington, NY: Kennikat.

———. 1988. Religion, politics, and gender: The leadership of Nannie Helen Burroughs. *Journal of Religious Thought* 44 (Winter–Spring): 7–22.

———. 1993. *Righteous discontent: The women's movement in the black Baptist Church, 1880–1920*. Cambridge: Harvard University Press.

Hoover, Theressa. 1980. Black women and the churches: Triple jeopardy. In *Black Theology: A Documentary History, 1966–1979*, Gayraud S. Wilmore and James H. Cone. Maryknoll, NY: Orbis.

Jones, Jacqueline. 1985. *Labor of love, labor of sorrow: Black women, work and the family from slavery to the present*. New York: Basic Books.

King, Deborah K. 1988. Multiple jeopardy, multiple consciousness: The context of black feminist ideology. *Signs: Journal of Women in Culture and Society* 14(1): 42–72.

King, Mary. 1987. *Freedom song: A personal story of the 1960s Civil Rights movement*. New York: William Morrow.

Mills, Kay. 1993. *This little light of mine: The life of Fannie Lou Hamer*. New York: Dutton.

Painter, Nell Irvin. 1977. *The exodusters: Black migration to Kansas after Reconstruction*. New York: Random House.

Reagon, Bernice Johnson. 1983. Coalition politics: Turning the century. In *Home Girls: A Black Feminist Anthology*, ed. Barbara Smith. New York: Kitchen Table.

Richardson, Mailyn, ed. 1987. *Maria W. Stewart, America's first black woman political writer*. Bloomington, IN: Indiana University Press.

Robinson, Jo Ann Gibson. 1987. *The Montgomery bus boycott and the women who started it: The memoir of Jo Ann Gibson Robinson*. Knoxville, TN: University of Tennessee Press.

Rothenberg, Paula S. 1988. *Racism and sexism: An integrated study*. New York: St. Martin's.

Schur, Edwin. 1984. *Labeling women deviant: Gender, stigma and social control*. New York: Random House.

Sernett, Milton C. 1989. On freedom's threshold: The African American presence in central New York, 1760–1940. In *The African American Presence in New York State: Four Regional History Surveys*, ed. Monroe Fordham. Albany, NY: New York African American Institute.

Sterling, Dorothy. 1984. *We are your sisters: Black women in the nineteenth century*. New York: W. W. Norton.

Walker, Alice. 1982. *The color purple*. San Diego, CA: Harcourt Brace Jovanovich.

———. 1983. *In search of our mothers' gardens: Womanist prose*. San Diego, CA: Harcourt Brace Jovanovich.

Wallace, Michelle. 1979. *Black macho and the myth of the superwoman*. New York: Dial.

Webber, Thomas L. 1978. *Deep like the rivers: Education in the slave quarter community, 1831–1865*. New York: W. W. Norton.

White, Deborah Gray. 1985. *Ar'n't I a woman? Female slaves in the plantation south*. New York: W. W. Norton.

Wilhelm, Sydney. 1971. *Who needs the Negro*. New York: Doubleday.

———.1973. "Equality: America's Racist Theology." Pp. 136–157 in Joyce Ladner, editor, *The Death of White Sociology*. New York: Random House.

Wilmore, Gayraud S. 1983. *Black religion and black radicalism: An interpretation of the religious history of Afro-American people*. 2nd ed. Maryknoll, NY: Orbis.

Wilson, William Julius. 1980. *The declining significance of race: Blacks and changing American institutions.* Chicago: University of Chicago Press.

Woodson, Carter G. 1930. The Negro washerwoman. *The Journal of Negro History* 15(3): 269–77.

NOTES

1. Prathia Hall Wynn, in an unpublished paper, has identified sexism as an oppression visited on the *entire* black community. She points out, and rightly so, that the critical involvement of women in the material survival of the community and its institutions (church and family) means that women's poverty and degradation extends to the entire community.

2. This term is offered by Katie G. Cannon.

3. I use the term *poor* not only as a designation for those whose incomes place them below the poverty line, but in a way similar to that in which James Cone uses the term *black*—as a label designating those who stand in solidarity with "the least of these," and, for the purposes of this discussion, the least of these are "poor" black women.

4. One of the most helpful discussions of this I have experienced was at a black feminist panel discussion on racism and self-hatred held at Simmons College in Boston, Massachusetts, in the early 1980s. The exact date and conference escape me now.

5. Although left out of many of the current discussions of the underclass, I think that Sydney Wilhelm's 1971 *Who Needs the Negro* (Garden City, NY: Doubleday) provides an important and provocative context that needs re-examination. His thesis, using the Native American experience as a historical example, argues that any group that becomes economically useless becomes a prime target for genocide. In a later essay, Wilhelm (1973) also points out that claims of racial equality function as racist ideologies since economic discrimination maintains the same essential state of white over black.

12 Reclaiming the Souls of Black Men Folk: The Mission of African American Religious Institutions

ROBERT MICHAEL FRANKLIN

This chapter describes the current status of African American males relative to several social indicators, reporting the conclusions of group interviews with black males concerning their nonparticipation in traditional black churches. Maintaining that a crisis faces black men, one that is fundamentally spiritual, we suggest that religious institutions are obligated to create new ministries and persist in current outreach ministries to these men. While other government and private approaches to what we here term the "black male crisis" have addressed symptoms, in this chapter we propose that public and private institutions collaborate to affect the causes.

The chapter concludes with four policy-related goals for religious institutions seeking to uplift the status of African American men. To achieve them, government agencies and corporations must become financial partners with the central hope-giving institutions in the African American community. The recommended goals are (a) to enable men to overcome the disabling effects of excessive individualism, (b) to develop positive self-images and personal responsibility, (c) to facilitate intrafamilial reconciliation while teaching interpersonal skills, and (d) to teach marketable work skills.

THE SPIRITUAL CRISIS FOR
AFRICAN AMERICAN MALES

For African American males in contemporary America, these are the best and the worst of times. Television's popular situation comedies often feature black males. During the 1988 presidential election campaign, diverse commentators admitted that the most intellectually stimulating and emotionally arousing campaign was that orchestrated by Jesse Jackson, a black male. The political outcome of the phenomenon placed a black male, Ron Brown, as chairperson of the National Democratic Party (later to become Secretary of Commerce under President Bill Clinton). A black man serves as pastor of the historic Riverside Church of New York City. And, black male rap and jazz musicians and professional athletes define American popular cultural trends, which are followed by youth around the world.

At the same time, for many Americans, black males constitute the nation's most enigmatic and threatening segment of the population. Recently, considerable media attention has been focused on a melancholy litany of dubious distinctions. These daily reports feed us images of black men who are violent, unemployed, misogynous, irresponsible, and drug dependent.

Perhaps the most ominous among these reports is a *Time* magazine feature story, "Today's Native Sons: Inner-City Black Males are America's Newest Lost Generation" (December 1, 1986). The authors write that although black men account for only 6 percent of America's population, they make up half of the male population of its penal system. While the national unemployment rate is 6.9 percent, for black men it is 15 percent; and for black teens, it remains more than 40 percent.[1] The leading cause of death among black males between the ages of 15 and 24 is homicide. The current average life expectancy (65 years) for black men is less than that for white men more that 40 years ago. Black men are increasingly absent from the home, with almost 60 percent of all births to black women occurring out of wedlock. Finally, the number of black men enrolled in college is declining rapidly.

Scholars and public leaders have sought to portray the predicament of "today's native sons" as a threat not merely to the future of the African American family and community, but to the entire society, thereby making it a cause for concerted public and private action.

Speaking to the 1988 annual convention of the American Psychological Association, Dr. Joseph N. Gayles, Jr., vice president of the Morehouse School of Medicine, said, "It is important for our society to view black male health—both physical and mental—as a major public policy problem and address its solution as a social malignancy affecting . . . the very fabric of American society."[2]

Notwithstanding this catalogue of despair, the public sector has not deemed this state of affairs severe or significant enough to merit intervention. Federal and state government agencies have done little more than expand job opportunities in the military services and construct new prisons to house these problematic citizens.

Regrettably, many religious institutions have exhibited similar ambivalent regard for black males who fit the underclass profile. In general, churches are more successful in providing ministry to middle-class, educated men. Far from developing innovative and effective outreach ministries to poor men, most black churches seem to share the wider society's posture of fear, mistrust, impatience, and contempt for them. It would be exceedingly tragic for the black community and the nation if hundreds of thousands of young black male lives were to become "wasted treasures" due to the combined effects of structural oppression, personal irresponsibility, and community neglect.

The underlying premise of this chapter is that, because religious institutions are the principal zones in which moral values are taught, they have a nonnegotiable obligation to persist in reaching this endangered population, who continue to be God's children, no matter how debased. Churches, temples, and mosques have done well in the past and must renew their missions with intelligence and gusto. The history of African American home missions work includes stories of breathtaking redemption as manifest in the lives of persons such as Malcolm X, as well as the common stories of millions of nameless men who have been empowered to resist and overcome the traumas of oppression.

In my judgment, the crisis of the black male in America is fundamentally, although not exclusively, spiritual. I use the term *spiritual* to refer to an ensemble of features, including a human being's basic sense of personhood in relation to an ultimate concern, commonly named God. The spiritual dimension is the locus of a person's most fundamental values and commitments, an internal center that is the source of love and the hopeful affirmation of life and the future. From this realm springs forth the human longing for truth, goodness, and beauty in the world. In the African American community, spirituality has been understood to be a holistic style of living that is attentive both to the personal and social dimensions and qualities of wholeness and justice.

To be sure, the spiritual crisis of black men entails other significant dimensions—political, economic, cultural—but throughout history, black men have suffered the indignity of deprivation in each of these zones without losing hope, defiance, spirit, collective purpose, and confidence in God. Following the analysis of sociologist William Julius Wilson, I am suggesting that something new has occurred in the modern, post-Civil Rights movement era. Wilson characterizes this contrast in the following words:

> In the mid-1960s, urban analysts began to speak of a *new dimension to the urban crisis* in the form of a large subpopulation of low-income families and individuals whose behavior contrasted sharply with the behavior of the general population. Despite a high rate of poverty in ghetto neighborhoods throughout the first half of the twentieth century, rates of inner-city joblessness, teenage pregnancies, out-of-wedlock births, female-headed families, welfare dependency, and serious crime were significantly lower than in later years and did not reach *catastrophic proportions until the mid-1970s.* (Italics mine)[3]

It is important to remember that the internal spiritual crisis discussed here is linked ineluctably to broader national and global circumstances, such as this nation's economic slip into postindustrial decline, the retreat of the Reagan and Bush presidencies from funding social welfare programs, ongoing malaise concerning public morality that began two decades ago with the Watergate revelations, the infusion of narcotics into urban centers matched with the gradual tolerance for drug use and marketing in many communities, and the devastating effects of the Vietnam War upon the collective American consciousness—effects we have yet to fully exorcise. Together, this ensemble of social ills has conspired to "reexpose the spiritual, economic, and political chaos existent in the African American community," which highlights the inability or "failure of the church in recent history to respond significantly to those conditions."[4]

To face crisis means to make decisions. What is at stake here is nothing less than the souls of black men folk. Will they reclaim the inner resources necessary to resist the onslaughts of injustice, domination, depression, and weariness? Or, will they succumb to the near-overwhelming forces of destruction? Whatever the case, men must take responsibility for themselves and decide to do the right thing.

As we approach a new century, this spiritual challenge will be so monumental that to survive will require a dynamic amalgam of spiritual, moral, cognitive, and behavioral resources, which can be found most readily in the great faith traditions, and especially in Christianity and traditional African religions.

Here, we will briefly identify and discuss some of the major issues facing African American religious institutions as they seek to minister to men, and will suggest ways in which the private sector may contribute to the moral regeneration of African American men. While I am somewhat uncomfortable with isolating the status of black men from their interdependent linkages to women and children, I take comfort in knowing that my distinguished colleagues give attention in this volume to the broader dimensions of the black family's future. Also, when I refer to African American religious institutions, I primarily have the black churches in mind, as they have been what C. Eric Lincoln and Lawrence Mamiya in *The Black Church in the African American Experience,* refer to as the central institutional sector of African American life.[5] However, I will attempt to include other faith traditions throughout.

In *Black Men,* a fine collection of essays edited by Lawrence E. Gary, Dr. James S. Tinney presents a brief but insightful synopsis, "The Religious Experience of Black Men."[6] Tinney does not address the experience of non-Christian men. He argues that the black church is a male institution, because some men (particularly clergy) have benefited positively from it, especially in terms of leadership development, psychological liberation, intellectual growth, financial reward, and encouragement of male authority in the home. But, for most laymen, the story is very different. Indeed, he notes that, "many black males seem uninterested in, or hostile to, the black church" (269). A slight overstatement could claim that the church is *female space owned and operated by men.*

While preparing my master's thesis at Harvard Divinity School, I tried to account for the paradox cited by Tinney. Through a series of group interviews, I recorded black male explanations for their exodus from the church. The explanations include the following institutional factors:

1. The social teachings of Christianity encourage passivity and meekness, which are dysfunctional in street cultures.
2. The image of the moral person embraced in the churches is comprised of a disproportionate number of so-called feminine character traits, such as quiescence, humility, nonassertiveness, and self-sacrifice, which repel men in pursuit of machismo.
3. Since the Civil Rights movement, most churches have withdrawn from vigorous social activism and have turned their attention to institutional expansion and physical improvement.
4. Even when involved in politics, churches are insufficiently radical and prophetic in their political orientations, choosing to support rather than fight the powers that be.
5. Worship in the churches tends to be excessively long and often thematically unintelligible.
6. The dominant religious symbols of the church are problematic in either expressing devotion to Eurocentric aesthetic values (the Westernized Christ figure) or in failing to adequately portray black life in America.
7. Churches are preoccupied with fund raising and tend to be insensitive to poor people.
8. Churches seem to tolerate obvious hypocrisy among valued members, while inducing excessive guilt among ordinary folk, especially in relation to personal behavior that pertains to sexuality and recreational drug or alcohol use.

Although a growing number of progressive clergy and congregations are working to correct many of these items, in general, the churches have not changed significantly. These exodus explanations are still valid for many men, although less prominently than during the late 1960s to mid 1970s. By the end of the 1970s and the beginning of the 1980s, significant developments occurring generally within society and specifically within the African American community resulted in increased black male religious participation. Together, these related social forces created a push/pull dynamic from which churches and other religious institutions benefited.

First, the repressive climate resulting from economic and social policies fostered by President Reagan's administration *pushed* many black men back into religious institutions searching for community support and answers to tough life questions. Second, reforms within the Black Church initiated by a new generation of sophisticated black clergy, who were products of the black liberation theology movement, *pulled* many disaffected men back into the churches. We should not equate mere church attendance with the inner transformation necessary for personal wholeness. But, reaffiliation with a community of faith is an important first step in claiming one's identity as a member of a community of hope, struggle, and accountability. If this phenomenon continues, it could offer hope for the religious regeneration of black men and the heightened vigor of black church ministries to them.

Historians and social scientists have demonstrated that during periods in which the social status of blacks is threatened, black nationalist ideas ascend to the community's ideological forefront. During the Reagan era, former President Carter's measures supporting black causes were systematically dismantled and a climate of selfishness and insensitivity to people of color was fostered. As black frustration and hopelessness increased, religious leadership in the community began to mobilize masses in constructive ways. Two of the most significant mass leaders at this time were Reverend Jesse Jackson, who served as a catalyst for the movement that led to Harold Washington's 1983 mayoral victory, and Minister Louis Farrakhan, whose unique oratorical abilities offended the establishment while endearing him to the urban underclass. Although Farrakhan's legitimacy has been called into question by many, it is undeniable that portions of his message counteract precisely the despair at the core of the spiritual crisis that is the focus of this chapter. To the extent that young people who, like Malcolm X, have joined the Nation of Islam and have been transformed from hopeless, self-destructive misfits into proud, optimistic, and self-respecting citizens, then, Farrakhan's effectiveness as a religious leader is validated.

During the 1983 Washington campaign crusade, one could attend any Saturday morning meeting of Operation P.U.S.H. and find thousands of people, including a remarkable number of men, gathered for what was more than a political rally. It was a religious phenomenon, a spiritual revival of collective hope, purpose, and self-determination. Men who would not attend church the next morning attended faithfully each week. In these meetings, Reverend Jesse Jackson, the charismatic Baptist preacher, revived hope, analyzed injustice, and outlined a concrete political agenda that included these men.

With respect to Farrakhan, I personally witnessed large numbers of young men who had been involved previously in self-destructive behavior join his organization and experience moral regeneration. While social scientific studies of the so-called Black Muslim movement observe that such "conversions" tend to be intense and short lived, one cannot deny that something extraordinary can happen to young men whom society has written off, if the correct spiritual magnet is present to attract them. Even more fascinating, in my opinion, was Farrakhan's decision to register and vote for Mayor Washington, a departure from former Black Muslim practice. Not only had he "converted" these young men, he politicized them, thereby countering the charge that black religious "cults" are typically apolitical and otherworldly. Reverend Jackson, in turn, politicized large numbers of Holiness-Pentecostal congregations, which have tended to emphasize turning away from this world in preparation for the next.

To understand the spiritual impact of Reagan's presidency on African American men, we must pause to recognize the enormous amount of pain in poor, black communities. In large measure, this pain is the consequence of racism, sexism, poverty, and abandonment by the government and much of the black middle class. Psychoanalysts refer to the ego defense mechanism, wherein pain is often masked by anger. For most men I know, anger is easier—that is, more socially acceptable—to express than pain. But even here there is a racial double standard. Whereas racism permits white men to be angry with impunity, it insures that black male rage is carefully monitored, suppressed, and punished. Hence, one of the great challenges to the health of black men lies in discovering appropriate ways to express pain and anger. Religious institutions that facilitate this sort of therapy tend to be attractive to men. This was part of the genius of Elijah Muhammad's Nation of Islam, which produced men such as Malcolm X, who understood and diagnosed black self-hatred, hurt, and rage with brilliant clarity and force.

Racially insensitive government policies have driven many men and women to search for more constructive and organized ways of making rage articulate. I am persuaded that this environment contributed to the resurgence of the Nation of Islam and to the religio-political crusades that elected mayors Harold Washington and Wilson Goode, and projected Reverend Jesse Jackson into the international messianic spotlight.

The second part of the push/pull dynamic is the emergence of a cadre of sophisticated pastors who are products of black liberation theology, persons such as the Reverends Wyatt Tee Walker in Harlem; William Augustus Jones in Brooklyn; John Bryant and Cecilia Bryant in Baltimore; Jeremiah Wright, Jr., in Chicago; H. Beecher Hicks in Washington, D.C.; Cameron Alexander and McKinley Young in Atlanta; Prathia Wynn in Philadelphia; Charles Blake in Los Angeles; Samuel McKinney in Seattle; Amos Brown in San Francisco; and J. Alfred Smith in Oakland. Like Dr. Martin Luther King, Jr., these women and men were, for the most part, educated in historically black colleges, active during the Civil Rights movement, and sought to delicately blend radical politics with middle-class lifestyles. With black theologian James Cone providing textual vision for the movement, these leaders began to combine Christianity with black nationalism, thereby infusing traditional black church life with new vitalities. The result is that their churches have attracted significant numbers of men who experience personal wholeness. These leaders and their congregations provide us with contemporary models of facilitating the constructive expression of pain and anger, organizing and transforming powerless persons into political agents, and instilling confidence in a God who cares.

MAJOR ISSUES FOR THE AFRICAN AMERICAN MINISTRY

We now consider major issues facing African American religious institutions as they minister to men. Obviously, a huge list of such issues

could be generated. As we are focusing on the short period of time sep-
arating us from the next century, we will here deal with a proposed
agenda for the next ten years, articulating four major concerns in the
form of goals: (a) overcoming the disabling effects of hyper-individu-
alism, (b) developing self-esteem and personal responsibility,
(c) reconciling and reintegrating family relationships, and (d) acquiring marketable skills. Note the absence of any specific mention of
drugs, crime, and so forth. Returning to my premise that the black
male crisis is fundamentally spiritual, I maintain that substance abuse
and other pathologies are *symptoms,* not *causes,* of the crisis. If we
heal the human spirit, it will not permit imposed or self-inflicted forms
of dehumanization.

Overcoming Individualism

The stress of postindustrial urban life, together with Enlightenment
era liberal ideologies of individual autonomy and self-sufficiency,
have created a culture of busy, fragmented, self-centered individual-
ists. In this culture, men are encouraged and rewarded for
independence and mobility, which does not make for good relationships or mental health. Far from being a healthy personal goal, I think
that excessive autonomy, or what I shall term "rabid individualism,"
represents a form of neurosis and self-deception. The crisis is compounded for men who do not have access to conventional means for
achieving and expressing their independence. When persons do not
have an honest, reliable support system to affirm and challenge their
behavior, they may resort to destructive avenues of expression, as is
evident in the drug subculture.

Religious institutions have a role to play here that may be supported
and reinforced by the public sector and other private institutions. The
goal is to help the rabid individualist to have some meaningful and
wholesome group experience. In my limited experience, the small-
group format, such as the encounter group, is more effective than the
large mass meeting. Religious institutions can provide the space and
some of the leadership for black male spiritual encounter groups. Just
as some affluent business leaders have established trust funds to reward inner-city youth for completing high school while avoiding drug
addiction or pregnancy, public and private sector agencies could help

fund and reward men for being responsible in attending group meetings and doing some sort of community service. If religious institutions are to compete with the street subculture for the allegiance of men, they must offer an alternate reward system that combines status and money. Even these realities have their proper place in African American spirituality, which has always been holistic and affirming of material and spiritual fulfillment—of personal and social transformation. The image of Jesus affirmed in black churches is that of both an ascetic and a prophetic critic of human culture, and at the same time the reigning sovereign lord of creation.

Developing Self-Esteem

It is exceedingly important for black men to reaffirm their identity as members of a community rather than as atomistic, disconnected free agents. One of the positive effects of a renewed communal identity is a deeper sense of personal responsibility and self-esteem. As the community affirms these men as valuable members, they can fulfill their potential as parents, protectors, and leaders. Men who love themselves properly will not seek to dehumanize women or show indifference toward children. Because society's current depths of psychological pain, personal powerlessness, and self-hatred are unprecedented, prayerful patience and creativity must be brought to bear.

One of the measures of the depth of this "new pain" is found in the realm of the arts. To my knowledge, no major black novel or film has portrayed the growing phenomena of black male suicide and fratricide. Even blues artists (the voice of our folk wisdom tradition) have not yet articulated its depth. Yet, black male suicide and homicide rates are chillingly high. Fortunately, young rap artists have begun to address the despair in hopeful songs, such as the hit single "Self Destruction," by the Stop the Violence Movement, a collection of rap stars.

It is too easy to be glib about the church's role in this transformation process. It is one thing for churches to preach self-esteem, but another to go into threatening places to spend time with troubled souls. It will not be easy for churches to overcome their fear of men who have victimized them in the past. But church members must remember that every crisis is a moment of opportunity for something new to emerge.

Each time the churches initiate social movements, such as antidrug rallies and political campaigns, they provide men with alternatives to apathy, powerlessness, and self-hatred. Such self-esteem campaigns must enlist the services of our most visible, charismatic, and influential leaders and artists. These efforts should be funded by corporate sources and government grants, because all persons, and society as a whole, benefit from men who are productive, peaceful citizens.

Reconciling Family Relationships

As men are reintegrated into the religious community and develop new self-respect, esteem, and responsibility, they can do much to overcome and reconcile strained family relationships. Black men and women must become friends and partners in the struggle for a meaningful and healthy collective existence. We need to be educated in the art of wholesome interpersonal relations and family formation. Someone must teach us how to communicate better, how to resolve conflicts without resorting to violence or abusive language, and how to resist temptations that compromise high-quality relationships. This must include basic public health information, so that we may take the steps necessary to eradicate AIDS in our infant population and to promote better nutrition and personal grooming.

Religious institutions are in a unique position to promote such moral education. They can provide forums for lectures, films, and role plays to teach some of the virtues that such positive media role models as *The Cosby Show* emphasized. Again, private-sector agencies and corporations should be mobilized to financially support programs for family reconciliation and public health.

Developing Marketable Skills

One hundred years ago, Booker T. Washington, president of Tuskegee Institute, preached a gospel of the "hand, head, and heart," urging African Americans to develop those technological, industrial, agricultural, spiritual, and intellectual habits and skills that would make them noble, productive citizens. We need to hear his gospel again. Black economists of every political persuasion have challenged African Americans to transform their status as consumers to producers of desirable goods.

Religious institutions can take up the challenge and create schools where technical skills can be taught. For many reasons, some men may be intimidated by formal, school-based educational programs. Churches can provide a safe space where they can learn marketable skills and be affirmed for their willingness to try again. Corporations can expand their commitment to hiring and training men who may not be as productive initially as other workers. Government should reward and encourage companies to do this through tax breaks and similar measures.

Most of the suggestions offered here are not novel or unreasonable, though implementing them will require courageous and visionary leadership. I think such leaders are in place, or awaiting the call to action. Achieving the goals stated here will also require the unselfish commitment of private and public sector institutions, thereby reversing the trends of the past decades. It remains to be seen whether such commitments can be evoked. The souls of black men folk cry out for our attention. May we heed W. E. B. Du Bois, who delivered these stirring words to the commencement audience at Howard University on 6 June 1930:

> To increase abiding satisfaction for the mass of our people, and for all people, someone must sacrifice something of his own happiness. This is a duty only to those who recognize it as a duty. The larger the number ready to sacrifice, the smaller the total sacrifice necessary . . . It is silly to tell intelligent human beings: Be good and you will be happy. The truth is today, be good, be decent, be honorable and self-sacrificing and you will not always be happy. You will often be desperately unhappy. You may even be crucified, dead and buried, and the third day you will be just as dead as the first. But with the death of your happiness may easily come increased happiness and satisfaction and fulfillment for other people—strangers, unborn babes, uncreated worlds. If this is not sufficient incentive, never try it—remain hogs.[7]

REFERENCES

Du Bois, W. E. B. 1970. Education and work. In *W. E. B. Du Bois Speaks,* ed. Philip S. Foner. New York: Pathfinder.

Lamar, Jacob V., Jr., et al. 1986. Today's native sons: Inner-city black males are America's newest lost generation. *Time* (1 December): 26–29.

Lincoln, C. Eric, and Lawrence H. Mamiya. 1990. *The black church in the African American experience.* Durham, NC: Duke University Press.

Tinney, James S. 1981. The religious experience of black men. In *Black men,* ed. Lawrence E. Gary. Beverly Hills, CA: Sage.

Wilson, William Julius. 1987. *The truly disadvantaged: The inner city, the underclass, and public policy.* Chicago: University of Chicago Press.

NOTES

1. Jacob V. Lamar, Jr., "Today's Native Sons. Inner-City Black Males are America's Newest Lost Generation," *Time* (1 December 1986), 26–29.

2. Dr. Joseph N. Gayles, Jr., quoted in Ann Hardie, "Problems Facing Black Men Threaten U.S. Society, Psychologists Say," *Atlanta Constitution,* 15 August, 1988, section D.

3. William Julius Wilson, *The Truly Disadvantaged: The Inner City, the Disadvantaged, and Public Policy* (Chicago: University of Chicago Press, 1987), 3.

4. Khalil Abdullah, prepublication review of this chapter, 1990.

5. C. Eric Lincoln and Lawrence H. Mamiya, *The Black Church in the African American Experience* (Durham, NC: Duke University Press, 1990).

6. James S. Tinney, "The Religious Experience of Black Men," in *Black Men,* ed. Lawrence E. Gary (Beverly Hills, CA: Sage, 1981), 269–76.

7. W. E. B. Du Bois, "Education and Work," in *W. E. B. Du Bois Speaks,* vol. 2, ed. Philip S. Foner (New York: Pathfinder, 1970), 74.

13 The Black Church as a Resource for the Twenty-First Century

CLARENCE G. NEWSOME

One of my colleagues is quick to point out, whenever he is asked to discuss the black church in one way or another, that in truth there exists no such entity as the black church, if one wishes to speak of a monolithic structure. Rather, there are, he posits, churches within a quite diverse religious community, which differ as to theology, doctrine, polity, and perceptions of what constitutes authentic religious experience, and which also differ as to the legitimacy or efficacy of political action and involvement.[1]

While I agree in principle with this point of view, I think it is possible nonetheless to speak of the reality of the black church, if we accept this nomenclature as a metaphor for a religious orientation common to black Americans who profess to be Christian. As W. C. Turner has noted, this religious orientation is characterized in large measure by a worldview in which belief in the God of Christianity gives rise to an unequivocal commitment to racial equality and the principles of democracy by way of a tripartite emphasis on prophetic social consciousness, moral integrity, and spiritual empowerment.[2] Inasmuch as the black church can be so defined, it can be a most significant resource for the twenty-first century. Moreover, through any of its constituent congregations, denominations, or church agencies, it holds such potential because of this traditional threefold emphasis. It does not represent a cure-all to the many problems likely to confront African Americans.

These problems will likely be too vast. Nonetheless, the black church can play a significant, if not major, role in their amelioration.

According to many forecasts, the twenty-first century promises to be a time of unrivaled prosperity. Life during the era of high technology, the "third wave," as Alvin Toffler characterizes it, will be unprecedented in that it will combine the best of both the first and second waves of human history, the eras of agrarian and industrial development. The result will be a period of heightened productivity, leisure, and personal fulfillment.[3]

But, as with all things that sound too good to be true, there will be a downside. In part, the downside has to do with the fact that the full emergence of the third wave will require widespread social readjustments, perhaps more vast than those attending the previous shift (the "second wave") from a primarily rural to an intensively urbanized society. Where the second wave favored the creation of large centralized labor forces to service industrialization, the third wave will not only lead to the dissolution of these forces but, because of the specialized and select skill requirements of high technology, will also likely bring about the obsolescence of mass labor. Large numbers of laborers, highly employable and much needed during the industrial boom, will become as obsolete as the smokestacks that now stand cold and crumbling in factory and mill towns throughout the United States.

In large measure, it is this downside that is portended in the 1988 report by the Commission on Minority Participation in Education and American Life, "One-Third of a Nation." The contention that, by the year 2000, one-third of all Americans will be members of minority groups is highly suggestive. This figure, if taken alone, is no opprobrious statistic. Seen in isolation, it can be said to be a positive sign of the nation's increasing diversity, cultural as well as demographic. But when the sociohistorical and economic context is considered fully, it does indeed call attention to an impending problem, namely that the same one-third will "suffer disproportionately from unemployment, inadequate education, ill health, and other social and economic handicaps."[4]

The report is consistent with a statement issued by the Ford Foundation in spring 1988, which states that America is beginning to experience what the foundation terms "the new permanence of poverty."[5] For the first time, a group of people are emerging in the nation's life who can be legitimately categorized as chronically poor. In the newsletter, poverty is classified on the basis of income levels persisting for eight years or more. In just two years, from 1986 to 1988, the poverty rate in the United States increased 8.2 percent, from 12.6 to 21.8. Of those categorized as impoverished, 3 percent are clearly identified as chronically poor, and this percentage is rising annually.[6]

What is startling is that during the twenty-first century one-third of the nation may be chronically poor, caught in a cycle of poverty with no escape from generation to generation. It is quite conceivable that during the next century America will experience a kind of postindustrial slavery, a bondage as awful and as despicable as that suffered by blacks prior to the Civil War. In a very real sense, it is quite possible to say that the downside of the third wave will be such a postindustrial slavery, identifiable not only in America but throughout the world. It is already evident to a significant degree in many South American countries, notably Columbia, El Salvador, and Peru. There is, however, no better example at present than South Africa.

Perhaps it would be helpful to focus momentarily on South Africa, for the events taking place there could very well prove ominous for America during the twenty-first century. By any standard of Western industrialism, South Africa is a wealthy nation. Yet, the gap between rich and poor is as wide and as glaring as in any place on the globe. In fact, South Africa has the highest measure of economic inequality of the fifty-seven countries for which data are available.

In South Africa as a whole, including the tribal reserves, the proportion of the total population living below subsistence in 1980 was estimated by economist Charles Simkins to be 50 percent. For black Africans throughout the country, the proportion was estimated to be nearly two-thirds; but in the reserves, no less than 81 percent of the households were in dire poverty. By contrast, whites constituted less than one-sixth of the total population but earned almost two-thirds of the total income. Black Africans comprised three-quarters of the total population and earned only one-quarter of the total income.[7]

Perhaps it can be said that comparing America to South Africa, even if prospectively, is like comparing apples to oranges. Among other things, South Africa's recently eliminated (in law, if not yet in practice) system of apartheid has been a dominant factor in the poverty rate and the disfranchisement of its black African population.

But, any rejoinder must note that race and/or ethnicity is a common factor shaping the wedge dividing the "haves" from the "have nots" in both countries. Moreover, it is equally important to raise the question of the difference between segregation de jure and segregation de facto. To be sure, at one level it can be said that America has a much better track record on desegregation than South Africa. But, on another level, we are compelled to ask: What is the essential difference? For example, what is the essential difference between a "reserve" overpopulated by South Africans and an urban ghetto overpopulated by African Americans, Hispanic Americans, and, to a lesser degree, Asian Americans? In both cases segregation is real. In both instances the faces of poverty are many: malnutrition, physically and/or intellectually stunted growth, single-parent homes, family breakups, joblessness, crime, drug abuse, high infant mortality rates, high murder rates, high incarceration rates, and so on.

Since the birth rate among white Americans is declining at a time when it is escalating among African Americans and other minority groups in the United States, it could very well be the case that by the end of the twenty-first century much more than one-third of the nation will be dispossessed; mirroring the current South African situation, it could be as much as three-fourths. The same case may hold for the world population by the end of the next century, unless something is done now.

But what is to be done? More to the point, what resources are available for an attempt to do anything at all? Primary among the resources at our disposal is the black church. No institution in American life is more tried or tested or suited to help reverse the apparent trends of the twentieth century in America and throughout the world. It is an institution created by a dispossessed, disfranchised, and economically impoverished people. It has a long history, albeit not always glowing, of involvement in turning (however slightly or imperceptibly) the course of events to the advantage of those whom the privileged would consign to the underside of history. One way in which the black church can be such a resource is by remaining true to its historic threefold emphasis: prophetic social consciousness, especially as it bears upon issues of racial equality and human rights; moral integrity; and spiritual empowerment.

RACIAL EQUALITY AND HUMAN RIGHTS

From its inception in the eighteenth century, a prophetic social consciousness has been one of the distinguishing attributes of the black church. From the time that blacks gathered on the Byrd plantation in Mecklenburg County, Virginia, to organize a Baptist church in 1758 to the organization of the A.M.E. and A.M.E. Zion churches in 1816 and 1822, respectively, up to the Civil Rights movement of the 1960s and the black theology/black power thrust of the 1970s and 1980s, the black church has been vocal in one way or another in calling the nation to task for acts of social, political, and economic injustice.

In the coming days, the black church cannot afford to retreat from its longstanding commitment to social and political justice. Few other institutions in America can be relied upon to speak the truth in love or to act compassionately on behalf of those who live their lives on the margins of society. Certainly the federal government cannot be counted on to any satisfactory degree. In truth, a retreat on the part of the black church would prove as detrimental to the nation in general as to the black community in particular. The nation needs the black church to remind it over and again that it is a nation created "under God."

In this regard, to be a resource to the nation and the world during the next century, the black church must evince more than a superficial awareness of current events. Its leadership, as well as its laity, must demonstrate current, thorough understanding of transactions in the sociopolitical and economic marketplace. Over the years, it has resisted, despite prior characterizations to the contrary, the temptation to become wholly "other-worldly" or nontemporal in orientation.[8] Certainly the church has not always been as forthright as it should when addressing temporal matters. But it has never abandoned its commitment to earthly, mundane affairs, nor should it be inclined to do so now in any guise.

On the other hand, the black church should not permit itself to become so engrossed in the mundane that it abdicates its mandate to prophesy. It can ill afford to bury its ecclesiastical head in the sand of denominational politics and the like. Further, it should resist all tendencies at both the local and general levels to make of itself a world wholly unto itself. Instead, it should work to transform the world by positioning itself squarely at the intersection of time and eternity, that point where the affairs of human history are assessed, analyzed, critiqued, and interpreted in light of the perceived will of God, particularly as discernable through the teachings of the Christian faith.

The black church will be capable of apprehending the truth, for example, while the cleavage is growing wider between white and minority groups in America (and throughout the world), a cleavage is also growing within racial and/or ethnic groups. It is no secret that the chasm between middle-class blacks and the black poor has become as critical as the gap between blacks and whites. At the intersection of time and eternity, the black church can "tell it like it is." Compassionately, but firmly and forthrightly, it can say that the lure America used to divide blacks and poor whites during slavery and Reconstruction is the same one being used to divide blacks today: the promise of upward mobility for some at the expense of others, the possibility of sociopolitical and economic advances for a few to the deprivation of many.

It will be absolutely critical for the black church to position itself at that point where, one might say, the courses of divine and human history cross paths—and not merely for the sake of perspective. It is equally important for the purpose of being located existentially at a vortex where it is possible to compare and contrast an awareness of the way things are with "revelations" of the way things ought to be and to consequently raise a whirlwind of questions that may then become a force bringing about social change, thus remaining true to the church's tradition of prophetic social consciousness.

Cornell West raises one of these all-important questions in his book, *Prophetic Fragments,* when he asks, "How does a present day Christian think about and act on enhancing the plight of the poor, the predicament of the powerless, and the quality of life for all?"[9] This question leads to another: Will changes in ecclesiastical structures be required to address effectively the needs of the poor and the powerless?[10]

The black church's emphasis on prophetic social consciousness also invites responses to the questions raised, not just from the power brokers of the land, but from that reality which the black church regards as the power giver of the world, that is, from God. It must be the responsibility of the black church to interpret and clarify what it understands God to say to the powers that be, and to do so in good faith.

One of the most distinguishing aspects of the Tawana Brawley affair in New York in 1987 was the sense in which her advocates, chief among them a black minister, seemingly acted in bad faith. Protesting police abuse, when justified, is a noble cause. But the way in which Miss Brawley's advisors represented her suggested that her complaint was contrived and that their actions were opportunistic and self-aggrandizing. In the opinion of many blacks as well as whites throughout the country, the entire episode seemed a mockery of truth and justice, especially to the extent that these virtues were paraded under the banner of the prophetic tradition of the Christian faith. In a social climate where the critics of organized religion seem to be daily growing in number, the credibility of the black church will depend heavily on the degree to which its membership, both ministerial and lay, speak and act in good faith with both its religious tradition and the public at large.

MORAL INTEGRITY

If the black church is to be a resource to the nation and to the world during the twenty-first century, it must maintain its emphasis on moral integrity. Like prophetic social consciousness, an emphasis on morality, on right living, has always been one of the prominent features of the black church. Since the days of the "invisible institution" during slavery, the black church has recognized the need to model what it has preached, though it has not always done so. It has recognized that, in many respects, African Americans have had to be, or at least appear, more virtuous than others in American society in order to garner even a modicum of respect. Even more, it has recognized that it has had to call its membership to be morally upright in order that God not be mocked, that the claims about the truth of God and God's will for the world not be proven to be dysfunctional.

The black church has always recognized the integral relationship between proper ethical conduct and a social order that allows for judicious exercise of self-determination and pursuit of self-fulfillment in life. (It is largely for this reason that throughout the years the black church has favored the principles of democratic government.) In recent years, debacles involving the likes of Jim Bakker and Jimmy Swaggart have seriously undermined public confidence in the ability of any church, denomination, or religious group to maintain the strength of their professed convictions, let alone to act on them. Insofar as the black church is not exempt from the circle of suspicion, and indeed never has been, it is imperative that in the coming years it be most vigilant in disarming the cynics' cannons, not for the sake of proving them wrong, but because it is both right, beneficial, and strategically advantageous to live according to God's will.

It must be acknowledged, however reluctantly, that large numbers of people, poor, well-to-do, black, white, and so on, have intentionally shielded themselves from the influence of organized religion. In the opinion of some, they have done so because they do not perceive organized religion, the black church included, as being relevant to their life situations. But perhaps their rationale has as much, if not more, to do with their perception that organized religion of *any* stripe or hue is essentially an organization of hypocrites who are too hypocritical to acknowledge what they are.

Projections of the downside of the third wave may have as much to do with the "critical distance" between the preachments of organized religion and the visible actions and activities of its various memberships as with any other factors. This is to say that these projections, although rooted in present realities, may be as dire as they are because the failure of organized religion to "keep the faith" has over the years seriously undercut the ability of people to have faith in much of anything, including the prospect of a bright future.

George Bush's presidency went on record as calling for a "kinder, gentler nation." The current Clinton administration seems to be trying to enable this nation to come into being. The black church has and will have a unique opportunity to model the kind of morality that makes such a nation possible, now and during the twenty-first century. Because of the peculiar trials, tribulations, struggles, and triumphs of its membership that are uniquely related to the plight of being black in America, the black church has the sensitivity for building and promoting human relationships, for creating true community, and for transcending the boundaries of race, gender, and class (socioeconomic standing)—without being oblivious to their reality, without negating their positive value in the scheme of God's universe. But it must do far more than declare its allegiance to the God of Christianity in the coming days; it must follow through in ways that clearly reflect continuity between the tenets of the faith, the profession of the faith, and individual and collective conduct and deportment under the banner of the faith.

A historical anecdote will illuminate the point. During the antebellum period, the African Methodist Episcopal denomination was confronted with a particular challenge to "practice what it preached." There emerged, at the level of the General Conference, a concern over the practice of some members, free black men, of purchasing slaves ostensibly for the purpose of freeing them. In most instances, free blacks bought enslaved blacks on the condition that they be reimbursed before officially "setting the captives free."[11]

Difficulties with reimbursement resulted in some blacks essentially holding other blacks in slavery for indefinite periods. The issue of blacks purchasing blacks under a "conditions" clause in the A.M.E. Book of Discipline was reviewed by the Committee on Slavery in 1856. The majority report favored deleting the clause, ruling that purchasing people without setting them free immediately and unconditionally was morally unsound—was sinful. The minority report, however, favored maintaining the clause. On the conference floor, the minority position prevailed.[12] If the black church is to be a resource for the twenty-first century, its loyalties must not be so confused; its practices must not be so duplicitous.

SPIRITUAL EMPOWERMENT

As a resource for the twenty-first century, the black church must augment its emphasis on spiritual empowerment. It is clearer now than ever before that the battles are indeed waged today not so much with "powers and principalities," but with "spiritual wickedness in high places." In a very real sense, the only way to truly overcome the chasms that exist between wealthy and poor, black and white, men and women, and preachers and their flocks, is to be empowered at a level of reality where all seems possible.

The noted scholar of the African American religious experience, C. Eric Lincoln, has commented that the black church has tended historically to be a determinative factor in local, state, and national politics only when whites are unable to resolve their ambivalences.[13] Jesse Jackson's unsuccessful bid for the Democratic Party's presidential nomination in 1988 would appear to support this contention. Although he enjoyed the full backing of the various constituencies comprising the black church, and in the opinion of many blacks and some whites appeared to be the strongest Democratic contender, the white conservative wing of the party seemed doggedly opposed to the idea of a black nominee. Many believe that race became too significant an issue in his candidacy.

To avoid this pitfall, Douglas Wilder, in his gubernatorial run for the Commonwealth of Virginia, seems to have used a strategy wherein black churches throughout the state played a critical role but assumed a low profile. The tacit, if not articulated, concurrence of black church leaders across denominational lines may well have translated into Wilder's narrow margin of victory.[14] If so, it can be said that the black church in Virginia, in this instance, is an example of validating claims of experiencing the power and work of the Holy Spirit by a pragmatic, success-oriented political posture.

The work of the Church Association for Community Service (CACS) is another case in point. Founded in Washington, D.C., in 1989, the CACS is an interdenominational organization of approximately one hundred local congregations and social service agencies networked to share human and financial resources in combating the drug epidemic in the District of Columbia. Its program is threefold: (a) to build upon, incorporate, and support the many drug abuse programs operated by the various churches and secular service agencies; (b) to establish an outreach network to every family, young person, and adult so that they will have access to assistance, especially at the point of crisis; and (c) to rebuild and empower a system of community care in which families help families to identify and address problems at their onset, and to prevent difficult situations from becoming tragedies.[15] To meet its objectives, the CACS is divided into fifteen geographical districts, with one or more churches in each district committed to conducting a family crisis counseling center, an evening youth program, a parent education program, an after-school program, and a community outreach forums program. One church in each district serves as the site for coordinating the programs in the other churches. The success of the Church Association's work is predicated on the significant involvement of lay volunteers.

Although the Wilder victory and the work of the CACS provide positive examples, far more needs to be done to demonstrate the tangible benefits of following the guidance of the Holy Spirit, especially in the way of empowering laity to exercise more authority in designing and implementing programs at local and judicatory levels of church life.[16] To the disadvantage of the church's work, the dominant model of pastoral leadership, regardless of denomination, tends to be that of the self-styled autocrat. This style of leadership seriously undermines the credibility of the Holy Spirit, both as an abstract idea and as a concrete reality. In the main, it contradicts the claims often made in black church circles about the nature of the Spirit, especially those that conform generally to the evangelical notion of the Spirit as the ubiquitous personal presence and power of God available in equal measure to all "born-again" believers. Even more than contradicting the meaning of the Holy Spirit, it can be said that in the eyes of many congregants, autocratic leadership violates the Spirit itself, for it is oriented more toward exclusiveness than inclusiveness, more toward inequity than parity. Moreover, from the vantage point of the laity, such leaders inhibit the "movement of the Spirit" with respect to any motivation to become involved in the life of the church beyond attending Sunday worship. Consequently, lay participation in the work of the black church is often unnecessarily and regrettably minimized.

In the years to come, the viability of the black church will very much depend upon its ability to maximize lay participation. The failure to do so may result in the virtual dissolution of the black church during the next century, rendering it the cultural artifact of a bygone era. Without involving laity more completely, particularly at the local level, the black church will likely suffer a catastrophic loss of membership by the year 2010. Black "baby boomers" have already opted in large numbers for no church affiliation. Among blacks in urban settings, church membership is regarded to a significant extent as irrelevant. Unless numbers of black baby boomers are drawn to the church over the next decade, the children of this generation, the post-baby boomers, also will be disinclined to affiliate, leaving a small, aged remnant on church rolls by the second decade of the new century. The work required to evangelize these black baby boomers (and their families) cannot be accomplished without the full-scale involvement of the laity.

Evangelization is undoubtedly one of the great challenges facing the black church today. How the church responds to this challenge will clearly portend its value as a resource for the twenty-first century. Should it mobilize its greatest resource, the laity, for the work of evangelization, the chances are great that it will be a pivotal institution in the life of the nation. But here again, the practical benefit of believing in the Holy Spirit will be key. Mobilization for evangelization will not be possible without pastors and church officials demonstrating that belief in the Holy Spirit translates into spiritual empowerment. The validity and efficacy of spiritual empowerment is evident to the degree that power to promote the ideals of Christianity and the work of the church on both individual and social levels is shared equitably.

Sharing power, in this instance, does not mean that pastors and church officials should forsake the authority vested in them by virtue of their office. It does mean that they should use their authority as a means of empowering others. Doing so would lend much credence to the Christian ideals of giving, sharing, and sacrifice. In tangible, practical ways, it would enable laity to participate in the life of the church at a level of commitment that would hold their loyalty throughout their lifetimes. Such commitment and loyalty would lead to heightened enthusiasm for the work of evangelization. It would also result in more evangelical strategic planning, programmatic development, and management. In the face of limited, finite resources, efficiency and effectiveness are relevant concerns. This is particularly the case if evangelism is understood not merely as an appeal to the unchurched, but as a lifelong process of promoting spiritual and social well-being among all, unchurched and churched alike. Empowering laity would free them to be moved by the Holy Spirit to work more closely, vigorously, and conscientiously with pastors and ordained church officials in undertaking evangelization in the most effective ways possible. Moreover, an empowered laity would be free to participate fully in the historic mission of the black church: to find a way to overcome the spiritual schizophrenia that has plagued the race since the 1660s, the time when American slavery became restricted almost exclusively to the bondage of Africans. Near the beginning of the twentieth century, W. E. B. Du Bois wrote passionately and perspicaciously of this schizophrenia. In now famous and oft-quoted words, he wrote of the dilemma of being an American and a Negro as "two souls, two thoughts, two unreconciled strivings; two warring ideals in one dark body."[17] Over the years many have largely construed this characterization in psychological terms. But consideration of the title of the book in which Du Bois couched his insight, *The Souls of Black Folk*, would suggest that he understood that the issue was fundamentally spiritual. It was, and basically remains, an issue of achieving wholeness in the face of two formidable obstacles: (a) the pressure to look "at one's self through the eyes of others," to measure "one's soul with the tape of a world that looks on in amused contempt and pity";[18] and (b) the absence of economic and political power to be self-determining as a race.

To the extent that the laity are empowered to participate in the life of the church, they are likely to take seriously the claims their ministers make about the possibility of being made whole by the power of the Holy Spirit. In the process, they are likely to develop greater confidence in their innate ability to find ways, individually and collectively, to reconcile nationality and race; to find ways of becoming whole.

It is frequently said in the African American community that, unlike most other ethnic and racial groups in American society, blacks seem incapable of working together or supporting one another over protracted periods of time. The comment is often made with special reference to economic development. Unlike Jews, it is noted, African Americans seem unwilling to trust each other enough to patronize black businesses or enterprises enough for the race on the whole to develop the economic leverage needed for real political strength.

If there is truth to this claim, then perhaps it is rooted in the problem of spiritual schizophrenia. From this condition undoubtedly emanates the problem of identity. That the race has grappled with its identity throughout its history is clearly evident in the variations of and changes in preferred nomenclature: *colored, Negro, Afro-American, black American, African American*. It is a difficult proposition to trust yourself or anyone else when both who *you* are, and who you are dealing *with*, are unclear, and identity is an issue of paramount importance.

No better example of African Americans working together and supporting one another can be found than the black church. No institution in African American life has a longer track record. The economic reality of the black church is a case in point. On average, the economic transactions of local black congregations, or those of the judicatories of denominations for that matter, fall far below the standard of high finance, but many have remained viable economic entities for more than one hundred years. In this sense, they illustrate the ability of blacks to work together and to sustain their effort.

Given its track record, the black church is and can be a model for building trusting relationships. It is a model that can be exploited to the benefit of the race, if the laity are empowered to devise and implement strategies for projects and programs to realistically address the needs of African Americans to reconcile their strivings and to clarify their identity—in the interest of affirming their humanity.

In the final analysis, the empowerment of the laity would benefit the well-being of all Americans. For in the affirmation of black humanity is the affirmation of all humanity. Furthermore, there is an implicit demand for public policy and political practice that, throughout the years to come, will hold the nation accountable for equal opportunity and social justice.

The black church can be a resource for the twenty-first century, provided it remains true to its threefold emphasis on prophetic social consciousness, moral integrity, and spiritual empowerment. It alone is not equipped to solve the many problems the race will confront. But through its many local congregations, its various denominations, and its agencies, it can help to insure that blacks (and other minorities) will not merely survive, but will thrive.

REFERENCES

Commission on Minority Participation in Education and American Life. 1988. One-third of a nation.

Du Bois, W. E. B. 1969. *The souls of black folk.* New York: New American Library. Reprint.

Jones, Lawrence N. 1985. The black churches: A new agenda. In *Afro-American religious history: A documentary witness,* ed. Milton Sernett. Durham, NC: Duke University Press.

———. 1994. The African American churches: In history and context. (In this volume.)

Lincoln, C. Eric. 1984. *Race, religion, and the continuing American dilemma.* New York: Hill and Wang.

Lincoln, C. Eric, and Lawrence H. Mamiya. 1990. *The black church in the African American experience.* Durham, NC: Duke University Press.

Richardson, Harry V. 1976. *Dark salvation: the story of Methodism as it developed among blacks in America.* Garden City, NY: Doubleday.

Toffler, Alvin. 1980. *The third wave.* New York: William Morrow.

Tucker, Frank. n.d. The Church Association for Community Service: The plan, n.p.

Turner, W. C. 1989. Black evangelism: Theology, politics and race. *Journal of Religious Thought* 25 (Winter-Spring): 40–56.

West, Cornell. 1988. *Prophetic Fragments.* Grand Rapids, MI: Eerdmans.

Wilmore, Gayraud S. 1983. *Black religion and black radicalism: An interpretation of the religious history of Afro-American people.* 2d ed. Maryknoll, NY: Orbis.

Wilson, Francis, and Mamphela Ramphele. 1988. Uprooting poverty: The South African Challenge. *Carnegie Quarterly,* 33 (Spring-Fall): 2–8.

NOTES

1. Lawrence N. Jones, "The Black Churches: A New Agenda," in *Afro-American Religious History: A Documentary Witness,* Milton Sernett, ed. (Durham, NC: Duke University Press, 1985)

2. W. C. Turner, "Black Evangelism: Theology, Politics, and Race," *Journal of Religious Thought,* 25, 2 (Winter-Spring 1989), 40–56. In their recently published landmark study, *The Black Church in the African American Experience* (Durham, NC: Duke University Press, 1990), C. Eric Lincoln and Lawrence H. Mamiya limit their

operational definition to the seven "independent, historic, and totally black-controlled denominations" and "a scattering of smaller communions." The seven denominations that receive most of the attention are: the African Methodist Episcopal Church (A.M.E.); the African Methodist Episcopal Zion Church (A.M.E.Z.); the Christian Methodist Episcopal Church (C.M.E.); the National Baptist Convention, U.S.A., Incorporated (NBC); the National Baptist Convention of America, Unincorporated (NBCA); the Progressive National Baptist Convention (PNBC); and the Church of God in Christ (COGIC). Lincoln and Mamiya acknowledge that "in general usage, any black Christian person is included in the "black church" if he or she is a member of a black congregation" (p. 1). Rather than employ a basically sociological definition, as Lincoln and Mamiya do, I have chosen to define the black church largely in phenomenological terms in order to include those "predominantly black local churches in white denominations such as the United Methodist Church, the Episcopal Church, and the Roman Catholic Church" (Lincoln and Mamiya, p. 1).

3. Alvin, Toffler, *The Third Wave*. New York: William Morrow, 1980.

4. "One-Third of a Nation," a report by the Commission on Minority Participation In Education and American Life, 1988, 3.

5. *Ford Foundation Newsletter,* Spring 1988, 1.

6. *Ibid.*

7. Francis Wilson and Mamphela Ramphele, "Uprooting Poverty: The South African Challenge," *Carnegie Quarterly,* 33, 3/4 (Summer-Fall, 1988), 2–8.

8. See Gayraud, S. Wilmore's *Black Religion and Black Radicalism: An Interpretation of the Religious History of Afro-American People,* 2d ed. (Maryknoll, NY: Orbis, 1983). In many respects, Wilmore's book is an exploration of the temporal foci of the African American religious experience.

9. Cornell West, *Prophetic Fragments* (Grand Rapids, MI: Eerdman, 1988), xi.

10. In a presentation on April 5, 1991, at the Duke Divinity School, Durham, NC, in honor of the publication of Lincoln and Mamiya's *The Black Church in the African American Experience,* Bishop Reuben Speaks, of the African Methodist Episcopal Zion Church,

raised the question as to whether the present-day structure of the church ought to be declared obsolescent, if the church does not adequately address the needs of the dispossessed in the immediate years ahead. He made no reference to any particular denomination.

11. Harry V. Richardson, *Dark Salvation: The Story of Methodism as It Developed Among Blacks in America* (Garden City, NY: Doubleday, 1976).

12. *Ibid.*

13. C. Eric Lincoln, *Race, Religion, and the Continuing American Dilemma* (New York: Hill and Wang, 1984), 204.

14. My position is corroborated by Martel A. Perry, Executive Director of Computer Services, the Commonwealth of Virginia.

15. Tucker, Frank. "The Church Association for Community Service: The Plan," n.d.

16. To these examples can also be added the Congress of National Black Churches highlighted in Lawrence N. Jones, "The African American Church: In History and Contexts", in this volume.

17. Du Bois, W. E. B. *The Souls of Black Folk* (New York: New American Library, 1969), 45.

18. *Ibid.*

Education, Science, and Technology | D

14 Overview and Recommendations

Faustine C. Jones-Wilson

In the United States, educational relationships between African Americans and other Americans of color with the dominant white group are complex, often strained. Scholars have documented this nation's long history of imposed educational inequalities, grounded in various state or local decisions to differentiate among the races, as well as in federal unwillingness to enforce the "equal" portion of the U.S. Supreme Court's 1896 *Plessy v. Ferguson* decision. Public policies in education for people of color usually have not been democratic or scientific, or always wise, but have often been guided by expediency and the politics of a given era.

This state of affairs had become even more complex in 1989, when the One-Third of a Nation Conference was held, because of the socioeconomic status of people of color compared to that of white Americans. Scholars have documented a strong relationship between socioeconomic status and educational attainment. Proportionally, more people of color than whites are poor (or economically disadvantaged), a condition affecting their children's readiness to learn; their choice of school subjects; their later motivation and/or willingness to learn; their standardized test scores; and their levels of aspiration, career choices, and the educational patterns leading thereto. Their socioeconomic status also affects their teachers' perceptions of these students.

Yet, as was clearly stated in the 1954 Supreme Court decision, *Brown v. Board of Education of Topeka,* one can hardly expect children and youth to succeed in the world as it has become without equal educational opportunity. In today's global inter-relationships, with the rapid growth of technology and escalation of knowledge, that education must be of the highest quality.

Certain key educational problems created by these complex relationships are examined in the five presentations that comprise this section. Each chapter makes recommendations for change to improve the educational conditions and status of people of color.

Faustine C. Jones-Wilson's "Educational Policy Crosscurrents Since 1983" examines school reform reports of the 1980s, policymaking efforts designed to correct inadequacies of elementary- and secondary-level public schooling. She finds this wave of reform reports to be cyclical, another in a series of such efforts since the 1950s. The 1980s reports give sparse attention to African Americans, other people of color, or the poor. Educational policy papers by black organizations and scholars have been largely ignored by the education community, including black educators, and by educational policymakers at the federal and state levels. Schools are service institutions, established in response to social demands. Society is responsible for them, yet finds it convenient to make its public schools scapegoats for larger social ills over which the schools have no control. Recommendations for educational "reform" often occur in response to crises, real or perceived. Jones-Wilson explains that if the general recommendations of the 1980s had been implemented there would still have been no guarantee that the education offered to black and other minority children would improve or that the post-schooling employment opportunity structure would open for them. She concludes that there are forces of reconstructionism that can be utilized for positive educational change, as exemplars of desirable policies and practices that should be replicated.

Sylvia T. Johnson, in "Testing Testing: Assessment, Standardized Tests, and the Educational Process Among African American Students," examines uses of measurement and advocates usage in the interests of the learners, particularly African Americans. She discusses internal and external factors affecting test scores. With respect to the nature of measurement, Johnson stresses that educational or psychological measurement is never done directly; no mind meters exist. All such measurement techniques are applied to behavior, and inferences are then made to level of achievement, aptitude, personality, interest, or some other human characteristic that cannot be measured directly. Test scores obtained through such measurement, then, frequently are not sufficient measures of aptitude, achievement, or other psychological or educational constructs for people of color. She points out that the distribution of African Americans across socioeconomic status (SES) levels differs from that of other groups and that researchers have established that a strong relationship exists between socioeconomic status and standardized test scores; economic advantage has enabling effects for higher test scores.

Disproportionate numbers of African American students have not had economic advantages; this helps to explain some of the gap between test scores of African American children and youth and those of their white peers. The situation is complicated by the interaction of health effects and nutrition with socioeconomic status on test scores of black and white students. Johnson also examines efforts to reduce and eliminate racial and cultural bias in tests and discusses testing and the military, along with certification testing. She analyzes the role of teachers, their caring and concern (or lack thereof) relative to the achievement of all children. She identifies, explains, and justifies alternative assessment and measurement procedures. Johnson concludes that there is no assessment system that will solve the problem of what is wrong with how we educate African American children. The primary focus must be on the student, the classroom, and the educational climate of the school and the community, with assessment playing a supportive role in that system.

Anne Reynolds asserts in "New Teacher Assessments: Palliative or Panacea for Minority Performance?" that by the year 2000 we must expect drastic changes in the way teachers are assessed. She begins with a story set in the future, extrapolating currently emerging patterns of (a) assessing students' pre-entry teacher education program enabling skills; (b) testing their exit skills after the program has ended, where a passing score grants a provisional teaching license; (c) end-of-first-year professional employment critiques through portfolio submission, examination, and assessments by professional experts in the subject matter field, resulting in full licensure; and (d) a five-year assessment by a National Board for Professional Teaching Standards, requiring evidence of *excellence* in teaching, after which full board certification is granted. She explains in detail the group differences hypothesis and the test instruments hypothesis, each purporting to explain the low minority-teacher pass rates on current teacher program admission tests and initial teacher licensure tests, and proposes solutions for these problems. She examines the current status of minority teacher performance on observation systems, a new type of teacher assessment. She gives the pros and cons of renovations and innovations in teacher assessment that are currently in the research and development process and analyzes their prospects for improving pass rates of minority teachers. She also discusses implications of the new assessments for teacher education programs and makes suggestions for using the new assessments in teacher education. She concludes with suggestions for further research, and offers her thoughts about the challenges faced by educators, assessment specialists, and policymakers. Assessments for new teachers and new assessments for teachers are not a panacea for the declining numbers of minority teachers or for the problems of low minority-teacher pass rates on current tests.

In "African Americans, Education and Science: Recent Findings and Policy Implications," Willie Pearson, Jr., explains that the emergence of new technologies may be the most formidable enemy of African Americans, who are underrepresented in science and technology. Projections indicate that complex technologies will prevail, and that the nation's prosperity will depend on a populace that has mastered them. If African Americans fail to master these technologies, they face the prospect of becoming obsolete—a huge illiterate underclass that is minimally employable. Their failures will affect the society negatively, because it will then suffer from a shortage of productive workers. To solve this problem, African Americans must participate in greater numbers in the precollege science and mathematics schooling experience, particularly in advanced mathematics and science courses in high school, and especially in physics and chemistry. Black females, particularly, need to enroll in these classes, for their representation is lower than that of males. Pearson notes that, in general, the inner-city high schools attended by African Americans are underfinanced, underequipped, and staffed disproportionately by inexperienced teachers. On the other hand, blacks in desegregated high schools are concentrated in the noncollege preparatory tracks, where these advanced mathematics and science courses usually are not taught. The historically black colleges and universities (HBCUs) make major contributions to the talent pool, because they award more undergraduate and master's degrees in biology and engineering to blacks than do predominantly white institutions. Disproportionate numbers of African Americans earning Ph.D.'s in science and engineering received their undergraduate degrees from HBCUs. Pearson cites case studies of three intervention programs that serve minority students well at different pipeline stages. He then details policy implications and strategies, lists recent federal initiatives, and restates, in closing, the importance of increased African American participation in science and technology.

Walter R. Allen and John Wallace collaborate on the fifth chapter, "Black College Students: Achievement, Social Integration, and Aspirations." They present data from a three-year study, the National Study of Black College Students (NSBCS), on academic achievement, social involvement, and occupational aspirations for a national sample of over 2,500 black students attending selected predominantly white and historically black, state-supported universities. The study examined how the data related to student background characteristics, campus characteristics, campus experiences, and student personality orientation. Allen and Johnson review the pertinent literature on campus race differences prior to revealing the findings of the NSBCS. The racial composition of the campus emerged as the most significant predictor of student outcomes related to social involvement and occupational aspirations, and as the second most important predictor for academic achievement. Students who had better relations with faculty and who had higher high school grades also had higher college academic achievement. Other data indicated that college grades were highest for students who reported high educational aspirations and who felt they had chosen the right college to attend. Female occupational goals were highest for those on black campuses who had high educational aspirations and high grades in high school. Black male occupational goals were best predicted by high educational aspirations and high grades in high school. Academic achievement was highest for low socioeconomic status African American students who attended historically black colleges and had favorable relations with faculty. But high-achieving black college students from middle- or upper-class backgrounds more often had high occupational aspirations and reported favorable relations with white peers. The authors believe that interpersonal relationships form the bridge between individual predispositions and institutional setting. In their study, the most powerful and consistent predictor of all student outcomes was campus racial composition. Students who attended historically black institutions reported better academic performance, greater social involvement, and higher occupational aspirations. The authors conclude that in addition to an individual's personal characteristics, his or her academic performance will also be affected by the quality of life at the institution attended; the level of academic competition; university rules, procedures, and resources; relationships with faculty and friends; racial hostility on the campus; and the extent of social support networks on the campus. They conclude with recommendations to improve African American student participation in American higher education.

FORECAST

In 1992, the National Science Foundation released information indicating that the mathematics achievement test scores of African American students who were nine, thirteen, and seventeen years old had improved since 1973. Also, evidence was released that African American high school seniors who were college bound had increased their Scholastic Achievement Test scores in the 1980s. Yet the achievement gap remains between white elementary and secondary students and their counterparts of color. Low-to-moderate income students of color and many of their white counterparts will remain academic underachievers unless appropriate federal and state policies and programs are implemented and maintained, with sufficient funding to permit all eligible students to partake. Corporate and philanthropic assistance is essential, as well. Lacking such sustained commitment, students of color will not be fully prepared educationally to meet the challenges of the rest of the decade of the 1990s or be proficient enough to succeed in the twenty-first century. This nation will suffer because these youth are an increasingly larger proportion of the population; they will be unskilled—poorly prepared for the emerging labor market—and unable to contribute to the maintenance of our economy. Further, our democracy cannot be maintained without an enlightened, committed, civilized citizenry capable of making intelligent judgments on social problems. Long-existent social inequities in our society also must be remedied; education does not exist in isolation or in a vacuum. Many educational problems result from, and are part and parcel of, systemic circumstances over which schools and teachers have no control.

RECOMMENDATIONS

Inequities in education, coupled with the lower socioeconomic status of African Americans, Hispanics, and Native Americans, must be remedied. Many children and youth from these groups continue to attend second-rate schools. To solve these problems, appropriate public policies must be enacted, funded adequately, maintained, and enforced over time. The conference participants developed the following recommendations as initial steps in the solution process.

1. Fully fund Head Start, a federal program that has provided evidence that preschool early intervention providing comprehensive services improves the educational attainments and life chances of poor children and children of color.
2. Alter the educational climate of schools. Replicate elementary and secondary school programs that have demonstrated success in teaching African American children and others of color. These include Dr. James Comer's School Development intervention methods, as well as the "Effective Schools" programs modeled after the late Dr. Ronald Edmonds's ideas and extended by such educators as Dr. Barbara Sizemore in selected Pittsburgh, Pennsylvania, schools. Reform and restructure schools along the lines of these and other successful school models.
3. Replicate special intervention programs that have attracted and prepared children of color to succeed in college-oriented mathematics, science, and technology programs.
4. Place standardized tests in perspective. Endorse and use alternative assessment techniques that offer the possibility of better measurement of achievement and other cognitive constructs among African American students.
5. Begin to recruit minority teachers as early as the seventh grade and provide financial assistance to those students who desire or agree to become teachers.
6. Target intervention programs in mathematics, science, and technology toward African American students in elementary and junior high schools. Do not wait until the high school level.

7. Encourage precollege enrichment programs for high school students on college campuses.
8. Revise teacher education programs by raising admission standards, altering the curriculum to include teacher-test assessment content, evaluating students through their program years, including multiple-choice test items in preservice teacher-education examinations, creating support services for these prospective teachers.
9. Use new assessment forms as a basis for evaluation in teacher education classes.
10. Create consortia and trade ideas with other teacher educators.
11. Restructure teacher education programs so that multicultural education is granted a larger role and enable teachers to understand all aspects and ramifications of the fact that "different" does not mean inferior with respect to learners.
12. Rethink relationships between precollegiate and higher education. Colleges and universities must develop better working relationships with local public schools, including articulating expectations and requirements for high school graduation and college admission.
13. Recruit retired scientists and engineers to work in public schools, supplementing the traditional instruction there.
14. Increase the amount and quality of required precollege mathematics and science course work for all students in every state and the District of Columbia by state mandates.
15. Locate new and continuing sources to provide and maintain financial aid for promising students from low-to-moderate socio-economic backgrounds.
16. Sensitize public school teachers and college faculty to their critical role in student support and development.
17. Reassert and enforce the goal of educational equity at every level in the U.S. educational system.
18. Recommitment on the part of the African American community to educational excellence for its children and youth is mandatory. Home and school efforts must be collaborative ventures. We must re-establish our sense of community.
19. Publicizing educational gains and successes must be a priority of the media in all its forms (television, radio, print). Positive publicity will enhance a return of the public's confidence in public schools.

15 Educational Policy Crosscurrents Since 1983

FAUSTINE C. JONES-WILSON

I n the decade of the 1980s, some thirty national reports on education were issued by prestigious task forces and commissions. Most of them are harshly critical of public elementary and secondary schooling. In general, these reports propose, as solutions to the problems they describe, the raising of achievement standards for students, increasing the number of courses required for graduation, competency testing for teachers, raising the salaries of selected teachers through a merit pay system, and lengthening the school day or school year.[1] Additionally, between 1983 and 1986, more than 700 state statutes were enacted; these laws were designed to regulate and control schools by stipulating what should be taught, how, and by whom.[2] Collectively, this national inundation occurs in the name of "excellence" or "quality," but *equity* in education has had no priority in the school reform movement.[3]

Most of the national reform reports ignore African Americans, Hispanic Americans, Native Americans, other minorities, and economically poor members of all groups. If these groups are not neglected in a prestigious report, they are awarded perfunctory attention in what amounts to a cursory notation. If we are truly concerned about the education of America's black citizens, other minority groups, and the future of this political democracy, we must understand the educational debates of the 1980s and their relationship (or lack of it) to African Americans and other minorities—the citizens who will be one-third of this nation by the year 2000.

Toward the goal of contributing to that understanding, this chapter has four components. These are, first, the historical context, for to understand the educational policy cross-currents of the 1980s one must place those events in the cycle of policy debates that have occurred in the United States since the 1950s. In that sense, educational "reform" through educational policy shifts has been both cyclical, usually in response to a perceived or real crisis, and short lived; the present policy debates, reformulations, and recommendations represent another such cycle.

In the second part of this chapter, we will examine the educational policy recommendations of the 1980s, their content, and what is missing from them. We will judge whether—if the recommendations are implemented—the education of African American and other minority children will improve. Would the opportunity structure open up for them, especially employment opportunity, if minorities were better educated? When the current furor over education reforms is abated and the smoke clears, will the same picture of an educationally neglected group emerge or could the current reform movement be used as a real opportunity to discover, examine, and develop the special talents and abilities of those children who will soon be one-third of the nation?

Third, we will look at who shall be educated and to what ends. We address this dimension of thought because educational debates of the 1980s, including their criticisms of public schooling, are the contemporary expression of the ongoing larger debate in our society and in all societies, sometimes overtly, often covertly. Who shall be educated? Why? To what ends? By whom? For how long? These are questions about individuals, which are accompanied by institutional questions: What knowledge is of most worth? How does one know what knowledge is most valuable? Who decides? Why? Related to public schools, the questions become one: Why are there *public* schools, a system of schooling at public expense designed to educate all the children of all the people? These are not merely theoretical questions. They address themselves to the future of black children, of all children, the future of a publicly supported schooling system as we know it, and indeed to the fate of our democracy itself.[4]

Fourth, we will look at recommendations to improve the education of minority youth and examine anticipated social benefits from this improved education.

We must also remember, as we proceed, the positive aspects of contemporary educational policy discussions: (a) they have placed schooling in the forefront of our minds; (b) they have generated national attention and activity around the issue of the sorry state of public elementary and secondary education; and (c) they have directed attention to schools as instruments for developing a good society.[5]

HISTORICAL CONTEXT

In the United States, educational reform movements occur in cycles, often in response to crises. In a 1984 article, Passow indicates that the wretched state of American education has been a recurring theme over the last ninety years or so.[6] In the 1950s, the schools were held to be responsible for the manpower shortage, the nation's inability to stop the spreading of Communist ideology, and the failure to educate scientists and engineers who could outdo the Russians in the space race. Led by such vitriolic critics as Arthur Bestor and Vice Admiral Hyman Rickover, the blame for school failure was variously placed on John Dewey's progressive education, the separation of teacher training from arts and what was called a "stranglehold" of professional educators over teacher education and certification. It was asserted that control of the schools had to be removed from professional educators in order to reform schooling.[7]

The result was that the federal government increased appropriations to the National Science Foundation to sponsor summer institutes for science and mathematics teachers, to develop new science and mathematics curricula for the public schools, and to establish graduate fellowships to encourage students to select science as a career. Also, the National Defense Education Act (NDEA) was passed in 1958. Its aim was to provide for identifying academically able students, to encourage them to stay in school, and in general to strengthen science education in schools. NDEA funds were available to students who promised to teach as a career, created special foreign-language instructional centers in colleges, provided funds for summer institutes for teachers, and strengthened what was then the U.S. Office of Education.

This new emphasis on intellectualism, new curricula, and science facilities was intended to reform the schools and "save" the United States. However, by the time all the proposed reforms were instituted there was an expanding school population, due to the influx of post-

World War II "baby boomers," and a teacher shortage. The reforms were short lived. In sum, during the 1950s, the societal focus was on discovering and educating the talented for national defense and for work in an emerging technological society.[8] There are striking similarities between this educational policy discourse of the 1950s with respect to school reform and that of the 1980s' discussions on the "excellence" movement and its goals of preparing talented people to keep our nation competitive with international rivals, as well as preparing people to be employable in our postindustrial service society serving corporate interests.

The education of African Americans in the 1950s was *not* a part of the goals of school critics or educational reformers. In fact, the last half of that decade was the time of massive resistance policies and efforts in southern states; those strategies were designed to thwart the desegregation of schools and maintain the racially separate, unequal schooling practices that had been in effect since 1896. In the North, policies of racial containment prevailed as school boards in their policymaking gerrymandered district boundary lines to prevent black students from attending predominantly white schools even when black schools were overcrowded and white schools were under-utilized. Black teachers found employment difficult to obtain except in all-black or changeover schools. In Little Rock, Arkansas, federal troops had to be sent to protect the lives of nine black youth—all of them carefully selected, capable students—who sought to enter Central High School in 1957 as part of their right to an education equal to that of their white peers. President Dwight D. Eisenhower had to be goaded into protecting the lives and rights of these black American citizens.

In the decade of the 1960s, especially after 1965, civil rights leaders and organizations were demanding that black children receive equal educational opportunity in every region of the nation and calling for an end to de facto school segregation. The 1960s and early 1970s were a time of social and educational protest movements. There were sit-ins, boycotts, marches, and demonstrations seeking an end to the war in Vietnam, an end to racial/ethnic/gender discrimination at home, and education of "the disadvantaged" as appropriate educational policy. Social and educational protests, while permissible in America, usually operate within contained parameters. This was a time when the society gave the *appearance* of wanting to educate "the disadvantaged," but policies, programs, and practices were not implemented, fully funded, or maintained long enough to make a difference in the lives of most of the underprivileged. Selected segments of this population benefited from such federal programs as Head Start and Follow Through, but these and other programs never were fully funded so that all eligible children and their families could participate in them.[9] Further, there was unevenness in their implementation and faulty articulation of offerings to the designated groups. In many instances, federal programs and funding were used to placate militant leaders, to quell community protests with promises of benefits to come, or as substitutes for (instead of additions to) state and local programs and funding.

Because the reforms of the 1960s emphasized equality in education, it is important to remember some of the criticisms of schools in that era. Such analysts as John Holt, in *How Children Fail,* Charles Silberman, in *Crisis in the Classroom,* and Jonathan Kozol, in *Death at an Early Age,* argued, usually correctly, that schools and teachers erected barriers that prevented students from learning. Urban schools, particularly, were said to be destroying African American students. Those school systems were characterized as bureaucratic, with uncaring teachers. Professional teacher educators were held to be variously anti-intellectual, too child centered, and generally inept—people who could do nothing else in the world of work, so they became teachers of teachers. Some radicals wanted schools abolished (Ivan Illich; Paul Goodman); others wanted schools reformed and made more humane (Silberman). The media, including filmmakers, attacked public schooling. Such films as *High School, Up the Down Staircase,* and others made the public fearful of desegregated urban public secondary schools.

In the midst of the furor and clashing arguments, African Americans continued to press for equality and equal educational opportunity. Parents submitted to busing plans to desegregate schools so their children could gain access to higher-quality buildings, equipment, libraries, laboratories, and so on. Parents sought community control of schools in New York and entered into the political fray in other cities, seeking to elect more African Americans to school boards and/or to get them employed in policymaking positions in school systems. These efforts were designed to place people in positions so that high-quality policies, programs, and procedures would be formulated

and implemented to educate black youth. While some successes resulted, no national plan to improve the education of African
Americans or other minorities emerged. Fads, such as performance
contracting, that purported to be sure-fire panaceas with guaranteed
results, came and went, with substantial financial investment made to
little avail.

In the larger society, the reality became clear that our nation could
not, or would not, support "guns and butter" simultaneously. The
war in Vietnam (the "guns") predominated, and domestic programs
(the "butter"), including those in education, suffered. In 1969, when
Richard M. Nixon's presidential administration replaced Lyndon B.
Johnson's, a different tone began to permeate the nation. Nixon was
clearly opposed to busing as an educational policy and sought to define equality of opportunity in terms of compensatory education for
African Americans, with the focus on basic skills achievement. African
American students were variously treated as disadvantaged, different,
and deficient—especially in mental ability. Career education was proposed as the solution to "student rebellion, delinquency, and
unemployment."[10] The 1970s' tone and approach conceptualized education for African Americans as vocational training for the lower
sector of the labor market, a kind of tracking that essentially abandoned the idea of equal educational opportunity. Coupled with a
retreat from increased spending for educational programs, career education as it was proposed would reinforce the social inequities of
lower-class status in the society for black youth.[11]

In the 1970s, neoconservative critics of federal programs to help the
disadvantaged included schooling in their harsh attacks on governmental intervention to help citizens.[12] While these articulate,
intelligent neoconservatives were not monolithic in their approaches,
in general they held that schooling and the War on Poverty had failed.
Schools could not help the disadvantaged very much, for their families were said to be the major cause of underachievement among poor
African American children. Other critics held that the rate of return
from the educational investment was too low, and therefore not worth
the price. Even some apparently well-meaning critics picked up the
theme of school failure, which fueled the existent anxieties of middle-
class parents about the value and feasibility of public schooling for
their children.

The 1970s stressed standardized testing in schools. Because minorities frequently score lower on these tests than do white students, the testing emphasis underscored inequality of educational achievement.[13] Racial differences in educational achievement, based on test scores, provided fuel for those intellectuals who revived and promoted the concept of genetic differences between blacks and whites. Blacks were judged by them to be mentally inferior to whites.

THE REFORM MOVEMENT OF THE 1980s

In one sense it can be said that the educational reform movement of the 1980s was initiated in the fall of 1982 with the publication of Adler's work, *The Paideia Proposal: An Educational Manifesto.*[14] However, it was not until the issuance of *A Nation at Risk* in April 1983 that public attention was focused on American schools.[15] This report proclaimed that mediocrity was the primary characteristic of the American educational system. That proclamation had the immediate effect of moving educational discourse away from whatever equity discussions remained and toward an undefined "excellence." The report also claimed that once again the United States was losing out to foreign competition, this time to the Japanese and West Germans in economic matters. (In 1957, the United States had lost to the Russians in political matters.) In 1983, U.S. schools were blamed for the fact that the Japanese economy had grown more rapidly and exhibited more stability than ours, and it was emphasized that Japanese children scored higher on standardized tests than did U.S. children. Thus, in 1983, the mission of education was again redefined to serve the national interest. Education was a weapon whose mission was to serve our national interest in the trade war competition with Japan and Western Europe, and provide willing, competent workers for the domestic labor market. It is said that *A Nation at Risk* initiated the first wave of educational reform in the 1980s aimed primarily at school improvement, with education defined as of instrumental value.[16]

There were 30 or more reform reports in the 1980s; Mary Hatwood Futrell conceived a method for classifying them. Futrell, a former teacher, was president of the National Education Association (NEA) during the 1980s. She was intimately involved in the educational reform discussions. Futrell defines the decade of the 1980s as a time of *debate,* but not of reform, and characterizes the debate as having come in four waves.

The first wave, initiated by politicians as their response to *A Nation at Risk,* came from governors and state legislators who advocated more "tests for students and teachers, more credits for graduation, more homework, more hours in the school day, more days in the school year, more regimentation, more regulation."[17] As indicated earlier, more than 700 statutes were passed by state legislatures stipulating what should be taught, when, how, and by whom. The basic idea of this first wave was to control and regulate schools and teachers, what Futrell calls a "top-down" reform of education. In this respect, it must be remembered that education is a subordinate social institution in terms of power, and therefore subject to regulation by more powerful institutions.

Reacting to the first wave in its assessment of policy recommendations for increased graduation requirements and uniform educational requirements administered without flexibility or sensitivity, the College Board expressed fear that dropout rates of African Americans and Hispanics might increase under these pressures.[18] Only in the most general terms did the first wave of reform reports recognize that minority students have special needs that must be met by education. The reports did not usually specify what these special needs are, what is to be done to meet them, or who is to pay the attendant costs. The 1983 reports did not mention school desegregation. Thus, the first wave of education reform reports in the 1980s, issued by national majority-group leaders, gave marginal attention to the education of nonwhite Americans. Nonetheless, the reports seized center-stage attention and generated enthusiasm in society.[19]

Meanwhile, the first major crosscurrent was the appearance of important policy statements, reports, and recommendations by African Americans that addressed the question of quality education for our children. These documents were virtually ignored in the larger society. They seem also to have received minimal attention in school systems and in colleges and universities that are run and heavily populated by African Americans. Three of these assessments were the 1983 update of the 1977 NAACP *Report on Quality Education for Black Americans: An Imperative; Civil Rights, Education, and the Black Child,* issued by the National Black Child Development Institute in 1984; and *Saving the African American Child,* a 1984 report of the National Alliance of Black School Educators, Inc.[20] These documents describe the economic and social underpinnings that cause the educational condition of blacks, evaluate the educational plight of underachievers, and make clear recommendations for change that would improve educational achievement. Yet no major foundation or governmental body has seen fit to honor and dignify these reports by publicizing their existence and funding their recommendations.

Returning now to Futrell's classification scheme, by 1986 the "top-down" first wave generated a second wave of reform, led by *Teachers for Tomorrow's Schools,* the Holmes Group report, and the Carnegie report, *A Nation Prepared: Teachers for the 21st Century,* both of which focused on teacher reform.[21] A cynic might feel that the message of these prestigious reports is, "Fix the teachers, then the schools can be fixed." This feeling is conveyed by these reports' emphasis on reforming teacher education programs to make them longer in duration and more intellectually sound, followed by standardized examinations for entry into the profession. In turn, they propose, the profession would be characterized by differentiated, hierarchical staffing patterns, new accountability and evaluation plans, and so on.

From her vantage point, Futrell is somewhat positive about this second wave of reform.[22] Speaking as a professional educator, she states that if schooling is intended to serve as an instrument for social and economic revitalization, it should be wielded as an instrument by educators and not legislators. Thus, the emphasis of the second wave of reform was to look to local schools and teachers, as well as to the teaching profession, to lead the educational improvement effort. The argument was that, in the first wave, regulators had taken decision-making authority away from teachers and principals, thereby producing a web of inefficiency.

In 1986, other prestigious groups issued reports that condemned top-down school regulation. These included the National Governors' Association, the Education Commission of the States, and the Association for Supervision and Curriculum Development. Scholarly analyses—some supportive, others critical—of this second wave of reform reports have appeared intermittently in issues of *Phi Delta Kappan,* some of which are cited in this chapter. Readers will also find the

November 1986 issue of *Harvard Educational Review* and the Spring 1987 issue of *Teachers College Record* enlightening and instructive.

Many African American academicians have found the second wave of reform reports to be potentially destructive to minorities. To make teacher education preparatory programs a year longer, for example, would increase financial problems of those minority students who already find it difficult to pay the costs of a four-year undergraduate education. To say that the most desirable teacher education programs are five-year programs is to do potential harm to the large number of four-year programs at historically African American colleges and universities. The reports lack evidence that their recommendations are sound or that they would improve the quality of teacher preparation if implemented.

Six concerned analysts, Beverly M. Gordon (Ohio State University), Bernard Oliver (Syracuse University), A. Wade Smith (Arizona State University), G. Pritchy Smith (University of North Florida), Reginald Wilson (American Council on Education), and Mary E. Dilworth (AACTE), reviewed the second wave of reform reports with respect to their potential impact on the education of African Americans. In the Spring 1988 issue of the *Journal of Negro Education,* these critics of the reform reports conclude that if the Holmes and Carnegie Report recommendations are implemented, predominantly white research institutions could and probably would become the dominant gatekeepers to teacher certification and degree programs, ostensibly based on meritocracy. Students from other institutions, including most black colleges and universities, would be consigned to the lower levels of differentiated teaching structures; minority teachers would suffer in the hierarchy that would result from restructuring the teaching force. Fewer minority teachers will be produced at a time when minority students will be a larger proportion of the students to be taught. More of tomorrow's teachers will be white.[22]

According to Futrell's classification, the third wave of educational reform in the 1980s was again a kind of "top-down" reform, this time with the U.S. economy as the focus. The emphasis was based on the claim that schools needed to produce graduates who could staff American businesses and reassert this nation's economic preeminence. This wave Futrell calls "economic utilitarianism." While she supports the concept that the business community and the education community must work cooperatively, she does not believe that economic goals should "drive" education or determine its ends and means. Further, she makes it clear that the "crisis of the hour," that is, narrow, provincial priorities, should not design education.

Again, African American efforts to shape policy appeared to fall on deaf ears. For example, each January the National Urban League issues its annual assessment, *The State of Black America*. It is customary for each issue to include a chapter on education, with appropriate recommendations appended, written by an African American educator.[24] The nation's power structures could have aided in implementing the educational strategies recommended annually, along with correcting the overall economic and social conditions that underlie academic underachievement. This has not happened.

The growing concern of African Americans about the underachievement of such a large proportion of urban youth caused a number of organizations and individuals to come together in 1986 to form an umbrella group, the National Conference on Educating Black Children (NCEBC). This group endorsed the concepts of the "effective schools" movement and committed itself to an educational effort to work with public schools to bring about day-to-day improvement in urban schools. At bottom, this group accepts the wisdom of the late Ronald Edmonds, that "we know enough to successfully teach Black children. Whether we do it will depend on how we feel about the fact that we haven't so far."

To begin to accomplish its goal to make a difference in schools, the 300-odd national participants at the 1986 conference formulated a "Blueprint for Action." This is a practical plan that stipulates goals with implementation activities for students, teachers, principals, parents, the community, and policymakers. The initial Blueprint was revised and reissued as "Blueprint for Action II" in 1987.[25] Thus, amid the furor for large-scale reform, and as people contemplated what Spring calls "the thinkable,"[26] NCEBC was concentrating on what is doable, implementable, and achievable. NCEBC continues to focus on improving schools in cooperating districts across the nation.

The fourth and last wave of education reform in the 1980s, Futrell holds, traces its parentage to the second wave. She says the fourth wave "envisions democratic, grassroots reform and demands a return to schools that are organized to facilitate educational renewal and improvement from the bottom up."[27] This fourth wave focuses on ethical as well as economic imperatives and assumes that schools must offer both excellence and equity, emphasizing that every student must reach his potential. Futrell says this wave still is in the developmental stage. Yet a 1984 first-wave report, *Pride and Promise: Schools of Excellence for All the People,* made these and other similar recommendations. It failed to receive the media coverage that the 1986 second-wave Holmes and Carnegie reports were accorded (see note 5).

We must remember that the political tone of the 1980s was set by Ronald Reagan's presidency. His political and educational philosophies, and those of his appointees, affected policy recommendations for education. Reagan assumed office with a mandate for change containing policy recommendations from the Heritage Foundation, a conservative think tank. Initially, his policy proposals included closing the U.S. Department of Education, promoting tuition tax credits, the use of vouchers, and prayer in the schools. As he moved on into his presidency, after *A Nation at Risk* was published, Reagan gave fifty-one speeches on education reform around the country. In these talks, he advocated tougher graduation requirements for students, master teacher programs, increased academic demands and more discipline, learning the basics, and reforming teacher certification.[28] Reagan's policies aided and abetted a shift to the right in political climate and in educational thought.[29] It is Giroux's belief that the conservative agenda for schooling, emphasizing standardized testing, massive accountability schemes for teacher evaluation, standardized curricula, and top-down, get-tough approaches to school discipline has contributed to the disempowerment of teachers.[30] Reagan's educational policies showed no concern for the minority children who will be one-third of the nation by the turn of the century.

Continuing with the political tone of the nation, in November 1988, George H. Bush was elected to the presidency, proclaiming that he intended to be "the education president." However, not much substance emerged from his campaign rhetoric. For example, Bush promised to make Head Start available to all eligible four year olds, but that did not happen.

However, on September 27, 1989, President Bush and the nation's governors met at the University of Virginia, in Charlottesville, in an education summit where they expected to set goals for the nation's schools.[34] Interestingly, and disappointingly, no official from the District of Columbia was included in this summit meeting, although the District's schools are considered a state agency by the U.S. Department of Education.[32] It appears that there will be an effort made to establish *national* standards of performance for schooling outcomes, along with a *national* system of measuring and reporting results.[33]

The education community, particularly the minorities in it, must monitor the results from this closed-door summit meeting. We do not know how these new *national* policies will be implemented in a now decentralized educational system that has many disparities. Apparently, there was no promise of fully funding the educational programs, such as Head Start and Chapter 1, that have already been instituted and that have "track records" of success. Let's hope that this 1989 educational summit was not just another media event. Talk is cheap, but actions speak louder than words. It remains to be seen what Bush will do to make real his claim that he wants to be the "education president." If he is serious about this claim, now is a propitious time to move ahead with substantive actions to implement the rhetoric. Bush could establish a place for himself in history if he seizes the opportunity to re-establish education as desirable, meaningful, useful, doable, worthy of respect and support, and inclusive of all the children of all the people.

It would be misleading to leave the survey of the 1980s without acknowledging that some educational thinkers and researchers did reject the conservative ideas that dominated the decade, among them such intellectuals as Ernest Boyer, John Goodlad, Theodore Sizer, Sara Lawrence Lightfoot, Kenneth Strike, Linda Darling-Hammond, Robert E. Slavin, and Ralph Tyler. They argued for improving the working conditions and salaries of teachers to make the profession more attractive. They advocated increased educational autonomy for principals and teachers. They wanted school bureaucracies reduced and class size limited. They encouraged the development of curricula that offer intellectual adventure, problem-solving, diversified course material, and application of the lessons to the lives of the learners. Making learning meaningful includes more student discussion, more field projects, cooperative learning methods, and expanding students' capabilities. These scholars, along with others cited previously, represented mainstream crosscurrents to conservative views.

New Reform for the 1990s?

In January 1993, William Jefferson (Bill) Clinton assumed the office of President of the United States. With a Democrat in the White House for the first time since the Jimmy Carter administration ended in 1981, we may hope for distinctive leadership changes in presidential recommendations for policies and programs, including those in education. With a Democratic majority in Congress, as well, bipartisan bickering may be minimized.

Clinton came to the presidency from the governorship of Arkansas, one of the nation's poorest states, with a background in educational reform in that state. Additionally, he had chaired the Education Commission of the States in 1986–1987, chaired the National Governors Association (NGA) in 1987–1988, and was cochair of the NGA education task force in 1989–1990. He thus has an experienced background with educational issues, problems, and needs, particularly with respect to poor school districts and people as well as to persons of color.

David Osborne offers an insightful analysis of the complex politics, policies, and programmatic efforts of Bill and Hillary Clinton to improve the public schools in Arkansas.[34] Osborne points out that "when Clinton came into office, Arkansas was last in the nation in education spending per child, in teacher salaries, and in percentage of college graduates."[35] Its state and local tax burden also was, per capita, the lowest in the nation (1979 and 1980). Clinton's aggressive policies secured budget increases of 40 percent (though these had to be reduced in the second year) for elementary and secondary education. He raised teacher salaries, required preservice applicants for teaching positions to pass the National Teacher Examination, and created a summer residence school for gifted children. He introduced teacher testing and standardized tests to measure the performance of public schoolchildren and youth. As a result of these and other aggressive acts in the economic arena, Clinton alienated many Arkansans and lost the 1980 gubernatorial race.

However, he won again in 1982 and built his administration around education reform and economic development. He appointed his wife, Hillary Rodham Clinton, to chair an education committee. The Clintons wanted to upgrade accreditation standards, raise teachers' salaries, lengthen the school year, and improve curricula.[36] Hillary Clinton and her committee held hearings in the 75 Arkansas counties and, by doing so, built up citizen support while simultaneously gathering citizens' opinions about the state of Arkansas's education, including the performance of its teachers. Public opinion swung to the Clintons' side. Arkansans decided that their schools and many of their teachers were indeed inadequate and that it was worth an increase in the sales tax and a property tax rate hike to make the commitment to improve the situation.

Wattenberg's postscript to Osborne's article states that by 1990 the following major changes, and others, resulted from the Clintons' educational reform efforts in Arkansas:[37]

- Eighty percent of the Arkansas state budget is devoted to education, the highest percentage in the nation.
- Teachers' salaries increased more than 77 percent in nine years.
- Students may choose any public school they want to attend provided that acceptable racial balance is maintained.
- More than 50 percent of high school graduates went to college, as contrasted with 36 percent five years earlier.
- Arkansas students moved from the 44th to the 64th percentile in math and from the 46th to the 61st in reading.
- The state's high school graduation rate is the highest in the South and is above average for the nation.
- Elementary school class sizes have been reduced from 35 per class to a maximum of 23 per class for grades 1–3 and 25 in grades 4–8.
- 75,000 students now take advanced math as contrasted with only 5,100 earlier.
- Enrollment in foreign languages has more than tripled.

The Clinton legacy in Arkansas is that he brought about a revolution in the state's attitude toward education. If this legacy can be transferred to the national scene, major positive changes could occur in American schools. Clinton appointed a colleague, former governor of South Carolina, Richard Riley, as Secretary of the Department of Education. In South Carolina, Riley had worked successfully on education reform. Assessments of their performance related to education in their first year in office indicate that neither President Clinton nor Secretary Riley used the force of their offices to give education a high profile. Riley has indicated that the Clinton administration has shifted the national debate on education away from harsh, negative critical comments to a stance of acknowledging a crucial need for fundamental change.

The specific elements of that change are enumerated in the Clinton Administration's education initiative, "Goals 2000: Educate America Act,"[38] which was signed into law by the president on March 31, 1994, P.L. 103–227. It contains ten titles, only two of which will be itemized in detail below.

Title I, "National Education Goals," codifies into law the eight goals, as follows: By the year 2000 (a) all children will start school ready to learn; (b) the high school graduation rate will increase to at least 90 percent; (c) students will leave grades 4, 8, and 12 having demonstrated competency in challenging subject matter; (d) the nation's teaching force will have access to programs for the continued improvement of their professional skills; (e) U.S. students will be the first in the world in math and science; (f) every adult will be literate; (g) every school will be free of drugs, violence, and the unauthorized presence of firearms and alcohol; and (h) every school will promote partnerships that will increase parental involvement and participation in promoting the social, emotional, and academic growth of children. To the six goals initially enumerated, two more were added: one a teacher education and professional development goal, and the other a parental participation goal that is designed to promote school/home partnerships.

Title II, "National Education Reform Leadership, Standards, and Assessments," (a) establishes the National Education Goals Panel to report on the nation's progress in meeting the above goals and to review certification criteria (which it can disapprove) developed by the National Education Standards and Improvement Council (NESIC), as well as voluntary national standards certified by NESIC; (b) establishes the NESIC to develop criteria for certification of national and state standards; certify voluntary *national* standards (content, student performance, and opportunity-to-learn); certify content, student performance, and opportunity-to-learn standards developed and voluntarily submitted by *states* if the state standards are comparable or higher in rigor and quality to voluntary national standards; and certify for a period not to exceed five years assessments voluntarily submitted by states, if the systems adequately measure *state* content standards certified by NESIC, the state can demonstrate that all students have been prepared in the academic content being assessed, and the assessments will not be used by the state for high stakes purposes for five years from the date of enactment of this act; (c) provides for the development of voluntary national opportunity-to-learn standards; (d) authorizes the secretary to make grants to states and school districts to defray the costs of developing, field testing, and evaluation of assessments; (e) establishes an Office of Educational Technology in the U.S. Department of Education to provide federal leadership in developing a national vision and strategy to promote increased awareness and use of technology in educational planning and in schools.

Title III, "State and Local Education Systemic Improvement," provides incentives, including funding, for state and local improvement efforts that aim to help all students reach academic standards. Title IV, "Parental Assistance," supports goal 8, encouraging parental assistance and providing for ways to increase parents' knowledge, strengthen home/school partnerships, and fund at least one parental information and resource center in each state before September 30, 1998. Title V, "National Skill Standards Board," establishes a 28-member National Skill Standards Board to stimulate the development and adoption of a voluntary national system of occupational skill standards and certification. Title VI, "International Education Program," authorizes the Secretary of Education to study international education programs/delivery systems and carry out an international education exchange program. Title VII, "Safe Schools," authorizes competitive grants to school districts to help to ensure safe schools that are violence-free. Title VIII, "Minority-Focused Civics Education," permits the development and implementation of staff development seminars in American government and civics for teachers who work with minority and Native American students. Title IX, "Educational Research and Improvement," reauthorizes the Office of Educational Research and Improvement (OERI) for five years. Title X contains definitions and miscellaneous provisions related to a variety of issues including school prayer; protection of pupil rights; gun-free schools; limitations on the use of assessments; and prohibition of environmental tobacco smoke in kindergarten, elementary and secondary schools, and libraries serving children. (Source: United

States Department of Education, *Goals 2000: Educate America* [Washington, DC: 1994])

This means that national education standards now are a reality. Our country has not had them before, nor have we had skills standards for workers. The effectiveness of the education standards will be determined by how thoroughly and how equitably they are implemented, monitored, and assessed in the nation's 15,000 local school districts. Properly utilized, the goals and standards can represent hope and promise, a new beginning. Using them positively and courageously on behalf of high-quality educational reform to benefit all students and communities could be the linchpin of a Clinton legacy to brighten the national outlook while preparing all students to be contributing citizens and employees in the global village/economy.

WHO SHALL BE EDUCATED, AND TO WHAT ENDS?

This nation has never exhibited a commitment to fully educate its citizens of color. Educational inequalities and underachievement are rooted in the long, strained history of dominant/minority relationships that have existed in this country for close to 400 years. African Americans have systematically fought against their caste-like status since the formal release from slavery on December 18, 1865.

In education, that status meant that African Americans in the postwar South were forbidden to learn. What Horace Mann Bond called "compulsory ignorance" was a cornerstone of public policy in that region. In the North, education for free blacks was often separate, usually unequal. Prior to the Civil War, African Americans sought to educate themselves by organizing churches and establishing their own elementary schools.[39]

After the Civil War, there were differences of opinion among the Freedmen's Bureau, Republican politicians, benevolent philanthropists, northern missionary societies, the southern white planter class, and the former slaves as to whether or not African Americans should be educated. Further, if they were to be schooled, what should be the appropriate educational pattern, and how much schooling should be provided? The compromise that emerged favored practical education, manual labor schools for African Americans. A prolonged discussion of the educational compromises is not appropriate here. The interested reader should consult James D. Anderson's, *The Education of Blacks in the South, 1860–1935,* for details.[40] It is important here to understand that public policy has never been formulated or implemented to provide the means for blacks and other minorities to be educated academically the same as white citizens.

Who shall be educated and to what ends? Public policy constitutionally supported separate and unequal education for African Americans from 1896 (*Plessy v. Ferguson*) to 1954 and 1955, when *Brown v. Topeka Board of Education* I and II were rendered by the Supreme Court, overturning *Plessy.* Even then, no widespread, substantive, conclusive educational changes occurred on the part of white policymakers until the passage in the 1960s of the Civil Rights Act of 1964, the Voting Rights Act of 1965, the Elementary and Secondary Education Act of 1965 (amended in 1974), the Higher Education Act of 1965 (with amendments in 1972), and the institution of affirmative action policies made possible by Executive Order 11246, signed by President Lyndon B. Johnson.

Therefore, African Americans who have been educated successfully, especially in classical, academic, or concentrations other than vocational education, have, in general, been educated against the odds and in spite of the system. Even though public policy grudgingly admitted African Americans to academic curricula, "the higher learning" in education, barriers and roadblocks continued to be erected to prevent both mass access to that knowledge and persistence in schooling. The result is that in 1989 disproportionately large numbers of African Americans and other minorities continued to suffer from longstanding educational inequalities rooted in now longstanding decisions to educate them minimally, preferably in manual or vocational pursuits, to the end of maintaining the established social hierarchy.

Even the most cursory review of the literature of African American education by African American authors will provide evidence that African Americans believe in formal education and have great respect for its intrinsic value as well as its utility as a means for entry into desirable occupations and a chance at "the good life."[41] The prolonged legal battles through the court system's layers are testimony to the African American struggle for equal educational opportunity. The debate between Booker T. Washington and W. E. B. Du Bois about the nature of education to be offered African Americans continues today, although in different form. The point here is that African Americans and other minorities have, by public policy, been excluded from common schooling and the possibility of equity by dominant power holders. At the same time, African Americans and other minorities have fought to eliminate the obstacles erected to prevent them from learning the content that served the dominant group so well, while keeping minorities learning just enough to be eligible for low-level employment and second-class social status.

Most of the school reform reports of the 1980s mention equal educational opportunity or equity only peripherally. They focus on an "excellence" that often is not defined, without considering the social and economic conditions that impede academic work of quality. They fail to provide evidence that their recommendations will make schooling more effective for minorities or the poor. They do not tell us where to find funding for some of the proposed reforms. The reports ignore the public purpose of common schooling, as originally envisioned. They pay little or no attention to reform's effects on minority and low-income students. Their proposed curriculum changes fail to address the cultural resources of minority groups and fail to make traditional approaches to knowledge variable or related to the lives of urban students. They fail to explore what role schools could and should play in maintaining our democratic republic and arriving at a more humane social order. If the most-discussed reform reports are fully implemented, their effect will be to justify the status quo with respect to minority students and to further suggest that their subordinate plight is inevitable. It is not.

Conversely, the crosscurrents to the most-discussed reform reports come from African American organizations and individuals. The 1984 report of the National Alliance of Black School Educators, *Saving the African American Child,* clearly outlines the political aspects of schooling, including the issue of control over its nature and operation. This report focuses on attaining equity, promoting cultural excellence, and altering the curriculum to include African American content in all subjects. It stipulates ways to attain academic goals and advocates staff training in African American content, an end to racism, an end to malpractice in the use of standardized testing, along with community-based cultural education outside of schools. This report recognizes that poverty has a negative impact on the equality of life and calls on the federal government to provide an "adequate basic quality of life," which would undergird an educational safety net. Further, the report recommends research priorities and topics for anyone who is concerned about reforming education on behalf of African Americans.[42] We can generalize from this report to say that similar content and methods should be added to schooling to improve the educational chances of Hispanic, Native American, and Asian American youth in the next decade.

In like manner, a 1989 report from the Joint Center for Political Studies, *Visions of a Better Way: A Black Appraisal of Public Schooling,* is an important and useful tool for sincere individuals and organizations who want to improve schooling. This succinct report examines the historical context in which African Americans have sought to be educated, barriers to successful schooling today, and models and concepts that have improved schools for African American children. It concludes with specific recommendations for correction and change in a positive direction.[43] Again, in Ronald Edmonds's words, "We know enough to educate black children. Will we do it?"

WHAT WILL IMPROVE THE EDUCATION OF BLACKS AND OTHER MINORITIES—AND WHAT ARE THE ANTICIPATED BENEFITS?

Before discussing those policies and actions that will improve the education of minority students, we must first acknowledge what won't work. Pious, pompous platitudes will *not* improve the education of minority people or help this nation move forward to fulfill its economic and political goals. Neither will piecemeal schemes, "Band-Aids" that merely cover superficially what are deep, long-existent, continuing problems. Our children and our nation are indeed "at risk"; only serious, sustained, consistent, authentic policies and programs will solve the problems that are so apparent.

Change is made by people who will solve problems; educational change can occur. Corrections can be made if we accept and use our vast collective wisdom by acting honestly, purposefully, and with energy on what we know at this time of crisis.

We must stop "playing games" with each other. We must stop "playing school." The most basic decision to be made is whether this country intends to educate those minorities who will be one-third of the nation by the year 2000. African Americans, other minorities, and the poor must use their organized efforts and the help of their allies to determine that the answer is affirmative.

What will work? Here I acknowledge my indebtedness to the ideas of many others and draw upon my own experiences.[44]

1. President Clinton and his advisers must set a new tone for the 1990s. First and foremost, public schools need to be reclaimed and resupported as the social institution responsible for providing civic education, common schooling, as a public service to the nation and to individual citizens.
2. The purpose of the public school as an institution must be articulated, then supported.
3. Adequate funding must be allotted to finance schools if they are to be reformed and if the children of the poor are to be given educational opportunity equal to the children of the rich. In June 1989, for example, the Kentucky Supreme Court ruled the state's public school system unconstitutional because of financial disparities between rich and poor districts. Our nation has rich and poor states. Therefore, the obligation is upon the federal government, states, and local communities to adequately fund education.
   A. The federal government must assume a primary role in financing a school reform movement that is national in scope. As a start, full funding for Public Law 100–297, the School Improvement Act, would put substance where only rhetoric now exists. Programs such as Head Start and Chapter 1, with proven, cost-effective track records, should be available to every child who is eligible for participation.
   B. States and local communities must identify and use new revenue sources other than the property tax system for financing schools.
4. Corporations, businesses, and industry must bring employment opportunities back to this country so that students can see that there is hope of employment after they graduate from schooling at the various levels. Full employment is the key to motivating

learners. When it is clear that jobs are in their future, students will exert the effort to learn what schools are teaching.

5. All racial and ethnic groups must be included in discussions and conclusions about what knowledge is of most worth, what is to be learned, how it is to be learned, and in what time span.

6. School climates must be improved. Academic instruction must be the first order of business in schools. Schools must also be places where students are taught to believe in themselves and where they can feel that they are people of value.

7. What is taught must be related to the lives of the learners. We need to draw on the cultural resources of the communities and their people, so that students understand and are interested in what schools are trying to teach. Students must be taught how to use what is taught in school. Problem solving and critical thinking must be integral parts of learning at every level.

8. The curriculum must include the contributions of minority people throughout the subjects. Multiculturalism and diversity must be accepted and enhanced, as in the "salad bowl" concept.

9. Lengthening the school day and year would allow more time for instruction, based on the quality and quantity of what is to be learned in the 1990s. Also, this would allow students less time to forget what they have learned. Presently, a considerable amount of forgetting occurs over summer vacation. However, the school day needs to be reorganized. Lengthening the day must not mean adding more clock hours of "sameness," which would be disastrous.

10. Teaching must be made a more attractive profession, so that intelligent young people will choose it as a career. Teachers must be paid commensurate with the years of education they must acquire to be qualified to instruct and in tandem with the responsibilities of the job that they are expected to do with the young.

11. More African Americans, Hispanics, Native Americans, and Asians need to be recruited as teachers, principals, guidance counselors, school psychologists, school social workers, and so on. In all positions and at all levels the educational enterprise needs more minority professionals.

12. Schools and other social service agencies must work together

more closely so that students and their families are informed about services and facilities that are available to them and designed to meet their needs.

13. The emphasis on standardized testing should be reduced, and student progress measured in terms of their performance, based on agreed-upon standards and criteria. Minority professionals in the various disciplines must be included in decision making related to appropriate standards and criteria.

14. Ineffective teachers, principles, and other personnel must be removed after due process has been honored. "Ineffective" must include those people who refuse to change their behaviors toward minority students, as well as those people who show that they have failed to master the content of their subject-matter specialities and/or classroom management skills.

15. No one plan will succeed for all students. Therefore, schools must be allowed authority to plan for and work with their individual constituencies within the parameters of our democratic ideals and equal educational opportunity.

This country must make a sustained commitment to educate African Americans, other minorities, and the poor; it must be a national commitment so that every child can be reached. Recurring educational recommendations for promoting schemes for parental choice, vouchers, tuition tax credits, privatization, home schooling, and so on will permit wider variations in schooling than now exist, will contribute to the further demise of the "common school" concept, and will undermine public schools. If those recommendations are fully implemented, it is very probable that minority children and poor children will populate "dump schools" or "sink schools" that are little more than holding pens. This state of affairs will not help individuals or our social system.

No "quick fixes" will solve the educational problems that exist in so many public elementary and secondary schools. Secondary schools seem to be worse off than elementary schools today, with such problems as drugs, teenage pregnancy, and low achievement. Are there operational policies and programs that could be replicated to ensure short-term gains and long-term effects? I believe that there are. Brief examples follow.

James P. Comer's School Development Program (SDP), initiated in 1968 in two low-achieving public schools in New Haven, Connecticut, works well. By 1984, those schools, which in 1968 had been 32nd and 33rd of 33 schools in the city, were ranked 3rd and 4th highest out of 26 remaining schools in New Haven. Further, from 1984 to 1989, they had the best attendance records in the city and had no serious behavior problems for over a decade.[45] Comer's plan also works in five other states, where it has been replicated in its entirety. Policymakers, foundations, and public-spirited donors would do well to fund complete replications of SDP across the country. Incomplete, partial replications cannot succeed as well.

In a like manner, public elementary, junior, and senior high schools across the country have accepted and implemented the "effective schools" model espoused by such educators as the late Ronald Edmonds, Wilbur Brookover, Daniel Levine, Lawrence Lezotte, Eugene Eubanks, and others. The 1985 and 1988 Summer Yearbook issues of the *Journal of Negro Education* have publicized the five concepts around which the effective school model operates and case studies of urban schools that work today. Principals of these and other such effective or improving urban schools are willing, even eager, to have interested educators, policymakers, community people, philanthropists, and others visit their schools, observe what is occurring, ask questions, and replicate the "effective schools" principles in their buildings.[46]

Further, parochial and private schools are successfully educating urban children. One such school is Holy Angels School in Chicago, the largest all-black Catholic school in the country.[47] Also in Chicago, Marva Collins is experiencing continuing success with her private school. All of the successful schools cannot be enumerated here, but enough of them exist in varied regions of the country to provide evidence that African American children can learn, that they can achieve at high levels of accomplishment. These schools' beliefs, policies, programs, methods, and evaluation systems can be replicated to increase the number of successful schools.

The totality of poverty and other economic burdens and social, family, and educational problems has become so burdensome to some minority youth that they may never fit into the patterns of conventional schooling that have been established. Samuel D. Proctor offers a solution for such youth, revolving around an intervention investment by the society. The heart of his proposal is the creation of a new institution, a national youth academy with fifty campuses, utilizing inactive military bases.[48] Proctor envisions that 5,000 students could be housed at each location annually, for a total of 250,000 students. These students would be boys and girls age twelve to sixteen who would live on campus, away from their dreadful home environments.

Proctor describes the students' education as an immersion experience. He envisions that the educational scheme has three components: (a) learning lifelong skills, discipline, self-respect, and accomplishment; (b) mastery of subject matter at the established secondary school attainment levels; and (c) cultivation of aesthetic taste and development of the body. One-third of the education would be practical, providing all of the services required on the military bases—maintenance, cooking, housekeeping, farming, health services, and so on. For this work, students would be paid nominally, but it is the training and work combination that is instructive and valuable.

The second third would consist of basic academics in grades seven through twelve, with classes taught by thorough, respected teachers who would first undergo special training for this assignment. To the extent possible, husband/wife teams would be sought so as to portray the customary, traditional family experience.

The last third of the proposed plan involves human development activities, such as music, drama, sports, photography, gymnastics, and so on. The three components would be correlated, to produce self-sufficient, educated, capable individuals.

Proctor emphasizes that it would cost the society *less* to implement this plan than to keep drug addicts in the penal system for a year—about $14,000 per person, as compared with $30,000 per person for incarceration. Proctor's intervention plan seems to me to be a moral and economic investment that will create productive citizens who will be saved from degradation and who will be able to contribute to society. Policymakers would do well to consider such plans.

CONCLUSION

Since 1983, our nation has been permeated with discussions of "school reform." Based on a long history of struggle, first for the right to be educated, then for equal educational opportunity, now for equity in all aspects and at every level of education, African Americans were understandably skeptical about benefits that would come to them from the proposed school reforms of the 1980s. These "reforms" seemed to be more rhetoric than reality for people of color. The proposed policies (e.g., school choice, vouchers) and programs (break-the-mold schools) seemed to have the right political appeal in a decade of conservative dominance and were lauded by articulate, highly visible secretaries of education. A political purpose was served, and some school improvements occurred. For example, students' scores have improved on tests of basic skills.

Nevertheless, in general African Americans felt that the "reform" movements of the 1980s represented a mentality of "business as usual," retaining the status quo, giving the appearance of caring while doing only as much as must be done to maintain social discipline and order. Vilfredo Pareto might have explained this phenomenon by saying that powerful interests are better safeguarded now by chicanery than by force. The elite, under this ideology, make modifications to circumvent counterforces; those variations make cyclical movements possible.[49]

Now, with the passage of Public Law 103–227, the nation has a new federalism in education. Some citizens perceive it as a threat to state and local control of education; others regard it as hope and promise for authentic school reform. For many years, it has been clear that the nineteenth century school model is outmoded and inadequate for twenty-first century conditions and needs; new model(s) must emerge to meet new circumstances. Goals 2000 can be the catalyst and means for the emergence of those new models across the land and for the enlargement of the opportunity structure to prepare all of America's citizens to participate in the global village economy of the twenty-first century.

Sustained leadership in that direction is a necessary imperative for goal attainment. Our nation now has a historic opportunity to reclaim a world leadership role by demonstrating that a multicultural democracy can survive and that diversity can be an asset when its elements are joined and pull together in common purpose. Then, our children will have reason for learning and will exert the effort to be successful in school achievement. Education is a key to ending the cycle of poverty and hopelessness, but children who are forced to grow up without hope cannot break out of poverty.[50] The Clinton Administration can be the right leadership to restore authenticity, decency, and caring. Its officials and Congress can, through federal policies/programs and their enforcement, stimulate and encourage a new national will to educate all of America's youth, particularly the children of color whose families are becoming one-third of the nation. Everyone will benefit as a result.

Neither federal nor state officials need to reinvent old solutions. Models of school success exist in urban areas. These include the Effective Schools Programs and the Comer Plan, elements of which have been incorporated in Goals 2000 (e.g., parent involvement component). Such models, enhanced and strengthened by provisions of the ten Titles of Goals 2000, can be replicated across the nation to teach underachieving children and youth. African American colleges and universities should plan to become professional development centers for preservice and in-service educators (teachers, principals, guidance counselors, school psychologists, school social workers) of all races and ethnic groups who will teach African American and other children of color. These institutions have a long history of successfully educating such professionals to work effectively with these youth and their families.

America needs a renewal of spirit and a rededication to the ideals of fairness and equity. Hope becomes promise and reality as policies and programs are implemented to solve problems and move our nation toward its highest ideals. Goals 2000, properly implemented across the nation, will move our country in this direction.

REFERENCES

Adler, Mortimer. 1982. *The Paideia proposal: An educational manifesto*. New York: Macmillan.

Anderson, James D. 1988. *The education of blacks in the south, 1860–1935*. Chapel Hill, NC: University of North Carolina Press.

Bell, Terrel H. 1986. Education policy developments in the Reagan administration. *Phi Delta Kappan* 67:493.

Bond, Horace Mann. 1970. *The education of the Negro in the American social order*. New York: Octagon.

Butts, R. Freeman. 1989. *The civic mission in educational reform: Perspectives for the public and the profession.* Stanford, CA: Hoover Institution Press.

Carnegie Forum on Education and the Economy. 1986. *A nation prepared: Teachers for the 21st century—The report of the task force on teaching as a profession of the Carnegie Forum on Education and the Economy.* New York: Carnegie Corporation.

College Board. 1985. *Equality and excellence: The educational status of black Americans.* New York: Author.

Comer, James P. 1985. Empowering black children's educational environments. In *Black children: Social, educational, and parental environments,* ed. Harriet Pipes McAdoo and John Lewis McAdoo. Beverly Hills, CA: Sage.

Comer, James P. 1989. Child development and education. *Journal of Negro Education* 58: 125–39.

Du Bois, W. E. B. 1973. In *The education of black people: Ten critiques, 1906–1960,* ed. Herbert Aptheker. Amherst, MA: University of Massachusetts Press.

Futrell, Mary Hatwood. 1989. Mission not accomplished: Education reform in retrospect. *Phi Delta Kappan* 71: 9–11.

Futrell, Mary Hatwood. 1989. Looking back on education reform. *Phi Delta Kappan* 71: 9.

Giroux, Henry A. 1989. Rethinking education reform in the age of George Bush. *Phi Delta Kappan* 70: 728–30.

Holmes Group. 1986. *Tomorrow's teachers: A report of the Holmes Group.* East Lansing, MI: The Holmes Group, Inc. 1986.

Howe, Harold II. 1983. Education moves to center stage: An overview of recent studies. *Phi Delta Kappan* 65: 167–72.

Jones, Faustine C. 1977. *The changing mood in America: Eroding commitment?* Washington, DC: Howard University Press.

Jones-Wilson, Faustine C. 1986. Equity in education: Low priority in the school reform movement. *The Urban Review* 18: 31–39.

Journal of Negro Education 54 (3) (Summer 1985 Yearbook).

Journal of Negro Education 57 (3) (Summer 1988 Yearbook).

Keesbury, Forrest E. 1984. Who wrecked the schools? Thirty years of criticism in perspective. *Educational Theory* 34: 209–17.

National Alliance of Black School Educators, Inc. 1984. *Saving the African American child.* Washington, DC: Author.

National Association for the Advancement of Colored People. 1977 [1983]. *Report on quality education for black Americans: An imperative*. New York: NAACP Special Contributions Fund.

National Black Child Development Institute. 1984. *Civil rights, education, and the black child*. Washington, DC: Author.

National Commission on Excellence in Education. 1983. *A nation at risk: The imperative for educational reform*. Washington, DC: U.S. Government Printing Office, April.

National Conference on Educating Black Children. 1987. A blueprint for action II. Washington, DC: Author.

Pareto, Vilfredo. 1961. Cycles of interdependence. In *Theories of society,* ed. Talcott Parsons, 2: 1381–85. New York: The Free Press of Glencoe.

Passow, A. Harry. 1984. Tackling the reform reports of the 1980s. *Phi Delta Kappan* 65: 644–83.

1985. *Phi Delta Kappan* 66 (April) (Special issue).

Popkewitz, Thomas. 1988 Educational reform: Rhetoric, ritual, and social interest. *Educational Theory* 38: 77–93.

Raywid, Mary Anne. 1962. *The axe-grinders: Critics of our public schools*. New York: Macmillan.

Raywid, Mary Anne, Charles A. Tesconi, Jr., and Donald R. Warren. 1984. *Pride and promise: Schools of excellence for all the people*. Westbury, NY: American Educational Studies Association.

Shapiro, Svi. 1987. Reply to Stedman. *Educational Theory* 37: 77–79.

Shields, Portia. 1989. Holy Angels: Pocket of excellence. *Journal of Negro Education* 58: 203–11.

Spring, Joel. 1989. *The sorting machine revisited: National educational policy since 1945*. rev. ed. New York: Longman.

Stedman, Lawrence C. 1987. The political economy of recent educational reform reports. *Educational Theory* 37: 69–76.

Taylor, Susan Champlin. 1989. A promise at risk: Can America rouse itself to conquer the perils facing its children? *Modern Maturity* 32: 34–41, 84, 89, 90.

Timar, Thomas B., and David L. Kirp. 1989. Education reform in the 1980s: Lessons from the states. *Phi Delta Kappan* 70: 504–11.

1989. *Visions of a better way: A black appraisal of the public schooling*. Washington, DC: Joint Center for Political Studies Press.

Watson, Bernard C. 1980. Education: A matter of grave concern. *The state of Black America 1980*. New York: National Urban League, Inc.

Watson, Bernard C., and Fasaha M. Traylor. 1988. Tomorrow's teachers: Who will they be, what will they know? In Janet Dewart, ed., *The state of Black America 1988*. New York: National Urban League, Inc.

Wilcox, Preston R. 1969. "The Community-Centered School," in Ronald and Beatrice Gross, eds. *Radical school reform*. New York: Simon and Schuster.

Wilson, Reginald. 1989. Black higher education: Crisis and promise. In Janet Dewart, ed., *The state of Black America 1989*. New York: National Urban League, Inc.

Woodson, Carter G. 1968. *The education of the Negro prior to 1961*. New York: Arno Press and *New York Times*.

NOTES

1. R. Freeman Butts, *The Civic Mission in Educational Reform: Perspectives for the Public and the Profession* (Stanford: Hoover Institution Press, 1989), 1–37.

2. Thomas B. Timar and David L. Kirp, "Education Reform in the 1980s: Lessons from the States," *Phi Delta Kappan* 70 (1989): 504–11; Mary Hatwood Futrell, "Looking Back on Education Reform," *Phi Delta Kappan* 71 (1989): 11.

3. Faustine C. Jones-Wilson, "Equity in Education: Low Priority in the School Reform Movement," *The Urban Review* 18 (1986): 31–39.

4. Henry A. Giroux, "Rethinking Education Reform in the Age of George Bush," *Phi Delta Kappan* 70 (1989): 728–30; Paul D. White "Public Education Is a Mess," *Washington Post,* 30 May 1989, p. A19.

5. Svi Shapiro, "Reply to Stedman," *Educational Theory* 37 (1987): 78; Thomas Popkewitz, "Educational Reform: Rhetoric, Ritual, and Social Interest," *Educational Theory* 38 (1988): 77; Mary Anne Raywid, Charles A. Tesconi, Jr., & Donald R. Warren, *Pride and Promise: Schools of Excellence for All the People* (Westbury, NY: American Educational Studies Association, 1984).

6. A. Harry Passow, "Tackling the Reform Reports of the 1980s," *Phi Delta Kappan* 65 (1984): 644–83.

7. Mary Anne Raywid, *The Ax-Grinders: Critics of Our Public Schools* (New York: Macmillan, 1962).

8. Joel Spring, *The Sorting Machine Revisited: National Educational Policy Since 1945*, rev. ed. (New York: Longman, 1989), 151, 168; Forrest E. Keesbury, "Who Wrecked the Schools? Thirty Years of Criticism in Perspective," *Educational Theory* 34 (1984): 209–17.

9. See selected articles from the 20th anniversary of compensatory education section of *Phi Delta Kappan* 66 (April 1985), specifically Lawrence J. Schweinhart and David P. Weikart, "Evidence that Good Early Childhood Programs Work," pp. 545–47; Lawrence J. Schweinhart "The Promise of Early Childhood Education," pp. 548–53; Virginia R. L. Plunkett, "From Title I to Chapter 1: The Evolution of Compensatory Education," pp. 533–37.

10. Spring, *The Sorting Machine Revisited,* 153–60.

11. Spring, *The Sorting Machine Revisited,* 164–67.

12. Faustine C. Jones, *The Changing Mood in America: Eroding Commitment?* (Washington, DC: Howard University Press, 1977), 41–80.

13. Robert J. Havighurst and Daniel U. Levine, *Society and Education,* 5th ed. (Boston: Allyn and Bacon, Inc., 1975: 40–43.

14. Mortimer Adler, *The Paideia Proposal: An Educational Manifesto* (New York: Macmillan, 1982).

15. National Commission on Excellence in Education, *A Nation at Risk: The Imperative for Educational Reform* (Washington, DC: U.S. Government Printing Office, April 1983).

16. Mary Hatwood Futrell, "Mission Not Accomplished: Education Reform in Retrospect," *Phi Delta Kappan* 71 (1989): 9–11.

17. Futrell, 11.

18. College Board, *Equality and Excellence: The Educational Status of Black Americans* (New York: 1985).

19. Harold Howe II, "Education Moves to Center Stage: An Overview of Recent Studies," *Phi Delta Kappan* 65 (1983): 167–72.

20. NAACP, *Report on Quality Education for Black Americans: An Imperative* (New York: N.A.A.C.P. Special Contributions Fund, 1977, and 1983 update); National Black Child Development Institute, *Civil Rights, Education, and the Black Child* (Washington, DC: Author, 1984); National Alliance of Black School Educators, Inc., *Saving the African American Child* (Washington, DC: 1984).

21. The Holmes Group, Inc., *Tomorrow's Teachers* (East Lansing MI: Michigan State University, 1986); Carnegie Forum on Education and the Economy, *A Nation Prepared: Teachers for the 21st Century—The Report of the Task Force on Teaching as a Profession of the Carnegie Forum on Education and the Economy* (New York: Carnegie Corp., 1986).

22. Futrell, 11–13.

23. *Journal of Negro Education* 57 (1988): 141–58. See selected articles from *The Journal of Negro Education* 57 (1988). Articles of particular interest include Beverly M. Gordon, "Implicit Assumptions of the Holmes and Carnegie Reports: A View from an African-American Perspective," pp. 141–58; Bernard Oliver, "Structuring the Teaching Force: Will Minority Teachers Suffer?" pp. 159–65; A. Wade Smith, "Maintaining the Pipeline of Black Teachers for the Twenty-First Century," pp. 167–77; G. Pritchy Smith, "Tomorrow's White Teachers: A Response to the Holmes Group," pp. 178–94; Reginald Wilson, "Recruiting and Maintaining Minority Teachers," pp. 195–98; Mary E. Dilworth, "A Continuing Critique of the Holmes Group," pp. 199–201.

24. See, for example, Bernard C. Watson, "Education: A Matter of Grave Concern," in *The State of Black America 1980;* Bernard C. Watson with Fasaha M. Traylor, "Tomorrow's Teachers: Who will They Be, What Will They Know," in *The State of Black America 1988;* Reginald Wilson, "Black Higher Education: Crisis and Promise," in *The State of Black America 1989.*

25. National Conference on Educating Black Children, "A Blueprint for Action II" (Washington, DC: 1987).

26. Spring, *The Sorting Machine Revisited,* 185.

27. Futrell, 13–14.

28. Terrel H. Bell, "Education Policy Developments in the Reagan Administration," *Phi Delta Kappan* 67 (1986): 493.

29. Lawrence C. Stedman, "The Political Economy of Recent Educational Reform Reports," *Educational Theory* 37 (1987): 74.

30. Giroux, "Rethinking Education Reform," 728–30.

31. David S. Broder and David Hoffman, "Bush, Governors Chart Ambitious School Goals," *Washington Post,* 28 September, 1989, p. A4; Frank J. Murray, "Bush Hails Education Goals as a 'Major Step,' " *Washington Times,* 29 September 1989, pp. A1, A3, A10; David, S.

Broder, "It's Easy to Set School Goals," *Washington Post,* 27 September 1989, p. A31.

32. *Washington Post,* 28 September 1989, p. A4.

33. David S. Broder, "Education: Help Might Be on the Way," *Washington Post,* 20 September 1989, p. A25.

34. David Osborne, "Turning Around Arkansas' Schools: Bill Clinton and Education Reform."

35. Osborne, "Turning Around Arkansas' Schools," 9.

36. Osborne, "Turning Around Arkansas' Schools," 10.

37. Ruth Wattenburg, "Postscript" to Osborne, "Turning Around Arkansas' Schools," 16–17.

38. Mark Pitsch, "Picture Mixed for Education, Clinton Team," *Education Week,* XIII, 18 (1994) 1; 19.

39. Carter G. Woodson, *The Education of the Negro Prior to 1861* (New York: Arno Press and *New York Times,* 1968).

40. James D. Anderson, *The Education of Blacks in the South, 1860–1935* (Chapel Hill, NC: University of North Carolina Press, 1988).

41. See, for example, Horace Mann Bond, *The Education of the Negro in the American Social Order* (New York: Octagon, 1970); W. E. B. Du Bois, *The Education of Black People: Ten Critiques, 1906–1960* ed. Herbert Aptheker (Amherst, MA: University of Massachusetts Press, 1973).

42. NABSE, "Blueprint," 11–43.

43. *Visions of a Better Way: A Black Appraisal of Public Schooling* (Washington, DC: Joint Center for Political Studies Press, 1989).

44. I am indebted to the ideas of R. Freeman Butts, Mary Anne Raywid, Charles A. Tesconi, Jr., Donald R. Warren, Joel Spring, Henry A. Girouxi, NABSE members, the Joint Center for Political Studies, Congressman Augustus Hawkins, NCEBC members, and many others. Over a period of years, I have been influenced by Dr. Edmonia W. Davidson's analyses and wisdom in these and other educational matters. I acknowledge the influence of these people and their ideas on my work.

45. James P. Comer, "Child Development and Education," *Journal of Negro Education* 58 (1989), 125–39; James P. Comer, "Empowering Black Children's Educational Environments," in *Black Children: Social, Educational, and Parental Environments,* ed. Harriette Pipes McAdoo and John Lewis McAdoo (Beverly Hills, CA: Sage, 1985).

46. *Journal of Negro Education* 57, 3 (1988); *Journal of Negro Education* 55, 3 (1985).

47. Portia Shields, "Holy Angels: Pocket of Excellence," *Journal of Negro Education* 58 (1989): 203–11.

48. Samuel D. Proctor, "To the Rescue: A National Youth Academy," *New York Times,* 16 September 1989.

49. Vilfredo Pareto, "Cycles of Interdependence," in *Theories of Society,* eds. Talcott Parsons, Edward Shils, Kaspar D. Naegele, Jesse R. Pitts. (New York: The Free Press of Glencoe, 1961) 1381–85.

50. Susan Champlin Taylor, "A Promise at Risk: Can America Rouse Itself to Conquer the Perils Facing Its Children?" *Modern Maturity* 32 (1989): 32–41, 84, 89, 90. In addition, policymakers should consult the publications of the Children's Defense Fund and listen to Marian Wright Edelman, director of that organization, for implementable solutions that will help children and youth who are truly "at risk."

16 Testing Testing: Assessment, Standardized Tests, and the Educational Process among African American Students

SYLVIA T. JOHNSON

The assessment scales constructed by Alfred Binet at the beginning of the century were designed to identify low-scoring children and target appropriate instruction toward them at an early age so that their school performance would be maximized.

Among the Igbo people of Nigeria, the length, flexibility, and degree of control of the forearm and hand are appraised in young children before they begin formal academic schooling, with a view toward not beginning such a regimen until a child is ready to accept, advance in, and enjoy this experience.

Among many African peoples, there are long-term, systematic, and elaborate educational programs spread over a period of four years that are prerequisite to attaining adulthood. The educational experiences that constitute these programs are extended and modified, depending on the performance of the learners in specific activities.

All these efforts use measurement in the interests of the learner. We have developed the science, art, and practice of measurement extensively in educational practice in the United States. Where do we fall in terms of using measurement in the interests of the learner, particularly the African American learner? To explore this question, we will examine the performance of African Americans on a range of tests and look at the widely reported gap between the scores of American minority youth and majority youth. We will also discuss various internal and external factors affecting test scores.

THE TEST SCORE GAP

Standardized test results released from school districts; college admissions testing programs; certification testing for teachers, lawyers, and other professionals; and even large-scale armed forces testing repeatedly document the finding that average scores of African Americans and Hispanics are lower than those of whites or Asians. Such releases are usually followed by choruses of explanations, angry recriminations, and veiled or not-so-veiled reassertions of racial inferiority.

Often, news reports of test scores either do not emphasize several fundamental verities about testing in general or overstate others. As a result, the meaning people draw from score reports may be essentially projective. In other words, we see what we already believe the situation to be, making the scores useless for positive educational purposes and almost magical in their support of already-held beliefs.

Those who feel that test scores are irrelevant may discount results entirely. Those who perceive average results across groups as measures of each individual may imagine that each white child stands intellectually above each African American and Hispanic youngster, regardless of whether they regard this gap as a function of home, school, or nature.

Actually, these interpretations ignore the very nature of measuring characteristics of people as well as the fact that these average scores represent groups whose members typically have scores stretched throughout the range of possible scores on a test. There are many low-scoring white children and many high-scoring African American and Hispanic children. Further, group score differences are due to a complex interplay of factors, including educational experiences, motivation, socioeconomic background, and limitations in the precision of measurement.

PERFORMANCE OF AFRICAN AMERICANS ON STANDARDIZED TESTS

In nearly all schools, the major national standardized tests are used to test African American elementary and high school students along with their peers. African American youth at three grade levels from elementary to high school are proportionally represented in the National Assessment of Educational Progress (NAEP), conducted annually across the country. Those entering or considering the military take the Armed Services Vocational Aptitude Battery (ASVAB). For college admission, many students take either the Scholastic Aptitude Test (SAT), constructed by the Educational Testing Service (ETS) for the College Board, the American College Testing Program tests, or both. Although some of these tests are called aptitude measures, they are generally regarded as measures of knowledge and skill attainment, or achievement.

How do African American students fare on these standardized tests? The scores they achieve are roughly equivalent to or somewhat lower than the scores of non-African Americans with similar educational and income levels. The spread of scores tends to be lowest among those from low income levels with weak educational backgrounds (Bock and Mislevy 1980; CEEB 1987).

Substantial variability exists among the mean test scores for African American students from different communities and age groups. In those communities where the distribution of income and education among African Americans is comparable to that among the total American population and where the school systems are highly rated and well supported, African American students at all grade levels generally score at or above the national norm for all students. In strong urban school systems, test scores of African American students also show moderate, steady annual increases as greater resources are expended and improved instructional strategies are used (MCPS 1985). For example, in a Maryland county just outside Washington, DC, with a 15 percent African American population in its schools, African American students are at or slightly above the national norms for the California Achievement Tests. Among the local black population, the median levels of income and education are about the same as the figures for whites nationally (MCPS 1985). The median income and educational level for all county residents is near the top for the United States as a whole. The county-wide scores, well above national norms, reflect the importance of these antecedents.

THE NATURE OF MEASUREMENT

Scores on standardized tests are numbers with inherent egalitarian appeal. It seems logical that if a test operates as a mental yardstick, test scores should accurately reflect the appropriate level of knowledge of the person being tested. Such an interpretation, however, presupposes that the test score is an implicit substitution for the "real thing" we want to measure. In reality, the relationship between the test score and the characteristic we actually want to measure may not be the same for all examinees, particularly for African Americans and members of other racial minorities who have been systematically excluded from educational benefits. As a result, a test score alone, for minority groups, is often not a sufficient measure of aptitude, achievement, or other psychological or educational constructs.

Yet test scores are increasingly used in educational and employment decisions at all levels. These decisions involve not only educational programming and vocational placement of individual students or job applicants, but also, increasingly, the evaluation of schools, school systems, and training programs in terms of their efficacy in providing educational experiences.

This broader usage of tests has had several positive outcomes. Community groups have responded to reports of low test scores in local public schools by developing school- and community-based strategies to improve the curriculum. Because of these efforts, school systems have achieved improvements in the average scores on standardized tests. The knowledge that test scores will be viewed as barometers of a school's progress probably sensitizes teachers and administrators to the "fit" between curriculum and test, and encourages systematic coverage of the curriculum. Such use of tests does not necessarily validate the quality of the tests as measurement devices; rather, it speaks to the effectiveness of the tests as spurs to curriculum development and instructional improvement.

The essential point to recognize whenever educational or psychological measurement is used is that such measurement is never done directly. We do not measure minds the same way we measure the length of a room. Although physical measurement also can produce errors, the errors that occur in measuring characteristics of people may be particularly difficult to detect and interpret. All educational and psychological measurement techniques are applied to behavior, from which a level of achievement, aptitude, personality, interest, or some other human characteristic that cannot be measured directly is inferred.

A low score on a psychological measure simply does not have much meaning alone. It may mean that the person tested places a low value on what is being measured, or that what is being measured is present but is not being tapped by the specific behavior measure used. This axiom of psychological measurement is well known to test makers, many of whom agonize over the lack of information provided by low scores. Yet the less people know about measurement, the more they believe in the infallibility of the test score.

Any interpretation of the meaning of a test score should also take into account other indexes of the individual's performance. A given score should be examined along with current scores on other tests or with scores on similar tests given at a different time.

FACTORS AFFECTING TEST SCORES

To better understand the performance levels of African Americans on standardized tests, it is important to examine the factors that affect test scores. The test score is a product of the test itself, the person tested, and the test setting (see Fig. 1). From this perspective, factors within the test include the technical aspects of how test items are generated and scaled, standardization and tryout group features, question content and format, and the test criterion (Johnson 1979). Despite careful and conscientious attention to test development, the need to make a test broadly applicable to children in general may make the test less precise for measurement with particular children. This is a common problem in developing a nationally marketed test.

Test items are typically generated to meet the specifications established for the test. These specifications are a set of requirements regarding the specific content and type of task involved in the test; the level of intellectual process required, such as simple recall, information analysis, or the application of principles to a novel situation; the difficulty of the items; and the format and any other important characteristics. Specifications are usually laid out in a rectangular grid to show the requirements of particular cells, then test developers can assemble items appropriately for a complete test.

FIGURE 1. Factors Affecting Test Score

The Test (or Item Pool)

1. Nature of item tryout sample
2. Nature of standardization group
3. Item scaling model and methods
4. Manner of item subset generation
5. Logical strategies in test building
6. Format of questions
7. Appearance
8. Item content and features
9. Choice of criterion

The Tested

1. Race and racism
2. Sex and sexism
3. Motivation
4. Socioeconomic status
5. School experiences
6. Home experiences
7. Ways of thinking
8. Interests and preferences

The Test-Taking

1. Personal characteristics of the tester
2. Expectancies and beliefs of the tester
3. Physical surroundings
4. Mode of test presentation
5. Timing or pacing of presentation

Source: Johnson, S.T. 1984. The test, the tested, and the test taking: A model to better understand test performance. Paper presented at the Annual Meeting of the American Educational Research Association, April 1984, in New Orleans, LA.

Items are then tried out on people similar to those for whom the test is intended, often in conjunction with an existing test or scaled set of items that serves as a yardstick for judging the quality of the new items. If the performance of the tryout group on a new item is consistent with performance on the existing test or items, we say the item discriminates well or has a high discrimination index. (This is discrimination in a descriptive sense and not in the sense of racial or sexual discrimination.) If the performance on a new item is inconsistent with performance on the existing test or items, the item is said to have a negative discrimination index. Should this occur, the new item is examined carefully and either revised to remove errors in meaning, style, or context, or it is discarded. It is also possible that items may not discriminate in either direction. When this happens, people who do either well or poorly on the existing test perform at about the same level on the tryout item. This results in a flat shape for the item's characteristic curve—the graph of its performance relative to total score performance. These "flat" items may be discarded by test developers because they do not add to the information gained from a test.

The group of flat items may include some poor items, but it may also include items with good discrimination power for subgroups for whom their content is appropriate but with little or no discrimination for other groups. If the proportion of African Americans in the tryout group is small, items with greater validity for this group may be eliminated at this stage and thus not be included when the test is standardized. Therefore, attention needs to be given to the composition of both tryout and standardization groups, and to item performance within race and sex subgroups.

The criterion toward which a test is aimed is a policy issue with measurement meaning. For selection tests, *criterion* is defined as the important future outcome that the test is designed to predict. Conceptually, the criterion may be "superior performance as a physician," but operationally, that criterion must be reduced to something measurable, such as first-year grade point average in college or medical school. These operational choices of criterion measure are important policy decisions because they indicate what we accept as tangible evidence of success.

The factors tested include all that individuals bring with them to the test in terms of background, expectations, home and school experiences, ways of thinking, interests, and preferences. These factors also form the motivational framework that spurs or slows the taking-on of the testing task. This factor is discussed further in the motivation section of this chapter.

The test setting is more than the room, desk, and chair. It includes the tester and the meaning and expectations communicated by the total setting. If individuals receive many messages that striving for achievement includes rejection and pain rather than enhancement, they will behave accordingly in a situation that arouses these responses. These messages may be received more often by poor African American children than by children from middle-class backgrounds. Strategies that alter the messages and meaning of context have been found to affect achievement positively, particularly among African American children (Jagers 1992; Johnson and Anderson 1992; Ladson-Billings 1992; Lee 1992; Shujaa 1992; Swartz 1992).

TESTS AND SOCIOECONOMIC STATUS

Because the distribution of African Americans across socioeconomic levels differs from that of other groups, it is important to examine the relationship between test scores and socioeconomic status (SES). Studies citing everything from early childhood achievement measures to medical school admission tests have consistently found sizable and statistically significant positive correlations between SES indexes (such as income and educational level) and test scores across diverse populations. A logical question here is: "Do tests measure constructs in ways that are more appropriate and valid for students from higher-income families, or does economic advantage provide a consistent framework for the academic improvement that results, on the average, in higher test performance?" One of the earliest investigations of the relationship between test scores and SES was done by Allison Davis, an African American educational anthropologist at the University of Chicago. In that landmark study of white students of varying socioeconomic backgrounds in a mid-sized Illinois city, Davis found a strong relationship between SES and standardized test scores (Davis 1948).

While Davis clearly recognized the enabling effects of economic advantage, he was concerned that current instruments did not accurately identify superior talent among young people from lower socioeconomic backgrounds. Along with Kenneth Eels, Davis developed a test designed to be free of the cultural effects identified in the earlier study (Davis and Eels 1951). Although the measure had mixed results in subsequent research, it represented the first attempt to build a measure of general ability without a strong component based on common cultural experiences. Subsequently, Anne Anastasi put forth an approach to measuring constructs across different cultural groups (Anastasi 1950, 1954). She asserted that test makers needed either to identify commonalities across cultures and base tests on these factors or to develop instruments within cultures based on behaviors that represent intelligent, adaptive behavior within specific contexts. The Davis-Eels Games represented the first approach (Davis and Eels 1951); this effort was followed by other attempts in succeeding years. The within-culture approach has had fewer advocates. A demonstration of its use among African American groups was developed by Robert Williams (Williams 1973).

The use of test data, or the action that results as a specific outcome of the attainment of a test score, is a tremendously important issue, and here SES may also play a crucial role. Family resources and know-how may influence what happens within a school when a child scores low. In one setting, low scores mean that fewer school resources are expended, whereas in another setting, it is a signal for an immediate, targeted, and well-monitored expenditure of support services to maximize intellectual development.

Finding a relationship between SES and test scores should not be an excuse for inaction. It simply means that more should be done to help low-income children succeed academically. There are numerous examples of action taken in successful and effective schools with low-income populations resulting in improvements in academic climate, school achievement, test scores, and future prospects for graduates. In fact, the test-SES connection should spur school districts to apply extra resources by reducing class size; raising expectations of teachers and children; and providing tutoring, counseling, and social services to counter this relationship.

The test-SES relationship should not be interpreted to support an "evil genie" theory of test making. There is a relationship between school resources and income, between per-pupil expenditures and income, and between academic performance measured by grades and income; thus, a test score and income relationship should not surprise us. Higher income increases the likelihood that educational interventions will be available throughout the schooling years to help raise test scores and other indexes of achievement. These consistent interventions are designed with the expectation of cumulative results on achievement in the long run, and although these interventions may be modified, they are not discontinued in the face of short-term findings, as often happens with interventions in low-income schools. Nor can one assume that all poor children score badly on tests. However, it does mean that, on average, poor children, both black and white, score lower than middle- and upper-income students on standardized tests at all levels, from elementary school through graduate school.

A complex interaction with SES occurs when we consider drug and health effects on tests scores of black and white students. Although an estimated 75 to 80 percent of drug users are white, drugs have their most pervasive effects on poor, predominantly black urban communities (Poulin 1991; U.S. Dept. of Commerce, 1993; Gordon, and Nembhard 1994). The general climate and public safety are often so affected by the turf wars of drug dealers and the behavior of drug users that children in some communities go to school to retreat and are unable to function effectively intellectually (Nobles and Goodard 1989; Anderson 1990). Clearly, all aspects of school achievement, including test scores, will be affected in such cases.

Proper health care and nutrition are basic requirements for all children. Dr. Reed Tuckson, former commissioner of public health in Washington, D.C., has stated that 60,000 people of color died premature deaths owing to the disproportionate quality of health care (Abramowitz 1989). It is reasonable to state, then, that poor health care, inadequate or nonexistent health insurance, the absence of preventive health services in the community, and limited family income are risk factors for low school achievement because they deny children the basic requirements to prepare them to achieve.

BIAS AND COLLEGE ADMISSION TESTS

Are the lower average test scores of African Americans due to academic background or to problems with both the test and the test setting? Recent research suggests that the correct response is "all of the above." According to student self-report information, black students taking the SAT have, on average, taken fewer mathematics courses in high school than their white counterparts (Ramist and Arbeiter 1986). However, there is also increasing evidence that special test preparation and coaching can increase SAT scores.

In 1984, the National Association for the Advancement of Colored People (NAACP) conducted a test preparation program in New York City, Atlanta, and San Francisco among African American youth from low-income backgrounds (Johnson et al. 1985). Average math and verbal scores improved 70–85 points, with some students gaining as much as 200 points on one of the two subtests. The curriculum included test-taking strategies, review of fundamentals of algebra and geometry, and vocabulary and reading activities. Involvement of parents was solicited in encouraging and motivating students, monitoring homework completion for the program, and assisting in transportation arrangements to ensure timely attendance. The effectiveness of the program, which provided thirty-six hours of classroom instruction, may be attributed to students' improved academic skills, lowered test anxiety, and increased levels of motivation and self-confidence in the test setting. A subsequent study of performance on specific test items showed that, in addition to earning higher scores, students tended to answer more test questions after the coaching, and their increased performance was not confined to particular item types (Johnson and Wallace 1989).

IDENTIFICATION OF BIAS IN TESTS

Test makers use several systematic techniques to reduce or eliminate racial and cultural effects in tests, and current tests are much better in that regard than were their predecessors. These procedures include a sensitivity review of all test items by reviewers specially trained to identify content that might be offensive, misleading, or confusing to particular groups, as well as extensive statistical procedures to identify biased items.

Most current techniques for examination of bias involve the study of test items. In general, these techniques require either that items be compared with the entire test as a criterion or standard, or that groups of equal performance levels on some standard be compared on each item. One technique is differential item functioning (DIF). DIF, which was developed at the ETS by measurement scientists using a procedure originally devised for cancer research, is a method for identifying test items that show differential performance between groups of students matched on the basis of ability or achievement. One would expect that some general principles might emerge that would assist test developers in writing and refining test questions, and, in fact, some have (Medley and Quirk 1974). However, often items identified have nothing that can be reasonably determined to be a cause of differential difficulty. While the offending item can be removed from the test, it is not possible to prevent other items from causing similar problems if the basis of the differential difficulty is obscure.

Identifying and removing biasing features of test items using statistical procedures of this type have certain inherent logical problems. Biased items are identified when the students' performance on them is sharply different from performance on other items. However, defining these items as biased assumes that most items are unbiased. It is in fact remotely possible that if the entire test was poor, these aberrant items would be the best or the most fair. DIF researchers meet this criticism by using the procedure to identify items that function differently. They then remove the offending items and repeat the matching procedures. This helps to remove from the matching standard test items that may have been unfair to a group (African Americans, Hispanics, women) when individuals of equal performance were compared.

MOTIVATION

The importance of motivation in test taking is generally accepted, but it is often perceived as a characteristic wholly under the control of the person being tested. If characteristics of the test materials are not appealing or are even alienating, the person's performance on the test may be decreased even though, on one level, that person desires to do well. Conversely, test questions of high interest and attraction may really "grab" students, hold attention, and spur them to more intensive intellectual activity. In this way, the actual test content can have motivational value by influencing the person's internal decision to take on the task required by the test question.

Two researchers at the ETS demonstrated this several years ago in a study of an older version of the National Teacher Examination (NTE), a test widely used for teacher certification (Medley and Quirk 1974). Using a group of both black and white college students, they administered questions from the NTE with a set of parallel items constructed to be equally difficult in terms of the reasoning and judgement involved, but with content features targeted to interest African American students. As predicted, the white students did better on the "real" NTE questions, and the black students showed superior performance on the parallel questions. These results are consistent with the review of motivation toward academic achievement in African Americans (Banks, McQuater, and Hubbard 1978), which presented extensive evidence on the importance of interest and content features in the performance of students of all ethnic groups. This reconceptualization is a valuable base for research on motivational factors in testing material and their role in influencing examinee performance.

Motivation toward maximum performance comes from self-confidence and our own expectation of personal performance. These are formed by our experiences, including the expectations of others as we experience them. The expectations of performance held by teachers and administrators not only serve to form the performance of students in the Pygmalion sense, but actually determine what educational interventions are made.

An administrator with one expectation may regard low achievement test scores in reading and math at the fifth-grade level as a basis for excluding a child from the standard sixth-grade curriculum, with subsequent placement in a "basic skills" course. A private prep school administrator may see the same score as an indicator of the additional tutoring and academic support that needs to be provided to prepare the child for the Preliminary Scholastic Aptitude Test (PSAT), the Scholastic Aptitude Test (SAT), and eventual college admission. This administrator knows that for the upper-middle-class student, college is a "given" and the task of the school is to provide the necessary preparation. When these beliefs are further conditioned by teacher and administrator expectations of differing performance by race, African American children from poor families get a "double whammy" in low expectations of performance with concomitant effects on self-confidence and achievement. The task of the school is to do what is necessary to prepare the student. However, if the definition of *necessary* is conditioned by these expectation factors, opportunity is curtailed. It is here that racism can operate in the most insidious way because these racially biased expectations may create a situation in which black and white children in the same classroom experience different environments, which may have important consequences for their subsequent achievement. The prescription for children who score low cannot be a school situation in which they do less.

TESTING AND THE MILITARY

A large proportion of African American youth enter the armed forces after completing high school and participate in the Department of Defense (DOD) testing program. The DOD is the nation's largest test user. Through its construction and administration of the Armed Services Vocational Aptitude Battery (ASVAB) it has a profound impact on the broad range of American youth who desire to enter military service. The ASVAB's 10 subtests include traditional academic areas such as work knowledge, paragraph comprehension, numerical operations, and knowledge of mathematics, as well as familiarity with specialized areas such as automobiles, general shop, and electronics.

The ASVAB has undergone regular revisions and is currently being revised and revalidated. In an earlier major test norming and bias analysis study, the DOD reported test results by racial group (Bock and Mislevy 1980). Yet the sharply different educational experiences of young people included in these groups make such comparisons misleading. All 16- to 25-year-olds took the same tests, but some 25-year-olds had been out of school for eight years and had not taken a test since that time, whereas others were in graduate school. The greater proportion of black youth in the former category and of white youth in the latter category produced results that confirmed educational difficulties with race. In addition, the high school programs of 16-year-old test takers were diverse. Some of these test takers, disproportionally African American, were enrolled in half-day distributive educational programs, whereas others, among whom were proportionally fewer African Americans, were enrolled in chemistry and German. All of these differences were aggregated under the label of race and reported in five score ranges called "mental categories" (Bock and Mislevy 1980).

The differences found *within* racial groups were greater than those found *between* groups. For example, within the white group tested, the differences in test scores between young people whose mothers had low levels of education and those whose mothers were college trained were far greater than any of the differences between ethnic groups. Clearly, the disparate educational experiences among these young people are major determinants of their performance on the ASVAB (Bock and Mislevy 1980).

The effect of income level on test scores was also clarified by the armed forces results. For example, the average scores of whites whose mothers had finished grades 9 though 11, of Hispanics whose mothers had finished high school, and of African Americans whose mothers had begun college were about the same. The 1981 Census figures also indicate that these three groups of women had similar income levels, thereby supporting the link between test score, income, and parental background (Block and Mislevy 1980).

The DOD has a special opportunity, and even a responsibility, to use its extensive test data to the educational benefit of African Americans. Under the volunteer armed forces, large numbers of African American men and women are entering the service. In some states, as many as 37 percent of young African American men completing high school in a given year enter military service (Bock and Mislevy 1980). Recruits are assigned to training programs according to the test scores recorded upon entry. Although it is possible to be retested and to move to other levels of training, a systematic push to encourage and reward educational development aimed at entry to more advanced training programs seems a natural and appropriate use of the DOD system. This would truly be a use of measurement not only in the interests of the learner but also in the broadest national interest.

TEACHER CERTIFICATION TESTING

The role of certification testing in the current shortage of African American teachers is an important issue that has been widely discussed. A major reason for this shortage is that many African American applicants have had difficulty passing teacher certification tests. This raises the question of the validity and appropriateness of such tests in selecting teachers. Are tests eliminating people who would be good, even outstanding, teachers? This is not an easy question to answer, and it requires a look at what is involved in certification testing.

A particular problem is involved in certification testing for teaching, law, and other fields in which group differences in mean test scores by race have been found. In such tests, a particular body of content is tested, but what is really *desired* is the identification of successful practitioners in the field and the elimination of poor practitioners. The knowledge of a relevant body of content is no doubt related to successful practice, but having this knowledge alone is certainly not sufficient to ensure successful practice, and in some cases it may not even be necessary. If a knowledge-based test eliminates individuals who are already functioning as effective teachers according to comprehensive evaluation standards, and if those eliminated individuals are disproportionately African American or of other minority groups, it would seem appropriate to question the use of this test. The critical problem for certification testers is the definition of necessary and meaningful areas of content and the simulation of situations that may have greater relationship to field practice. There is some evidence that appraisals with a stronger field practice base show less difference or, in some cases, no difference by race (Witty 1986). Some creative efforts toward solutions are under way to improve teacher certification testing. These include the PRAXIS, a redesigned successor to the NTE, as well as custom programs designed for individual states. This ongoing work should result in better certification testing, but it will cost more and will probably take much more time and effort from both candidates and certifiers.

TEACHERS AND TESTING

Teachers play a critical role in the achievement of all children, African American as well as others, and they may be especially important to poor children, a disproportionate number of whom are from American minority groups. Where such children are concerned, it is clearly vital to have committed teachers who care deeply about teaching.

The role of this commitment as a factor in school achievement has emerged in a recent report of the NAEP from the 1988 reading assessment (NAEP 1989). Teachers of fourth-grade students were asked about their backgrounds and teaching practices, and their responses were matched with the performance of their students. Neither teachers nor students were identified during this process. Teachers of low-scoring students reported slightly greater usage of prescriptive techniques, including individual and small group instruction, which would be an expected and appropriate targeting. However, teachers were also asked, "If you could start over, would you become a teacher?" Less than 4 percent of all respondents said "no," and 12 percent indicated "probably not." However, among teachers in metropolitan schools of relatively low SES, 10 percent answered "no" and 24 percent answered "probably not." Among teachers of African American children, 8 percent and 20 percent answered "no" and "probably not," respectively. Further, those teachers answering "no" or "probably not" tended to have lower-scoring students, whether they worked in low-income or high-income schools. The data does not allow us to determine whether these feelings preceded their school assignments. However, we can recognize the need to make the circumstances and surroundings of teaching at least as positive for those teachers in low-income urban areas as for those in high-income urban or suburban areas and, for such settings that may require more from teachers and may not provide short-term reinforcement, to recruit individuals who care deeply about teaching.

A recent study sponsored by the National Science Foundation examined the content and skills assessed by commonly used textbook tests and standardized tests in mathematics and science for grades 4 through 12, and the influence of these instruments on instruction (Madaus and West 1992). These researchers found that the widely used tests they examined were very poor at measuring the skills and knowledge recommended by mathematics and science curriculum experts. The tests overwhelmingly measured rote memorization and recall rather than conceptualizing, problem solving, and reasoning. Only 3 percent of the items on standardized math tests examined conceptual knowledge, and just 5 percent of those questions tested problem-solving and reasoning skills. Even more potent in terms of our current discussion was the finding that teachers with more than 60 percent minority students in their classrooms reported greater test preparation and greater influence of the tests on their classroom instruction. Those teachers also had more low-income students, as indicated by those receiving Chapter 1 services. Seventy-five percent of teachers with high proportions of minority students reported pressure from their school districts to improve standardized test scores, compared with about 60 percent of teachers with low proportions of minority students. Among those teachers with high proportions of minority students, 60 percent reported teaching practices such as teaching test-taking skills, teaching topics known to be on the test, putting more emphasis on tested topics, and beginning test preparation more than one month before the test. These practices were reported significantly less often by teachers whose class composition was less than 10 percent minority. Thus, the current climate of emphasis on assessment strongly influences the choice of curricular experiences for African American students.

TEST USE AND ACHIEVEMENT

Some information from tests has highlighted the need for greater community and school efforts, especially at the junior and senior high school levels, to increase academic preparation for college and employment. When low test scores are earned by students who are not in school each day and are not receiving meaningful and substantive instruction, it does not make sense to blame the measure. To the extent that these factors co-vary with race, they will affect the racial differences in test scores. A climate of expectation of achievement must be established and maintained within schools and communities so that time is spent on high-quality instruction followed by well-planned home assignments that are completed and brought to school. If the length of time in which students are exposed to meaningful academic work is limited, they can hardly be expected to show high performance.

Regular, on-time school attendance supported by homework is a rather simple, mundane idea, but these activities serve to orient students primarily toward schooling and thus to allow the overall academic effort to have the best chance to make an impact.

Further, we need to place tests in perspective, to remove the measurement mystique from the general public as well as from the professional users. We need to improve the extent and quality of the training in measurement provided for teachers, counselors, and other professionals, who use and interpret tests. More and better public information on testing is needed to make test results more accessible and understandable.

Related to the need to place testing in perspective is the need to recognize that test scores are only part of the picture when examining and appraising abilities and achievements for all groups. Scores should be examined together with other indexes of achievement and motivation. Some of these data are rather "soft" but have substantial validity in a reasoned appraisal of performance. At times, traditional paper-and-pencil tests may be quite inappropriate measures of performance, and more appropriate measures of performance should be used.

TESTING AND COMPUTER TECHNOLOGY

The trends in computer-adaptive testing offer promise for making measurement more useful for guiding instruction, but they certainly do not ensure this outcome. The technology must be accompanied by policy commitments and appropriate enablers for the desired outcomes.

In the technological climate of growing feasibility and creativity of computer-adaptive tests, there are enormous advantages in terms of rapid and useful feedback to teachers and children, modification of test materials to provide the most appropriate measurement, and alternate modes of presentation to maximize motivation and minimize anxiety. But such advantages are not automatic outcomes of the technology. They will come only in a policy climate that insists on maximum development of all individuals. The flooding of schools with hardware and software will not do it, although such technology must have both hardware and software. Commitment, follow up, and a dependable consistency of resources are necessary if such technology is to change the educational realities of African American children for the better.

ALTERNATIVE ASSESSMENT

A variety of new and not-so-new forms of assessment and measurement procedures are receiving wider use and acceptance and may offer sounder measurements that are less bound to traditional psychometric models. These procedures differ radically from conventional multiple-choice instruments in several ways. They may include frequent assessments of learner performance on academic tasks over a period of time, with the responses constructed by the learner rather than selected from a predetermined set, and may be customized to the learner and the learning setting. Such measures, which are called performance assessments or constructed-response assessments, include portfolios, projects, open-ended problem-solving sequences, and other observations of performance in natural settings, simulated performance activities, and other formats.

These approaches to assessment may produce a great deal of information on the performance of learners. Rather than a single outcome or set of outcomes based on test items, information may be produced on the student's anxiety, ability, motivation, attitudes toward the tasks, and cognitive processes used during the assessment phases. Snow (1993) points out that it is important to generate rival hypotheses regarding these factors to explain variability in achievement, and that the development of a psychometrics rather than a psychology of testing has constrained testing's usefulness.

Do these new approaches offer promise for better measurement of achievement and other cognitive constructs among African American students? It is possible that they may, but this is not an automatic outcome of their use. Conceptually, these informal measures have the same need to meet requirements of validity and reliability as other measures, even though these quality indexes may be demonstrated in new ways.

Some of the new assessments have been developed using African American learners and involve the creation of projects by those learners to demonstrate understanding and application of complex problem-solving and analytic skills (Wolf 1993). These assessment projects are developed by students who have received high-quality instruction specifically targeted toward developing research and inquiry skills.

In these cases, the assessments could be termed "instructments" because they require and stimulate high-quality instruction, which leads to the production of well-reasoned, creative student projects based on sound principles of inquiry. These projects are the stuff of the assessment, but they depend on the quality of instruction. Regular feedback, modification of production, and appropriate preparation are elements in the chain to high-quality performance. Clearly, the availability of excellent, intensive instruction to the full diverse range of American children is essential to the development of this level of performance. Assessments obtained without this high quality of instruction will be comparable to the results obtained with conventional paper-and-pencil tests and poor instruction. They will be at a low level and will not indicate what students could do if creatively instructed.

Informal assessment procedures, coupled with inspired teaching, can be highly motivational and can develop critical thinking skills. These procedures may eventually lead to more formal ways of documenting and comparing individuals or groups in a "proficiency space" rather than along single dimensions, but there is need for research that more clearly delineates the constructs and processes involved.

The special nature of these informal procedures raises an important area for research. The teacher–evaluator in these procedures is an essential piece of the instrumentation. Because the contagious enthusiasm of one such collaborator in learning may be very different from the more pedantic style of another, appraisal of process and product must include examination of the instruction.

One problem with the newer assessments is actually a problem of the complex interplay of forces that has created the vast disparity in educational experiences received by American children. Children receiving very low standardized test scores now are not likely to show creativity and originality when new assessments are administered to them unless their experiences between the two events are radically different from any they previously had. Sound, regular instruction for all children in problem solving is essential for the large-scale use of constructed response measures, or the children will not construct adequate responses. On the positive side, these newer procedures do allow for divergent production and thus for the expression of human diversity. Therefore, diversity in background, when met with maximum resources and quality instruction, can become the source and impetus for maximum learning for all children, not the base of the problem of unequal performance.

The "backwash" concept was used by the measurement theorist Robert Wood (1987) to represent the effect of the examining technique in two respects: on the way subject matter is structured, taught, and learned; and on the way candidates prepare for, and are prepared for, the examining process. Two other types of backwash should be added to these: the effect of the examining technique on the candidate's motivation and personal sense of capability; and the effect of the perception that teachers and other preparers may have of an examinee's capability to demonstrate knowledge—that is, what teachers *believe* students can do in the assessment situation and the effect that that belief has on student performance.

New measures should be carefully appraised, as should any measure. The validity or appropriateness of a test as a measure of a given construct does not come by fiat. Good intentions do not create validity, and problems of validity do not disappear because the testing method is inventive (Conlan 1990). But individuals do differ in how they exhibit knowing, and multiple-choice tests can be perceived as limited-response tests that do not allow the necessary appraisal of the extent and quality of the learner's thinking (Robinson 1993). Research using alternate approaches should be carried out in African American communities to learn how a broader view of the psychology of assessment can improve instructional and assessment systems.

ASSESSMENT AND THE CURRENT EDUCATIONAL SCENE

The American obsession with measuring has involved African Americans in an odyssey as they have sought to validly demonstrate their competencies and to obtain rewards of attainment related to those competencies. While good assessment can document levels of performance, the history of test use shows a mixed picture.

As we move toward the assessment programs we will use in the twenty-first century, it is essential to recognize that no assessment system will solve the problem of what is wrong with how we educate African American children. Test results are *reflections* of what is happening in our schools; traditional tests represent the achievement of African Americans when quality educational experiences have been provided. Testing may document the problem when quality education has been lacking, but it will not change it. Radical changes in instruction are necessary, with consequent changes in assessment that more fully document, extend, and even modify instruction, as well as provide feedback. The newer methods of assessment offer that promise, but without radical changes in instruction, the resulting products will be even less useful than current tests in assessing student knowledge and understanding.

It is too simplistic to use the approach that changes in the way we measure should be the primary starting points in the move to improve what happens to children in schools and classrooms. We need a broad view of assessment, one that encompasses the psychology of learning and uses what we know about how people learn in order to develop assessment systems. These systems will then supply information to be used to refine and extend instructional interventions. The primary focus must be on the student, the classroom, and the educational climate of the school and the community, with assessment playing its proper supportive role in that system.

REFERENCES

Abramowitz, M. (1989). "D.C. Health System Gutted," in *The Washington Post*, 15 June, B, 1:5.

Anastasi, A. 1950. Some implications of cultural factors for test construction. In *Proceedings of the 1949 Invitational Conference on Testing Problems*. Princeton, NJ: Educational Testing Service.

Anastasi, A. 1954. *Psychological testing, 2nd ed.* New York: Macmillan.

Banks, W. C., E. V. McQuater, and J. L. Hubbard. 1978. Towards a reconceptualization of the social cognitive bases of achievement orientations in blacks. *Review of Educational Research* 48: 381-98.

Bock, D., and R. Mislevy. 1980. *Profiles of American youth*. Washington, DC: U.S. Department of Defense.

College Entrance Examination Board (CEEB). 1987. *Equality and excellence: The educational status of black Americans*. New York: CEEB.

Conlan, G. 1990. Comments on development of constructed-response assessments. Paper presented at Educational Testing Service conference, Construction vs. Choice in Cognitive Measurement, 30 November 1990, at Princeton, NJ.

David, A. 1948. *Social class influences upon learning*. Cambridge: Harvard University Press.

Davis, A., and K. Eels. 1951. *The Davis-Eels games*. Chicago: University of Chicago Press.

Gordon, E. T., E. W. Gordon, and J. G. G. Nembhard. 1994. Social science literature concerning African American men. *Journal of Negro Education* 3(4): 508–31.

Jagers, R. J. 1992. Attitudes toward academic interdependence and learning outcomes in two contexts. *Journal of Negro Education* 61(4): 531–38.

Johnson, S. T. 1979. The measurement mystique: Issues in selection for professional schools and employment. Occasional paper no. 2. Washington, DC: Howard University Institute of the Study of Educational Policy.

Johnson, S. T., and D. K. Anderson. 1992. Legacies and lessons from independent schools. *Journal of Negro Education* 61(2): 121–24.

Johnson, S. T., C. A. Asbury, M. B. Wallace, S. Robinson, and J. Vaughn. 1985. The effectiveness of a program to increase Scholastic Aptitude Test scores of black students in three cities. Paper presented at the annual meeting of the National Council on Measurement in Education, Chicago.

Johnson, S. T., and M. Wallace. 1989. Characteristics of SAT quantitative items showing improvement after coaching among black students from low-income families: An exploratory study. *Journal of Educational Measurement* 26(2): 133–45.

Ladson-Billings, G. 1992. Liberatory consequences of literacy: A case of culturally relevant instruction for African American students. *Journal of Negro Education* 61(3): 378–91.

Lee, C. D. 1992. Profile of an independent black institution: African-centered education at work. *Journal of Negro Education* 61(2): 160–77.

Madaus, G., and M. M. West. 1992. The influence of testing on teaching math and science in grades 4–12. Final report. Washington, DC: National Science Foundation.

Medley, D. M., and T. J. Quirk. 1974. The application of a factorial design to the study of cultural bias in general culture items on the national teachers examinations. *Journal of Educational Measurement* 11: 235–45.

Montgomery Country Public Schools (MCPS), Department of Educational Accountability. 1985. Progress being made by minority students. Internal memorandum from Superintendent Wilmer S. Cody to the Board of Education, 30 July.

National Assessment of Educational Progress (NAEP). 1989. Reading proficiencies by selected teach items (grade 4). *Draft data almanac.* Princeton, NJ: NAEP.

National Institute on Drug Abuse. 1991. *Drug use among American high school seniors, college students, and young adults (1975–1990).* DHHS pub. no. Adm 91-1813. Washington, DC: Government Printing Office.

Nobles, W. W., and L. L. Goodard. 1989. Drugs in the African American community: A clear and present danger. In *The state of Black America,* ed. J. Dewart. 1989.

Poulin, J. E. 1991. Racial differences in the use of drugs and alcohol among low-income youth and young adults. *Journal of Sociology and Social Welfare* 18(3): 159–66.

Ramist, L., and S. Arbeiter. 1986. *Profiles: College-bound seniors 1985.* New York: The College Board.

Robinson, S. P. 1993. The politics of multiple-choice vs. Free-Response Assessment. In *Construction vs. choice in cognitive measurements: Issues in constructed responses, performance testing and portfolio assessment,* ed. R. E. Bennett and W. C. Ward. Hillsdale, NJ: L. Erlbaum Associates.

Shujaa, M. J. 1992. Afrocentric transformation and parental choice in African American independent schools. *Journal of Negro Education* 61(2): 148–59.

Snow, R. E. 1993. Construct validity and constructed-response tests. In *Constructions vs. choice in cognitive measurements: Issues in constructed responses, performance testing and portfolio assessment,* ed. R. E. Bennett and W. C. Ward. Hillsdale, NJ: L. Erlbaum Associates.

Swartz, E. 1992. Emancipatory narratives: Rewriting the master script in the school curriculum. *Journal of Negro Education* 61(3): 341–55.

U.S. Department of Commerce. 1993a. *Statistical abstract of the United States, 1993.* Washington, DC: Department of Commerce.

U.S. Department of Commerce. 1993b. *We the American . . . Blacks.* Washington, DC: U.S. Department of Commerce.

Williams, R. L. 1973. On black intelligence. *Journal of Black Studies* 29–39.

Witty, E. P. 1986. Testing teacher performance. *Journal of Negro Education* 55(3): 358–67.

Wolf, D. P. 1993. Assessment as an episode of learning. In *Construction vs. choice in cognitive measurements: Issues in constructed responses, performance testing and portfolio assessment,* ed. R. E. Bennett and W. C. Ward. Hillsdale, NJ: L. Erlbaum Associates.

17 New Teacher Assessments: Palliative or Panacea for Minority Performance?

ANNE REYNOLDS

It's the year 2000. You are a college sophomore, eager to become a classroom teacher. But before you step from one side of the teacher's desk to the other, you must successfully navigate the teacher assessment track. The first hurdle on the track is an assessment of enabling skills, given prior to entering your teacher education program. In the testing center located in your university, you sit at a computer terminal taking the test of enabling skills. The test is designed to measure your understanding of important skills in reading, writing, and mathematics. Some questions require you to watch a short videodisc selection and then choose an answer located on the screen. Other questions ask you to show your work on the screen. Still others ask you to type in an essay or to write it on a separate piece of paper. After you finish the test, you receive a profile of your correct and incorrect answers. If you stumble at this hurdle, you are directed to an instructional computer package and encouraged to take the assessment again at a later date. If you clear the enabling skills hurdle, you enter a formal teacher education program.

The next hurdle on the teacher assessment track comes after your teacher education experiences are over. The year is now 2003. At this point in your teaching career, you are expected to know the content you will teach, general principles of teaching and learning, and content-specific teaching strategies. You return to the testing center at your university to complete a battery of tests. Like the test you took to enter your teacher education program, some of the test questions ask you to watch a videodisc and then answer via computer; others ask you to answer traditional multiple-choice questions. Unlike the enabling skills test, some questions use paper and pencil; these questions require you to base your answers on evidence contained in a number of teaching-related documents (for instance, student cumulative folders, narrative reports, student papers, textbooks). After you successfully complete this battery of tests, you receive a provisional teaching license. With this license, you enter full-time teaching under the supervision of a mentor teacher who also teaches in your school.

The third hurdle on the teacher assessment track comes in 2004, at the end of your first year of teaching. As the year progresses, you gather evidence of your teaching and critique each piece of evidence. Your evidence includes documents such as observation records of your lessons, made by your mentor teacher, principal, and district beginning-teacher supervisor; videotapes of your lessons, with your own written critique including what you would do differently next time; collections of student papers, with your commentaries on student progress; and letters to and from parents regarding student progress, accompanied by your comments about what you learned from the letters and how you used them to further student learning. At the end of the year, you bundle your evidence and your critique into a "teaching portfolio" and send it off to a regional testing center where it is evaluated by teachers and administrators who are subject-matter specialists in your field. The evaluators have been educated to work with beginning teachers. From them you receive a profile of your strengths and weaknesses, suggestions for improvement, and an overall pass/fail rating. If you pass this hurdle and meet other state requirements, you become fully licensed to teach.

The year is now 2008. Eight years have passed since your first hurdle on the teacher assessment track. You've taught for five years, think you're an exemplary teacher, and want to be formally recognized and rewarded for it. Your final hurdle is certification assessment offered by the National Board for Professional Teaching Standards, the governing body for the profession of teaching. Instead of assessing minimal competency in the skills and knowledge required for teaching, as did the previous three hurdles, this examination requires you to show *excellence* in teaching. Certification assessment occurs in ways similar to those you have already experienced—written and computerized tests, performance-based measures, portfolios—and introduces another form: the assessment center. During an assessment center session you participate in structured interviews with trained examiners who ask you to explain your portfolio documents. You also work alone and with other teachers in simulated teaching situations that probe your understanding of students, curricula, context, content, pedagogy, and how to teach your particular content. At the end of this grueling process, you receive National Board certification, which grants recognition of exemplary teaching, higher salary, and greater responsibility to share your expertise with other teachers.

Though the scenario above may seem like a pipe dream, it's not. By the year 2000, we can expect drastic changes in the way we actually assess teachers. Due to increasing criticism of current teacher licensure tests from the educational community and new understandings about teaching and cognition from the research community, changes are underway in major testing houses such as the Educational Testing Service and in various states such as Connecticut, California, Minnesota, and Georgia. But what promise do these changes hold for improving minority teacher performance? Are the changes palliative or panacea? In this chapter, we explore these issues.

To begin, we highlight the current status of minority teachers on standardized, multiple-choice teacher licensing tests; suggest some reasons for their low pass rates; and describe what is being done to remedy these problems. We move next to a brief discussion of observation systems, which are also used in teacher licensure, and describe the current status of minority teacher performance. We then jump to concrete visions of the future, namely, new forms of teacher assessment now in the research and development process. We will discuss the pros and cons of such assessments and their prospects for improving minority teacher pass rates, and conclude the section with suggestions for further research. In the third section, we suggest implications of the new assessment forms for teacher education. The chapter ends with some thoughts about the challenge we face as educators, assessment specialists, and policymakers.

CURRENT STATUS OF MINORITIES ON TEACHER LICENSING TESTS

Minority teacher pass rates on current teacher education program admission tests and initial teacher licensure tests are below those of majority teacher pass rates (Ansah 1985; Dilworth 1998; Eissenberg and Rudner 1988; Zapata 1988b). This is an alarming fact. Given the changing demographics of the U.S. population, the percent of ethnic minority children is rising. Yet, partially due to "entry-gate" tests, which screen ethnic minority teachers out of teaching positions, and partially due to other factors such as increased opportunities to work in professions previously closed to minorities, the number of minority teachers is dwindling. As many researchers point out, such demographics may negatively affect students and imperil the delivery of multicultural education and equal educational opportunities (Bass de Martinez 1988; Mercer 1983; Middleton et al. 1988; Valencia and Aburto 1989). Why are the pass rates so low for minority teachers?

Hypotheses about Low Minority Teacher Pass Rates

Two hypotheses are popularly proposed for low minority teacher pass rates on multiple-choice tests: (a) test results are true indications of differences among groups of individuals; and (b) the test instruments themselves are biased against certain groups of prospective teachers, for instance, African Americans, Hispanics, or women (Allan, Nassif, and Elliot 1988). Each of these hypotheses is explored below.

Group differences hypothesis.   The first hypothesis is that true knowledge-level differences exist among minority and majority teachers. These knowledge-level differences may stem from each group's socialization into somewhat different cultures and/or inequities in educational opportunities.

The cultural differences argument states that socialization of individuals into nonmainstream settings gives these individuals world views and language norms that are different from those of individuals who grew up in mainstream settings. These different norms affect test performance. For instance, Llabre and Froman (1987) postulate that Hispanic students may have conceptions of time (an aspect of world view) that impede their ability to complete standardized selected-response tests within given time constraints. In other words, Hispanic students may experience time in ways unlike mainstream students, therefore they may take more time than is allotted to answer each question and find themselves unable to complete the test. Llabre and Froman base their hypothesis on a study of cultural conceptions of time in Brazil and the United States conducted by Levine, West, and Reis (1980). Weak standard English language skills are also proposed as a reason for low minority teacher pass rates due to difficulties in "code switching" and translation from one language to another, which increase the amount of time needed to understand and answer each question (Holmes 1986; Smitherman 1989).

Prior educational opportunities also differentially prepare students to pass current admissions tests for teacher education programs and subsequent tests of general knowledge and enabling skills. Inequities include low socioeconomic home environments in which reading materials are not readily available and the lack of available curricular resources in elementary and secondary schools (Bell and Morsink 1986; Haberman 1988; Mercer 1982). Many of these students enroll in colleges and universities such as the historically black colleges, where resources are frequently unavailable to remediate problems with enabling skills, test content, and test unfamiliarity (Bell and Morsink 1986; Gifford 1986; Holmes 1986).

A large body of research literature focuses on group differences; however, another reason exists for low minority teacher pass rates on current selected-response tests: the tests themselves.

Test instruments hypothesis.   Criticisms of the test instruments themselves abound, and two major issues are cited: the ways in which test content is identified and the connections between actual teaching, student learning, and test content.

Test specifications are typically set by small advisory panels whose members identify important content that may not reflect issues important to the larger teaching community or to subgroups of minority teachers (Gifford 1986; Johnson 1988). For example, critics contend that the content of the test may reflect what is currently taught in some teacher education programs but not in others, thus giving some prospective teachers an unfair advantage (George 1985; Gifford 1986;

Spencer 1986). Others say that current tests are primarily tests of reading and quantitative skills (Bruno and Marcoulides 1985; Ivie 1982). Still others argue that the tests *do* tap professional knowledge, but they focus on the cognitive aspects of teaching at the expense of more important affective and motivational sides such as establishing and maintaining rapport with students and stimulating critical consciousness, which are thought to be the hallmarks of good teaching with minority students (Delpit 1988; Hilliard 1986; Johnson and Prom-Jackson 1986; Nelson-Barber 1988). Likewise, Porter and Freeman (1986) claim that the tests fail to assess professional orientations such as teachers' beliefs about the purposes of schooling and the extent to which teachers believe that all students can learn. Furthermore, critics point out that only the dimensions of teacher knowledge that have one correct answer are presently tested.[1] In the eyes of these educators, especially Shulman (1986), testing only the "generic" dimension of teaching is insufficient because in live teaching situations, teachers draw upon another knowledge domain called "content-specific pedagogy."[2] Only in rare instances (as in some items in subject area tests) is content-specific pedagogical knowledge tapped in current tests.

The connections between actual teaching, student learning, and test content are also a major source of contention. As Haertel (1987) asserts, advisory panels usually are asked to judge whether a teaching candidate would have had the opportunity to learn the content prior to the first years of teaching, but they are not asked to judge whether the content is actually needed in teaching.[3] Taking the argument a step further, Madaus and Pullin (1987, 32) question whether the content of the test is actually linked to teacher competence:

> If a test has no connection to minimal success as a teacher, why give it? Moreover, since decisions made on the basis of these tests scores are ultimately justified on the basis of the test-takers' potential "competence" to perform successfully at some minimal level in the classroom, construct-related evidence (about the nature of the construct "competence") must also be collected. In other words, does the test actually measure an aspect of competence related to classroom performance?

And Peterson (1984) questions whether there actually *are* links among test content, student learning, and teacher effectiveness.

Solutions to Low Minority Teacher Pass Rates

Many solutions have been proposed to remedy the problem of low minority teacher pass rates on current multiple-choice tests. Some solutions address problems with group differences:

- Start recruitment efforts for minority teachers as early as seventh grade and provide academic and financial assistance to students who plan to become teachers (Witty 1986; Zapata 1988a).
- Revamp teacher education: Raise standards for admission, screening and evaluating students throughout the program years. Revise the curriculum to reflect the content of current teacher assessment tests, using multiple-choice items in teacher education classes so students will become familiar with the item type. Require teacher education students to have a concentration in a subject-matter field. Seek funds outside the teacher education program and university to pay for internal changes. Hire "better" faculty and encourage faculty to participate in state committees to revise enabling skills requirements (Aburto and Nelson-Barber 1987; Antonelli 1985; Clark 1988; Cooper 1986; Dupre 1986; Fields 1988; Hackley 1985; Spencer 1986).
- Create support services for prospective minority teachers (Case et al. 1988; Cooper 1986).
- Sponsor test-taking workshops for minority students (Cooper 1986; Hackley 1985).
- Sponsor remedial classes in reading and writing (Cooper 1986; Hackley 1985; Aburto and Nelson-Barber 1987).
- Provide "warranties" for teacher education graduates (Hackley 1985).

Other solutions attempt to remedy deficiencies in the tests themselves:

- Lower cut scores on tests (Bruno and Marcoulides 1985).
- Review other documentation such as observation records on prospective teachers who score in the "marginal range" around present cut scores, and grant licenses when appropriate (Haertel 1987).
- Offer "provisional licensure" to teachers who score below the cut point but show, through additional documentation, that they are competent in the classroom (Haertel 1987).

It is clear that minority teacher performance on current selected-response teacher licensure tests is below that of nonminority teacher performance and that concerned teacher educators are trying to correct the situation. Yet their efforts may be misplaced. Recently, states have begun to use teacher observation systems as part of the licensure process for beginning teachers. Given this move toward performance examinations, it is important to explore how minority teachers have fared on these assessments.

Current Minority Teacher Performance on Observation Systems

Observation systems are now used by at least 18 states as part of teacher licensure, according to research by Darling-Hammond and Berry (1988). In a study of observation systems, Logan, Garland, and Ellet (1989) found that they are based mainly on the teacher-effectiveness research literature; that is they attempt to measure observable teacher behavior that research shows is statistically linked to gains in student scores on standardized tests. Some observation systems spotlight general principles of teaching (e.g., Virginia's observation system); others are more attuned to how general principles are couched in context and the content being taught (e.g., Georgia's observation system). Observation systems generally document a candidate's teaching behavior and/or action in the classroom and may be limited to predesignated times by trained examiners or may include frequent, informal (sometimes surprise) visits by peers and/or mentor teachers. As part of some teacher induction or assistance programs or teacher career-ladder programs, observation systems may include additional measures of a teacher's performance such as student questionnaires (Burry, Poggio, and Glasnapp 1989; McLarty 1987) or parent comments (Robards and Hanson 1985).

Of the few studies that have been reported on minority teacher performance on observation systems, evidence suggests that minority teacher pass rates are similar to those of white teachers (Johnson 1988). For example, in Virginia during the fall of 1985, African American teachers scored at or above the level attained by white teachers on the generic competencies of the Beginning Teacher Assistance Program; 57 percent of the African American techers and 55 percent of the white teachers successfully passed the competencies (Johnson 1988; Witty 1986). As Witty (1986, 361) states, "This assessment finding represents the first time in the history of Virginia that the pass rate for black teachers in that state was better than that for white teachers. Although the difference is not significant statistically, it is quite important psychologically."

In addition to its inspirational significance, such a finding suggests that performance-based assessments may provide minority candidates with opportunities to demonstrate competence not now tapped in selected-response tests. It is to the new wave of teacher assessments, which rely heavily on performance measures, that we now turn.

PROPOSED IMPROVEMENTS IN TEACHER ASSESSMENT TESTS

The goal of assessment should be to identify clearly what one wants to know about an examinee and then develop assessment instruments that match the content and allow the examinee to demonstrate the knowledge, skill, disposition, and so on with a minimal amount of interference from the instrument. With this goal in mind, old tests are being revamped and new forms of assessment are being created.

Renovations in Teacher Assessment

Work is under way at the Educational Testing Service (ETS) (Tannenbaum 1990; Wesley 1990), as well as in states such as Connecticut (Delandshere and Guiton 1990; Pecheone 1988; Popham 1989) and Georgia (Renfrow and Kromrey 1990), to revamp teacher licensing tests. The renovations will reflect new conceptions of teacher knowledge (e.g., content-specific pedagogical knowledge) and new technology (e.g., videodisc, videotape) into selected- and constructed-response tests. For example, ETS is crafting constructed-response exercises to assess a teacher's knowledge of content, content-specific pedagogy, and general principles of teaching and learning.[4] A prospective teacher might be given a short description of a student's incorrect answer to a problem (such as a two-digit by two-digit multiplication problem) and asked to identify the error and give a mathematical explanation for how to correct the error. Or a test taker might watch a videotaped excerpt of a classroom interaction in which a student disrupts the class and be asked to write answers to questions concerning possible responses to the situation.

The striking difference between current teacher licensure tests and their revamped cousins is the emphasis on items that ask for a test taker to construct an answer rather than select one. In some cases, the renovations to current tests being made by ETS and others will include assessment forms novel to teacher testing.

Innovations in Teacher Assessment

In an attempt to make teacher assessment more appropriate, some researchers have co-opted forms of assessment used in other professions, such as medicine, architecture, business, and law (Aburto and Haertel 1987; Bird 1987; Dinham and Stritter 1986; Lareau 1985). These forms include structured interviews, simulated teaching activities, and portfolio entries (work samples that document teaching actions and thoughts). All of the above forms are now used for teacher assessment, though each form targets different experience levels of teaching and varies in stage of implementation.

Simulations are being developed and field tested on novice to experienced classroom teachers at different institutions across the United States for purposes of teacher education, teacher licensure, and advanced teacher certification. Two such projects are geared for use with teacher education students. At the University of Virginia, teacher educators are field testing a microcomputer-based simulation that asks preservice teachers to teach a spelling lesson to a class of "Pac-Man" type figures projected on a screen. The figures have computer-modulated voices and particular behavior patterns such as getting out of their seats or whispering to adjacent students. As the teacher teaches, an evaluator standing at the rear of the room enters information concerning the teacher's classroom management behaviors into a computer. At the end of the short lesson, the information is analyzed and the computer gives feedback to the preservice teacher concerning classroom management behaviors, for instance, the number of times the teacher exhibited behavior considered "appropriate" by the teacher effectiveness literature (Murphy, Kauffman, and Strang 1987). At Indiana University in Pennsylvania, teacher educators currently run an assessment center to evaluate teaching competence in the early years of the teacher education program (Byham 1986; Millward 1989). Assessment center activities include in-baskets such as responding to letters from parents, and group assessments such as coordinating teaching activities with other teachers.

Other research and development is aimed at teacher licensure. For instance, the Connecticut State Department of Education is field testing simulations and structured interviews to gather information about prospective teachers' knowledge of content and content-specific pedagogy (Tomala 1989). In one structured interview, a prospective teacher is given a set of cards on which topics from a unit on ratios, proportions, and percents are written. The interviewer asks the teacher to arrange the cards in the order in which she or he would teach the unit. When the candidate is ready, the interviewer elicits a pedagogical rationale for the ordering to tell whether some topics seem to belong in subgroups that would be taught together and to talk about any missing topics or topics that should be deleted from the set.

Advanced certification of experienced teachers drove the work at Stanford University, where researchers created and field tested prototype assessments for National Board for Professional Teaching Standards certification (Haertel 1990; Shulman 1987a; Shulman, Haertel, and Bird 1988). The prototypes focused on four subject areas—elementary school mathematics and literacy and secondary school history and biology—and required candidates to respond as they would on the job. For instance, in the "Lesson Planning" exercise, teachers were given curricular materials (e.g., pages from a math textbook) and asked to plan a lesson for a given group of students. At the end of an allotted period of time, interviewers asked the teachers questions about the planned lesson. Some of the questions required the teachers to give rationales for their planned activities.

Portfolio entries were also explored and field tested at Stanford as prototypes for National Board certification (Bird 1990; Collins 1990; Vavrus and Collins 1989). Teachers involved in the portfolio study ranged from novice to experienced. The portfolios were collections of work samples—pieces of teaching evidence—that teachers accumulated over the course of a year. Other teachers attested to the originality of the pieces. At an assessment center, held at the end of the portfolio collection year of the study, teachers participated in exercises using their portfolio entries. For example, in the Literacy Assessment Project exercise, "Reporting on Student Progress," teachers referred to individual student work samples when they discussed how they would talk with parents about their child's progress (Wolf 1989). The use of teacher work samples is also currently under research and development at ETS as part of renovations to existing tests.

New forms of teacher assessment, including the recent renovations of the NTE Core Battery and state-constructed tests, take a significant step forward in creating assessments that adapt to the individual and not vice versa, as is now the case. As Snow and Peterson (1985) argue, individuals with similar characteristics (e.g., high spatial ability, high text anxiety) perform differently on alternative assessment forms (Gavurin 1967; Schmitt and Crocker 1981); for this reason, tests should be constructed to take individual differences into consideration. When used in a complementary fashion, performance assessment forms such as simulations and portfolios allow a prospective teacher to demonstrate knowledge, skills, abilities, affect, and orientations to teaching in ways previously unavailable. However, the verdict is still out regarding minority teacher performance on new teacher assessments.

Effects of New Assessments on Minority Teacher Performance

The big question regarding new forms of assessment is: "What effect will they have on minority teacher performance?" As discussed above, African American test takers tend to do worse on multiple-choice tests than do white test takers (Ansah 1985; Eissenberg and Rudner 1988). Yet it is less clear that African Americans do better on performance-based tests. Valencia and Aburto (1989) argue that minority teacher performance improves with the use of performance-based assessments and support their argument with analyses of data from simulations and observation systems, described previously. Their case is appealing, but built on scant research in this area and even undermined by evidence from performance measures used in law examinations, which shows that performance examinations do not substantially narrow or widen the gap in passing rates between racial groups (Klein, in preparation). Furthermore, performance assessments in the form of simulations and observations may negatively affect minority teacher pass rates due to a host of factors, including selection of content for observations or performance (Bracht and Glass 1968), examiner bias in interview situations (Valencia and Aburto 1989), examiner/examinee interaction effects (Evertson and Green 1986; Valencia and Aburto 1989; Zieky 1989), and coaching on particular tasks selected for simulation or documents chosen for portfolios (Zieky 1989).

Even with preventive action such as requiring sensitivity training for all examiners, rating classroom context difficulty levels independent of actual candidate observations, and requiring multiple independent scorings of each performance response (Valencia and Aburto 1989; Zieky 1989), problems that now plague teacher assessment tests may continue. Why might this be the case? Inequities in educational opportunities, resources, and expectations, among others, persist in our society. Test scores reflect these inequities, yet research into assessment issues can help mitigate damage caused by social ills. Some of the more pertinent research issues are as follows:

- What is "good" teaching in nonmainstream cultural settings? How should these findings influence teacher education and teacher assessment?
- How should we assess a prospective teacher's cultural sensitivity and ability to teach culturally diverse students?
- How do we create scoring rubrics that are appropriate for culturally different orientations to teaching or to culturally different responses?
- What form of assessment methodology best measures a particular construct for a given person or group of people with similar characteristics? For example, if a prospective teacher has high test anxiety with multiple-choice tests, will the anxiety lessen with constructed-response tests or with portfolio work samples?
- Do constructs change as assessment forms change, or do different test forms tap different aspects of the same construct? For example, do observations measure the same things as performance-based, constructed-response methods? How do we deal with the psychometrics of such lane switching?
- As we develop and test new assessment forms, how do we build in checks for adverse impact that allow us to analyze for causality?

Answers do not come easily to such questions. They require thoughtful research and deliberation. Unfortunately, teacher education and teacher assessment cannot be put on hold until answers are created. Both must continue making modifications based on emerging research findings. In the next section, we discuss what teacher education institutions might do now to prepare students for the new assessments.

IMPLICATIONS OF THE NEW ASSESSMENTS FOR TEACHER EDUCATION PROGRAMS

Missing from the current educational scene is a shared meaning about what is important for teachers to know and do to be effective in the classroom. Until some form of consensus is reached, a familiar cry will resound through the educational community: There is a lack of fit between what teacher education programs teach, what standard setters (e.g., state departments of education, National Board for Professional Teaching Standards) promulgate for licensure and certification, what teacher assessments measure, and what teachers actually do in the classroom. Still, there is hope that a consensus can be reached. Educators are beginning to define what effective teachers know (Shulman 1987b), how teachers think (Clark and Peterson 1986), and what teachers do (Rosenfeld 1990). As the findings of these various research programs are pooled, there is a greater chance that constituencies (e.g., teacher education programs, state departments of education, assessment houses) will share meanings and expectations for teachers.

Until that time, though, teacher educators will need to continue preparing students for teaching. While the importance of licensure tests is not to be understated and prospective teachers should have an opportunity to become familiar with the testing hurdles they will encounter, teacher educators must keep in mind that the content of tests is only a *sample* of what teachers need to know and do. Test content is largely dependent upon methods of assessment available to test developers. In other words, no matter how important an aspect is to teaching, if a measurement tool is not available, the aspect will not get measured in a formal assessment. Therefore, teaching to the test is not only unwise, it is also deleterious to the education of prospective teachers.

However, I believe there is merit in preparing teacher education students for the new assessments. The new assessments explode current notions of what "testing" should be by allowing prospective teachers to express their understandings and abilities in ways that may be more compatible with their ways of knowing, and more like what they will actually encounter in the classroom. By using new and old assessments in teacher preparation, we enlarge a prospective teacher's repertoire of assessment tools as well as validate the practice of using multiple forms of assessments. The new assessments also incorporate refreshed conceptions of teacher knowledge (e.g., content-specific pedagogy) and require teachers to make public what is often kept private—justifications for teacher actions. Both of these additions warrant deliberation in the teacher education program curriculum.

With these ideas in mind, suggestions for how to use the new assessments in teacher education follow:

- Build activities that require students to reflect orally and in writing on their teaching experiences using advanced technology such as computers, videodiscs, and videotapes.
- Use the new assessment forms as a basis for evaluation in teacher education classes.
- Encourage students to use the new forms as evaluation methods in their own classrooms.
- Create consortia with other teacher educators to trade ideas. This idea has been initiated with mixed success by educators at Stanford University, Florida A & M, the Dayton (OH) Public Schools, City College of New York, Pan American University in Texas, and the University of Alaska (Minority Consortium 1988).

Though only a sample of what a teacher knows and does in teaching, the new assessments are worth using as curricular aids in teacher education programs.

CONCLUSIONS

Understandably, we hold high expectations for new teacher assessments. Yet, new teacher assessments—both assessments for new teachers and new assessments for teachers—are not a panacea to the problems of low minority teacher pass rates on current tests or to the declining numbers of minority teachers in our nation's schools. At best they are a palliative to a social disease that stems from inequities in our society. Our challenge as teacher educators, policymakers, and assessment creators is to find the right fit between what we want to know about teachers, what different forms of assessment can tell us, and which forms best elicit from an examinee what we want to know. All the while, we must realize that the changes we make in teacher assessment will have little effect on the composition of the teaching force if the social inequities in our society are not also changed.

REFERENCES

Aburto, S., and E. Haetrel. 1987. *Study group on alternative assessment methods: Executive summary.* Stanford, CA: Stanford University Teacher Assessment Project.

Aburto, S., and S. Nelson-Barber. 1987. *Symposium on equity issues in teacher assessment. Executive summary.* Stanford, CA: Stanford Teacher Assessment Project.

Allan, R. G., P. M. Nassif, and S. M. Elliot, eds. 1988. *Bias issues in teacher certification testing.* Hillsdale, NJ: Lawrence Erlbaum.

Ansah, S. L. 1985. *Quality teachers: Is testing the answer?* Paper presented at the annual meeting of the Mid-South Educational Research Association, November, Biloxi, MS.

Antonelli, G. A. 1985. The revitalization of teacher education at UAPB. *Action in Teacher Education* 7: 63–64.

Bass de Martinez, B. 1988. Political and reform agendas' impact on the supply of black teachers. *Journal of Teacher Education* 39: 10–13.

Bell, M. L., and C. V. Morsink. 1986. Quality and equity in the preparation of black teachers. *Journal of Teacher Education* 37: 16–20.

Bird, T. 1987. *Teacher assessment and professionalization.* Paper prepared for the Task Force on Teaching as a Profession, Carnegie Forum on Education and the Economy.

Bird, T. 1990. The schoolteacher's portfolio: An essay on possibilities. In *The new handbook of teacher evaluation: Assessing elementary and secondary school teachers,* ed. J. Milman and L. Darling-Hammond. Newbury Park, CA: Sage.

Bracht, G. H., and G. V. Glass. 1968. The external validity of experiments. *American Educational Research Journal* 5: 437–74.

Bruno, J. E., and G. A. Marcoulides. 1985. Equality of educational opportunity at racially isolated schools: Balancing the need for teacher certification with teacher shortage. *Urban Review* 17: 155–65.

Burry, J. A., J. P. Poggio, and D. R. Glasnapp. 1989. *The Kansas internship program assistance/assessment model: A product of the interdependence of research and practice.* Paper presented at the annual meeting of the American Educational Research Association, March, San Francisco, CA.

Byham, W. C. 1986. *Use of the assessment center method to evaluate teacher competencies.* Pittsburgh, PA: Development Dimensions International.

Case, C. W., R. J. Shive, K. Ingelbretson, and V. M. Spiegel. 1988. Minority teacher education: Recruitment and retention methods. *Journal of Teacher Education* 39: 54–57.

Clark, C. M., and P. L. Peterson. 1986. Teachers' thought processes. In *Handbook of research on teaching, third edition,* ed. M. C. Wittrock. New York: Macmillan.

Clark V. L. 1988. Teacher education at historically black institutions in the aftermath of the Holmes and Carnegie reports. *Teacher Education Quarterly* 15: 32–49.

Collins, A. 1990. *Novices, veterans, experts, and masters: The role of content and pedagogical knowledge in evaluating teaching.* Paper presented at the annual meeting of the American Educational Research Association, April, Boston, MA.

Committee of Bar Examiners of the State Bar of California. 1988. *Information regarding performance tests.* San Francisco, CA: Committee of Bar Examiners.

Cooper, C. C. 1986. Strategies to assure certification and retention of black teachers. *Journal of Negro Education* 55: 46–55.

Darling-Hammond, L., and B. Berry. 1988. *The evolution of teacher policy.* Santa Monica, CA: Rand Corporation.

Delandshere, G., and G. Guiton. 1990. *Content-specific assessment— Measurement concerns.* Paper presented at the annual meeting of the National Council on Measurement in Education, April, Boston, MA.

Delpit, L. 1988. The silenced dialogue: Power and pedagogy in educating other peoples' children. *Harvard Educational Review* 58: 280–98.

Dilworth M.E. 1988. Black teachers: A vanishing tradition. *Urban League Review* 11: 54–58.

Dinham, S. M., and F. T. Stritter. 1986. Research on professional education. In *Handbook of research on teaching, third edition*, ed. M. C. Wittrock. New York: Macmillan.

Dupre, B. B. 1986. Problems regarding the survival of future black teachers in education. *Journal of Negro Education* 55: 56–66.

Eissenberg, T. E., and L. M. Rudner. 1988. State testing of teachers: A summary. *Journal of Teacher Education* 39: 21–22.

Evertson, C. M., and J. L. Green. 1986. Observation as inquiry and method. In *Handbook of research on teaching, third edition*, ed. M. C. Wittrock. New York: Macmillan.

Fields, C. M. 1988. Close to 100 percent of Grambling University students now pass teacher-certification examination, up from 10 percent. *Chronicle of Higher Education* 35: A23-A25.

Gavurin, E. I. 1967. Anagram solving and spatial aptitude. *Journal of Psychology* 65: 65–68.

Gifford, B. R. 1986. Excellence and equity in teacher competency testing: A policy perspective. *Journal of Negro Education* 55: 251–71.

George, P. 1985. Teacher testing and the historically black college. *Journal of Teacher Education* 36: 54–57.

Grossman, P. L. 1988. *A study in contrast: Sources of pedagogical content knowledge for secondary English.* Unpublished doctoral dissertation, Stanford University, Stanford, CA.

Haberman, M. 1988. Proposals for recruiting minority teachers. Promising practices and attractive detours. *Journal of Teacher Education* 39: 38–44.

Hackley, L. V. 1985. The decline in the number of black teachers can be reversed. *Educational Measurement: Issues and Practice* 4: 17–19.

Haertel, E. H. 1987. *Validity of teacher licensure and teacher education admissions tests.* Paper prepared for the National Association and Council of Chief State School Officers.

Haertel, E. H. 1990. Performance tests, simulations, and other methods. In *The new handbook of teacher evaluation: Assessing elementary and secondary school teachers*, ed. J. Millman and L. Darling-Hammond. Newbury Park, CA: Sage.

Hilliard III, A. G. 1986. From hurdles to standards of quality in teacher testing. *Journal of Negro Education* 55: 304–15.

Holmes, B. J. 1986. Do not buy the conventional wisdom: Minority teachers can pass the tests. *Journal of Negro Education* 55: 335–46.

Ivie, S. D. 1982. Why black students score poorly on the NTE. *High School Journal* 65: 171.

Johnson, S. 1988. Validity and bias in teacher certification testing. In *Bias issues in teacher certification testing,* ed. R. G. Allan, P. M. Nassif, and S. M. Elliot. Hillsdale, NJ: Lawrence Erlbaum.

Johnson, S.T., and S. Prom-Jackson. 1986. The memorable teacher: Implications for teacher selection. *Journal of Negro Education* 55: 272–83.

Klein, S. P. (no date, unpublished manuscript). *Does performance testing on the bar examination reduce differences in scores among sex and racial groups?* Santa Monica, CA: The Rand Corporation.

Lareau, A. 1985. *A comparison of professional examinations in six fields: Implications for the teaching profession.* Stanford, CA: Stanford Teacher Assessment Project.

Levine, R. V., L. J. West, and H. T. Reis. 1980. Perceptions of time and punctuality in the United States and Brazil. *Journal of Personality and Social Psychology* 38: 541–50.

Llabre, M. M., and T. W. Froman. 1987. Allocation of time to test items: A study of ethnic differences. *Journal of Experimental Education* 55: 137–40.

Logan, C. S., J. S. Garland, and C. D. Ellet. 1989. *Large-scale teacher performance assessment instruments: A synthesis of what they measure and a national survey of their influence on the preparation of teachers.* Paper presented at the annual meeting of the American Educational Research Association, March, San Francisco, CA.

McDiarmid, G. W., D. L. Ball, and C. W. Anderson. 1989. Why staying one chapter ahead doesn't really work: Subject-specific pedagogy. In *Knowledge base for the beginning teacher,* ed. M.C. Reynolds. Oxford: Pergamon.

Madaus, G. F., and D. Pullin. 1987. Teacher certification tests: Do they really measure what we need to know? *Phi Delta Kappan* 69: 31–38.

McLarty, J. R. 1987. *Career ladder instrumentation: The Tennessee experience.* Paper presented at the annual meeting of the American Educational Research Association, April, Washington, DC.

Mercer, W. 1983. The gathering storm: Teacher testing and black teachers. *Educational Leadership* 41: 70–71.

Mercer, W. A. 1982. Future Florida black teachers: A vanishing breed. *Negro Educational Review* 33: 135–39

Middleton, E. J., E. J. Mason, W. E. Stilwell, and W.C. Parker. 1988. A model for recruitment and retention of minority students in teacher preparation programs. *Journal of Teacher Education* 39: 14–18.

Millward, R. E. 1989. *Implementing a preteacher assessment center.* Paper presented at the annual meeting of the American Educational Research Association, March, San Francisco, CA.

Minority Consortium of the Stanford Teacher Assessment Project. 1988, November. Unpublished meeting notes.

Murphy, D. M., J. M. Kauffman, and H. R. Strang. 1987. Using microcomputer simulation to teach classroom management skills to preservice teachers. *Behavioral Disorders* 11: 20–34.

Nelson-Barber, S., ed. 1988. *Thinking out loud: Proceedings of the teacher assessment forum on equity in teacher assessment.* Stanford, CA: Stanford Teacher Assessment Project.

Pecheone, R. L. 1988. *The catalytic role of new teacher assessment strategies: Designing assessments to measure subject matter pedagogical understandings.* Paper presented at the annual meeting of the American Educational Research Association, April, New Orleans, LA.

Peterson, P. L. 1988. Teachers' and students' cognitional knowledge to classroom teaching and learning. *Educational Researcher* 17: 5–14.

Peterson, R. E. 1984. *CBEST, NTE, and other mensurations: Notes on testing would-be teachers in California and elsewhere.* Address delivered at the spring conference of the California Council on Education of Teachers, April, San Diego, CA.

Popham, W. J. 1989. *Videotape-based teacher tests: Old medium, new methods.* Paper presented at the annual meeting of the American Educational Research Association, March, San Francisco, CA.

Porter, A. C., and D. J. Freeman. 1986. Professional orientations: An essential domain for testing. *Journal of Negro Education* 55: 284–92.

Renfrow, D. D., and J. D. Kromrey. 1990. *Descriptions and uses of content-specific pedagogical items.* Paper presented at the annual meeting of the National Council on Measurement in Education, April, Boston, MA.

Reynolds, A. 1990. *Developing a comprehensive teacher assessment program: New pylons on a well-worn path.* Princeton, NJ: Educational Testing Service.

Robards, S. N., and R. A. Hanson. 1985. *Oklahoma's entry-year assistance program: Some findings after two years of implementation.* Paper presented at the Oklahoma Education Research Symposium II: Implications for H.B. 1706, January, Stillwater, OK.

Rosenfeld, M. 1990. *Job analysis as a basis for defining performance domains for the beginning teacher.* Paper presented at the annual meeting of the American Educational Research Association, April, Boston, MA.

Rosenfeld, M., R. F. Thornton, and L. S. Skurnik. 1986. *Analysis of the professional functions of teachers: Relationships between job functions and the NTE Core Battery.* Princeton, NJ: Educational Testing Service.

Schmitt, A. P., and L. Crocker. 1981. *Improving examinee performance on multiple-choice tests.* Paper presented at the annual meeting of the American Educational Research Association, April, Los Angeles, CA.

Shulman, L. S. 1986. Paradigms and research programs in the study of teaching: A contemporary perspective. In *Handbook of research on teaching, third edition,* ed. M. C. Wittrock. New York: Macmillan.

Shulman, L. S. 1987a. Assessment for teaching: An initiative for the profession. *Phi Delta Kappan* 69: 38–44.

Shulman, L. S. 1987b. Knowledge and teaching: Foundations of the new reform. *Harvard Educational Review* 57: 1–22.

Shulman, L. S., E. Haertel, and T. Bird. 1988. *Toward alternative assessments of teaching: A report of work in progress.* Stanford, CA: Stanford Teacher Assessment Project.

Smitherman, G. 1989. *Black English and multiple-choice testing.* Presentation made at the Educational Testing Service, August 17, Princeton, NJ.

Snow, R. E., and P. L. Peterson. 1985. Cognitive analyses of tests: Implications for redesign. In *Test design: Developments in psychology and psychometrics,* ed. S. E. Embretson. Orlando, FL: Academic Press.

Spencer, T. L. 1986. Teacher education at Grambling State University: A move toward excellence. *Journal of Negro Education* 55: 293–303.

Tannenbaum, R. J. 1990. *Analysis of stage 1 job analysis of teaching: Enabling skills*. Paper presented at the annual meeting of the American Educational Research Association, April, Boston, MA.

Tomala, G. 1989. *Designing semi-structured interviews for statewide assessment*. Paper presented at the annual meeting of the American Educational Research Association, March, San Francisco, CA.

Valencia, R. R., and S. Aburto. 1989. *Issues of access: the case of Latino teacher testing*. Paper presented at the conference on Assessment and Access of Hispanics in Higher Education, Educational Testing Service, Princeton, NJ.

Vavrus, L., and A. Collins. 1989. *Portfolio documentation and assessment center exercises: A marriage made for teacher assessment*. Stanford, CA: Teacher Assessment Project.

Wesley, S. 1990. *Stage II of the NTE successor: Using job analysis to identify subject matter knowledge for teacher licensure*. Paper presented at the annual meeting of the American Educational Research Association, April, Boston, MA.

Witty, E. P. 1986. Testing teacher performance. *Journal of Negro Education* 55: 358–67.

Wolf, K. P. 1989. *Candidate information sheet. Assessment-of-students extension exercise for portfolio entry two: Reporting on student progress*. Unpublished manuscript.

Zapata, J. T. 1988a. Early identification and recruitment of Hispanic teacher candidates. *Journal of Teacher Education* 39: 19–23.

Zapata, J. T. 1988b. Impact of testing on Hispanic teacher candidates. *Teacher Education & Practice* 4: 19–24.

Zieky, M. 1989. *Are performance tests for teacher certification less biased than paper and pencil tests?* Paper presented at the annual meeting of the American Educational Research Association, March, San Francisco, CA.

NOTES

1. Teacher Assessment tests usually cover general principles in eight domains of teacher knowledge: knowledge of pedagogy, knowledge of students, knowledge of curriculum, knowledge of context, knowledge of professional issues, knowledge of general subjects, knowledge of enabling skills, and knowledge of content (Reynolds 1990).

2. Content-specific pedagogical knowledge is also called "pedagogical content knowledge" (Grossman 1988), "subject-specific pedagogical knowledge" (McDiarmid, Ball, and Anderson 1989), and "content-specific cognitional knowledge" (Peterson 1988). The central factor in content-specific pedagogical knowledge is knowledge of the *content for teaching* as contrasted with knowledge of the content per se or generic knowledge of teaching as commonly tested.

3. In rebuttal to this argument, a study by Rosenfeld, Thornton, and Skurnik (1986) is salient. These researchers completed a job analysis of teaching in which teachers were surveyed to determine the importance of the content of the NTE Core Battery for their jobs, the degree to which each content statement was related to overall job success, and the cognitive level at which the content was used on the job. The only two knowledge areas that were not rated as highly linked to the job of teaching were history and philosophy of education.

4. The assessment forms will be similar to those presently used in the California State Bar Examination (Committee of Bar Examiners 1988). For example, in one bar examination performance-based question, test takers are given a set of documents common to lawyers (e.g., relevant and irrelevant statutes and case descriptions, notes from meetings with clients, a police report) and are asked to respond in written memo form to senior partner's request for a summary of the strengths and weakness of the client's position, a plan for next steps in the case a summary of additional information that was needed, and so forth.

18 | African Americans, Education, and Science: Recent Findings and Policy Implications

WILLIE PEARSON, JR.[*]

In the early 1980s, many African American leaders rightfully expressed concern about the racial insensitivity of many of the nation's political officeholders. Yet, many neglected perhaps the most formidable enemy of African Americans: the emergence of new technologies. Up to 45 percent of existing U.S. jobs may be significantly altered by technological changes over the next two decades, many through an upgrading of skills (Johnston and Packer 1987; "Needed: Human Capital" 1988). The likelihood of a huge technologically illiterate underclass is a tremendous threat to the economic aspirations of African Americans. The danger signals of technological obsolescence for African Americans are clear. The jobs in which African Americans are heavily employed are those which are predicted to be dramatically affected by the forces of automation and declining or slow growth ("Best Jobs" 1988) (See Table 1).

In the future, American prosperity will depend in large measure on a populace that can master complex technologies. To meet this challenge, American public

[*]The author gratefully acknowledges the assistance of Heather Scull, Kwamine Washington, Frances Reeves, Lesley R. Williams, Gloria Lindsey, and Africa Dalton, undergraduate research assistants. Special thanks also are due to Susan King, LaRue Cunningham Person, Earl Smith, Daryl C. Chubin, George Campbell, Melvin Thompson, and Arlene Maclin.

education will have to be geared toward meeting the educational requirements of the twenty-first century or the country will inevitably lose out to nations that produce scientists and engineers (Lamm 1988).

Because of an aging labor force, the United States will need every available worker. At precisely the time when the country needs its talents and productive abilities the most, the nation is running the risk of leaving a generation of inner-city youths behind. Each year, more than a million high school students quit before graduation. Of the 2.5 million who do graduate, about one in four cannot read at the eighth-grade level (Magazine 1989). Disproportionally, both groups are minorities, especially African Americans and Hispanic Americans.

These trends are particularly disturbing because an estimated 80 percent of U.S. productivity improvement since World War II is attributed to technological advancement. Productivity is linked to the standard of living. Technology is driven by people with the skills to innovate. These skills are derived, to a large degree, from math and science (Magazine 1989).

In this chapter, we assess recent research on the role of the American education in training African American scientists and suggest policy strategies for increasing African American participation and performance in science.

RECENT FINDINGS

Research has borne out the contention that African Americans are significantly underrepresented in American science and mathematics (Pearson 1985, 1986, 1988, 1989a). Nevertheless, most scholars of American science neglect to include African Americans as subjects in their investigations; frequently, their exclusion is justified by African Americans' marginal participation in science and mathematics. In a recently published volume, edited by myself and H. Kenneth Bechtel (1989), several scholars assessed the role of American education in training African American scientists. This chapter draws heavily on that work.

American science is a pervasive and dominating force that often shapes the boundaries and directions of aspects of citizens' lives. As a social institution, science inevitably reflects the values of American society in its social structures, beliefs, and attitudes. The striking

TABLE 1. Percentage Change in Employment for Selected Occupations 1988–2000, and Percentage of Employment Comprised by Whites, Blacks, and Hispanics, 1988

Occupation	Percent Change 1988–2000	Percent Composed of		
		Whites	Blacks	Hispanics
Total, all occupations	15	87	10	7
Executive, administrative, and managerial occupations	22	92	6	4
Professional specialty occupations	24	89	7	3
Engineers	25	90	4	3
Computer, mathematical, and operations research analysis	52	86	7	3
Natural scientists	19	90	3	3
Health diagnosing occupations	24	88	3	4
Health assessment occupations	38	87	8	3
Teachers, college	3	89	4	4
Teachers, except college	18	89	9	4
Lawyers and judges	30	96	2	2
Other professional workers	23	90	8	4
Technicians and related support occupations	32	86	9	4
Health technicians and technologies	34	81	14	4
Engineering and scientific technicians	22	89	7	5
All other technicians	39	88	7	4
Marketing and sales occupations	20	91	6	5

(continued)

TABLE 1. (Continued)

Occupation	Percent Change 1988–2000	Percent Composed of		
		Whites	Blacks	Hispanics
Administrative support occupations, including clerical	12	86	11	6
Clerical supervisors and managers	12	85	14	6
Computer operators and peripheral equipment operators	29	83	14	6
Secretaries, typists, and stenographers	10	89	8	5
Financial recordkeeping occupations	1	90	6	5
Mail clerks and messengers	10	74	22	9
Other clerical occupations	13	84	13	7
Service occupations	23	79	18	10
Private household workers	–5	76	23	17
Protective service occupations	23	81	17	6
Food service occupations	23	83	12	10
Health service occupations	34	69	28	6
Cleaning service occupations	20	74	23	15
Personal service occupations	27	85	12	8
Precision production, craft, and repair occupations	10	90	8	8
Mechanics, installers, and repairers	13	91	7	8
Construction trades	16	91	7	8

TABLE 1. (Continued)

Occupation	Percent Change 1988–2000	Percent Composed of		
		Whites	Blacks	Hispanics
Other precision production occupations	3	88	8	9
Operatives, fabricators, and laborers	1	82	15	11
Machine setters, set-up operators, operators, and tenders	−3	83	15	7
Transportation and material-moving machine and vehicle operators	12	82	16	11
Helpers, laborers, and material movers, hand	2	82	15	13
Agriculture, forestry, fishing, and related workers	−5	92	7	13

Source: *Monthly Labor Review*, November 1989.

underrepresentation of African Americans in the American scientific community demands serious scholarly investigation (Bechtel 1989).

AFRICAN AMERICAN PARTICIPATION IN MATHEMATICS AND SCIENCE

High School

Davis's (1989) analyses of African American participation and performance in high school mathematics confirm previous findings that, regardless of race, proportionately more students in the academic (college preparatory) curriculum take advanced mathematics. However, for academic-track African Americans, 55 percent were enrolled in advanced math courses, compared to 79 percent of whites. In addition, white students are more likely than their African Americans peers to be enrolled in an academic curriculum (46 percent versus 36 percent).

Of the students in the academic curriculum who were enrolled in the most advanced sequence (algebra I and II, geometry, and trigonometry), 89 percent were white, and 9 percent were African American. One of Davis' most striking findings is that 34 percent of those students who had not studied mathematics by their junior year were African Americans.

African Americans attending predominantly white high schools received better training in prealgebra skills than those who attended predominantly black high schools.[1] However, few African Americans are enrolled in advanced courses in predominantly white high schools.

Davis argues that African American students have positive attitudes toward the study of mathematics. Overall, they have high expectations for themselves and are willing to work hard in math. Davis concludes that the classroom experience is not encouraging or interesting enough to sustain the positive feelings toward mathematics that African American students bring to the classroom. She draws this conclusion because the mathematics self-concept of African American students is not strong.

According to Anderson (1989), African American students generally have positive attitudes toward science. However, these attitudes appear to be in conflict when questions are directed at awareness of the philosophy and methodology of science, confidence in science, and science research. African American students tend to have fewer science-related experiences and less use of scientific problem-solving methods than the national average, and the disparity increases with age. Overall, African American students perform below the national average on science achievement tests. African American students tend to perform best on questions reflecting daily experience and common knowledge, but have difficulty on questions involving comprehension and application of process methods in both biology and physical science.

On average, African American students take less than three years of high school science and tend to avoid advanced science courses (except for biological science) than do other students. Those who have considered science as a major in college are less likely to have taken three or more years of high school science courses.

The low performance of African American high school students on science achievement tests is not surprising, given that many fail to enroll in advanced-level or quantitative science courses and their last science course is usually general biology or Biology I. Achievement tests tend to emphasize physics and chemistry. Therefore, it is important that African American students be counseled or motivated to take advanced courses in science (Anderson 1989).

African American students are heavily concentrated in inner-city schools, where students perform more poorly on science achievement items than do students taught in other environments. Many African American students are confronted with poorly maintained and poorly equipped science laboratories. Compounding the problem is the fact that many African American students are taught by teachers who are not highly motivated, have inadequate knowledge of African American achievement in science and engineering, lack adequate science training, lack confidence in their ability to teach science, and do not like science (Anderson 1989).

Regardless of race, students who excel in science in college usually have a background that includes three or four years of high school mathematics and science. Evidence has shown that inadequate mathematical preparation is detrimental to success in such advanced, quantitative science courses as physics and chemistry. More research is needed to determine what factors affect African American students' decisions to choose lower-level courses and to identify those practices that promote participation in advanced science courses (Anderson

1989). Davis (1989) and Anderson both found that females were less likely than males to take advanced courses in mathematics and science.

College and Graduate Education

Studies of the baccalaureate origins of African American Ph.D. scientists consistently reveal that historically black colleges and universities (HBCUs) make significant contributors to that pool of talent. In a study of African American Ph.D. natural scientists, Jay (1971) found that almost three-fourths received their undergraduate degrees from HBCUs. In their study of the undergraduate origins of African American Ph.D. natural and social scientists, Pearson and Pearson (1985) also indicate that HBCUs play a prominent role; of the African American scientists studied, roughly two in three received their undergraduate degrees from HBCUs.

In a related study, Hill and White (1989) report that although bachelor's degree-granting HBCUs accounted for only 6 percent of all such U.S. institutions, they educated 44 percent of the African Americans who earned doctorates from 1983 to 1985 (even more of those who earned doctorates in nonscience fields). In science fields, one-third of African American doctorates had their baccalaureate origins in HBCUs. HBCUs seem to play a significant role in the life sciences—44 percent and 47 percent of Ph.D. biologists and agricultural scientists, respectively, received their undergraduate training in HBCUs (see also Hill and Hizell 1993). In 1991, Howard University and Clark/Atlanta University awarded 47 and 18 science and engineering (S/E) Ph.D.'s, respectively (National Science Foundation 1992b; Pearson and Leggon 1993).

In 1991, African Americans earned roughly 1 percent of all doctorates awarded in the physical sciences and 2 percent of those in engineering, 1.4 percent granted in the biological sciences, 1.7 percent in mathematics and computer sciences, and 4.2 percent of doctorates awarded in the social and behavioral sciences (National Science Foundation 1992b; see also National Research Council 1993).

Between 1981 and 1991, the total number of S/E doctorates awarded to African Americans increased from 282 to 328. However, some field differences did emerge. For example, increases occurred in biological sciences (from 43 to 44); social and behavioral sciences (from 183 to 195); chemistry (from 13 to 18); engineering (from 16 to 43); mathematics (from 7 to 9); and computer/information sciences (from 2 to 5). Declines were experienced in agriculture (from 9 to 6) and earth, atmosphere, and marine sciences (from 3 to 2). Interestingly, in 1981, about 28 percent of the 1,013 doctorates awarded to African Americans were in S/E fields. By 1991, that figure had increased to 35 percent (of 933 doctorates) (National Science Foundation 1992b).

Fechter's (1989b) findings revealed that the proportion of total Ph.D.'s who are African American has been rising quite slowly—from 1.0 percent in 1975 to only 1.3 percent in 1985. Moreover, the outlook for improvement in the near term is not encouraging. The number of new Ph.D.'s being awarded to African Americans is also rising slowly; for example, in 1985, the 293 degrees awarded in science and engineering fields to African Americans who were U.S. citizens represented only 2.2 percent of the total .[2] The few African Americans possessing doctoral degrees in the sciences are clustered in three fields: psychology, social sciences, and life sciences. In 1985, African Americans constituted only one-half of 1.0 percent of the Ph.D. population in the more quantitative fields—mathematics, computer science, engineering, and the physical sciences.

Fechter (1989b) also reports some encouraging findings, at least for African American females. African American females (in comparison with all females) have been more successful than African American males (in comparison with all males) in entering science and engineering fields at the doctorate level. In 1985, African American females constituted almost 3 percent of the female science and engineering doctorate population. The comparable figure for African American males is roughly 1 percent. The higher rates for African American females at the doctorate level are evident in each major field.

Fechter (1989b) argues that the origins of the relatively low rates of participation by African Americans in doctorate-level science and engineering education lie in a variety of experiences and behavior. Among these is their relatively high rate of attrition from the educational pipeline, which in turn has been attributed to the inferior quality of their precollege schooling—reflected in part by the relatively smaller number of African American high school students who have taken advanced courses in science and mathematics. Another factor that has been suggested as an explanation is African Americans' disadvantaged economic status. The average income of African American families is significantly lower than the average income of white families. Moreover, the percentage reporting federal sources of financial support for new Ph.D. awardees has been declining for both African Americans and whites, but the decline has been relatively greater for African Americans. These economic forces may also explain why African Americans, on average, take longer to complete the requirements for a Ph.D. than do whites.

Fechter (1989b) also found that African American Ph.D.'s are more likely than whites to report that they were being underutilized—that is, that they were either unemployed part-time but seeking full-time work or employed part-time but seeking full-time work, or employed in a nonscience or nonengineering job because science or engineering jobs were not available. This underutilization was heavily concentrated among African American males in the fields of psychology and the social sciences. African American women, on the other hand, were less likely to report underutilization than either comparable white females or African American males.

It is important to note here, as encouragement for students considering S/E fields in college, that the unemployment rate for African American scientists and engineers is considerably below that of their peers in nonscience fields (Fechter 1989b). Once into their science and engineering careers, African American Ph.D.'s seem to have employment profiles comparable to their white peers. Regardless of race, the most important employer of Ph.D.'s in the U.S. economy is the academic sector. Almost two-thirds of African American Ph.D.'s and over one-half of white Ph.D.'s are employed in academia. However, other sectors are becoming increasingly more important. For African Americans, the growth in nonacademic employment is occurring in state and local governments and nonprofit organizations; for whites, the growth is occurring in the industrial sector (Fechter 1989b).

Given the similarity in their employment distribution by sector of the economy, it is not surprising that, within fields, African American and white Ph.D.'s engage in similar types of activities. In the quantitative fields (physical sciences, mathematics, engineering, and computer sciences), the most important activity is research and development

(R&D). In psychology, consulting and professional services have been increasing in importance (Fechter 1989b).

Salaries of Ph.D.'s have been rising, by about 5.5 percent per year since 1975 for African Americans, and by about 6.5 percent per year for whites. As a result, the salary differential between African Americans and whites has widened from less than 5 percent in 1975 to about 12 percent in 1985. Much of this difference can be explained by variations in years of experience. For example, the 1985 differentials narrow considerably; there is virtually none for Ph.D.'s with less than ten years of experience, and the differential for more experienced Ph.D.'s is about 5 percent, favoring whites. Similarly, within sector, African American/white differences in 1985 salaries range from 2 to 7 percent (Fechter 1989b).

Case Studies of Intervention Programs

Clewell's (1989) analysis includes case studies of three intervention programs. These programs serve minority students at different points in the educational pipeline, and their approaches vary accordingly. The first, Project Interface, works with junior high school students and emphasizes career awareness, motivation, enrollment in high school academic courses in mathematics and science, and parental involvement in their children's learning process. These areas have directly affected minority students' access to mathematics and science careers. Parental involvement has been found to be crucial to a child's choice of and successful participation in a mathematics or science major. The second program, Project SOAR, has developed an effective technique for increasing achievement in mathematics and science through a carefully planned series of exercises that emphasize the problem-solving aspect of mathematics and science rather than the disciplines themselves. Finally, the Undergraduate Math/Science Workshops of the Professional Development Program (PDP) focus on high-achieving minority students in a competitive setting and represent a different approach. PDP contains counseling, motivational, and academic assistance components.

These programs illustrate three important facts regarding intervention strategies. First, such strategies must take into account the place in the educational pipeline of the students whose needs they are addressing. Research has pointed out that different points along the pipeline require different approaches. Second, approaches must be tailored to the type of student being served. The PDP Math/Science Workshops illustrate that not all minority students require the same intervention, even if they are at the same place in the pipeline. And third, programs must ultimately address a larger problem than that are represented by the immediate needs of their participants. This can be done by dissemination of the intervention model as well as by changing the way parents help their children to learn and the way school teachers teach minority students mathematics and science (Clewell 1989).

The low representation of African Americans and other minorities in mathematics and science careers is a problem so severe that intervention is required at many levels and on many different fronts. We need more research on the most effective approaches, to maximize the return on intervention efforts. We must seek creative ways to apply the research findings and to ensure their wide distribution. An efficient dissemination system of both research and successful intervention efforts is necessary in the movement to increase the participation of African American and other minorities in mathematics and science fields.

POLICY IMPLICATIONS AND STRATEGIES

Education Policy

The challenge to American education is to not only recognize but also accept differences without creating disadvantages, whether self-imposed or imposed by the dominant group (McBay 1989; Sindler 1987). Research is needed that examines the role of classroom processes in maintaining or enhancing African American students' abilities and skills (Reyes and Stanic 1988). This is critically important because of the overrepresentation of African Americans in poorly staffed and underfinanced public schools.

K–12

- Teachers (especially elementary) must become more cognizant of the fact that *different* does not mean inferior with regard to linguistic and learning styles. Multicultural education must play a greater role in teacher education.

- Researchers and policymakers should pay more attention to the relationship between mathematics and science instruction (especially in the early grades) and African American student achievement. In general, students who do well in mathematics and science early in their educational experience are more likely to take more advanced courses in these subjects.

- Early patterns of gender differences in mathematics and science achievement (and course selection) persist throughout the educational system. African American female students' current course-taking behavior serves as a barrier to their entry into the mathematics and science pool.

- In desegregated high schools, advanced mathematics and science courses tend to be racially segregated due to curriculum tracking. It is clear that these advanced mathematics and science courses serve as critical filters in African Americans' access to careers in science and technical fields. Academic counselors can assist in reversing some of these trends by encouraging African Americans (especially those in the college-preparatory academic curriculum) to enroll in more advanced science and mathematics courses.

- Despite considerable evidence that the science talent pool tends to form around the seventh grade, few intervention programs are targeted toward elementary and junior high school students. Intervention programs are needed at each educational level. Far too many of the existing programs are targeted to gifted students. If the pool is to be considerably expanded, students from the bottom half of the class will have to be recruited and targeted for intervention.

- Colleges and universities should develop stronger ties with local public schools (especially minority schools).

- An increasing number of scientists and engineers from government, universities, and business are volunteering their talents to the effort. In some cases, "partnerships" have been formed between the schools and the scientists' employers. Partnerships represent much-needed joint efforts that are seeking solutions to the problems that face precollege science and math education (Worthy 1989a; 1989b).

- One of the greatest underutilized mathematics and science instructional talent pools in this country is that of retired scientists and engineers. Such individuals have high potential for supplementing formal and informal educational instruction. Many retirees may find it especially rewarding to work with young children. This would be particularly beneficial in locations experiencing difficulties in recruiting young science and mathematics teachers, and could be especially effective in areas with HBCUs.

- More evaluative research is needed on the effectiveness of intervention programs so that the most effective ones may be identified and disseminated. At present, few intervention programs have evaluative components.

- Instructional programs could be developed in churches, recreational centers, housing projects, and so on. Community-based instruction may increase African American parental involvement with their children's education because the parents may feel more comfortable in more familiar environments.

- States could increase the amount and quality of required precollege mathematics and science coursework taken by all students. This would increase the pool of all students with at least requisite minimum training in these disciplines for the successful pursuit of undergraduate degrees in these fields (Fechter 1989a). Given the fact that minorities will soon account for one-third or more of some school systems, this could have a high payoff.

Postsecondary

- The identification and findings regarding historically black and predominantly white colleges and universities that were leaders in the production of African American degree recipients suggest the need for follow-up studies to determine what factors contribute to the success of these institutions (Pearson 1989b).

- Greater efforts to support HBCUs and to strengthen and develop further programs in the natural and technical sciences are needed to assure their survival and future success in educating African American students.

- Predominantly white colleges and universities (PWCUs) may require greater financial and other incentives to increase their ability to recruit and retain African American students in the natural and technical sciences.

- Between 73 and 88 percent of African American college withdrawals are for nonacademic reasons (National Science Foundation and Department of Education 1980). This suggests that financial support plays a major role in the attrition process. More public and private funding should be directed toward those institutions with large African American enrollments and those with proven records of producing African American scientific and technical talent.

- One effective way to increase the number of minorities, especially African Americans, in science and engineering is by increasing their course selection in such fields in two-year colleges and improving their transfer rates to four-year colleges. Roughly 45 percent of African Americans enrolled in postsecondary education attend two-year colleges (Haberman 1988). But retention and transfer rates for minorities attending two-year institutions are among the highest of all postsecondary institutions. This large percentage of minorities attending these institutions is a well-known fact in the educational community. Yet, few four-year institutions (either HBCUs or PWCUs) have forged partnerships with these institutions. Obviously, one policy strategy should be to forge more partnerships. Researchers should provide critical knowledge regarding the most effective way to increase retention and transfer rates for minorities attending two-year colleges. Local, state, and federal governments can play a larger role by supporting program efforts to increase minority participation in science and engineering at these institutions. (This is especially true in the case of the National Science Foundation [NSF], which has traditionally provided minimum research and program support to two-year colleges.)

- Undergraduate professors should encourage talented African American students to continue their training beyond the baccalaureate degree. Students must be made aware of the long-term benefits of a doctorate in science or engineering. Those who pursue doctoral studies should be advised to become involved in teaching and research activities in graduate school. Teaching and research skills provide invaluable training and experience that will ultimately prove vital to success in a scientific or technical career, whether academic or otherwise. In the long run, such skills will enhance career development and career mobility (Blackwell 1981).

Recent Federal Initiatives

Legislation

- On September 12, 1989, the House approved legislation that created three merit-based congressional scholarship programs aimed at encouraging more college students to pursue studies in science, engineering, and mathematics. These programs are to be administered by the NSF. In the case of essentially equal appointments, the NSF director would have the authority to consider an applicant's financial need or give preference to women, minorities, and the disabled in awarding the scholarships (Angle 1989).

- For the first program, consisting of four-year, $5,000-per-year scholarships, local nominating committees would propose candidates. Winners, one man and one woman per congressional district who plan to pursue studies and careers in math, science, or engineering, would be chosen by the NSF director (Angle 1989).

- The second program provides 500 two-year scholarships worth $7,500 per year to juniors and seniors willing to commit to teaching math or science in primary or secondary schools receiving federal aid under Chapter 1 (educational support for disadvantaged students). For each year of scholarship aid, a recipient would be required to teach two years. A recipient could be granted an additional $7,500 for one year of postgraduate study, provided it is required to earn a teaching certification. However, that year's award would require no teaching payback (Angle 1989).

- The third program would also grant 500 scholarships annually to juniors and seniors. In this case, however, recipients would be required to work as scientists or engineers for at least two years after graduation or to complete a minimum of two years of postgraduate education in math, science, or engineering. These scholarships would be worth $5,000 per year, plus up to $2,500 more matched dollar for dollar with the college where the student is enrolled. Eligibility would be restricted to those pursuing fields of study in which the NSF projects workforce shortages. Substantial penalties

would be imposed on those failing to complete the service requirements (Angle 1989).

- In a related matter, the legislation also requires the NSF to monitor
intervention efforts designed to improve math and science teaching
and enhance the career potential of disadvantaged students. The
NSF is to report its findings to Congress, regarding the most effective programs and what role the federal government could play in
encouraging their dissemination (Angle 1989).

Administrative

- Former Secretary of Energy, Admiral James D. Watkins, was an
outspoken proponent for improving precollege science and mathematics education in the U.S. In testimony before the House Science,
Space, and Technology Committee, he called for increasing the participation of African Americans and other underrepresented groups
in science and math education. Watkins encouraged greater volun-
teerism in teaching mathematics and science throughout the
educational system, believing that the national labs can be used as
effective educational resources because of their state-of-the-art
equipment and highly trained personnel. Many of these scientists
and engineers already serve as volunteers teaching students (especially economically disadvantaged and minority students) and
school teachers. Watkins estimated that the Department of Energy
would have about 20 national laboratories actively involved in various intervention efforts within the year (Watkins 1989; Barinaga
1989).
- The NSF has announced several new initiatives targeted to minority students.[3]
- In addition to focusing on the best and brightest students, the NSF
recognizes the need to focus on the bottom half of the student population if it is to raise the nation's general scientific literacy. To
accomplish this, partnerships should be forged with government
(especially at state levels), businesses, and public schools. The approach would focus more on improving science and mathematics
education, particularly at the local level, by recruiting academic scientists and engineers to work with their local public schools (Walsh
1989).[4]

MEDIA

Some public television stations have shown programs on minority participation in science. Currently, several television program consultants are developing proposals which, if funded, will give broad treatment to the hidden contributions of minorities to science and technology. However, many of the proposed programs are targeted to public television audiences. Unfortunately, few minorities view public television programming. Fortunately, most of these programs include companion educational packages, especially for precollege students. Thus, videotapes could also be made available to the schools. If major networks can devote primetime to the black athlete, surely minority scientists and engineers can be highlighted.

Recently, some television commercials (e.g., Dow and Whitney Houston) relevant to minority participation in science and technology have been aired. Commercials are one area where minority celebrities can play a larger role in encouraging young minorities to study science and mathematics. Such focus should include the relevance of science to daily life and emphasize that science and mathematics can be fun. Of course, Black Entertainment Television (BET), radio programs, and talk shows aimed at minorities can also play significant roles in making minorities more aware of opportunities in science and technology.

Some magazines aimed at minority readers have done a credible job of focusing on science and technology opportunities, but more can and should be done. Federal mission agencies and industry can produce and disseminate more posters of famous minority scientists and engineers. Special effort should be made to include women in the poster series.

IMPORTANCE OF INCREASED AFRICAN AMERICAN PARTICIPATION IN SCIENCE AND TECHNOLOGY

If efforts to recruit and retain young African Americans in science and engineering are to be successful, they must be linked to genuine, rewarding employment opportunities. Young African Americans, like other young Americans, must see a link between their investment in science and engineering education and a return on that investment.

There are many excellent reasons why young African Americans and other underrepresented minorities should pursue scientific and technical training to a greater extent than in the past. We briefly discuss some of these reasons below.

Return on Investment

Teachers and minority parents should be better informed of the nearly race-equalizing effects of the doctorate in the sciences and engineering so that they may encourage African American and other minority students to persist in their education. Student loans are a good investment because of the low unemployment rates among minority scientists and engineers. Financial assistance is usually more available to those who pursue studies in science and engineering than nonscience fields, especially at the graduate school level.

Academic Employment

Recent estimates place the universities' production of scientists and engineers at 10,000 Ph.D.'s annually beginning in the next decade. Some scholars claim that such a production level would be considerably below the 18,000 that the nation's R & D effort would require. There is a growing shortage of university professors to teach science and engineering to the next generation of scholars. There is every indication that the large cohort of Ph.D.'s expected to retire in the 1990s will lead to opportunities for new Ph.D.'s in most science disciplines (including the social and behavioral sciences).

Nonacademic Employment

It will be increasingly possible for minority scientists and engineers to build more successful careers in industry and the government because they may be employed without the appearance of competing with whites. In fact, nonacademic employment for new African American Ph.D.'s is increasing (National Research Council 1993), but the paucity of minority research executives in corporations continues (Ellis 1988). Because of a shortage of scientists in certain disciplines, some corporations are cutting back their R&D plans (Magazine 1989). Some governmental agencies are now confronted with labor shortages for their scientific and engineering workforces (Barinaga 1989).

Survivability

To compete effectively in an increasingly (international) technical labor market, African Americans will have little choice but to alter significantly their science and mathematics course-taking behavior or accept roles as untrained onlookers. Currently, African Americans make up a disproportion of these onlookers in the form of displaced workers—victims of the ongoing scientific and technical revolution. Even when displaced workers find new jobs, they are likely to earn considerably less than their previous salaries (National Urban League 1988; Pearson 1988).

REFERENCES

Anderson, Bernice. 1989. Black participation and performance in high school science. In *Blacks, science, and American education,* ed. Willie Pearson, Jr., and H. Kenneth Bechtel 43–58. New Brunswick, NJ: Rutgers University Press.

Angle, Martha. 1989. House passes bill to establish science, math scholarships. *Congressional Quarterly* 16 September: 2399.

Barinaga, Marcia. 1989. Getting energy into the schools. *Science* 246: 318.

Bechtel, H. Kenneth 1989. Introduction. In *Blacks, science, and American education,* ed. Willie Pearson, Jr., and H. Kenneth Bechtel, 1–20. New Brunswick, NJ: Rutgers University Press.

———. 1988. Best jobs for the future. *U.S. News & World Report* (25 April): 60–63, 66, 68–70.

Blackwell, J. E. 1981. *Mainstreaming outsiders: The production of black professionals.* Bayside, NY: General Hall.

Clewell, Beatriz C. 1989. Intervention programs: Three case studies. In *Blacks, science, and American education,* ed. Willie Pearson, Jr., and H. Kenneth Bechtel, 105–22. New Brunswick, NJ: Rutgers University Press.

Davis, Josephine D. 1989. The mathematics education of black high school students. In *Blacks, science, and American education,* ed.

Willie Pearson, Jr., and H. Kenneth Bechtel, 23–41. New Brunswick, NJ: Rutgers University Press.

Ellis, William W. 1988. Employment, human resources, and human development. Paper presented at the Congressional Black Caucus Legislative Weekend Symposium on Opportunities and Challenges for Minorities in Science and Technology: Preparing for the year 2000. Washington, DC, 16 September.

Fechter, Alan. 1989a. The human resources base for scientific and technical activity in the United States. Paper presented at the U.S.-Japan Science Policy Seminar, 22–25 May.

———. 1989b. A statistical portrait of black Ph.D.'s. In *Blacks, science and American education,* ed. Willie Pearson, Jr., and H. Kenneth Bechtel. 79–101. New Brunswick, NJ: Rutgers University Press.

Haberman, Martin. 1988. Alliances between 4-year institutions and 2-year colleges can help recruit more minority students into teaching. *Chronicle of Higher Education* 27 July.

Hill, Susan, and Eliza Hizell. 1993. HBCUs and the baccalaureate origins of recent black doctorate recipients. Paper presented at National Association for Equal Opportunity in Higher Education (NAFEO), Washington, DC, 3 April.

Hill, Susan, and Patricia White. 1989. Black participation in doctorate education. Paper presented at National Association for Equal Opportunity in Higher Education (NAFEO), Washington, DC, 19 April.

Jay, James M. 1971. *Negroes in science: Natural science doctorates, 1876–1969.* Detroit: Balamp.

Johnston, W. B., and A. H. Packer. 1987. *Workforce 2000: Work and workers for the 21st century.* Indianapolis, IN: Hudson Institute.

Lamm, R. D. 1988. Post-crash institutions. *The Futurist* (July/August): 8–12.

Magazine, A. H. 1989. Human resources: Restoring American's competitive edge. *Vital Speeches of the Day:* 502–7.

McBay, Shirley M. 1989. Improving education for minorities. *Issues in Science and Technology* (Summer): 41–47.

National Research Council. 1993. *Summary report 1991: Doctorate recipients from United States universities.* Washington, DC: National Academy Press.

National Science Foundation and Department of Education. 1980.

Science and engineering: Education for the 1980's and beyond. Washington, DC: National Science Foundation and Department of Education.

———. 1990. *Women and minorities in science and engineering.* Washington, DC: Government Printing Office.

———. 1992a. *Guide to programs: Fiscal year 1992* Washington, DC: Government Printing Office.

———. 1992b. *Selected data on science and engineering doctorate awards:1991.* Washington, DC: National Science Foundation.

National Urban League. 1988. The state of black America. In *Social Problems: Annual Editions,* ed. L. W. Barnes. Guilford, CT: Dushkin.

1988. Needed: Human capital. *Business Week* (19 September) (Special report).

Person, Willie, Jr. 1985. *Black scientists, white society, and colorless science: A study of universalism in American science.* Port Washington, NY: Associated Faculty.

———. 1986. Black American participation in American science: Winning some battles but losing the war. *Journal of Education Equity and Leadership* 6:45–59.

———. 1988. The effects of new technologies on black Americans. Paper presented at the Association of Social and Behavioral Scientists Meeting, Greensboro, NC, 23–26 March.

———. 1989a. The future of blacks in science: Summary and recommendations. In *Blacks, science, and American education,* ed. Willie Pearson, Jr., and H. Kenneth Bechtel. 137–52. New Brunswick, NJ: Rutgers University Press.

———. 1989b. The role of colleges and universities in increasing black representation in the scientific professions. In *Toward Black Undergraduate Student Equality in American Higher Education,* ed. Michael T. Nettles. Westpoint, CT: Greenwood.

Pearson, Willie, Jr., and H. Kenneth Bechtel, Ed. 1989. *Blacks, science and American education.* New Brunswick, NJ: Rutgers University Press.

Pearson, Willie, Jr., and C. Leggon. 1993. The baccalaureate origins of African American doctoral scientists. Paper presented at the annual meeting of the American Association for the Advancement of Science, Boston, 13 February.

Pearson, Willie Jr., and L. C. Pearson. 1985. The baccalaureate origins of black American scientists: A cohort analysis. *Journal of Negro Education* 54: 24–34.

———. 1986. Race and the baccalaureate origins of American scientists. *Journal of the Association of Social and Behavioral Scientists* 32:149–64.

Reyes, L. H., and G. M. A. Stanic. 1988. Race, sex, socioeconomic status, and mathematics. *Journal for Research in Mathematics Education* 19:26–43.

Spindler, G. D. 1987. Why have minority groups in North America been disadvantaged by their schools? In *Education and cultural process: Anthropological approaches,* 2d ed., G. D. Spindler. Prospect Heights, IL: Waveland.

U.S. Congress, Office of Technology Assessment. 1988a. *Educating scientists and engineers: From grade school to graduate school.* Washington, DC: Government Printing Office.

———. 1988b. *Power on!* Washington, DC: U.S. Government Printing Office.

Walsh, John. 1989. NSF education head makes risky bid. *Science* 246: 317–19.

Watkins, James D. 1989. Mathematics and science education. Testimony before The Committee on Science, Space and Technology, U.S. House of Representatives, 24 May.

Worthy, W. 1989a. Diverse, innovative programs revive precollege science, math education. *Chemical & Engineering News,* (11 September): 7–12

———. 1989b. Partnerships strive to improve precollege science education. *Chemical & Engineering News,* (25 September): 49–50.

NOTES

1. A report by the U.S. Congress (1988b) concludes that minority students (who are more likely to attend large urban schools) have less access to computers than white students. Not surprisingly, more affluent schools have acquired technology more rapidly than schools with students of predominantly low socioeconomic status (a disproportion of whom are African Americans). Predominantly, African American elementary schools are significantly less likely than

predominantly white schools to have a computer. Average student access to computers also varies by region. The highest student per computer rations are in those states where African Americans are most concentrated.

2. Based on the National Science Foundation (1990) report on women and minorities in science and engineering, Fechter's general findings and conclusions remain relevant (See also NSF 1992b).

3. Due to space limitations, these initiatives will not be discussed. For a detailed overview of these new initiatives and funding opportunities, see National Science Foundation (1992a), *Guide to Programs: Fiscal Year 1992*.

4. For an excellent discussion of the role that the federal government could play in human resource investment in science and engineering, see U.S. Congress (1989a).

19 Black College Students: Achievement, Social Integration, and Aspirations

WALTER R. ALLEN AND JOHN WALLACE

W hat happens to African American students at critical steps along the way between college entry, the election of a major field, and graduation or dropping out? How does the college experience for black students differ on historically black and on predominantly white campuses? How do factors such as gender, social class background, geographic region, or occupational goals influence black student success? Searching for answers to these and related questions, this chapter looks at the student outcomes: academic achievement, social involvement, and occupational aspirations for a national sample of African American students attending selected predominantly white and historically black state-supported universities. We report here on results of the National Study of Black College Students (NSBCS), conducted at the University of Michigan from 1981 to 1983. The study explores how these student outcomes are related to student background characteristics, campus characteristics, campus experiences, and student personality orientation.

CAMPUS RACE DIFFERENCES

Black students in college differ from their white peers in important ways. The parents of black students are typically urban, have fewer years of education, earn less, and work at lower status jobs than do the parents of white students.[1]

Black students on predominantly white campuses continue to be severely disadvantaged compared to white students in terms of persistence rates, academic achievement levels, enrollment in advanced degree programs, and overall psychosocial adjustments.[2]

Despite social, economic, and educational disadvantages, black college students have similar (or higher) aspirations to their white counterparts. However, they attain these aspirations less often than do white students. Educational attainment is also generally lower for black students. Black students attending predominantly white colleges apparently experience considerable adjustment difficulty. Some of their adjustment problems are common to all college students, but others are unique to black students.[3] For example, black students often find it necessary to create their own social and cultural networks to remedy their exclusion from the wider, white-oriented university community. Of all problems faced by black students on white campuses, those arising from isolation, alienation, and lack of support seem to be the most serious.[4]

Whether because of adjustment or other difficulties, African American students perform less well academically than do their white peers. Black students' academic difficulties on white campuses are often compounded by the absence of remedial and/or tutorial programs and limited informal information exchange with whites (i.e., faculty and other students). Nonetheless, despite the initial difficulties most black students experience, many make the required adjustments and achieve academic success in predominantly white institutions.[5]

Black students on historically black campuses are more disadvantaged than their peers (black and white) on predominantly white campuses in terms of family socioeconomic status, high school academic records, university instructional faculty/facilities, available academic majors, and opportunities for advanced study.[6] The typical parents of black students on black campuses earn less money, have lower educational achievement, hold lower status jobs, and are more often separated or divorced than are the parents of black students on white campuses. Consistent with observed economic discrepancies, black students on black campuses tend to have lower standardized test scores and weaker high school backgrounds than do typical black students on white campuses.[7]

Although much is made of real and imputed differences between students at historically black and predominantly white universities, the comparison of black students on black campuses to those on white campuses is often based more on conjecture than fact. The presumption is that white campuses provide superior environments for black student educational development, although empirical evidence shows a poorer match between black students and white campuses.[8]

A natural outgrowth of comparisons of black student populations on black and white campuses is recognition of the "special mission" of black colleges. To a large extent, black colleges enroll students who might not otherwise be able to attend college because of social, financial, or academic barriers. These institutions pride themselves on their ability to take financially disadvantaged and less academically prepared black students and correct their academic deficiencies. Thus, black colleges graduate students equipped to compete successfully in graduate schools or in their chosen professions.[9]

When black students on black and white campuses are compared on the dimension of psychosocial development, those on black campuses seem to fare much better. Gurin and Epps found that black students who attend black colleges possessed positive self-images, strong racial pride, and high aspirations.[10] More recently, Fleming showed black students on black campuses to have more favorable psychosocial adjustment compared with those on white campuses.[11]

In summary, the evidence suggests that black students on historically black campuses are more disadvantaged in socioeconomic and academic terms than are black (or white) students on predominantly white campuses. However, black students on black campuses display more positive psychosocial adjustments, more significant academic gains, and greater cultural awareness and commitment. In general, the "fit" between African American students and the college context seems more favorable at black than at white institutions. Together with campus race and family social class background, gender seems to be a critical determinant of student success.

METHODS OF THE STUDY

Data were collected using mailed questionnaires, which students returned directly to the University of Michigan. Students were randomly selected for participation in the study, based on lists of currently enrolled students supplied by the various university registrars' offices. Selected students received the questionnaire and four follow-up requests encouraging them to respond.

The 1981 phase of the study collected data from a cross-section of black undergraduates at six predominantly white, public universities: University of Michigan, Ann Arbor; University of North Carolina, Chapel Hill; University of California, Los Angeles; Arizona State University, Tempe; Memphis State University; and the State University of New York, Stony Brook. Data for 1982 were drawn from first-year undergraduate black students (freshmen and transfers) attending the six schools surveyed in 1981. Data for 1982 were also drawn from a cross-section of students attending two other predominantly white, state-supported universities: the University of Wisconsin, Madison; and Eastern Michigan University, Ypsilanti.

The 1983 phase of the NSBCS collected data from a cross-section of black undergraduates at eight historically black, public universities: North Carolina Central University, Durham; Southern University, Baton Rouge, Louisiana; Texas Southern University, Houston; Jackson State University, Jackson, Mississippi; North Carolina A&T State University, Greensboro; Central State University, Wilberforce, Ohio; Morgan State University, Baltimore, Maryland; and Florida A&M University, Tallahassee. These data sets were merged to compare and contrast students at predominantly white versus historically black universities.

The overall response rates and total N's (number of responses) for each year of the survey are as follows: 1981, 30 percent (N = 695); 1982, 35 percent (N = 976); and 1983, 25 percent (N = 860). Together the data sets total 2,531 students. Analysis for this chapter is restricted to 1,800 respondents from which we received complete data for all variables. Considered in the best light, these findings provide information about the college experiences and outcomes of more than 2,500 black students. This information is detailed, self-reported, and specific to the circumstances of the black students in U.S. higher education.

The NSECS represents one of the most comprehensive data sets currently available on the characteristics, experiences, and achievements of black college students. Nevertheless, these findings cannot be automatically generalized to the national case with certainty. However, the findings from this research are of substantial heuristic and informative value for attempts to understand the national case. As an exploratory study, it reveals fruitful avenues for future research. This research also provides useful baseline data about how a sizeable population of black students (those who chose to participate in this study) are faring in college.

Using multiple regression analysis to examine the net and joint explanatory influences of key predictor variables on student outcomes, we attempt to clarify complex relationships in the data. The multivariate model examined here investigates relationships between three outcome variables: (a) academic achievement, (b) social involvement in campus life, and (c) occupational aspirations. There were five sets of predictor variables: student educational background factors (high school grade-point average, amount of time spent studying, class level); student aspirations (how far student plans to go in school, when student will consider self successful in career); demographic characteristics (gender, socioeconomic status); personal adjustment factors (relations with white students, relations with white faculty, student's self-concept, student's attitudes concerning choice of institutions); and environmental factors (campus race, unity among black students).

FINDINGS

The regression analysis reported in Table 1 allows us to examine the specific correlation of predictor variables with outcome (or dependent) variables, while controlling for the influence of other variables. Our model best accounts for variance in academic achievement ($R^2 = .20$ or 20 percent). The model is least effective in explaining occupational aspirations (11 percent) and is most effective in explaining students' social involvement (18 percent) (See Table 1).

The predicted power of campus racial composition is consistent across the different student outcomes. In two instances, those of social involvement ($B = -.49$) and occupational aspirations ($B = -.35$), the racial composition of the campus emerges as the most significant predictor of student outcomes. For academic achievement, race is the second most important predictor of student outcomes ($B = .38$). Students who have better relations with college faculty ($B = .39$) and who

TABLE 1. Regression Models Predicting Academic Achievement, Social Involvement, and Occupational Aspirations

Independent Variables[a]	(I) Acad. Ach.			(II) Soc. Inv.			(III) Occ. Asp.		
	B	b	S.E.	B	b	S.E.	B	b	S.E.
Constant		1.29	.234		.989	.233		5.38	.405
OUTCOME VARIABLES									
Ugpa	—	—	—	-.02	-.02	.02	.02	.01	.04
Futoc	.01	.01	.01	-.02	.04	.01[b]	—	—	—
Soc. Involve	-.03	-.02	.03	—	—	—	.08	.04	.04[b]
EDUCATIONAL BACKGROUND									
Hsgpa	.20	.19	.02[c]	.02	.02	.02	.16	.09	.04[c]
Stutime	.03	.03	.02	.04	.05	.02[b]	.03	.02	.03
Class level	.03	.04	.02	-.06	-.08	.02[c]	.01	.01	.04
ASPIRATIONS									
Edasp	.11	.11	.02[c]	.03	.03	.02	.45	.26	.04[c]
DEMOGRAPHICS									
Sex	-.07	-.03	.05	.02	.01	.04[c]	-.34	-.10	.08[c]
SES	.01	.01	.02	.06	.09	.01[c]	.02	.03	.03

	B	b	S.E.	B	b	S.E.	B	b	S.E.
PERSONAL ADJUSTMENT									
Whtstud	-.02	-.01	.04	.18	.12	.03^c	.01	.00	.06
Profeval	.39	.27	.03^c	.10	.07	.03^c	-.01	-.00	.06
Self confidence	-.00	-.00	.03	.05	.05	.02^b	-.04	-.02	.04
Right choice	.07	.07	.02^c	.17	.17	.02^c	.07	.04	.04
ENVIRONMENT									
Camp Race	-.38	-.18	.05^c	-.49	-.25	.05^c	-.35	-.10	.09^c
Unity	-.04	-.04	.03	.10	.09	.03^c	-.05	-.03	.05
R^2	.199^c			.175^c			.110^c		
S.E.	.89			.85			1.61		
N	(1800)			(1800)			(1800)		

[a] See "Methods of the Study" for description of variables.
[b] p < .05 level
[c] p < .01
B = partial regression coefficient
b = unstandardized regression coefficient
S.E. = standard error

had higher grades in high school (B = .20) also have higher academic achievement in college. Other significant predictors of academic achievement reveal that college grades are highest for students who report high educational attainment aspirations (B = .11) and who feel they chose the right college to attend (B = .07).

Beyond college racial composition, social involvement is strongly correlated with student relations with white fellow students (B = .18) and students' belief that they made the right college choice (B = .17). Students who get along well with faculty (B = .10) and who sense greater unity among black students on campus (B =.10) also are more involved socially.

Occupational aspirations are minimally related to predictor variables in the model. Students with high educational aspirations have substantially higher occupational aspirations (B = .45). Predictably, students who aspire to the highest prestige occupations also expect to attain more years of schooling. Consistent with the findings from other studies, women report significantly lower occupational aspirations (B = −.34).[12] Although gender differences in academic performance and social involvement are negligible, females are substantially more likely to aspire to lower-status, less prestigious, and consequently less powerful occupations. Paradoxically, student gender identity was a more effective predictor of occupational goals than were student grades (college/B = .02; high school/B = .17), mother's education (B = .02), or faculty relations (B = −.01). In fact, gender identity nearly matched campus racial composition in ability to predict student occupational aspirations (B = −.35 vs. B = −.34). In short, student gender identity exerted a seemingly mysterious influence over student occupational choices.

To further clarify the complex underlying patterns in the data, we ran the regression model *within* categories of the key test variables of campus racial composition, student gender, and student socioeconomic status. This procedure facilitates efforts to determine whether contextual factors, or unmeasured correlates of key test variables, significantly influence results. Simply put, we used this procedure to ask whether the prescribed model had different predictive power for men compared to women, or for low-income compared to high-income status students, or for students attending traditionally white, as opposed to those attending traditionally black colleges.

There were significant gender differences, not so much in overall association of the model with occupational goals (male $R^2 = .10$, Female $R^2 = .11$) as in the relative importance of individual predictor variables. Thus, female occupational goals were highest for those on black campuses (B = $-.48$) who had high educational aspirations (B = .42) and good grades in high school (B = .20). By contrast, male occupational goals were best predicted by high educational aspirations (B = .47) and good grades in high school (B = .15). Beyond the differences revealed in predictors of occupational aspirations, no other striking gender differences were revealed.

Contextual analysis revealed important differences between students in the high and low mother's educational attainment groups. Overall association (R^2 values) between predictors in the model and student outcomes was basically the same for both groups. However, the specific pattern of associations between individual predictor variables and student outcomes differed dramatically. In the low-socioeconomic-status group, the strongest predictors of college grades were campus racial composition (B = $-.43$) and relations with professors (B = .40). In the high-status group, the strongest predictors were occupational aspirations (B = $-.36$) and relations with white students (B = .79). Thus, academic achievement is highest for low-socioeconomic-status African American students who attend historically black colleges and who have favorable relations with faculty. On the other hand, high-achieving black college students from middle- or upper-class backgrounds more often have high occupational aspirations and report favorable relations with white peers.

Social class differences are also apparent in black college student occupational aspirations. In the low-status group, occupational goals are highest for males (B = $-.45$), for students with high educational aspirations (B = .41), for students on historically black campuses (B = $-.24$), and for students with better high school academic records (B = .14). In the high-status group, occupational goals are highest for students with high educational aspirations (B = .53), for those attending historically black colleges (B = $-.52$), for males (B = $-.21$), and for students who reported better grades in high school (B = .23). Our contextual analysis of economic background failed to reveal important or substantial differences related to student involvement in campus social life.

The final contextual analysis, comparing students attending historically black colleges to those attending predominantly white colleges, is also revealing. Although the patterns associated with academic achievement in both groups were similar, (R^2 black campuses = 19%; R^2 white campuses = 15%), overall association was quite different for social involvement (R^2 black campuses = 9%; R^2 white campuses = 15%) and for occupational aspirations (R^2 black campuses = 3%; R^2 white campuses = 15%). Our model is more effective in explaining student outcomes on predominantly white than on historically black campuses. This may be because black students on white campuses more resemble in characteristics the white students on whom traditional status attainment and achievement models are validated. Taking the comparison further, essentially the same factors predict successful student outcomes on both types of campuses. Thus, academic achievement on both predominantly white and historically black campuses is highest for students who report favorable relations with professors, for students who express high educational aspirations, and for students with better grades in high school. This suggests that there may be universal or common features of a "successful college student profile."

On historically black campuses, males with high self-esteem who are happy with their college choice report the highest involvement or integration with campus social life. On predominantly white campuses, social involvement is highest for those whose relations with whites (faculty and peers) are most favorable and who are pleased with their college choice. On both sets of campuses, occupational aspirations are highest among males with high educational aspirations and strong high school academic records. The magnitude of association between predictor variables and the outcome variable occupational aspirations differs by a factor of five, comparing students on historically black campuses to those on predominantly white campus (R^2 black campuses = 3% vs. R^2 white campuses = 15%).

SUMMARY AND CONCLUSIONS

Interpersonal relationships form the bridge between individual predispositions and institutional settings. Characteristics of the individual and characteristics of the institution combine to determine academic performance, extent of social involvement, and occupational goals. The way a student perceives *and* responds to events in the college setting will differentiate the college experience and shape college outcomes. What he or she does when confronted with difficult subject matter, how she or he handles the uncertainty of new situations, and how adept he or she is in seeking and receiving help will ultimately determine whether his or her college experience is positive or negative.

Intertwined with institutional patterns, practices, and policies are social relationships. Social relationships embody the extrabureaucratic features of institutional structure and functioning.[13] The informal elements of formal organizational structure are important predictors of student outcomes in this study. For instance, the most powerful and consistent predictor of all student outcomes was campus racial composition. Students in the sample who attended historically black universities reported better academic performance, greater social involvement, and higher occupational aspirations. In short, the college experience was most successful (measured by these outcomes) for African American students on campuses with black majority student populations.

The salutary effect of attending a historically black university for student success clearly speaks volumes about the importance of sociopsychological context for student outcomes. In this respect, previous research demonstrates unequivocally the profound difference that historically black and predominantly white campuses represent for black students.[14] On predominantly white campuses, black students report feelings of alienation, sensed hostility, racial discrimination, and lack of integration. On historically black campuses, black students report feelings of engagement, connection, acceptance, and extensive support and encouragement. Consistent with accumulated evidence on human development, these students, like most human beings, develop best in environments where they feel valued, protected, accepted, and socially connected. Such supportive environments communicate that it is safe to take the risks associated with intellectual growth. These environments also have more people who provide black students with positive feedback, support, and understanding, and who communicate that they care about the students' welfare.

Historically black universities provide positive social and psychological environments for black students, comparable to that experienced by white students who attend white universities. Socially, the important ingredients are the extensive network of friends, the numerous social outlets, and the plethora of supportive relationships. Psychologically, the key ingredients are the multiple boosts to self-confidence and self-esteem, feelings of psychological comfort and belonging, and a sense of ownership—the feeling that "this is our campus." When these social and psychological ingredients are present in optimal combination, the chances that a student will be successful in college increase dramatically. Of course, the optimal presence of these ingredients does not guarantee success. Similarly, their absence does not guarantee that a student will fail. We are dealing here with probabilities, and the probability is that more students will succeed than fail under optimal sociopsychological circumstances.

In this connection we conclude that African American student college outcomes can be reasonably viewed as resulting from a two-stage process. Using academic performance to illustrate the point and the theoretical model implicit in such a conceptualization, we argue the following: Whether a student successfully completes college and whether that student graduates with "honors" are no doubt sizably influenced by individual characteristics. How bright the student is, the student's academic background or preparation, and the intensity of personal ambition and striving will all ultimately influence academic achievement. Beyond these personal traits, however, is a set of more general factors—characteristics more situational and interpersonal in nature. The student's academic performance will also be affected by the quality of life at the institution, the level of academic competition, university rules/procedures/resources, relationships with faculty and friends, racial composition of and hostility on the campus, and the extent of social support networks on campus.

TOWARD CORRECTIVE STRATEGIES

The challenge remains to develop strategies to improve the recruitment and retention of African American students in U.S. higher education. Problems of low black enrollment in college, depressed levels of academic achievement, and high rates of attrition have seemed intractable recently. Despite concerted efforts by many of the nation's colleges and universities, desired increases in the numbers of African American students have been difficult to achieve. If they are to improve the future prospects for expanded African American participation in U.S. higher education and reverse recent declines, colleges and universities must renew and expand their commitment of goals, energy, and resources. Without massive commitments, past gains will be grossly compromised or lost. If this happens, society as a whole will be the ultimate loser. Bright, promising African American students are being denied educational opportunities. Our society also misses the opportunity to enhance its competitive posture in the world economy.

We offer the following recommendations to improve black students' college enrollment and retention, and to stem the wasted potential represented by declining African American participation in higher education.

- *Precollege Enrichment Programs*
  Universities are encouraged to implement or expand programs that bring high school students to their campuses for short-term summer institutes or for coursework. Such programs would expose students at an early stage to the requirements, expectations, and procedures of higher education.
- *Better Coordination Among High Schools and Colleges*
  University faculty and staff and high school teachers, counselors, and administrators should expand their interactions and their mutual efforts to communicate university expectations and to enable colleges to anticipate incoming freshman students' strengths and weaknesses.
- *Coaching for Standardized Tests*
  High schools and colleges should organize practical courses on the theory and organization of standardized tests and train students in test-taking skills.
- *Early Admissions and Financial Aid Awards*
  Universities are encouraged to notify promising students of admission and financial award as early as the end of their junior year of high school. We encourage the use of a combination of traditional and nontraditional indicators of student potential.
- *Alternative Admissions Criteria*
  Universities continue to rely heavily on narrowly defined indicators of student academic achievement and academic potential. Alternative

376 | EDUCATION, SCIENCE, AND TECHNOLOGY

admissions criteria would emphasize extracurricular activities, teacher recommendations, personal interviews, and student personality traits, along with standardized test scores and high school grades as the basis for admissions decisions.

- *Systematic Orientation Programs*
  Colleges and universities should strengthen their freshman orientation programs to acquaint students with the problems of college life and strategies for coping.

- *Better Coordination of University Services*
  Offices serving student needs must strive for better coordination of efforts to avoid working at cross-purposes. Services must be organized into a "retention" system to track and assist students at each stage.

- *Faculty Involvement*
  As the university's "human link" with students, faculty must be sensitive to their critical role in student support and be encouraged to assume wider, more intense responsibility in aiding student adjustment to college. The university reward system must grant teaching more importance in faculty evaluations for promotions and raises.

- *Increased Black and Black Female Presence*
  The participation of these underrepresented groups at all levels in the university faculty and administration must be achieved. At the same time, the university community as a whole must be more sensitive to black and black female concerns and needs.

- *Value-Added Teaching Philosophies*
  Universities must adopt educational approaches that emphasize individualized instruction and identify deficiencies, and they must develop programs to correct these deficiencies. The measure of a program's academic excellence should be student growth and progress rather than the attrition rate.

- *Compile Data on Student Experiences*
  Systematic, comprehensive, longitudinal data files need to be maintained on students. Such data would provide an empirical basis for policy decisions (e.g., How do students who score low on college entrance exams actually perform over time?).

- *Commitment to Positive and Effective Change*
  The goal of equity in education must be reasserted. Universities must reaffirm and act on the goal of increased black representation in U.S. higher education.

REFERENCES

Allen, Walter. "The Color of Success: African American College Student Outcomes of Predominantly White and Historically Black Public Colleges and Universities." *Harvard Educational Review* 62, 1 (Spring 1992): 26–44.

Allen, Walter R. 1985. Black student, white campus: Structural, interpersonal and psychological correlates of success. *Journal of Negro Education* 54:134–47.

———. 1986. *Gender and campus race differences in black student academic performance, racial attitudes and college satisfaction.* Atlanta, GA: Southern Education Foundation.

Allen, Walter R., Edgar G. Epps, and Nesha Z. Haniff, eds. 1991. *College in black and white: African American students in predominantly white and historically black public universities.* Albany, NY: State University of New York Press.

Blackwell, James E. 1982. Demographics of desegregation. In *Race and equity in higher education*, ed. Reginald Wilson, Washington, DC: American Council on Education.

———. 1987. *Mainstreaming outsiders: The production of black professionals.* 2d ed. Dix Hills, NY: General Hall.

Fleming, Jacqueline. 1984. *Blacks in college.* San Francisco: Jossey-Bass.

Gurin, Patricia, and Edgar G. Epps. 1975. *Black consciousness, identity and achievement: A study of students in historically black colleges.* New York: Wiley.

Nettles, Michael T. 1998. *Toward black undergraduate student equality in American higher education.* Westport, CT: Greenwood.

Pearson, Willie, Jr., and L. C. Pearson. 1985. Baccalaureate origins of black American scientists: A cohort analysis. *Journal of Negro Education* 54:24–34.

Smith, A. Wade, and Walter R. Allen. 1984. Modeling black student academic performance in higher education. *Research in Higher Education* 21:210–25.

Thomas, Gail E. 1981. *Black students in higher education: Conditions and experiences in the 1970s.* Westport, CT: Greenwood.

———. 1984. *Black college students and factors influencing their major field choice.* Atlanta, GA: Southern Education Foundation.

Trent, William T. Focus on equity: Race and gender differences in degree attainment, 1975–76; 1980–81, in W. R. Allen, E. G. Epps and N. Z. Haniff eds. 1991. *College in black and white: African American students in predominantly white and historically black public universities.* Albany, NY: State University of New York Press.

Weber, Max. 1947. *The theory of social and economic organization.* New York: Free Press.

NOTES

1. Michael T. Nettles, *Toward Black Undergraduate Student Equality in American Higher Education* (Westport, CT: Greenwood, 1988); James E. Blackwell, "Demographics of Desegregation," in *Race and Equity in Higher Education,* ed. Reginald Wilson (Washington, DC: American Council on Education, 1982), 28–70.

2. Walter R. Allen Edgar G. Epps, and Nesha Z. Haniff, *College in Black and White: African American Students in Predominantly White and Historically Black Public Universities.* (Albany, NY: State University of New York press, 1991); Jacqueline Fleming, *Blacks in College* (San Francisco: Jossey-Bass, 1984); Nettles, *Toward Black Undergraduate Student Equality;* Gail E. Thomas, *Black Students in Higher Education: Conditions and Experiences in the 1970s* (Westport, CT: Greenwood, 1981).

3. Walter R. Allen, *Gender and Campus Race Differences in Black Student Academic Performance, Racial Attitudes and College Satisfaction* (Atlanta, GA: Southern Education Foundation, 1986); Gail E. Thomas, *Black College Students and Factors Influencing Their Major Field Choice* (Atlanta, GA: Southern Education Foundation, 1984).

4. Walter R. Allen, "Black Student, White Campus: Structural, Interpersonal and Psychological Correlates of Success," *Journal of Negro Education* 54 (1985): 134–47; Allen, *Gender and Campus Race Differences;* A. Wade Smith and Walter R. Allen, "Modeling Black Student Academic Performance in Higher Education," *Research in Higher Education* 21 (1984): 210–25.

5. Allen, Epps, and Haniff, *College in Black and White;* James E. Blackwell, *Mainstreaming Outsiders: The Production of Black Professionals,* 2d ed. (Dix Hills, NY: General Hall, 1987); Nettles, *Toward Black Undergraduate Student Equality.*

6. Allen, Epps, and Haniff, *College in Black and White;* Blackwell, "Demographics in Desegregation"; Willie Pearson, Jr., and L. C. Pearson, "Baccalaureate Origins of Black American Scientists: A Cohort Analysis," *Journal of Negro Education* 54 (1985):24–34; Thomas, *Black College Students and Factors.*

7. Patricia Gurin and Edgar G. Epps, *Black Consciousness, Identity and Achievement: A Study of Students in Historically Black Colleges* (New York: Wiley, 1975); Nettles, *Toward Black Undergraduate Student Equality;* Thomas, *Black College Students and Factors.*

8. Allen, "Black Student, White Campus"; Nettles, *Toward Black Undergraduate Student Equality.*

9. Blackwell, *Mainstreaming Outsiders,* p. 6–7; Tent, "Focus on Equity," p. 56–58

10. Gurin and Epps, *Black Consciousness.* [no further data available].

11. Fleming, *Blacks in College.* [no further data available].

12. [No data available].

13. Max Weber, *The Theory of Social and Economic Organization* (New York: Free Press, 1947).

14. Fleming, Blacks in College, p. 150–57. Walter Allen, "The Color of Success: African American College Student Outcomes of Predominantly White and Historically Black Public Colleges and Universities." *Harvard Educational Review* 62, 1 (Spring 1992):26–44.

20 | *Agenda for Excellence and Equity*

W. A. BLAKEY

On 26 June, 1992, after 17 years of litigation, the Supreme Court of the United States ruled in *Ayers v. Fordice* that Mississippi had not met its obligation to eliminate the vestiges of segregation in its formerly dual system of higher education. Although the nation's historically black colleges and universities (HBCUs) had benefited from the constitutional interpretation and application of *Brown v. Board of Education* (1954), the decision in *Ayers* represented the Court's first formal application of *Brown* principles to desegregation in higher education.

Although it did not go as far as many in the black higher education community would have liked in supporting enhancement of historically black colleges and universities, the eight-to-one decision clearly wrote ". . . a whole new chapter for education in the states where a large number of black students go to college." Similarly, many commentators and others concerned about the development and survival of black colleges look upon *Ayers* with a jaundiced eye; nevertheless, the Court's decision clearly represents a new legal watershed for historically black colleges and universities. As Howard University Law School's Professor J. Clay Smith has written of the court's opinion:

> Although "a student's decision to seek higher education has been a matter of choice," vestiges of a university system's *de jure* segregative policies go beyond recognition of the State's adoption and implementation of race-neutral admissions policies . . . . Further, the Court determined that there still remain discriminatory effects from "policies traceable to the *de jure* system," which

must be "reformed to the extent practicable and consistent with sound educational practices."

This paper outlines the history and promising future of the nation's historically black colleges and universities—emphasizing their economic, political, and social importance to the African-American community and the nation as a whole. It is a historical trek through the development of separate but unequal black colleges in the South, Southwest, and border states, coupled with an examination of the early legal battles to eliminate "separate but equal" as it was applied to higher education. Finally, it provides an analysis and impact statement for black colleges and minorities in higher education in light of the *Ayers* decision.

BLACK COLLEGES AND UNIVERSITIES— A TRADITION OF STRUGGLE AND SURVIVAL

Black colleges exist today in the wake of a proud tradition—born in slavery, nurtured through Reconstruction (1865–1877) and the Civil Rights movement of the 1960s, and matured in the development of a long line of black educators and leaders from Booker T. Washington and Mary MacLeod Bethune to Mary Hatwood Futrell and Benjamin E. Mays. These colleges have suffered through meager resources, illegal segregation, and duplicitous behavior by the federal and state governments. They have, notwithstanding these almost insurmountable barriers, made first-class doctors, lawyers, engineers, and teachers out of second-class citizens who were former slaves.

THE EARLY YEARS—A SEGREGATED PAST

No one has ever written a complete history of black America's struggle for education. Statements such as, "during slavery it was illegal to teach a slave to read," continue to oversimplify the fact that the educational circumstances of both free and enslaved black people varied widely.

In some Spanish territories, there were schools for Africans and Native Americans as early as the sixteenth century. In the eighteenth century, African slaves from Islamic cultures probably had a higher literacy rate than whites because many Moslems could read and write Arabic. Similarly, during the colonial period, black people probably received the best education in Pennsylvania and Massachusetts, where there were no laws against educating slaves. According to Massachusetts historian and state legislator Byron Rushing, in 1674, a reformer named John Eliot asked local slaveowners to send him their slaves once a week for instruction. Eliot's death canceled his plan, but others established classes for African slaves in 1717 and 1728.

The history of the education of Negroes is not without ironies. Rushing maintains that in 1798 and 1800, black parents, who felt their children were unwelcome in Boston's public schools, petitioned the school committee to establish segregated schools. When their request was denied, they established a private school. In 1808, the school moved to the African meeting house and was partly subsidized with public funds. Several other black schools were established, but by the 1840s, both black and white abolitionists had changed their thinking, and segregated schools were outlawed in 1855.

Before Reconstruction, only a few institutions, including Berea College in Kentucky and Oberlin College in Ohio, admitted Negroes (Wright 1992). Before the Civil War ended, two black colleges were established by church groups to provide black freed persons with an education in the liberal arts. (Cheyney State College was founded in 1837, but its purpose was normal and industrial education; it did not confer a bachelor's degree.) Wilberforce University in Ohio and Lincoln University in Pennsylvania were the pioneers for the 123 colleges and universities established to serve Negroes between 1854 and 1952, when black Americans had very limited access to white institutions (Franklin 1967; Blakey 1983).

The federal government's role in providing access to higher education for the freed slaves began with the creation of the Freedman's Bureau and the subsequent founding of Howard University in 1867, the only federally created and supported institution of higher education for black Americans in the United States.

Howard University was founded as the Howard Normal and Theological Institute for the Education of Teachers and Professions of the First Congressional Society of Washington. Named after Union General Otis Howard, the name was shortened when the current university charter was approved by Congress and signed by President Andrew Johnson on 2 March 1867. The charter designated Howard as, "The University for the education of youth in the liberal arts sciences." Although Howard was chartered by Congress to educate the newly freed slaves, it has, from the beginning, offered education to all. The first student body included four white girls who were the daughters of university trustees and faculty members.

Almost all the black colleges founded during Reconstruction were established with the assistance of northern white philanthropists who committed themselves to the educational advancement of four million newly freed slaves and about one-half million free blacks classified as "free men of color" before the Civil War. Among the earlier private black colleges were Hampton Institute (Virginia, 1864), Shaw University (North Carolina, 1865), Fisk University (Tennessee, 1866), St. Augustine's College (North Carolina, 1867), Morehouse College (Georgia, 1867), Morgan College (Maryland, 1867), and Knoxville College (Tennessee, 1875) (Anon 1904; Moore 1977). Many were products of the more progressive elements in traditional religious bodies. Only Cheyney State College (Pennsylvania, 1837) was founded before the Civil War. However, all but two of these institutions were listed as normal or industrial schools and did not confer bachelor's degrees. Furthermore, many of these institutions began as high schools because they were forced to develop high school graduates who could attend college (Blakey 1987).

In 1872, Alcorn College (now Alcorn State University) became the first black land-grant institution established under the Morrill Act of 1862. Seventeen public black colleges, the so-called "1890 institutions," were established under the second Morrill Act of 30 August 1890. This act paved the way for the development of legally separated black and white land-grant public institutions in various states.

As a result, within a nine-year period, between 1890 and 1899, one land-grant college for black students was either established or planned in each of the seventeen southern and border states. The colleges were separate, unequal, and, for the most part, not allowed to award baccalaureate degrees (U.S. House 1988).

Evidence of the persistence of the essentially second-class nature of black public colleges can be found in the extended *Adams v. Richardson* (1973) litigation. *Adams* was originally filed in 1970 to challenge the failure of the Department of Health, Education, and Welfare (HEW) to enforce Title VI of the Civil Rights Act of 1964. The suit represented the first attempt to apply the principles in *Brown* to the desegregation of higher education institutions. The *Adams* litigation sought the termination of federal funding to statewide systems that continued to perpetuate dual systems of higher education in ten southern states. In the 1980s, eight other states were brought under the purview of the *Adams* order.

Dual systems of education for black and white Americans were stimulated by the U.S. Supreme Court decision in the case of *Plessy v. Ferguson* (1896). This case clearly established the principle of "separate but equal" in all aspects of American life. Under *Plessy*, states were not compelled to construct even rudimentary components of an integrated or desegregated society. In fact, they were permitted to create rigidly separated structures because states had only to satisfy the mandate of establishing separate facilities that could be labeled equal. Such facilities were indeed separate, but never equal. Certainly, the advent of *Plessy v. Ferguson* was signaled by the Compromise of 1877, followed by the withdrawal of federal troops from the South, the re-establishment of home rule, and the states' actions to circumvent the Civil Rights Act of 1875.

The southern and border states reluctantly sought to implement the separate-but-equal doctrine. Several of the seventeen states responded first by constructing separate but equal professional schools for black students and second by establishing out-of-state tuition grants for black students. Both measures were calculated to circumvent efforts by blacks to gain admission to historically white public institutions. By 1933, black college graduates increasingly demanded access to professional school education. During that same year, some 97 percent of the approximately 38,000 black students enrolled in colleges were studying at historically black institutions.

Between 1935 and 1954, five Supreme Court cases that addressed the problem of equality of educational opportunity for black Americans received national attention and illustrated the issues raised in challenging the separate-but-equal doctrine in *Plessy*. These cases were: *University of Maryland v. Murray* (1935); *Mississippi ex rel Gaines v. Canada* (1938); *Sipuel v. Board of Regents of the University of Oklahoma* (1938); *Sweatt v. Painter* (1950); and *McLauren v. Board of Education of Topeka, Kansas* (1954). Each was significant for special reasons, and all are important for their collective attack against categorical discrimination in graduate and professional schools.[1]

Each of these cases included attempts that the Court ultimately rejected to preserve the separate-but-equal concept through the use of out-of-state tuition payments to black students, the construction of separate graduate and law school facilities, and the establishment of segregated facilities within a law school for Negro students. However, the basic question of whether there were any circumstances in which state-mandated, racially separate educational facilities or programs were equal was not addressed.

On 17 May 1954, the Supreme Court ruled in *Brown* that the principle of separate but equal had no place in education and was unconstitutional. The Court said, "We conclude that in the field of public education the doctrine of separate but equal has no place. Separate educational facilities are inherently unequal." The Court pointed to the many injustices inherent in racial separation in public institutions and, in 1955, ordered the dismantling of separate, dual school systems to proceed "with all deliberate speed."[2]

Unfortunately, there was more deliberation than speed in the process of dismantling dual school systems and equalizing the quality of education available to black students in the southern and border states. Many formerly black schools were simply closed and their teachers and principals demoted or reassigned, while the students themselves suffered the low expectations of their teachers and taunts from their white classmates.

One other observation with regard to the post-*Brown* period seems relevant. During this time, the meaning of the decision was clouded or lost. Instead of states using the desegregation tool to compel the equalization of expenditures, quality in education too frequently became equated with attending schools where white students were the dominant part of the student body. In some circumstances, desegregation became the sole focus of the effort, rather than quality education, which had been the goal from the beginning. From one perspective, it seemed irrelevant who was sitting next to a black student if the teachers were unprepared, the facilities were inferior, and the library contained outdated books and periodicals.

THE *ADAMS* YEARS—ATTEMPTS AT DESEGREGATION

Designed to break down the barriers of racial segregation and open the doors to equal opportunity in all aspects of American life, litigation in federal and state courts has always been a prominent tool in the civil rights arsenal. From *Murray v. Maryland* (1937), the first successes in higher education in *Missouri ex rel Gaines v. Canada* (1938) and *Sipuel v. Oklahoma State Regents* (1950) through *Brown* in the elementary and secondary arena, litigation had always proved a successful tool.

The most important legal action to affect the educational hopes and aspirations of blacks and black colleges involved decisions growing out of the *Adams v. Richardson* (1973) case.[3] *Adams* was important to the interests of blacks because it sought to identify an acceptable plan to implement desegregation in public higher education and to formulate policies to ensure access and increase participation rates for all black Americans. Although the decision in *Adams* was eagerly anticipated, in fact, it provided few positive benefits for public black colleges and little desegregation at traditionally white institutions in the South and Southwest. Thus, despite their attempts to facilitate equitable solutions to implement public school desegregation, federal courts have experienced little success in doing so for higher education. Some of the courts' difficulties in working with higher education desegregation can be attributed to the often recalcitrant behavior of southern state governments. Most of the problems, however, result from the complexities inherent in determining participation in higher education, where attendance is not compulsory and admission policies are *institutionally based*. Thus, the dictates of *Brown* that subsequently led to the development of racial percentages to desegregate public schools were not applicable to higher education.

The *Adams* case was filed by the NAACP Legal Defense Fund (LDF) because HEW was not enforcing Title VI of the 1964 Civil Rights Act against states operating dual systems of higher education. Title VI prohibits federal support to public educational institutions that practice segregation and discrimination. At the beginning of the case, the LDF charged that HEW had failed to enforce Title VI in ten states (Arkansas, Florida, Georgia, Louisiana, Maryland, Mississippi, North Carolina, Oklahoma, Pennsylvania, and Virginia). The states cited were not the only ones known to be violating Title VI at the time. Rather, they were the ones in which HEW officials had completed field investigations and site visits detailing violations of the statute.

The filing of the *Adams* case, as the Southern Education Foundation indicated, dispelled the notion that the nation's public colleges and universities had been desegregated long ago. Perhaps more important, the action revealed that predominantly white institutions in America had been neither responsive nor committed to providing sufficient access to black Americans wishing to enter higher education or to benefit from a comprehensive array of higher education opportunities.

The most significant development in the history of the *Adams* litigation was the intervention, in 1973, of the National Association for Equal Opportunity in Higher Education (NAFEO) through an amicus curiae brief (Haynes 1978). In that brief, NAFEO questioned two possible impacts of the case on public black colleges: (1) lack of a factual predicate for the exercise of HEW's enforcement authority regarding public black colleges and (2) insufficient facts to support intervention by HEW into the arena of higher education policies and practices affecting historically black public institutions. NAFEO sought to focus the court of appeal's attention on the following:

- The *Adams* complaint, followed to its logical conclusion, raised the real possibility that public black colleges would be dismantled as part of the relief, representing an anomalous development since black colleges had been in the forefront of providing equal opportunity for all since their inception.
- The factual assertion that public black colleges discriminated, on the basis of race, against whites and were segregated in violation of the Fourteenth Amendment to the Constitution was inaccurate.

NAFEO's brief argued further that the application of arguments used in *Brown I* to desegregate public schools could not be applied ipso facto to higher education (Haynes 1978).

The specter of destroying public black colleges was especially troubling to the NAFEO presidents—given their experience with public school desegregation in the South:

What emerges as the grounds of this suit, as well as the relief granted, is that the maintenance of black colleges as the larger university within a particular state is the maintenance of a dual system of education based upon race; therefore, the state is discriminatory and engaging in conduct forbidden by the Fourteenth Amendment. It follows, then, that the states must establish a unitary system—one system. To accomplish this, the black institutions must be assimilated into the white unitary system where there is presumptively equal educational opportunity, independent of the state's wishes to establish and maintain a "special purpose" institution of higher education (Haynes 1978).

The NAFEO brief emphasized the role of public black colleges as "special-purpose" institutions and pointed out that the right of the states to maintain such institutions was threatened by the position of the plaintiffs. For NAFEO, the issue in the *Adams* case was not a denial of equal educational opportunity, but a failure (by the states) to achieve equality of educational attainment. From NAFEO's perspective, achieving the attainment goal required the continued existence and enhancement of public black colleges (Haynes 1978).

NAFEO's intervention affected the *Adams* litigation in a more substantive way as well. Although the intervention by black college presidents in partial opposition to the LDF's position in the case appeared to conflict with the plaintiff's ultimate goal, NAFEO's opposition helped to fashion a remedy and decision that was consistent with LDF's objectives.

The roller-coaster nature of the planned submission by the states; the planned acceptance by HEW and the U.S. Department of Education (ED); and the rejection, modification, and attempted implementation by the courts all cast doubt on the utility of litigation as an effective tool to achieve minority access objectives in higher education.

In 1987, Judge John H. Pratt dismissed the *Adams* suit because he found the plaintiffs no longer had standing to pursue the case. He based his decision on *Allen v. Wright* (1984),[4] which established two requirements for standing to sue: (1) that the discrimination must be "fairly traceable" to the government's action or inaction and (2) that the alleged wrong could be redressed by those bringing the case.

A three-judge panel of the U.S. Court of Appeals for the District of Columbia Circuit reversed Judge Pratt—holding that the LDF still had legal standing to pursue the case. The appeals court decision, authored by then Judge Ruth Bader Ginsburg, said that a direct relationship exists between the federal enforcement of antibias laws and state decisions: "Federal funding of facilities that engage in proscribed discrimination is in part causative of the perpetuation of such discrimination." Judge Ginsburg also expressed the appeals court's support for judicial supervision of civil rights enforcement when agencies fail in their responsibilities: "[J]udicial review would serve to promote rather than undermine the separation of powers, for it helps to prevent the Executive Branch from ignoring Congressional directives."[5]

Although the District of Columbia Circuit Court succeeded in reviving *Adams*, the opinion may have raised more questions than it answered:

- Do the laws cited by the civil rights groups justify a lawsuit seeking to force the federal government to cut off funds to certain state agencies?
- Does a district court have the power to impose specific timetables other than those set out in legislation?
- Can a current administration be held to court agreements made by prior administrations?
- Should the state governments involved join the federal government as a defendant in the suit?[6]

These questions raised serious substantive concerns about the value of using Title VI and the federal courts as vehicles for remedying discrimination in arguably dual systems of higher education.

A DECADE OF DECLINE—'OUT OF THE MAINSTREAM, STRUGGLING FOR SURVIVAL'

The survival and enhancement of America's black colleges and universities should remain the twin goals of not only the African American community, especially black churches, but also those who believe in diverse and multicultural higher education. Maintaining black colleges involves three things: (1) ensuring a solid financial base, including a strong endowment; (2) encouraging black student enrollment from a broad cross section of educational and family financial backgrounds;

and (3) continuing and expanding the federal government's support of these institutions.

A number of historically black colleges and universities (HBCUs) have been on the verge of closure during the past five years. Five have closed or merged with other institutions, and still others totter on the brink of losing their accreditation or being excluded from the Title IV, Student Assistance Program because of high student loan default rates (U.S. General Accounting Office [GAO], August 1993).[7] Small, private, historically black colleges have experienced the greatest turmoil in the recent past; yet, some are among the strongest financially and academically, as well as the most popular among the new black college-conscious high school seniors![8]

In the late 1970s and the early 1980s, some black institutions faced decline and even possible extinction. The closure of Bishop College in Texas; the merger of Morristown College with Knoxville College (after Knoxville was placed on probation and lost its accreditation temporarily); the merger of Hinds Junior College and Utica Junior College in Mississippi; and the precarious financial positions of Fisk University, Lane College, Shorter College, Langston University, and Morris Brown College were all negative signs on the HBCU horizon. The future of Allen University (which has within the past year returned to fully accredited status) was also in doubt. These facts, coupled with the decline in church and alumni support, foreshadowed a dinosaur's demise for these black citadels of learning.

The near closure, in 1985, of Fisk University, which was founded in 1866, presents a good case and an unfortunate example of the plight of HBCUs. Fisk, once a proud monument to education—with high academic standards, the world-renowned Jubilee Singers and its historic buildings—fell victim to a mounting fiscal crisis and alumni neglect. Sincere attempts, in the late 1970s and early 1980s, to restore its once-proud past exacerbated an already difficult situation.

Black private colleges—which are more enrollment dependent than their public counterparts—are much more vulnerable to enrollment fluctuations and federal student aid shifts from grants to loans. These shifts may be discouraging college attendance among lower-income minority students, who are disproportionately black. Dr. Reginald Wilson, co-author of a succession of reports, on *Minorities in Higher Education*, has said:

Thus, many minorities and low-income students have been forced to revert to loans to continue to be able to afford to go to college. Not surprisingly, the highest default rates on loans occur among those least able to repay—low-income and minority students. When the foregoing factor is combined with the threat by the previous administration to penalize institutions with high student loan default rates, there is added a reluctance on the part of institutions to recruit so-called "high-risk" students, therefore compounding the measurable decline in those students' attendance in colleges and universities (Wilson 1989).

Until the 1988–89 academic year, competition with white public colleges and community colleges, coupled with virtual caps on federal student aid and the shift in federal student aid to lower income students (from grants to loans), had probably hampered black college enrollments—despite the growth in black high school graduation rates (Ellis and Stedman 1989).

The financial strength of black colleges is often too enrollment dependent because black colleges tend to have small endowments and lack broad-based alumni financial support.[9] An examination of the American Council on Education's Twelfth Annual Status Report, "Minorities in Higher Education" (1993), reveals a continuing rise in enrollment at public and private historically black colleges and universities. At the same time, tuition and fees have become an increasingly important source of current fund revenues for all black colleges and universities. This is true, notwithstanding the fact that federal support to black colleges—primarily in the form of Title IV, Student Assistance, and Title III, Part B Institutional Aid—declined significantly (as a percentage of current fund revenues) until 1986.

THE BLACK COLLEGE AND UNIVERSITY ACT

A Concept Emerges: Defining an HBCU

Early in 1979, Rep. Shirley A. Chisholm, (D-N.Y.), chair of the Congressional Black Caucus Education Brain Trust, convened a meeting of several individuals who were concerned about the plight of the HBCUs. Attending that meeting to discuss what could be done legislatively to address the situation were: Mary Frances Berry, then HEW Assistant Secretary for Education; William H. Blakey, then

Deputy Assistant Secretary for Legislation (Education) at HEW (now HHS); and Kenneth S. Tollett, Director of the Institute for Study of Education Policy at Howard University. Opposed to legislative solutions were Berry and Blakey; Tollett assumed a "pro" stance. Rep. Chisholm—and later Brenda Pillors, her education legislative assistant—listened attentively to the debate.

That 1979 discussion stimulated thought and further research and ultimately led to numerous hearings and legislative initiatives in the 98th and 99th Congresses. Thus, the first steps leading to the enactment of a "race-specific" statute to benefit historically black colleges were taken.

Seven years later, President Ronald Reagan signed into law the Higher Education Amendments of 1986 (P.L. 99–498). The new law, signed on 17 October 1986, included a new Part B of Title III of the Higher Education Act, authorizing the Black College and University Act. For the first time, Congress went on record in support of HBCUs.

Title III, which had been created in 1965 presumably to benefit black colleges, had been subjected to departmental mismanagement and had become increasingly attractive to smaller developing institutions with substantial minority and low-income student populations. The political incursion of these institutions serving needy students, including many well-financed institutions, reduced the percentage of Title III assistance reaching historically black colleges. Although congressional appropriations grew, an increasing amount of Title III funding—often through specific set-asides—went to new beneficiaries, e.g., community colleges.

The most difficult challenge facing those who tried to draft the race-specific statute was to develop a definition of the universe of postsecondary institutions that make up the black college and university community (U.S. Commission on Civil Rights 1981). The most universally accepted definition was articulated by the National Advisory Committee on Black Higher Education and Black Colleges and Universities. It includes:

> ...institutions that were founded primarily for black Americans although their charters were, in most instances, not exclusionary. These are institutions serving or identified with service to Black Americans for

at least two decades, with most being fifty to one hundred years old (National Advisory Committee 1978)

Although some viewed the definition adopted as purposefully selected to include certain institutions, it was in fact chosen for constitutional reasons.

The Black College and University Act defines these institutions in Section 322(2) of Title III:

> (2) The term "Part B institution" means any Historically Black College or University that was established prior to 1964, whose principal mission was, and is, the education of black Americans, and that is accredited by a nationally recognized accrediting agency or association determined by the secretary [of education] to be a reliable authority as to the quality of training offered or its, according to such an agency or association, making reasonable progress toward accreditation. (20 USC 1061)

This definition, developed in close consultation with Howard University Law School Professors Herbert O. Reid and Kenneth S. Tollett, included not only the 107 post-Civil War institutions, but also four two-year public institutions in Alabama, Denmark Vesey Technical Institute in South Carolina, and the University of the Virgin Islands. The statutory definition focused on the historic and continuing mission of this subset of higher education institutions that were providing quality postsecondary educational opportunities to black Americans. As the legislative history makes clear:

> The statutory definition contained in Section 322(2) defining "Part B institution" for Historically Black Colleges and Universities includes the universe of eligible Part B institutions. No other criteria, standard or definition should be used. This definition includes many institutions which are more than 100 years old, at least one established as late as 1963, one created in the 1940's, three whose student enrollments are no longer majority black, and several historically black colleges which have been (or will be) merged with traditionally white institutions (U.S. Senate 1986).

This definition was adopted after considering (in an earlier draft of the bill) a definition that focused on the racial makeup of the student body. Professors Reid and Tollett argued persuasively for the definition adopted by Congress:

> The Minority Business Enterprise provision of the Public Works Employment Act of 1977, which was upheld in *Fullilove*, is a legislative equivalent of a race-specific Title III of the Higher Education Act. In both instances, the objective of Congress is to remedy the effect of past discrimination against minorities, particularly Hispanics and Blacks, including Historically Black Colleges and Universities in the case of Title III of the Higher Education Act. The Minority Business Enterprise provision required that all grants made by the Department of Commerce for public works projects be conditioned on the local grantee's assurance that at least 10% of the amount of the grant would be spent procuring the services of minority business enterprises. A proposed Title III which will make direct grants to Historically Black Colleges should define such colleges as institutions established for Blacks before 1964—the year of the enactment of the 1964 Civil Rights Act—and whose principal missions were and are the education of Black Americans (U.S. House 1984).

Remedying Discrimination in the Past

The revisions in Title III, Part B of the Higher Education Act, first enacted as part of the 1986 Amendments (P.L. 99–498), were designed to overcome the historic deficiencies in the current law and to begin a targeted process of remedying past discrimination against the nation's historically black colleges and universities. This category of institutions, which came into being as a result of white philanthropy and segregation in the South, had experienced uneven treatment by federal policymakers and unequal financial support from the federal government.

The principal support mechanism for black colleges, before 1986, had been Title III of the Higher Education Act—the only source of direct institutional support for small colleges. Since 1966, Title III had been *perceived* to be a black college program, in part, because of conversations, assurances, and intimations that took place *outside* of the formal legislative and policymaking process. Most black college presidents and their representatives believed that the term "developing" was utilized as a surrogate for "Negro" in the original act. Rep. Edith Green, who chaired the Subcommittee on Special Education, was the only member in either body of Congress on record—in the entire legislative history of Title III—who equated "developing" with "race" (Negro or black):

> I am not sure whether I am directing my question in the right way, but this particular Title (Title III) was written in my office last year and was a separate piece of legislation. This was not really the purpose of Title III, for a cooperative venture among the top 10, but, rather, we conceived it primarily to strengthen the Negro colleges in the South (U.S. House 1965).[10]

The "developing institutions" surrogate was used, many believe, because Congress would not have enacted race-specific, remedial legislation. The original statute also included several other phrases such as "out of the mainstream" and "struggling for survival" that complicated the regulatory process of trying to establish institutional eligibility criteria for Title III. As the funding for Title III grew, it became increasingly attractive to community and junior colleges and small, four-year, predominantly white liberal arts colleges as a source of institutional aid.

In FY 1980, less than 5 percent of the funding awarded under Title III went to historically black colleges and universities. Lengthy deliberations during the 1980 reauthorization process and the enactment of the 1980 Amendments to the Higher Education Act of 1965 indicate just how tenuous Title III assistance is for black postsecondary institutions. In light of current budgetary constraints and likely future funding trends, additional mechanisms must be found to provide federal support to these institutions. Notwithstanding the importance of Title III to a wide variety of postsecondary institutions, historically black colleges and universities have a legitimate claim to a program of institutional assistance designed to enhance their academic programs; rehabilitate existing structures; build new, state-of-the-art facilities; and strengthen student support programs. The Supreme Court has upheld the constitutionality of analogous "race-specific" or "race-conscious" remedies in school desegregation, employment, and voting rights cases. For example, *Fullilove v. Klutznick* (1980),[11] addressed the constitutionality of Section 103(f)(2) of the Public Works Employment Act of 1977. The Court affirmed the authority of the U.S. Congress to enact race-conscious legislation to remedy past discrimination under the general authority of the Civil War Amendments to the Constitution.

In *Fullilove*, the Court recognized the constitutional legitimacy of race-specific remedial legislation, if not the constitutional imperative of Congress's power under the Civil War Amendments, to provide race-conscious relief where a specific record of discrimination in the past can be pointed to as the factual and legal premise for congressional action. Since the American Negro or black American or African American's experience with slavery, as well as with institutions that arose out of slavery and segregation, are unique, the availability of *institutionally based* remedies may be narrower than first thought. The Supreme Court, without overruling *Fullilove*, has already indicated clear limits to its application in cases involving race.[12]

Since 1965, predominantly white institutions have continued to *enroll* larger numbers of black students but have graduated fewer students than their enrollment would suggest is appropriate or reasonable, while experiencing high black dropout rates. The unique role of historically black colleges and universities in redressing the current imbalance is critical. However, that role is not likely to be fulfilled if the federal government maintains its presently *passive* approach to ensuring the maintenance and growth of historically black colleges and universities.

The historical record is replete with discriminatory allocations of Morrill Act funds and disproportionately small awards of federal grant and contract funds to the seventeen black land-grant institutions, when compared with their seventeen white counterparts. This discriminatory system of allocating funds was aided, contributed to, and exacerbated by the states in their failure to designate black public institutions to receive matching state funds and their differential treatment of black public institutions in the allocation of state-appropriated funds (Trueheart). Furthermore, the only serious federal effort to mount a concentrated program of federal funding to black colleges and universities (Title III) has been plagued by lack of funding, program management problems, and lack of statutory and administrative direction. Because of recent statutory modifications, the effort is unlikely to preserve its principal focus on the original black college and university beneficiaries.

The 1954 *Brown* decision placed both the states and the federal government on notice regarding the maintenance of dual school systems, and the 1964 Civil Rights Act formally outlawed discrimination in federally assisted programs and activities. The *Adams v. Riley* litigation (begun in 1974 as *Adams v. Richardson*), challenging the Department of Education's failure to fully exercise its mandate under the Civil Rights Act of 1964, has unequivocally established the federal government's failure to fulfill its statutory and constitutional responsibilities to eliminate discrimination in all public institutions of higher education. The failure of enforcement places the federal government in a posture of exacerbating past discriminatory conduct and leaving unremedied the pattern of denials and differential treatment afforded HBCUs.

Historically black colleges and universities are assisting the federal government to carry out its "access" mission by providing postsecondary educational opportunities to black, low-income, and educationally disadvantaged young people. Historically black postsecondary institutions became inseparably linked to this mission through Title IV programs, which, at the same time, have created a dependence upon federal assistance that can only partly be met using current programs. The current state of black colleges and universities—which is partly attributable to the actions and inaction of the states and the federal government—requires the enhancement of black postsecondary institutions to ensure their continuation and participation in fulfilling the federal mission of equal access.

The New Remedy

The Black College and University Act of 1986 made several important changes that will benefit black postsecondary institutions:

- It assured funding on a nondiscretionary, formula-driven basis to all eligible institutions as long as appropriations are provided by Congress.
- It established new statutory activities, including faculty fellowships; construction and renovation of academic facilities; and

purchase, lease, or rental of instrumentation and laboratory facilities for instruction and research purposes.
● It allowed the institution to determine funding priorities.

These changes are significant because, since 1965, more and more nonhistorically black institutions have qualified for Title III assistance and the HBCU share of the Title III appropriation has declined. Although the dollar amount has increased along with the total Title III appropriation, the HBCU share of Title III reached an all-time low in 1980 ($15,783,100 or 15 percent). The percentage decline disturbed black college presidents and some Capital Hill lawmakers because Title III had been widely perceived as a "black college program," and Congress believed it was providing for black colleges when it appropriated funds for Title III beginning in 1965. The 1986 Amendments, under Part B, have allowed Congress to focus Title III funds on the intended target and provided a focal point for the HBCU community to ensure adequate funding for HBCUs. Appropriations have steadily increased as a result.

Another important impact resulting from the Black College and University Act has been the range of activities that institutions can propose and undertake as part of an overall institutional development plan. Previously, all Title III projects and activities required Department of Education approval and, more recently, had to be "developmental" in nature. Thus, construction of new academic facilities and the acquisition of research and instructional instrumentation were not specifically authorized under the old law. The use of Part B funds for maintenance, construction, and acquisition of instrumentation—according to black college presidents and chancellors—is critical to long-term development, continued accreditation, effective competition for federal research grants and contracts, and attracting the best students of all races (Anon 1993a).

The 1986 Amendments represented a signal achievement in the white-dominated halls of Congress, especially because initial legislative drafting, strategy development, and political implementation were almost exclusively the product of the labor of black staffers in the House and Senate and the members of the Congressional Black Caucus. Nothing, however, would have been accomplished without the help of the black college presidents and their Washington-based staff.

The most significant hurdle in the process was the perceived opposition of House Postsecondary Education Subcommittee Chairman William D. Ford (D-Mich.) to "set-asides" in Title III in general and to the enactment of a race-specific statute for HBCUs in particular. A hearing at Atlanta University in 1985, convened by Chairman Hawkins ultimately convinced Rep. Ford of the substantive reasons and political support for the Black College and University Act. The conditions that led to this legislation, however, began in the colleges themselves, whose decline over the years had been incremental. That decline has not been helped by the difficulties encountered by many of the institutions in administering Title IV, Title III, and other federal funds. Declining percentages of Title III dollars and almost no access to large federal research grants exacerbated an already difficult situation. Despite attempts by Presidents Jimmy Carter, Ronald Reagan, and George Bush to focus attention and additional federal funds on black colleges through the White House Initiative on Historically Black Colleges and Universities, no rush of federal funds occurred and very little has been done to help the neediest institutions.

The three most significant achievements benefiting black colleges were initiated within the legislative branch: (1) the Challenge Grant Act of 1983, which helps build institutional endowments with federal matching grants, authored by then Rep. Paul Simon (D-Ill.); (2) the Department of Defense set-aside established by Rep. Ronald Dellums (D-Calif.); and (3) the bail-out of Meharry Medical College and the provision of start-up funds for Morehouse School of Medicine, engineered by Rep. Louis Stokes (D-Ohio).

The Reagan administration's regulatory restrictions on uses of Title III funds for developmental purposes only was the straw that broke the camel's back. The colleges could no longer do what they thought would lead to the strengthening of their institutions. Instead, they had to implement so-called "developmental" activities that were designed by the Department of Education to bring about the phasing out of Title III assistance to HBCUs. Under the department's interpretation of certain provisions in the 1980 Amendments (P.L. 93–374), only thirty-eight historically black colleges and universities would have remained eligible for Title III support.

A Renewed Federal Commitment to Historically Black Colleges and Universities

The Black College and University Act is not a panacea for the survival of black colleges. It does, however, represent a new statement of the federal government's commitment to the strengthening and survival of these colleges as part of the mainstream of higher education. The act commits new resources in a new way, which the presidents of black colleges believe will be most helpful. For example, Part B of Title III of the Higher Education Act Amendment of 1992 (P.L. 102–498) carries an authorization of $135,000 beginning in fiscal year 1993, plus an additional $20 million for up to sixteen black graduate and professional schools, and provides appropriated funds under a formula that eliminates discretion on the part of the secretary of education in awarding Part B funds. The maintenance and enhancement of these institutions is not only consistent with the federal objectives of equal opportunity in higher education, but also with the broad goals of desegregation and integration in our society.

Some black Americans and others in higher education and throughout society perceive black colleges and universities as anachronisms in a desegregated society or as academic shells of the institutions that bloomed in the late 1800s and early 1900s. Middle- and upper-income black Americans who originally declined to send their sons and daughters to black colleges often find their offspring socially rejected and academically underdeveloped at predominantly white institutions. Victimized by racial incidents and academic slurs, the students are now looking for a positive learning experience and supportive social environment at predominantly black institutions. Jacqueline Fleming in *Blacks in College* has documented the problems and reasons for black students' success at black colleges and universities. She writes:

> Our findings that black colleges have the capacity to positively influence cognitive development certainly argue for their continued existence. . . . Despite their poorer resources, Black colleges still possess the capacity to permit the expression of natural adolescent motivations for cognitive growth. This appears to be because the Black college environment offers a student a wider network of supportive relationships (Fleming 1984).

Mounting evidence suggests that black students are enrolling in and transferring to historically black institutions in ever-increasing numbers and that black students with degrees from black colleges obtain employment or gain admission to and graduate from professional and graduate schools at the same rate as blacks who attend predominantly white institutions (Dilworth). Congress, through the Black College and University Act, has reaffirmed the importance of and continuing need for these institutions.

PRESERVING AND ENHANCING THE NATION'S BLACK COLLEGES

The Role of Historically Black Colleges and Universities

The nation's historically black colleges and universities have survived more than a century of neglect by federal and state government as well as the effects of black admission to traditionally white institutions. They now face an uncertain future with fluctuating enrollments, often burdened by the overconcentration of low-income, educationally underprepared students, and less-than-adequate resources to meet the academic and financial needs of all those who seek admission. The proud tradition of black colleges in America is only partly explained by recounting how they arose from the ashes of slavery and racial segregation, or by recalling the celebrated stories of Booker T. Washington, Mary Macleod Bethune, and Benjamin E. Mays, or by chronicling the accomplishments of the Rev. Dr. Martin Luther King, Jr., Mary Hatwood Futrell, Leontyne Price, Ralph Wiley, and Ronald E. McNair.

Today's historically black colleges and universities maximize success with minimal resources. Black colleges and universities, public and private:

- enroll almost 200,000 students, some 130,000 in public HBCUs and 62,000 in their private counterparts, but only 33 percent of all blacks in higher education;
- award 40 percent of all baccalaureate degrees received by African Americans;
- receive, on average, $1.8 million annually in federal funds, 80 percent of which comes in the form of student aid; and

- struggle to keep tuition low (which has the anomalous effect of decreasing the amount of federal student aid received while their full-time enrollments increase) (Allen 1987–88; Payne 1987–88).

Black colleges and universities have assumed the difficult task of assisting the federal government with implementing Congress's declared policy of providing access and some measure of choice in higher education for low-income students. Even when this was not federal policy, black colleges promoted equal opportunity in higher education by educating black men and women beginning in the Reconstruction era and then eliminating family finances as a barrier to a college education. HBCUs have made enormous strides in educating generations of black teachers, lawyers, engineers, doctors, and politicians. The Reverend Jesse Jackson; Marva Collins; former Surgeon General, Joycelyn Elders; the late Justice Thurgood Marshall; the late Representative Barbara Jordan; former Virginia governor, Douglas Wilder; former Atlanta mayor, Maynard Jackson; former United Nations ambassador and Atlanta mayor, Andrew Young; and former Health and Human Services secretary, Louis Sullivan, M.D., are a partial listing of prominent black college alumni. Black colleges have accomplished much with limited resources amid myriad barriers to student academic success and extraordinary constraints reinforced by institutional racism within society and the higher education community.

Black colleges provide certain intangibles that contribute to their success in enrolling, retaining, and graduating black students. Black colleges assume, as their role and primary mission, the education of low-income students. At the critical point where academic potential and motivation meet college costs and family resources, black colleges intervene to ensure access. To ensure access, public and private black colleges keep their tuitions low and affordable. At private historically black colleges, for example, tuition is about two-thirds of the national average for independent institutions (Kirschner and Still-Thrift 1987). While the *price* paid by the student remains low and affordable, the actual *cost* is subsidized. At public institutions, the actual cost of education to a student is subsidized by the state. At private institutions, the real cost is subsidized by the United Negro College Fund (UNCF), alumni contributions, and gifts. UNCF supports forty-one private historically black colleges through local fundraising events, corporate contributions, and a national telethon. Without state tax support at black public colleges and UNCF's efforts, the access of black students to college would be almost nonexistent. The cost of educating black students, who frequently require additional help to make up educational deficits caused by poor elementary and secondary schooling, may often be greater than better-prepared majority and minority students.

Despite lower family incomes and often less prior family experience in a college environment, black college students are highly motivated and can excel in a positive environment. Dr. Jacqueline Fleming's *Blacks in College* has documented the difference in outcomes when black Americans attend black colleges. Their full participation in all aspects of student life (e.g., student government and sororities and fraternities), the presence of black role models and black faculty and staff to counsel and tutor them, and the existence of a positive and personally reinforcing learning environment all contribute to student success.

The exposure of black American students at the University of Michigan, Dartmouth College, George Washington University, and the University of Mississippi to explicit racial incidents simply underscores the findings in *Blacks in College*. These incidents have posed a real dilemma for campus administrators who seek to regulate or control the growing number of epithets, incidents, and obscenities directed at minority students. Some attempts to control racial hostility on predominantly white campuses have been successfully challenged in court.[13]

Black and Hispanic baccalaureate degree recipients who succeed in engineering, law, or medicine or who earn PhD's tend to be graduates of HBCUs or comprehensive urban institutions. In fact, the nine engineering programs, four law schools, and three medical colleges that are historically black produce a disproportionately large number of the engineers, lawyers, and doctors who are black. Black colleges, which historically admitted a broad cross section of students from adverse academic and economic backgrounds, now admit a disproportionate number of low-income, underprepared students (Kirschner, Payne and Schiavi 1987; Kirschner and Still-Thrift 1987). Even the academically gifted students who enroll have been overlooked by traditional institutions and indexes of success in college.

Black colleges appear to succeed by risking limited, targeted resources on "diamonds in the rough" who demonstrate potential. They also provide faculty who are interested in students, not just in teaching, and the kind of institutional support that encourages persistence and success.

A Premise for Further Federal Action

One hundred and thirty-five years of discrimination in higher education and more than one hundred years of segregated systems of higher education cannot be erased with a modest five-year attempt at remedying past discrimination. From the outset, the two principal sponsors of the Black College and University Act indicated that, if successful, their bill would authorize the *first five years of a ten-year program of targeted assistance* (U.S. Senate 1992).[14] Budget constraints, including two imposed by the Gramm-Rudman-Hollings Act, stalled the anticipated growth of appropriations for Part B. The imposition of caps on domestic spending required by the Omnibus Budget Reconciliation Act of 1990 (P.L.101–508) and the Omnibus Budget Reconciliation Act of 1993 (P.L. 103–66) further limited prospects for reach growth in Part B funding.

In the Higher Education Amendments of 1986, Congress established a $100 million authorization for Part B beginning in FY 1987. The Part B authorization was increased to $135 million beginning in FY 1993 in the Higher Education Amendments of 1992 (P.L. 102–498); the legislation was also amended to provide an increase in the Part B floor, or minimum award, for the smaller Part B institutions (Stedman 1993). Section 326, which provides assistance for HBCU graduate and professional schools, was amended to add eleven new schools and programs to the existing five schools. The House-Senate conferees made clear their intent that Section 326 funds are to be awarded only to institutions "that are approved by the appropriate program governing bodies and that have students matriculated"(U.S. Senate 1992).

The need for further federal action, however, extends far beyond the changes required in Part B and the parallel need to increase appropriations. Above and beyond the Title III program, the executive branch must begin to fulfill its own commitment to enhancement through the White House Initiative for Black Colleges and Universities. Three successive presidents (Carter, Reagan, and Bush) have issued Executive Orders 12232, 12320, and 12677, respectively, to strengthen the federal government's commitment to enhancing HBCUs. However, federal support did not increase. Rather, there may have been a marginal decline in federal support in the mid-1980s:

- In FY 1986, HBCUs received 5.54 percent of total federal funds obligated to institutions of higher education—a decline from the peak of 6.1 percent in FY 1983.
- Between FY 1969 and FY 1986, the HBCU share fluctuated between 4 and 6 percent—the HBCU percentage share of federal obligations being higher in the 1980s than in the 1970s (Presidents Boards of Advisors 1992).[15]

Two distinct patterns of funding have been noted by William W. Ellis and James B. Stedman in their analysis of federal executive branch allocations in response to the presidential executive orders:

- First, about nine of the twenty-seven agencies that spend over $200 million in awards to higher education institutions contribute the bulk of the funding for HBCUs. The middle range of six agencies that contribute $10 million to $100 million to colleges and universities devotes relatively meager amounts to HBCUs (Ellis and Stedman 1989).
- Second, those agencies with the highest of their higher education expenditures on HBCUs are, ironically, the federal agencies with the *smallest* higher education budgets (Ellis and Stedman 1989).

Among the ten federal agencies with the largest dollar commitment to HBCUs, only the Agency for International Development and the Department of Education are among the agencies making significant allocations to all institutions of higher education. It bears mentioning that the bulk of education department funds arrives at black colleges through need-based Title IV student aid awards and Title III and, therefore, is not affected in any way by the executive orders.

The HBCU presidents and the leadership of both the NAFEO and UNCF institutions have consistently pressed for the transfer of the Executive Order Program from the Department of Education to the Executive Office of the President to enhance its visibility and impact on federal agency budget decisions. The relatively junior status of the Department of Education, its inability to influence budgetary decisions of other federal departments and agencies, and the lack of any real federal commitment to fulfilling the promise of the White House Initiative have left the HBCU presidents suspicious and cynical about achieving the executive order's lofty goals.

The election of President Bill Clinton in 1992 and the issuance of a significantly revised Executive Order on Historically Black Colleges and Universities (E.O. 12876) holds out some promise for accomplishment of the original purposes of the White House Executive Order Program. Although the actual transfer was not achieved, the much improved Clinton Executive Order was signed on 1 November 1993.

For the first time, the Office of Management and Budget (OMB) will have a significant oversight role in ensuring department and agency compliance with the executive order's mandate to increase funding for HBCUs (Section 6). In addition, Executive Order 12876 requires each department and agency to "establish an annual goal for the amount of funds to be awarded in grants, contracts, or cooperative agreements to Historically Black Colleges and Universities" (Section 4). Finally, the appointment of executive level management and access to the department head or agency administrator has been ensured by requiring the appointment of "a senior official," who shall "report directly to the departmental or agency head . . ." (Section 5) (Clinton 1993).

The Challenges That Remain—An Agenda for Future Federal Action

Congressional enactment of the Black College and University Act in 1986 and its extension and expansion in 1992 should be considered a down payment on a long-term mortgage to free the minds of Africans in America and, most particularly, to permit America to realize her goal of equal opportunity in higher education. Beyond the general strengthening of the 99 Part B-eligible four-year and two-year public and private historically black colleges, there is a need to undertake other broad assistance to HBCUs. Some progress has been made. Congress has already enacted a legislative set-aside under the Department of Defense Authorization Act to increase the participation of black colleges in defense research and development. In 1988, Congress also enacted the Academic Research Facilities Modernization Act, which included a set-aside for historically black and other minority institutions. During a sustained fight with the National Science Foundation, the American Association of Universities, and the National Association of State Universities and Land-Grant Colleges (NASULGC) in the FY 1990 appropriations process, black colleges, working with the National Association of Independent Colleges and Universities (NAICU), secured $20 million in funding for this new program to assist with the construction and renovation of scientific research and laboratory facilities.

Three critical improvements were also made in Titles VI, VII, and IX of the Higher Education Act during the 1992 reauthorization. First, a program designed to open an entirely new career path for African Americans was established with the authorization of the Institute for International Public Policy/Minority Foreign Service Professional Development Program in Part C. This represents the first time that a program focused on the interests of minorities has been included in Title VI, long the province of the Ivy League and other elite research institutions. The institute program, which received $1 million in start-up funding in the FY 1994 Labor, HHS, and Education Appropriations Act (P.L. 103–112), will permit a consortium of public and private HBCUs to inaugurate a program that will include language instruction, academic year and summer internships with international agencies, a junior year abroad, and summer policy analysis/development institutes.

Second, many HBCUs have long needed direct institutional aid to implement short-term construction and renovation projects on academic, research and laboratory, and mixed-use buildings. In many instances, these buildings possess historical significance, have received little maintenance in the past decade, and may need additions to meet increased enrollment demands. The construction and renovation needs of HBCUs, although parallel to those of the broader higher education community, possess one important difference. Individual black colleges—especially the smaller private HBCUs—frequently have great difficulty securing private financing for construction. In addition to classroom and research facilities, many HBCUs also require new dormitories and other living facilities to accommodate the rise in black college enrollments. Once implemented by the Department of Education, the Historically Black College and University Capital

Financing Act (Title VII, Part B) will provide a federal guarantee to ensure repayment of all HBCU loan obligations under this new program.

Finally, a new program in Title IX, Graduate Education (Part E) will facilitate the acquisition of the Ph.D. or other terminal degree by HBCU faculty, as well as those in the higher education professorate providing instruction at colleges and universities with significant minority student populations.

Once this foundation is secure and the universe of institutions defined as "historically black colleges and universities" has been placed on solid academic and financial ground, the black higher education community should turn its attention to refining its academic strengths and developing HBCU cultural and research specialities. This will require the African-American higher education community to:

- focus increased attention on agencies where there is substantial R&D funding, including the National Aeronautics and Space Administration, the Department of Energy, and the Department of Defense; and
- form coalitions among HBCUs and other minority and majority institutions that provide access to new funding sources and expertise that may benefit HBCUs.

As a succession of White House Executive Order Annual Reports have made all too clear, historically black institutions are far too dependent on Title III and Title IV funds from the Department of Education as their principal sources of federal assistance. As the Part B appropriation grows and black college enrollment patterns continue their upward trend, concentrated efforts must be made to expand and diversify the funding base of HBCUs. It is logical to do this through agencies and sister institutions with which operational consortia and political coalitions can be negotiated and implemented. Some examples of such cooperation already exist:

- Ana G. Mendez University System, New Mexico Highlands University, North Carolina A&T State University, Los Alamos National Laboratory, Oakridge National Laboratory, Sandia National Laboratory Science Alliance.

- Jackson State University, Lawrence Berkeley Laboratory, and Ana G. Mendez University System Science Consortium.

The Ana G. Mendez Foundation of Puerto Rico, California State University at Dominquez Hills, Xavier University of Louisiana, Fordham University, City College of New York and Hostos Community College (City University of New York, Knoxville College, Morgan State University, and the University of Northern Iowa form the Consortium For Minorities In Teaching Careers (CMTC). The consortium's long-term program is to identify junior and senior high school students with the potential aptitude for teaching and guide them through high school and college and then on to graduate and postgraduate degrees. Initially, the consortium will identify 550 students from grades nine to twelve with the potential to develop the self-confidence and sense of achievement essential to quality teaching.

The most serious short-term threat to HBCU viability is the rise in student borrowing among HBCU students and the use of student borrower default rates to determine institutional participation in the Title IV, Student Assistance Program. The rising rate of student default in the Federal Family Education Loan (FFEL) Program (formerly the Guaranteed Student Loan [GSL] program) has paralleled the dramatic growth in student borrowing, especially a significant increase in borrowing by lower income students. While student indebtedness has grown from the early 1980s until today (U.S. Department of Education 1991),[16] the greatest growth has been among *modest-* and poverty-income freshmen (Kalcevic and Rhind 1991).[17] The increase in student borrowing reflects three independent trends: (1) establishment by Congress in 1981 of a statutory "needs test" for GSL borrowers; (2) failure of Congress to appropriate the authorized maximum Pell Grant, which forced more lower income students to borrow to pay rising college costs; and (3) increased access to college and other forms of postsecondary education because of the expanded availability of student assistance, especially federally guaranteed loans. Protecting HBCUs from exclusion from participating in the Title IV, Student Assistance Program can be achieved *only* by extending the HBCU exemption from the default "triggers" in section 435(a) (2) (B). Rep. Robert G. "Bobby" Scott (D-Va.) introduced legislation (H.R. 4025) on 11 March 1994, and Sen. Dale Bumpers (D-Ark.) and Thad

Cochran (R-Miss.) introduced legislation (S. 2004) on 25 March 1994, to extend section 435 (a) (2) (C)—which exempts HBCUs and tribally controlled community colleges from the default triggers—through 1 July 1998. Enactment of this legislation is essential to HBCU survival.

The most significant step Congress could take to enhance and strengthen historically black colleges and to counter the effect of increased low-income student borrowing would be to make the Pell Grant Program a true entitlement, thereby guaranteeing this most basic form of student assistance as well as access to a college education for every academically able and personally motivated black high school graduate in America.

The irony of using this student aid mechanism to strengthen a historically black college should not be lost. More than 80 percent of all Pell Grant recipients come from families with incomes below $15,000. Among students attending UNCF member institutions, for example, 61 percent were Pell Grant recipients in academic year 1991–92. In fact, over one-third (36.8 percent) of all students attending UNCF member colleges come from families with incomes of less than $25,000 (Fordyce 1993).

Due to the dramatic shift in the ratio of student aid available in the form of grants to aid available in the form of loans—from 79 percent grant aid and 17 percent loans in 1975–76 to 50 percent grant aid and 49 percent loan aid in 1992–93 (Knapp 1993)—lower income students find themselves debt burdened at graduation. This shift is exacerbated by the declining purchasing power of the Pell Grant—compared to increasing college costs—and Congress's inability to provide sufficient appropriations to fund the authorized maximum award (only three times since 1974!).

Making the Pell Grant an entitlement and/or raising the appropriated maximum award to $3,000 accomplishes several objectives at once. It (1) provides a specific incentive to low-income minority students to succeed in high school and to seek a college education with the cost paid and guaranteed, in part, by the federal government; (2) eliminates the risk of loss of special allowance and GSL interest subsidies and special allowance costs paid by the taxpayer on loans defaulted on by high-risk students; and (3) engages the students and parents in a joint venture that can alter the family's financial circumstances in the future. As the next section will make abundantly clear, reducing student borrowing and the risk of default also reduces the risk of institutional exposure and possible exclusion from the Title IV, Student Assistance Program.

The Challenge from Within

Two developments since enactment of the Black College and University Act in 1986 present cause for concern as the African American community seeks to strengthen and enhance the nation's historically black colleges and universities and expand opportunities for African Americans in higher education.

STUDENT LOAN DEFAULTS AND STATE OVERSIGHT

Historically black colleges and universities, especially black private colleges and universities, may be more *threatened* today by excessive student reliance on guaranteed student loans (now FFELs) and federal policies that target institutions with high student loan default rates for exclusion from the Title IV, Student Assistance Programs. Because HBCU students rely disproportionately on Pell grants, college work-study, and various loans, the possibility of excluding an institution from participation in the federal student assistance programs is potentially devastating. For example, 61 percent of all UNCF students receive Pell Grants and 60 percent receive Stafford Loans (Fordyce 1993.)

UNCF students' reliance on loans to pay college costs has increased dramatically over the past decade. Among UNCF member institutions, student borrowing in the old Guaranteed Student Loan Program grew from $4,139,201 in academic year 1979–80 to $56,808,000 in 1989–90—a fourteen-fold increase (Burnley and Kirschner 1981; Fordyce and Kirschner 1991). In 1991–92, UNCF students borrowed $83,429,000 in Stafford Loans (Fordyce 1993). This trend in student borrowing—with minority and low income students borrowing larger amounts to pay college costs—is not restricted to UNCF students. Both the Congressional Budget Office and the American College Testing Service (Mortenson 1990) have highlighted the problem of extensive student borrowing among minority and lower income students.

The irony of the current situation is disturbing. Congress's failure to appropriate the funds necessary to pay the Pell Grant's maximum award to the poorest students compels more and more lower income students to borrow to meet college costs. Institutions of higher education that assist the federal and state governments with carrying out their access missions, namely, HBCUs, community and junior colleges, urban four-year institutions, etc., tend to enroll more lower income and academically at-risk students, who are less well prepared for college level academic work. The institutional consequence of performing this national service is a higher than normal default rate because of the failure of at-risk students to graduate. High cohort default rates, however, do not mean large dollar amounts are in default (U.S. GAO, July 1989).

Above and beyond the negative personal impact and the adverse public policy consequences of increased student borrowing and resulting high student loan defaults, there is a simple question of the fundamental fairness of this widespread use of student loan default rates to make decisions that affect both student access to and institutional participation in the Title IV, Student Assistance Programs. The use of student loan default rates, as opposed to dollars in default, not only focuses attention on the wrong institutions in terms of seeking *recovery* of taxpayer dollars, but frequently implies or asserts wrongdoing by the institutions—which is totally unwarranted and unjustified.

The misuse of student loan default rates by policymakers has been most prominent since 1987, when former Education Secretary William Bennett first published default data to call attention to a growing segment of the student aid budget devoted to defaults and to attack certain institutions in the higher education community for excessive student loan defaults. At the time this criticism was launched, the role of institutions in the lending process was limited and their responsibility for the alleged defaults minor. The General Accounting Office (GAO) has documented both the misleading nature of using default rates, as opposed to dollars in default, and the skewed impact of default rates on HBCUs (U.S. GAO, August 1993).[18] Whatever the intended purpose of Congress in establishing default rates as an indicator of institutional misbehavior or wrongdoing, the experiment is a failure insofar as it applies to HBCUs.

Nowhere is the use of student loan default rates more acute and potentially devastating to the HBCU community than in the new Part H, Program Integrity-TRIAD provisions in the Higher Education Act. Part H was adopted as part of the Higher Education Amendments of 1992 (P.L. 102–325). It was intended to increase institutional

accountability for Title IV funds administered by eligible postsecondary institutions and to eliminate fraud and abuse among a small
number of such institutions. Part of the impetus for Congress's legislative action was a series of hearings held by the Senate permanent
Subcommittee on Investigations (Chaired by Sen. Sam Nunn, D-Ga.)
and a critical report that blamed the Department of Education for
much of the mismanagement, fraud, and abuse in the Guaranteed Student Loan Program (GSLP) (U.S. Senate 1991). The Nunn
subcommittee was not alone in its criticism of the Department of Education (U.S. GAO March 1993, May 1993).[19]

Equally important, Part H was intended to increase Congress's direction and oversight of three entities with extensive authority to
determine institutional eligibility for and participation in the Title IV
programs: the Department of Education, regional and national accrediting agencies, and the states that license an entity to do business
or authorize institutions to exist.

Congress's lack of control over the access points for institutional eligibility for more than $20 billion annually in federal student aid is best
understood by reviewing the limited number of hearings Congress held
on the accreditation process before 1991. These hearings reveal Congress's lack of understanding of the eligibility and certification process
that operated wholly in a regulatory context (with only limited statutory authority) and with almost no congressional oversight and little,
if any, state oversight of the licensure process for proprietary institutions of higher education. The foregoing contributed to the present
state of affairs and the June 1992 Congressional reform effort (Schenet
1990; Joint Interim Committee 1991).[20]

Congress's lack of oversight of the department's processes for determining an institution eligible, (e.g., USED relied on the states for
licensure and the various accrediting bodies for quality and for certi-
fying that an institution possessed the fiscal strength and
administrative ability to administer the Title IV programs) permitted
fraud and abuse to flourish in Title IV. Congress's inattention and the
department's inability to keep track of the growing federal family education loan programs, in particular, created an authority vacuum
that has been filled with the enactment of Part H.

The failed attempt to specifically define the proper roles of the
TRIAD members (Schenet 1990)—the primary role of the federal gov-

ernment as the funding agent and *regulator*, the limited but necessary role of the states as the *creator/licensor* of both public and private institutions of higher education, and the regional and national accrediting bodies as the *arbiters of quality* in higher education—must be addressed in a legislative context.

Part H of the Higher Education Amendments of 1992 plowed new ground in this area in several ways: (1) it established a statutory base for the Department of Education's eligibility and certification processes; (2) it created a State Postsecondary Review Entity (SPRE) in each state and provided federal funding to support the review activities authorized; (3) it provided termination authority in the SPRE to affect an institution's eligibility to participate in federal Title IV programs, without Secretarial review of the SPRE's decision, and with no statutory due process requirement in the state's termination process; (4) it utilized student loan default-rate thresholds to target institutions for state review by the SPRE; and (5) it established statutory criteria for the recognition of accrediting agencies whose decisions will be accepted for Title IV eligibility purposes.

The consequences of the statutory delegation of both program review and termination authority—where access to a federal program and to federal taxpayer dollars are at stake—could be catastrophic for the nation's HBCUs. The GAO notes in its recent report to Senator Paul Simon, "(A)s many as 62 of the 105 HBCUs could be subject to state review in 1994 because their cohort default rates met or exceeded 25 percent" (U.S. GAO, August 1993). The student enrollment and economic consequences of negative action by the several states is not measurable.

Furthermore, the use of student loan default rates to target institutions for state review under section 494C (b) (1) and (2) assumes that default rates imply Title IV funds mismanagement, fraud, or abuse. No credible factual evidence to support this use of student loan default rates has been articulated. In fact, the available evidence suggests otherwise (U.S. GAO, Oct. 1989; April 1991).[21] While default rates may serve as indicators of mismanagement or wrongdoing in some instances or at some institutions, default rates in and of themselves are neutral and unrelated to institutional behavior and should not be utilized to evaluate institutional behavior (U.S. Department of Education 1990).[22] Student loan default rates—when converted in a public relations context to institutional performance measures—are unreliable for this purpose and, in fact, direct attention to the wrong institutions when more reliable indicators would focus attention on those institutions with significant dollar amounts of federally insured loans in default.[23]

The systemic nature of the causes of student default and most of the truly effective measures for preventing student loan defaults (National Commission on Responsibilities 1993) have been ignored or obfuscated by federal policymakers. The student loan default debate frequently results in name calling and blaming the victim, rather than problem solving. Until there is a full re-examination of the criteria used to target institutions for review and student financing mechanisms, the bottom line will remain unchanged—historically black colleges and universities and those institutions that provide postsecondary access to African Americans will suffer.

HIGHER EDUCATION DESEGRATION AND AYERS

On 26 June 1992, after seventeen years of litigation in the District Court, the Fifth Circuit Court of Appeals, and in the Supreme Court of the United States,[24] the High Court ruled that Mississippi had not met its burden of eliminating the vestiges of segregation in its formerly dual system of higher education. The eight to one decision, although it did not go as far as many in the black higher education community would have liked in terms of supporting the "enhancement" of HBCUs, writes "a whole new chapter for education in the states where a large number of black students go to college."[25] While the nation's historically black colleges and universities have benefited from the constitutional interpretation and application of *Brown* principles,[26] the decision in *Ayers v. Fordice*[27] represents the first formal application of *Brown* by the Court to higher education desegregation. In effect, the Court declined to endorse Mississippi's "race-neutral" policies for achieving desegregation as sufficient to disprove *present* discrimination in its public system of higher education based on *past* discriminatory acts.

While *U.S. v. Mabus*, now *U.S. v. Fordice*, may be viewed as a judicial victory for the student plaintiffs (i.e., Mississippi's failure to disestablish its previously segregated system of higher education now requires it to create a system that permits all its citizens an "unfettered and free choice"[28] in public higher education), the cure could be worse than the disease. Three things are clear: (1) the implications of Judge Biggers's decision in the Federal District Court for the Northern District of Mississippi extend far beyond the borders of that state or Louisiana or Alabama; (2) time will not permit the plaintiffs or the HBCU community the latitude of extensive appeals or extended litigation because the entire community is under scrutiny and potentially under the budget knife; and (3) the HBCU community's institutional interests are not being *fully* represented in the courts, in the legislatures, in the media, or in other critical public policy arenas. The reason is simple—the HBCU community (the presidents, trustees, faculty, staff, alumni, students, and the African-American community, in general) has not defined and articulated its own solution. In the community's view, what should be the future of HBCUs?[29]

Some black educators and parents view black colleges as inferior and as a historical anachronism—no longer needed in view of the destruction of the walls of segregation in higher education. Enactment of the Civil Rights Act of 1964, following numerous legal victories in a series of NAACP-orchestrated cases between 1935 and 1959, some argue, makes black institutions unnecessary.

The nation's 104 historically black colleges and universities (Anon 1993b; Thomas and Green 1993),[30] however, have a present-day mission—to complement their glorious past—that requires their continuation and enhancement. HBCUs must remain committed to their historic mission of providing access to higher education for all, while performing a cultural, political, and social role as well. There is evidence that this multifaceted mission is still being successfully pursued. HBCU enrollments are on the increase—rising 28 percent between 1986 and 1992. HBCUs enroll only 17 percent of all African Americans in higher education but graduate 27 percent of all baccalaureate degree recipients. Moreover, HBCUs graduate 44 percent of all blacks receiving degrees in the physical sciences, 41 percent of black BA's in mathematics, 38 percent of black BA's in life sciences, 37 percent of black BA's in education, and 25 percent of black BA's in engineering.[31]

Historically black colleges and universities, however, still struggle internally (Smith 1993), as well as externally, with the specter of inferiority. The suggestion that they do not provide a quality education is belied by the achievement of their graduates in spite of the institutional odds and racial discrimination faced by both the institutions and their graduates. Although many in the HBCU fold have succeeded, others continue to struggle with unstable executive leadership, ineffective boards of trustees, and small or restricted endowments.

The problem presented by *Ayers* and its sister suits in Alabama and Louisiana[32] present an entirely different question. That question is whether state governments or the federal government may absolve themselves of their responsibilities for HBCUs by simply adopting race neutral admissions policies. Judge Biggers, the trial judge at the Mississippi Federal District Court level, received a *sua sponte* solution from the Mississippi Board of Higher Education. That proposal would have the practical effect of closing Mississippi Valley State University and merging Alcorn State University out of existence, while partially enhancing Jackson State University (Smith 1993). The board's proposal has been met with utter silence since it was first revealed in district court.[33]

Although the proposal was inappropriate when proffered by the board at the 22 October 1993 hearing, the three Mississippi black public institutions appear to be losing the public relations battle as they seek to maintain their integrity without direct representation before the district court had a separate voice in the Mississippi proceedings. This situation differs markedly from the posture of Grambling State University and Southern University in the Louisiana litigation and Alabama State and Alabama AM&N.[34]

The failure of the entire black college community to rally to the support of the Mississippi HBCU situation has left many in the community puzzled. Alvin O. Chambliss, lead counsel in *Ayers*, has vociferously articulated his views in this area (Hawkins 1993). The very real threat posed by the retrial before Judge Biggers appears to ignore several realities:

- If a merger or closure solution is deemed acceptable in Mississippi, e.g., if the board's plan is acceptable to the district court, it will be pursued vigorously in other jurisdictions that desire to eliminate their dual systems or simply want to reduce spending for higher education by closing black colleges.
- Although perceived as a public HBCU problem by many, the threat

of extinction extends to all HBCUs—public and private—because if Mississippi can escape its responsibility, then all states and the federal government may be able to do so as well.

- A Mississippi solution that resolves the issues favorable for the Mississippi plaintiffs may not be in the long-term interests of the Mississippi HBCUs; that is, merger and closure are institutional issues, not necessarily student access and choice issues.

It is the latter issue that requires the presence of HBCU institutional representation in *Ayers*. That presence could be established through the National Association for Equal Opportunity in Higher Education (NAFEO) or through a combination of the national black college alumni organizations, e.g., The Council of National Alumni Associations (CNAA), The UNCF National Alumni council, and The National Black College Alumni Hall of Fame. The institutional interests of HBCUs, however, are not necessarily protected by the current plaintiffs or their representatives.[35] A recent policy pronouncement by the USED office for Civil Rights that interpreted Title VI in light of the *Ayers* decision may significantly alter the prospects for state action and result in the closure of HBCUs or their merger with predominantly white institutions. The 31 January 1994 policy interpretation explicitly supports enhancement of HBCUs and rejects merger or closure as a by-product of state desegregation efforts:

> The Department reaffirms its position reflected in the "Revised Criteria," which is consistent with *Fordice*, that States may not place unfair burdens upon black students and faculty in the desegregation process. Moreover, the Department's "Revised Criteria" recognize that State systems of higher education may be required, in order to overcome the effects of past discrimination, to strengthen and enhance traditionally or historically black institutions . . . (U.S. Department of Education 1994).

EPILOGUE

Black colleges have a dual mission. They must continue to serve as access points to higher education for gifted and educationally disadvantaged black youngsters. They must continue to serve as educational citadels and cultural repositories for the black community and as centers for social and political development for students, faculty members, local communities, and the regions/states in which they are located.

Among people in higher education and in the public policy arena are some who believe that the time for black colleges and universities has passed. Their attitude ignores the need for the continued presence of other special-interest institutions. Although an institution was organized to overcome discrimination based on sex or religion or to carry out a specific purpose (for example, to train ministers or the laity), the cultural or symbolic reason for the existence of a special-interest institution is not questioned. Vassar, Notre Dame, and Brandeis have a specific purpose and will continue as institutions, and so must Howard and Tougaloo.

Even though black colleges and universities persist without direct federal assistance (except in the case of Howard University and the University of the District of Columbia, which receive annual appropriations and don't qualify for Title III funds), such institutions have a special claim to direct, race-specific, federal assistance because their present plight is, in large part, occasioned by discrimination in the past. Unfortunately, that discrimination did not end with the *Brown v. Board of Education* decision, nor with the enactment of the Civil Rights Act of 1964.

Congress, through the Black College and University Act and other legislation that benefits black colleges, must reaffirm continuously the importance of and continuing need for these institutions.

REFERENCES

Allen, W. R. 1987. Black colleges vs. white colleges. *Change Magazine*, May/June.

Anon. 1904. Early history of Knoxville College. In *Historical sketch*, ed. R. W. McGranahan.

Anon. 1993a. On the superiority of black colleges—An interview with William H. Gray, III. *Journal of Blacks in Higher Education*, no. 1 (Autumn): 60–66.

Anon. 1993b. Vital signs—The statistics that describe the present and suggest the future of African Americans in higher education. *Journal of Blacks in Higher Education*, no.1 (Autumn): 15–24.

Blakey, W. A. 1983. Black colleges and universities: Desegration, disintegration, or equity. *ISEP Monitor* 7 (June): 7–8.

———. Fall 1987. Centuries of struggle—Black America's fight for educational equality. In *Point of View*. Congressional Black Caucus Foundation.

Burnley, M., and A. H. Kirschner. 1981. *The 1981 statistical report*. United Negro College Fund.

Clinton, W. J. 1 November 1993. Executive order 12876. *Public papers of the president of the United States: William J. Clinton, 1993*.

Dilworth, M. E. Historically black colleges and universities: Taking care of home. *The state of black America*. New York: National Urban League, tables A and B.

Ellis, W. W., and J. B. Stedman. 10 October 1989. *Historically black colleges and universities and African-American participation in higher education*. Washington, DC: Library of Congress, Congressional Research Service (CRS).

Fleming, J. 1984. *Blacks in college: A comparative study of students' success in black and in white institutions*. San Francisco, CA: Jossey-Bass, Inc.

Fordyce, H. R. 1993. *The 1993 statistical report*. United Negro College Fund.

Fordyce, H. R., and A. H. Kirschner. 1991. *The 1991 statistical report*. United Negro College Fund.

Franklin, J. H. 1967. *From Slavery to freedom*. 3d ed. New York: Alfred A. Knopf.

Hawkins, B. D. 1993. Ford Foundation grant to SEF sparks controversy. *Black Issues in Higher Education*, 9 September, 34–35.

Haynes, L. L., ed. 1978. *A critical examination of the Adams case: A source book*. Institute for the Study of Education.

Joint Interim Committee on Proprietary Schools. 25 February 1991. *Access, achievement, and accountability*. Interim report to the 72d Texas Legislature.

Kalcevic, D., and D. Rhind. December 1991. *CBO papers: The experience of the Stafford Loan Program and options for change*.

Kirschner, A. H., K. Payne, and V. Schiavi. 1987. *1987 UNCF statistical report*. United Negro College Fund.

Kirschner, A. H., and J. Still-Thrift. 1987. *Access to college: The impact of federal financial aid policies at private historically black colleges.* United Negro College Fund/NIICU.

Knapp, L. G. September 1993. Trends in student aid: 1983–1993. *The College Board.*

Moore, I. P. 1977. *The rise and decline of the program of education for black Presbyterians of the United Presbyterian Church, U.S.A. 1865–1870.* San Antonio, TX: Trinity University Press.

Mortenson, T. C. February 1990. *The impact of increased loan utilization among low family income students.* ACT Student Aid Research Report Series 90–1.

National Advisory Committee on Blacks in Higher Education and Black Colleges and Universities. June 1978. *Higher education equity: The crisis of appearance versus reality.*

National Commission on Responsibilities for Financing Postsecondary Education. Februray 1993. *Making college affordable again.* Final report.

Payne, N. J. 1987–88. The role of black colleges in an expanding economy. *Educational Record* (Fall–Winter): 104–6.

President's Board of Advisors Historically Black Colleges and Universities. December 1992. *Fiscal year 1991 report on federal support for historically black colleges and universities—Not gaining ground, falling back.*

Schenet, M. A. 31 August 1990. Proprietary schools: The regulatory structure. *CRS report for Congress.*

Smith, J. C. 1993. A report on litigation affecting historically black colleges and universities with postscript on 12 April 1993, Mississippi hearing. Presented at UDC conference on *Ayers v. Fordice,* 5 April.

Stedman, J. B. 11 February 1993. Title III, Higher Education Act: Institutional aid reauthorized by 102d Congress. *CRS report to Congress.*

Thomas A. E., and R. L. Green. August 1993. *Historically black colleges and universities: An irreplaceable national treasure.*

Trueheart, W. E. *The consequences of federal and state resource allocation and development policies for traditionally black land-grant institutions: 1862–1954.* Ann Arbor, MI: University Microfilms.

U.S. Commission on Civil Rights. April 1981. *The black/white col-*

leges: Dismantling the dual system of higher education. Clearing-house Publication 66.

U.S. Congress. House. February–May 1965. Committee on Education and Labor, Subcommittee on Special Education. 89th Cong., 1st sess.

U.S. Congress. House. April 1984. *Hearings on the reauthorization of the higher education act.* Hearings before the Subcommittee on Postsecondary Education on H.R. 5240, Committee on Education and Labor. 98th Cong., 2d sess.

U.S. Congress. House. September 1988. *The unique role and mission of historically black colleges and universities.* Hearings before the Subcommittee on Postsecondary Education of the Committee on Education and Labor. 100th Cong., 2d sess.

U.S. Congress. Senate. 1991. *Abuse in federal student aid programs.* Report made by the Permanent Subcommittee on Investigations of the Committee on Governmental Affairs. 102d Cong., 1st sess., Rep. 102–58.

U.S. Congress. Senate. 1986. *Higher education amendments of 1986.* Conference report to accompany S. 1965. 99th Cong., 2d sess., Rep. 99–861.

U.S. Congress. Senate. 1992. *Higher education amendments of 1992.* Conference report to accompany S. 1150. 102d Cong., 2d sess., Rep. 102–630.

U.S. Department of Education. 1991. *FY 1991 guaranteed student loan programs data book—Guaranteed student loan programs annual commitments, FY 1966–FY 1991.* Washington, DC: OPE/OSFA, Division of Policy and Program Development.

U.S. General Accounting Office. March 1993. *Guaranteed student loan program's internal controls and structure need improvement.* Financial audit of the U.S. Department of Education. Washington, DC: Government Printing Office.

U.S. Department of Education. Office for Civil Rights. 1994. Notice of application of Supreme Court decision. *Federal Register* (31 January): 4271.

U.S. Department of Education. Office of Planning, Budget, and Evaluation. 1990. *Reducing student loan defaults—A plan for action.* Washington, DC: Government Printing Office.

U.S. General Accounting Office. July 1989. *Guaranteed student loans—Analysis of student default rates at 7,800 postsecondary schools.* Washington, DC: Government Printing Office.

U.S. General Accounting Office. May 1993. *Longstanding management problems hamper reforms.* Washington, DC: Government Printing Office.

U.S. General Accounting Office. April 1991. *Student loans—Characteristics of defaulted borrowers in the Stafford student loan program.* Washington, DC: Government Printing Office.

U.S. General Accounting Office. August 1993. *Student loans—Default rates at historically black colleges and universities.* Washington, DC: GAO/HRD 93–177 FS.

U.S. General Accounting Office. October 1989. *Supplemental loans to students—Who borrows and who defaults.* Washington, DC: Government Printing Office.

Wilson, R. F. 1989. Declining financial aid is cutting off access to higher education. *SEF News 3* (April): 6.

Wright, G. C. 1992. *A history of blacks in Kentucky.*Vol. 2, *In pursuit of equality (1890–1980).* Frankfort: Kentucky Historical Society.

NOTES

1. The National Association for the Advancement of Colored People (NAACP) authored the initial legal challenges to legally imposed racial segregation in higher education, having adopted a practical strategy of using mature black students as plaintiffs in carefully calculated cases designed to persuade whites that public systems of higher education discriminated against black Americans in terms of access to educational opportunities.

Beginning in the border states, where resistance to black advances was thought to be less harsh than in the deep South, the NAACP began its legal attack upon racial segregation in education. The first major legal test came in 1935 and involved the denial of admission to a black, Donald Murray, by the University of Maryland's Law School. With the NAACP's aid, Murray filed suit against the university, claiming that his constitutional rights as a citizen of Maryland had been violated although he had sufficient educational qualifications. Because Maryland provided no law school for blacks, the state court issued a writ of mandamus, ordering the university to admit Murray. The lower court's decision was affirmed by the Maryland Court of Appeals. The NAACP thus helped legitimize its strategy of attacking segregation in states where resistance to black advances was less harsh than in the deep South.

As a result of the *Murray* case, a similar suit was filed by the NAACP on behalf of Lloyd Gaines in Missouri. Gaines had graduated in 1935 from Lincoln University, Missouri's state-supported land-grant college for blacks. After graduation, he sought to pursue his education by attending law school. Because Missouri had no law school for blacks, Gaines applied to the University of Missouri Law School, where he was denied admission and told that he might pursue his legal training at an out-of-state law school. The university also explained that if Gaines attended an out-of-state law school, the state would pay his tuition.

Gaines rejected this offer and filed suit in the Missouri Circuit Court seeking a writ of mandamus against S. W. Canada, registrar of the University of Missouri. The lower court held against Gaines, and the NAACP appealed the case to the U.S. Supreme Court. The Supreme Court decided that Gaines was entitled to equal protection of the laws and that the state was bound to furnish him, within its borders, with facilities for legal education substantially equal to those that the state afforded for persons of the white race, whether or not other Negroes sought the same opportunity. The *Gaines* case of 1938 established the principle that if states did not provide educational facilities for blacks equal to those provided for whites, blacks were to be admitted to white institutions. This decision greatly contributed to the growth of support by southern state governments for developing small graduate and professional schools within public black colleges. This support was based on the assumption that blacks would not seek admission to white state-supported universities.

A second milestone in the NAACP's legal attack on segregation occurred in 1948 in *Sipuel v. Board of Regents of the University of Oklahoma*. As with *Gaines* and *Murray*, this case also involved the state's refusal to admit a qualified black to its law school.

On appeal to the U.S. Supreme Court, the Court held that denial of the applicant's admission violated the equal protection clause of the Fourteenth Amendment. The Court sent the case back to the

Oklahoma Supreme Court, which ordered the university to either admit Sipuel to the law school or suspend the white law school from operating until the state opened one for blacks. *Sipuel* strengthened the established precedent that a court would order admission of blacks to white graduate and professional schools if no black schools existed.

In 1959, the U.S. Supreme Court ruled in the case of *McLaurin v. Oklahoma State Regents*. Although McLaurin, a black, was admitted to the graduate school of the University of Oklahoma, he was required to suffer the indignity of forced segregation as a student. McLaurin, for example, was required to eat apart from whites and even to sit apart from them while in the classroom. The Court ruled that the required segregation imposed upon McLaurin was unconstitutional under the Fourteenth Amendment. It held that McLaurin was entitled to the same treatment inside the institution as any other student, regardless of race.

The attack against inequities perpetuated by evolution of "separate but equal" graduate and professional schools for blacks by white governments was in *Sweatt v. Painter*. Marion Sweatt, a black postman, wanted to pursue his legal education by attending the University of Texas Law School in Austin. Sweatt's application to the university was rejected on the basis of race, and the NAACP Legal Defense Fund (LDF) brought suit on his behalf to gain entry to the white law school.

The lower court, in 1946, had ordered the state of Texas to establish a law school at traditionally black Prairie View University, located 40 miles from Houston. The legal education offered at Prairie View was not comparable to the education offered by the University of Texas in any major respect. The state later abandoned its support for the Prairie View effort and established the Texas State University for Negroes in Austin. Texas State University put together a law school, and classes were to begin for Sweatt on 10 March 1947, if he chose to attend. Sweatt chose not to attend either Prairie View or Texas State and continued to pursue his case through the courts. When the case reached the Supreme Court, the Court ruled that the black law school (Texas State) did not "measure up" to the established white law school (University of Texas). The Court's reason was a critical landmark in desegregation litigation.

The Court concluded that Sweatt's exclusion from the University of Texas Law School violated his rights under the Fourteenth

Amendment and prevented him from being educated with future leaders of Texas and American society. The Court ordered Sweatt's admission.

The *Sweatt* case marked the first time the Supreme Court had ordered admission of a black to a school previously restricted to whites on grounds that the black school established by the state failed to offer equal educational opportunity.

2. *Brown v. Board of Education of Topeka, Kansas: Brown I*, 347 U.S. 483 (1954), and *Brown II* 349 U.S. 294 (1955).

3. Chronology of *Adams v. Richardson*:

1970: The NAACP Legal Defense and Educational Fund sues the U.S. Department of Health, Education, and Welfare (HEW), charging that HEW's Office for Civil Rights has failed to enforce Title VI of the Civil Rights Act of 1964. The suit charges that the department has not started proceedings to cut off federal aid to public colleges in ten states that have been found to be maintaining racially segregated systems of higher education. The states are Arkansas, Florida, Georgia, Louisiana, Maryland, Mississippi, North Carolina, Oklahoma, Pennsylvania, and Virginia.

1973: U.S. District Court Judge John H. Pratt rules that HEW must begin enforcement proceedings against states that do not submit to the Office of Civil Rights an acceptable plan for desegregating their higher-education systems.

1974: HEW accepts desegregation plans from all of the states except Louisiana and Mississippi. It refers Louisiana, which refused to submit a plan, and Mississippi, which submitted an unacceptable plan, to the Justice Department for enforcement proceedings.

1977: Judge Pratt finds that the plans accepted by HEW have not been effective and orders HEW to develop specific criteria for new desegregation plans.

1978: HEW publishes new criteria for plans, and subsequently accepts new five-year plans from Arkansas, Florida, Georgia, Oklahoma, and the North Carolina community-college system.

1979: The U.S. Department of Education is created and assumes responsibility for the case.

1980: Judge Pratt requires the Education Department to obtain plans from eight additional states: Alabama, Delaware, Kentucky, Missouri, Ohio, South Carolina, Texas, and West Virginia.

1981: The Education Department accepts five-year plans for the University of North Carolina system, and for Delaware, Mississippi, South Carolina, and West Virginia. The department refers Alabama and Ohio to the Justice Department for enforcement proceedings.

1982: The Education Department accepts a five-year desegregation plan from Kentucky.

1983: Judge Pratt orders the Education Department to negotiate additions to the six desegregation plans it accepted in 1977.

1983: The Education Department accepts additions to the 1977 plans, and new five-year plans from Pennsylvania and Texas.

1985: Desegregation plans expire in Arkansas, Florida, Georgia, and Oklahoma, and for North Carolina's community colleges.

1986: Desegregation plans expire in Delaware, Missouri, South Carolina, Virginia, and West Virginia, and for the University of North Carolina system.

1986: The Education Department accepts a new five-year plan from Maryland.

1987: Desegregation plan expires in Kentucky.

1987: Judge Pratt dismisses the case, saying that the NAACP Legal Defense and Educational Fund lacks the legal right to continue the suit and has failed to prove that action against the Education Department will bring changes to the public colleges involved in the case.

1988: The Education Department declares that Arkansas, North Carolina, South Carolina, and West Virginia are in compliance with Title VI. The department states that six other states—Delaware, Florida, Georgia, Missouri, Oklahoma, and West Virginia—must take additional steps to come into compliance with Title VI.

1989: The Education Department declares that Georgia, Missouri, and Oklahoma are in compliance with Title VI.

1989: The U.S. Court of Appeals for the District of Columbia reverses Judge Pratt's 1987 dismissal of the case and states that the Legal Defense and Educational Fund may continue the case. The court orders additional hearings on what measures should be ordered to bring about desegregation.

4. *Allen v. Wright*, 104 S. Ct. 3314 (1984).

5. *Women's Equite Action League (WEAL) v. Cavazos*, 879 F2d 880 (886 D.C. Circuit, 1989).

6. 879 F2d 880 at 886.

7. See also, generally, a preliminary chart entitled "Secretary's Institutional Default Reduction Initiative FY 1991 Cohort Default Rates Historically Black Colleges and Universities" (1 September 1993).

8. See Scott Jaschik, *Chronicle of Higher Education*, 19 July 1989, A–17.

9. Courtney Leatherman, "After Years of Failing to Win Alumni Gifts, Black Colleges Step Up Their Efforts. We're Sitting on Great Potential," *Chronicle of Higher Education*, 25 October 1989, A–31.

10. Title III of the Higher Education Act of 1965 is most directly traced to Rep. Edith Green's Domestic Faculty Exchange Act of 1964 (H.R. 11905), introduced in the 2d session of the 88th Congress on 2 July 1964. Subsequently, President Johnson, in his Education Message on 12 January 1965, requested legislation to help less-developed postsecondary institutions through professional exchanges, national teaching fellowships, and cooperative use of facilities and faculty. Both the president's proposal and Rep. Green's bill were ultimately reflected in Title III of H.R. 3220 and in H.R. 9567, which became the Higher Education Act of 1965 (P.L. 89–329).

11. *Fullilove v. Klutznick*, 448 U.S. 448 (1980).

12. *City of Richmond v. J. A. Croson*, 488 US 469, 472 citation (1989), in which Justice O'Connor, writing for a divided Court, said: "The principal opinion in *Fullilove* cannot be read to relieve the city of the necessity of making specific findings of discrimination required by the Clause since the congressional findings of past discrimination relied on in that case, was made pursuant to Congress's unique power under section 5 of the Amendment to enforce, and therefore identify and redress violations of the Amendment's provisions."

13. In *John Doe v. University of Michigan*, 721 F. Supp 852 (1989), federal district court judge Avern Cohn ruled that the university's policy aimed at barring harassment or discrimination based on race, ethnicity, religion, sex, sexual orientation, creed, national origin, age, marital status, handicapped or Vietnam-veteran status violated freedom of speech protections in the Constitution and said that the policy was so vague that "persons of common intelligence must guess at its meaning" (at 866 quoting *Broadrick v. Oklahoma*, 413 US, 601, 607) (1973). Similar policies at the University of Wisconsin, Stanford University, and Duke University faced similar challenges.

14. See sec. 303 of P.L. 102–325, the Higher Education Act Amendments of 1992 (106 Stat. 475), which amends sections 324(d) and 326(e).

15. The U.S. Department of Education has not yet published the FY 1991 White House Initiative (Executive Order 12876) report.

16. The Guaranteed Student Loan Analysis Branch of the U.S. Department of Education reveals growth from 1,299 loans totaling $828,000 in annual GSL volume in FY 1976 (with cumulative totals of 8,960 loans and $9,955,000) to 4,815 loans totaling $13,500,000 in FY 1991 (and cumulative totals of 57,466 loans totaling $127,468,000!) (U.S. Department of Education, 1991, p. 16). As of 30 September 1991, $57 billion of the $127 billion was still owed by current and former students (see chart on p. 6).

17. Deborah Kalcevic and Deborah Rhind (1991) write that "student's personal characteristics are also correlated with whether or not they borrow. Students from low-income families are considerably more likely to receive a Stafford Loan than are those from higher income families, reflecting both their greater financial need and the income restrictions of the program. Black students are more likely and Asian students less likely to borrow than are other students" (p. 18).

18. In an August 1993 report, the GAO told Sen. Paul Simon: "(O)f the total dollar amount of FFELs made to students each year, the percentage that goes to HBCU students is small, even though HBCU loan volume *more than doubled in recent years*. In fiscal year 1991, the total dollar volume of FFELs was $13.5 billion; loans to students attending HBCU's totaled $372 million—less than 2.8 percent of the FFEL's made to postsecondary students that year. . . . In fiscal year 1987, loans to HBCU students represented about 1.7 percent of other total loans to postsecondary students" (U.S. GAO, August 1993, p. 4) (emphasis supplied). In a 9 March 1994 letter updating this report to Cong. Edolphus Towns, chairman of the House Government Operations Subcommittee on Human Resources, Linda G. Morra did not alter GAO's previous loan volume estimates, but she did indicate that four HBCUs had been subjected to Limit, Suspension, and Termination action by the department because of "failure to submit audit reports or to take corrective actions required by prior audits. Two of the HBCUs had default rates above regulatory thresholds."

19. These two most recent GAO reports are critical of the Depart-

ment of Education's administration of the student loan programs and the management of the department in general. The OMB and the department's inspector general have consistently criticized the Department of Education's management of the student loan programs.

20. The report to the Texas Legislature is an atypical example of legislative oversight of the proprietary sector. This report was prepared following significant publicity associated with student loan defaults among cosmetology schools in Texas.

21. In April 1991, following a review of twelve studies of student loan defaulters, the GAO noted nine default characteristics, only one of which was institutional in nature. It concluded that students most likely to default on their loans were those who "(1) attended vocational/trade schools, (2) had low incomes, (3) had little financial support, (4) had minority backgrounds, (5) lacked high school diplomas, (6) failed to complete their educational programs, (7) attended school for one year or less, (8) borrowed small amounts, and (9) were unemployed when defaulting" (U.S. GAO 1991, p. 2). It seems clear that personal or situational factors are the overriding cause of student loan default, not institutional type or control, nor academic program.

22. Based on the 1987 National Postsecondary Student Aid Survey, the Department of Education found that 40 percent of the defaulters surveyed never earned a postsecondary degree and that 51 percent earned less than $10,000 at the time the loan entered "repayment status."

23. Recent hearings by the Senate Permanent Subcommittee on Investigations uncovered rampant fraud and abuse in the Pell Grant program by as many as fifty orthodox Jewish nonprofit schools. "As much as $300 million in Pell Grants—aid for low income students—may have been misused, . . ." according to the Senate Governmental Affairs Subcommittee on Permanent Investigations. See Mary Jordan, "College Aid Abuses Long-Known to Education Department, Senate Panel Told," *Washington Post*, 29 October, 1993, A–11. "Worst of all," according to Sen. Sam Nunn (D-Ga.), "the abuse of at least $300 million intended for poor students indicates how little control the Education Department has over its aid programs. The department is so understaffed and unskilled," he said, "that it has essentially 'issued an invitation to come rip me off.'" Mary Jordan, "A College Aid Rip-Off," *Washington Post*, 28 October 1993, A–1, A–11.

24. See *Ayers v. Allain*, 674 F. Supp. 1523 (N.D. Miss. 1987), *Ayers v. Allain*, 893 F. 2d. 732 (CA5 1990) panel decision, and 914 F2d 676 (CA5 1990) (rehearing *en banc*) Affirmed. See also "Is Higher Education Desegregation a Remedy for Segregation but not Educational Inequality? A Study of the *Ayers v. Mabus* Desegregation Case," *Journal of Negro Education* 60, no. 4 (1991) from Howard University.

25. Statement of Gray A. Orfield, "High Court Ruling Transforms Battles Over Desegregation at Colleges in 19 States," *Chronicle of Higher Education* 38, no. 44 (8 July 1992): A–16. See also Scott Jascik, "Whither Desegregation? Supreme Court's 1992 Ruling on Colleges Has Some Confusion and Lacks Force," *Chronicle of Higher Education*, (26 January 1994): A–33, A–37.

26. See *Brown I*, 347 U.S. 483, 495 (1954), holding that the concept of "separate but equal" has no place in pubic education, and *Brown II*, 349 U.S. 294, 301 (1955), ordering an end to segregation in public education "with all deliberate speed."

27. *Ayers v. Fordice*, 112 S. Ct. 2727 (1992).

28. 112 S. Ct. 2727 (1992).

29. Carver State Technical College and Bishop State Community College in Alabama merged, reducing the number of HBCUs recognized by the Department of Education to 104.

30. See also Arthur E. Thomas and Robert L. Greene, "Black Colleges and Universities," *Cincinnati Enquirer*, 26 September 1993, F–1; and Tamara Henry. "Renewing the Investment in Black Schools," *USA Today*, 2 December 1993, A–1.

31. Brooke A. Masters, "A Struggle for the Heart of Howard University," *Washington Post*, 20 December 1993, A–1, A–18.

32. "Black Colleges under Fire," *Emerge*, September 1993, 26.

33. See Memorandum Opinion *U.S. v. State of Louisiana* (Civil Action No. 80-3300, Section "A") (D.C.ED, LA), 23 December 1992.

34. See *Knight v. State of Alabama*, 787 F. Supp. 1030 (N.D. Ala, 1991).

35. For example, a possible response to the Mississippi Board's closure and merger plan would be a proposal that (1) "merged" Delta State into Mississippi Valley State University (MVSU), retaining MVSU leadership and mission and granting MVSU administrative authority over all state two-year institutions; (2) preserved Alcorn State University as a historically black land-grant institution by adding new

agricultural and technical programs that foster integration at the Lorman campus; and (3) enhanced Jackson State University (JSU) by folding the higher education center and the medical school in Jackson into JSU. These changes would protect the historic mission of the three public HBCUs, foster desegregation at all three campuses by encouraging majority student matriculation, and enhance each of the HBCUs academically.

21 The Role of Historically Black Colleges and Universities with Respect to Public Policy Research

STEPHEN J. WRIGHT

I n this chapter, we critically examine the role of historically black colleges and universities with respect to public policy research concerned with or affecting the social, economic, and educational conditions of African Americans.

Our study is based on four assumptions:

1. Public policy research—whether established by executive order, by legislatures or other public bodies, or promulgated by the courts in response to litigation—may seriously affect the personal and social conditions of African Americans, positively or negatively.

2. The process of developing or revising public policy may be significantly informed by the results of relevant and competent research.

3. The historically black colleges and universities, where the majority of the black faculty are located, should play a significant role in conducting policy research concerned with the black condition.

4. The use made by advocacy groups, concerned with the black condition, of public policy research conducted in the historically black institutions constitutes one reasonably valid measure of the significance of such research.

HISTORICAL BACKGROUND

Public policy research, or research that could serve a public policy purpose, has a long, if not extensive, history in the black institutions, as the following history indicates.

W. E. B. Du Bois

W. E. B. Du Bois, the first black to receive a Ph.D. from Harvard University, joined the faculty of Atlanta University in 1897 to teach sociology and to assume responsibility for what came to be known as *The Atlanta University Publications,* eighteen in all, published between 1896 and 1914. Kaiser (1967) characterizes these publications as "the first attempts to study scientifically the problems of the American Negro anywhere in the world." Of the eighteen publications, *The Mortality Among Negroes in the Cities, The American Negro Family,* and *The Negro American Artisan* had the breadth and depth to serve public policy purposes.

In the prefaces to the majority of the publications, Du Bois pleaded for more adequate and stable financial support—a problem that has continued to plague research in black institutions since that time.

Monroe N. Work

In 1908, Monroe N. Work accepted Booker T. Washington's invitation to become the Director of Research and Records at Tuskegee Institute. Beginning in 1912, he published nine editions of *The Negro Yearbook, Annual Encyclopedia of the Negro* which was, for its time, the most comprehensive data source on blacks. His records on lynchings came to be used as source data to support reform legislation over a number of years.

Work's *Bibliography of the Negro in Africa and America,* published by W. H. Wilson in 1928, with more that 17,000 entries, has been characterized by Porter (1982) as being "more indispensable today than in 1928 because no comparable work has been published."

Abram L. Harris and Charles H. Thompson

Abram L. Harris, professor of economics at Howard University from 1927 to 1945, was widely recognized for his pioneering work on the black worker. His *The Black Worker* and *The Negro and the Labor Movement* (with Sterling D. Spero) provided, according to Weiss (1982, 229), "an incisive analysis of alternate programs of reform."

Charles H. Thompson, director of the Bureau of Educational Research at Howard University and founder and editor of the *Journal of Negro Education,* provided much of the critical analysis that led to the landmark U.S. Supreme Court decision in *Brown v. Topeka Board of Education* (1954). Thompson, according to Kluger (1975, 172), "in a few strokes of the pen . . . sketched the principal arguments for attacking segregation itself as unconstitutional."

The Dispersion of Black Scholars

As late as 1944, when Myrdal's *An American Dilemma* was published, the great majority of black scholars engaged in research on black personal, social, and political conditions (or in research of any kind, for that matter) were connected with the black colleges and universities. Indeed, the great majority of those scholars who assisted Myrdal with his monumental study—Sterling Brown, Ralph Bunche, W. E. B. Du Bois, E. Franklin Frazier, Abram L. Harris, Charles S. Johnson, Alain Locke, Nelson Palmer, Ira D. Reid, and Doxey A. Wilkerson—were all connected at that time with three institutions: Howard, Fisk, and Atlanta Universities. About this time, however, the predominantly white universities began to recruit outstanding black scholars to their faculties. This recruitment of black scholars has increased significantly in recent years. The research of these scholars, for purposes of this study, must be distinguished from that conducted in the black institutions.

Institute for the Study of Educational Policy

One of the most significant later developments in public policy research was the establishment of the Institute for the Study of Educational Policy (ISEP) at Howard University in 1974. Kenneth S. Tollett (1979, xv), its executive director, described its purpose:

> Through its annual reports and monographs, through its seminars and workshops, and through its announcements and public testimony, the Institute for the Study of Educational Policy attempts to fill a vacuum

in the organized body of knowledge about higher educational opportunities for blacks and other minorities. In doing so, ISEP attempts to make a significant contribution to the formulation and evaluation of contemporary educational policy.

In publishing such documents as *The Changing Mood in America: Eroding Commitment*; *Equal Opportunity for Blacks in Higher Education: An Assessment*; and *Equal Opportunity: More Promise than Progress*, the institute was making a major contribution to public policy research in higher education. Unfortunately, the institute was discontinued in 1985.

PRESENT STATUS

The majority of the black colleges and universities are primarily undergraduate institutions in fact, if not in name. Only twelve confer the doctoral degree—the level at which most major research is conducted. (See Appendix B.) Of the twelve institutions, only Howard University has a fully developed set of doctoral programs. But regardless of the degree level of the institution, specialized research, such as public policy research, tends to be conducted in college- and university-based centers, institutes, or other dedicated units.

A search for centers or institutes engaged in public policy research was conducted, and the following were identified:

- The Institute for Urban Affairs and Research at Howard University, Washington, D.C.
- The Institute for Urban Affairs and Research at Morgan State University, Baltimore, Maryland
- The Center for Research and Economic Development at Jackson State University, Jackson, Mississippi
- The Lower Mississippi Delta Consortium of Thirteen Historically Black Colleges and Universities, based at Jackson State University, Jackson, Mississippi
- The Southern Center for Studies in Public Policies at Clark College, now Clark-Atlanta University, Atlanta, Georgia
- The Black Family Institute at Hampton University, Hampton, Virginia
- The Institute for Social, Economic and Political Studies at Xavier University, Cincinnati, Ohio

- The Institute on Health Care for the Poor and Underserved at Meharry Medical College, Nashville, Tennessee
- The Center for Applied Research and Urban Policy at the University of the District of Columbia, Washington, D.C.

The list is not exhaustive, but it is representative of the growing concern with respect to public policy research in historically black institutions.

General Description of Centers and Institutes

The centers and institutes listed above vary greatly with respect to resources, focus, and productivity. Only four—those at Howard, Morgan, the University of the District of Columbia, and Meharry Medical College—have full-time directors, and the majority are dependent upon "soft" money for their support.

As a group, the centers and institutes are concerned with a range of public problems, including health, welfare, civil rights, federal aid to education, minimum wage legislation, and economic development. The institute at Morgan State University, according to its director, Dr. Robert Hill, focuses on the urban problems of Baltimore as a part of the university's mission as an urban university. The lower Mississippi Delta Consortium focuses on the economic development problems of the delta as they affect blacks in the area.

The agencies are, for the most part, relatively new and without track records of major publications and related activities that would give them national visibility. The conspicuous exceptions are the Institute for Urban Affairs and Research at Howard University, with its many publications, and the Institute on Health Care for the Poor and the Underserved at Meharry Medical College, which seeks "to contribute to the development and understanding of health policies which have an impact on a local and national level" (Institute on Health Care 1989). The institute has recently conducted its second national conference.

Uses of Research Produced by Institutes and Centers

Because blacks tend to look toward their major advocacy groups for leadership in influencing the formulation, revision, and evaluation of public policy that affects them significantly, we attempted to determine major advocacy groups' use of the public policy research conducted in black institutions.

To this end, calls were made to the chief executive officers of the National Association for Equal Opportunity in Higher Education (NAFEO), the Legal Defense Fund, the National Urban Coalition, the National Urban League (the individual consulted was the executive vice-president), and the Congressional Black Caucus to ascertain the extent to which they used the public policy research conducted in black institutes and centers.

Except in the case of the Legal Defense Fund, which has used some data produced by the now-closed Institute for the Study of Educational Policy, the advocacy groups have been using very little of the research produced at historically black institutions. The reason for this situation may be twofold: the lack of visibility referred to previously and the relative paucity of research that focuses on public problems at the national level. Underlying the total situation is, as Wright (1979) notes, the serious paucity of researchers in the black institutions.

THE NEED

As citizens of the United States, African Americans are of course affected by public policies directed to the general population. But as a minority group with a long history of de jure segregation and discrimination, they have special problems involving equality of opportunity and the vestiges of segregation and discrimination.

While researchers in historically black institutions should by no means waive their opportunities to research public problems that affect the general population or a particular subgroup of problems in which blacks are substantially represented, the major focus of the public policy research in these institutions should be those special problems that impact blacks disproportionately and those rooted in the vestiges of segregation and discrimination. Such a focus will help to accelerate the solution of those stubborn problems that continue to impede the progress of blacks toward equal opportunity in the American social order.

CONCLUSION

In any serious consideration of what needs to be done, it should be borne in mind that significant research requires the right combination of talent, resources, time, and motivation—motivation driven, in part, by the opportunity to publish in recognized places and to experience the academic rewards in the form of salaries and promotions that good scholarship deserves. If any one of these conditions is missing, it is highly unlikely that the research produced will be either timely or substantive.

Realizing the need for talent, resources, time, and motivation, educators and policymakers should consider the following recommendations:

1. Colleges and universities should provide more opportunity for students to study public policy as a discipline to the end that they will come to understand, as a part of their general education, its potential as an instrument for not only improving the general human condition but the special condition of blacks as well.
2. Public policy research centers in black colleges and universities should limit their focus to a single, clearly defined area that impacts blacks, in order that they may have a better chance, with limited funds, to achieve visibility and excellence.
3. The presidents of the black colleges and universities should make a stronger effort to make their institutes and centers an important part of the public service mission of the institutions so as to stabilize at least their basic financial support.
4. The presidents should make a stronger effort to reduce the teaching loads of the directors, so they may provide effective leadership for their institutes and centers.
5. The institutions should provide opportunities for a limited number of able and interested young faculty members to pursue the study of public policy research at major university centers to increase the research capability of their own institutes and centers.
6. Directors of the institutes and centers should make a stronger effort through publications, conferences, seminars, and related activities to improve their visibility and the use made of their research.

REFERENCES

Institute on Health Care. 1989. Program for the second annual conference of the Institute on Health Care for the Poor and Underserved at Meharry Medical College, Nashville, TN, 2–3 October.

Kaiser, Ernest, 1967. Introduction. In *The Atlanta University publications*. Reprint. New York: Arno.

Kluger, Richard. 1975. *Simple justice*. New York: Vantage.

Porter, Dorothy. 1982. Monroe H. Work. In *Dictionary of American Negro biography*, ed. Rayford Logan and Michael Winston. New York: W. W. Norton.

Tollett, Kenneth S. 1979. Foreword. In *Elusive equality: The status of black Americans in higher education*, Lorenzo Morris. Washington, DC: Howard University Press.

Weiss, Roger. 1982. Abraham Harris. In *Dictionary of American Negro biography*, ed. Rayford Logan and Michael Winston. New York: W. W. Norton.

Wright, Stephen J. 1979. *The black educational policy researcher: An untapped national resource*. Washington, DC: National Advisory on Black Higher Education and Black Colleges and Universities.

APPENDIX A

List of Those Consulted Incident to This Study

Dr. Ronald Braithwaite, Associate Professor of Community Health, Morehouse Medical School.

Dr. Audry L. Brown, Director, Center for Applied Research and Urban Policy, University of the District of Columbia.

Julius Chambers, Director-Counsel, Legal Defense Fund.

Dr. Mary Coleman, Professor of Political Science, Jackson State University and Post-Doctoral Student, University of Maryland.

Dr. Ramona H. Edelin, President, National Urban Coalition.

Dr. Pekie Fessehatzion, Professor of Economics, Jackson State University.

Dr. Lawrence Gary, Director, Institute for Urban Affairs and Research, Howard University.

Dr. Robert Hill, Director, Institute for Urban Research, Morgan State University.

Dr. Mack Jones, Professor of Political Science, Prairie View A&M University.

Frank Lomax, Executive Vice President, National Urban League.

Dr. Leslie B. McLemore, Professor of Science, Dean of the Graduate School and Director of Research Administration, Jackson State University.

Dr. Samuel L. Myers, President, NAFEO.

Amelia Parker, Executive Director, Congressional Black Caucus.

Dr. Charles Projean, Director, Institute for Social, Economic and Political Studies, Xavier University.

Dr. David Satcher, President, Meharry Medical College.

Dr. David Swinton, Dean, School of Business, Jackson State University and Former Director of the Southern Center for Studies in Public Policies, Clark College.

Dr. Kenneth S. Tollett, Distinguished Professor of Higher Education and Former Executive Director of the Institute for the Study of Educational Policy, Howard University.

Dr. Hoda Zaki, Chairman, Political Science Department, Hampton University.

APPENDIX B

Black Colleges and Universities That Confer Doctoral Degrees

Alabama A&M University, Clark-Atlanta University, Florida A&M University, Howard University, Interdenominational Theological Seminary, Jackson State University, Meharry Medical College, Morgan State University, University of Maryland Eastern Shore, Tennessee State University, and Texas Southern University.

*Media,
Communications,
and Culture* | **E**

22 | Overview and Recommendations

Carolyn Stroman

Speakers for this issue area explored, from a cultural perspective, a variety of issues related to communications and information systems, focusing attention on the potential for meaningful change in mass media content within the current market through changes in policy and increased minority ownership of and control over production. Interaction between news sources, nonnews sources, and the media, the impact of this interplay on the production and dissemination of news and nonnews products, and its implication for the African American subculture, also were major topics. Presenters also explored issues relating to television viewing and its impact on Americans, and the relationship between communication systems and their applications in the delivery of information to communities of color.

Speakers addressed contemporary issues in communication and information technologies and assessed the means by which these technologies, contrary to popular opinion, may well end up widening rather than narrowing the gap between the nation's haves and have nots. The contributors raised hard-hitting questions and developed a set of recommendations that should bring about positive changes in social, political, and economic elements in the mass media and other communication systems, and in the culture that influences and is influenced by African Americans.

Our first chapter discusses the impact of technology on the cultural development of African Americans and other minorities. In "African Americans and the Information

Age: Life in the Pay-Per Society," Oscar Gandy describes how trends in the political economy of information will affect the life chances of all individuals. The "pay-per" society has revolutionized American culture, Gandy notes: "The commoditization of culture is reflected in the replacement of family songs by MTV; grampa's stories by videodisc; and friendly games of checkers, scrabble, and bid whist by solitary bouts with creatures in a cyberspace designed by Nintendo and downloaded through a "900" number over AT&T optical fibers." Gandy paints a clear, poignant picture of the possible future. Poor African Americans are at special risk for becoming isolated and disenfranchised as a result of the movement toward a pay-per society. Gandy portrays the emerging communications environment as perhaps less overtly politically sinister than in the Orwellian vision, but certainly as no less manipulative.

The information age promises to use computers, cable, satellites, fax machines, and other sophisticated technology to increase all Americans' access to information. However, various forces will increase the knowledge gap between the "technical elites and the technopeasants"; information will become increasingly restricted to those with the ability to pay. At its most simplistic level, a pay-per society excludes those who cannot afford the cost of communications services. This will have a great adverse impact, especially if the move to accelerate privatization of such public information institutions as public libraries goes unchallenged. However, Gandy's insight is critical to reaching the heart of the issue, which is once again cultural. After all, as he states, merely having or guaranteeing "access to whatever the market provides" is not sufficient. Gandy argues that the goal is equal access to whatever individuals need "to be able to construct accurate and useful images of their environment."

Gandy's vision of "a grassroots movement" to challenge and redefine the methods, aims, and content of the communications environment would require interaction among all social and class strata. He speaks of utilizing existing resources to organize a campaign that would force communication systems to be responsive to the needs of all Americans. Gandy's optimism for the success of such an approach is grounded in his confidence in the force of ideas.

Responding to the age-old question of what to do, Gandy says, "The kinds of answers we have been offered vary in part according to our belief that theory provides guidance, and that social pressure carries weight within the social system."

Concordance with Gandy's assertion is the impetus for Haile Gerima's "Independent African American Cinema: The Creation of an Alternative Cultural Infrastructure." As Gandy peers through the prism of information technology, Gerima examines the pioneers of African American cinema. He also detects the same "psychological scarification . . . and cultural alienation of a people," but argues "they were entitled to that imperfection. It was a logical consequence of their reality." In fact, all the contributors—published and unpublished—arrived at a consensus that Gerima states simply, "Africans, wherever they may be, have to integrate, into our day-to-day activity, our nation of culture." He underscores this imperative, admonishing that "there is no twenty-first century without attempting to fully integrate our culture with the rest of our needs."

As with the other conference participants, Gerima's professional life has been dedicated to the exposition of the African American cultural experience. His concept of struggle *and* empathetic evocation of the "tension" felt by African American moviegoers perhaps best conveys the emotional turmoil engendered by cultural alienation. "We enter the cinemas with a deeper subtext of anxiety and nervousness . . . knowing deep down we will not see ourselves, nor our humanity . . . we hide, grunt, we shout, nervously laugh, for more than anyone we are scared of the true ignored part of us contained within our bodies."

Culture as a stagnant entity is apt to be described as *history*, in its pejorative sense—something that once contributed to our condition, now too far removed to be indelible or relevant. Yet, one senses that at the core of the cultural dilemmas entwining African Americans is a refusal to acknowledge and embrace the truth of their past. The pervasiveness and starkness of its effects are seldom fully realized. The enlightened descendants of its immediate victims, while rightfully claiming an array of glorious heritages from a vast continent, often refuse to acknowledge capitulations or defeats as part of a past that proudly celebrates resistance victories. All in all, the horror of the experience has been diluted in historical memory as the need to wage personal and subjective struggles for survival and progress goes unabated.

A perceived need to establish a cultural framework is required to achieve the often-stated goal of institution building. Edmund Barry Gaither's contribution, "One-Third of a Nation, One Hundred Percent Ourselves," applauds the founding and growth of African American museums and galleries. He warns, however, that "Until a spectrum of such cultural institutions is forged and supported by African Americans, there can be no genuine flourishing of authentic black cultural expression nor the creation of a salient and sharp criticism and analysis of creative production."

Through the conference's panel on cultural hegemony and institutional autonomy, Gaither explores both the meaning of identity and the tools to preserve it, particularly as they relate to the historical evolution of African American artists. They express concern about the survival of families, the spiritual quicksand of consumerism, and the decertification of morality. Gaither notes that "Among the manifestations reflecting alienation from 'self' are cultural forms that, instead of heralding our uniqueness and creativity, bend to conform with perverse images that degenerate culture into mere commercial vehicles devoid of more profound sentiments."

America remains a country beset by cycles of recrimination, blame, and guilt, which seep from the cultural subconscious of individuals to be amplified on a scale never before technologically possible. Haile Gerima's term, "cultural aggression," is more than an abstraction; it refers to the perverse distortion of truth encoded with a malignant refusal to recognize another people's humanity. Collectively, these writers understand that restructuring and defining cultural ideals cannot be entrusted to any other than the people themselves.

RECOMMENDATIONS

Four papers were presented in this issue area. The recommendations that follow, both general and policy oriented, were drawn from them all.

General Recommendations

1. The "objectivity" paradigm of news reporting should be replaced by one that is sensitive to the interests and concerns of African

Americans and other minorities. In short, conference participants recommended that a news paradigm that gives emphasis to the agendas of minority community news sources be developed with a view to coordinating their activities and linking them up with state and national news sources.

2. African Americans must continue their efforts to increase the number of owners of communications media; at the same time, Congress must increase its efforts to safeguard the rights of minorities and to lessen the barriers to equity in the marketplace.

3. African Americans must participate more actively in the production and distribution of information in the United States; they must also exert effort to ensure that they have ready access to the information needed to be able to construct accurate and useful images of their environments.

4. African American radio personnel must consolidate the gains made in developing black radio into a political tool in the African American community and must develop collective strategies for furthering these gains in the future.

5. Steps must be taken, particularly by those in higher education, to educate and sensitize current and future news media employees, especially news media executives and managers, to the increasingly multicultural characteristics of the American marketplace. Furthermore, Afrocentric views of news value must become accepted as legitimate in American newsrooms.

6. Because television occupies a central role in the lives of African American children, parents must assume responsibility for controlling children's exposure to television; exerting such control is one of the most effective ways to mitigate the influence of television.

Policy Recommendations

The Committee on Media, Communication, and Culture studied a broad and complex range of issues, including the effects of mass media content on African Americans and their culture as well as issues of ownership, control, and access to telecommunications entities and how these issues influence the content presented to the public. All participants agreed that diversity of ownership is key to diversity and improvement in content. Most recommendations were directed toward establishing diversity in telecommunications ownership.

1. There must by concerted effort, not only by black groups but by all public interest groups, to lobby Congress and other government agencies to support and maintain current affirmative action policies of the FCC that encourage black and other minority ownership, management, and control of telecommunications entities.

2. African Americans must provide financial and public support for the development of "grassroots" public interest groups in telecommunications such as the National Black Media Coalition (NBMC) that need not rely upon corporate foundations for funding.

3. African Americans must increase their participation in professional communications organizations such as NBMC and the National Association of Black Owned Broadcasters in order to further promote their ability to successfully lobby for change.

4. African Americans must find ways other than boycotts and demonstrations to lobby for change in television and other media content. These methods must promote generous, responsible, and cooperative perspectives that complement the roles of community organizations and institutions, and that contribute to the spiritual and cultural needs of African Americans.

5. Black-owned public radio stations should coordinate their programs and policies to expand their growing significance in radio markets with large African American populations.

6. Opportunities must be developed for African Americans' access to new communications technology. Public schools should provide access within the classroom with emphasis on cooperative team learning.

7. Corporations and individuals must cooperatively initiate a massive public relations campaign to promote the goal of taxation to finance investments in black America—a New America Campaign. (See Oscar Gandy's chapter in this section.) Attracting communications-related industries to the central cities would strongly support integration of new technology with learning.

8. African American researchers must integrate research on media effects and media markets with a broad social agenda to recognize the paramount role the mass media plays in the lives of African Americans and other minorities.

23 African Americans and the Information Age: Life in the Pay-Per Society

OSCAR H. GANDY, JR.

Assessment and planning aimed at improving life chances for African Americans require an informed sense of the present and future status of the environment in which those life chances are determined. The American economy is undergoing a dramatic social and structural transformation with important implications for our understanding of the problems and prospects that the future holds for African Americans (Boswell and Bergesen 1987; Hollist and Rosenau 1981). Dramatic, epochal changes in a social system tend to be labeled in terms of economic attributes, frequently related to changes in the organization of production. Bell (1973) has discussed this change in terms of "the coming of post-industrial society." A focus on industrial sectors has led some observers to describe this change as a move toward a "service economy." Still others, who have recognized the importance of computers, data processing, and telecommunications have referred to this era as the Information Age, and the United States and other Organization for Economic Cooperation and Development countries as information economies (Jonscher 1983; Katz 1986; Porat 1976). A few, who have identified the role of information and information systems as components in the machinery of social control, have labeled this era as the Surveillance Age and ours as a "total surveillance society" (Donner 1980; Flaherty 1988; Gandy 1989, 1993). This chapter explores several trends in the political economy of information in the United States that have serious implications for the future of African Americans.

THE INFORMATION AGE AND THE INFORMATION ECONOMY

Evidence abounds that industrialized economies have increasingly allocated economic and productive resources to the production and distribution of information. Porat (1976), building on the work of Machlup (1962), provides a basis for identifying primary and secondary information sectors and their contributions to the gross national product (GNP). The 1960s are identified as the point of crossover, when the size of the workforce involved with information goods and services exceeded that of the noninformation industrial workforce. However, despite the immediate popularity of Porat's analysis, description is not explanation. Futurists and others who spoke in glowing terms about the unlimited potential of the Information Age (Salvaggio 1987) failed to fully understand the social and economic logic that lay beneath these changes (Hall and Preston 1988; Yearley 1988). Much of the talk about an information age may be seen as self-interested puffery. From the perspective of Theodore Roszak (1986, 45), "In our culture today, the discussion of computers and information is awash with commercially motivated exaggeration and the opportunistic mystifications of the computer sciences establishment. The hucksters and the hacks have polluted our understanding of information technology with loose metaphors, facile comparisons, and a good deal of out-and-out obfuscation."

While the extent of puffery is no doubt quite high, there have been identifiable changes in the structure of the American economy. The pursuit of profits in the logic of Western capitalism requires continual movement on two fronts, which has resulted in expansion of the information sector. To avoid a falling rate of profit, industrialists pursued production and distribution efficiencies and found them in computerization. To avoid overproduction and underconsumption crises, entrepreneurs sought new markets for new products and found help in sophisticated market research. Growth in the information sector was a consequence of anxiety over profits, rather than an explicit goal of social or economic policy.

The Drive for Efficiency

The role of computers and other information technologies in the rationalization of control over production, distribution, and mass consumption in the United States has been described in minute detail by James Beniger in his award-winning book, *The Control Revolution* (1986). Beniger describes an interactive process of growth, crises, and technological response that bears a striking, but unacknowledged, similarity to the Hegelian dialectics at the core of Marx's historical materialism (Marx 1906, 1973). The pursuit of efficiencies, involving the reduction of labor costs, contributes to a troublesome bottleneck in the distribution system, which when solved through improved coordination of transportation generates still further problems in the management of consumer demand. Computers in particular, and information technologies in general, are seen to have provided at least temporary solutions in each of these interconnected sectors of the domestic economy. However, the introduction of computers has important and perhaps unanticipated consequences for African Americans.

The pursuit of productive efficiencies has traditionally meant either the reduction of the workforce or the reduction of the skills needed by workers directly involved in production—or both. African American workers have suffered disproportionately the impact of computerization of American industry. Just as African Americans have begun to move in greater numbers into the white-collar labor force, expert systems (Born 1987; Schoppers 1986) are eliminating many of the routine data processing jobs that characterize this level of employment. Unfortunately, these same technologies have made it easier to isolate and exclude African Americans from the cultural and economic mainstream of the society.

The Commoditization of Culture

As we know, avoiding continuing economic crises requires continual identification of new goods and services that can be produced efficiently and marketed widely with the aid of creative advertising. Critical scholars (Schiller 1988; Robins and Webster 1988) have suggested that these new goods are not solely, or even primarily, the creations of imaginative minds or the product of expensive research and development. Part of this growth is the result of the commoditization of goods and services that were previously the products of household labor or social products exchanged within communities, and thus outside the reach of markets and pursuit of profits. The unpaid labor of wives and mothers has become high-priced cookies, brownies, microwaveable nouvelle cuisines, and homemaker services marketed to the two-income, no-kids families of the Information Age. The commoditization of culture is reflected in the replacement of family songs by MTV; grampa's stories by videodisc; and friendly games of checkers, Scrabble, and bid whist by solitary bouts with creatures in a cyberspace designed by Nintendo and downloaded through a "900" number over AT&T optical fibers. Even though participation by women in the labor force has increased significantly, there has been a continuing decline in real family income because the market has placed new demands on the consumer.

The Pay-Per Society

Mosco (1989) has coined the term *pay-per society* to describe the movement toward the commoditization of information. Despite the fact that information is very much unlike traditional commodities and is a classic public good, that is, its use by one individual does not reduce the potential for its use by another (Bates 1988), the perceived need to expand the array of marketable goods has led to both technological and regulatory solutions to the problems of exclusion and appropriability. Public goods tend to be supplied by governments because their profit does not return to the original investors in a way that can be controlled by the marketplace. That is, all who benefit from the production or consumption of information cannot be made to pay for those benefits. We all benefit from the education of our nation's youth, and recognizing this fact provides justification for general taxation to support public education. A similar justification supports our current system of free public libraries.

Because of the difficulties in excluding or collecting access fees from those who receive the signals broadcast from radio and television stations, a system of advertiser or third-party finance has developed. Copyright legislation serves as a regulatory mechanism thought to restrict the uncompensated duplication and sharing of information. Where regulatory efforts have not succeeded in restricting unauthorized access, technological solutions have been developed. Scrambling satellite signals has reduced access to cable feeds, including those of "premium" entertainment and sports events. The introduction of the new digital audio tape was delayed until a limit on tape-to-tape duplication could be developed and tested. These moves have been directed toward capturing the maximum amount of possible revenue from paying customers. Control over distribution allows information producers to engage in efficient price discrimination, charging different prices for access to segments of the market on the basis of their revealed time preferences for information. Efficient price discrimination ensures that the poorest members of the information market have access to theatrical films as much as two years after the well-to-do (Baldwin and Wirth 1989; Wildman and Siwek 1988). They will see a popular film in an edited version, filled with commercials, when it is finally programmed as a network television film of the week, while others may have paid $7 to see it during its opening week, $2.50 to rent it from a video store, or some fraction of their HBO subscription rate of at least $17.50 when it is released to cable.

The pay-per society is not limited to traditional entertainment channels. Information systems such as CompuServe and other information services charge users for connect time and set fees on a sliding scale for the particular classes of information they select. To use many of these services, the consumer must invest several hundreds of dollars for equipment and even more hours developing the necessary skills. Even the telephone is emerging rapidly as a profitable delivery system for information services. The "800" numbers that provide "free" information to potential consumers or persons with active warrantees are giving way to a variety of "900" or other premium information services, which charge the calling party variable fees depending upon the services delivered. Services such as directory assistance soon will be either paid for directly or financed indirectly by subjecting the caller to a commercial message from the sponsor of the directory service. Even the public library is being moved toward a fee-for-service model (Schiller and Schiller 1986, 1988). The Schillers (1986, 307) discuss the movement toward "disintermediation," a high-tech word for the elimination of the librarian as a professional. After all, "Who needs librarians if information can be supplied by private businesses, unencumbered by concern for the public good?" It is clear that in the pay-per society, the logic of capital will ensure that even information will become increasingly restricted to those with the ability to pay.

THE INFORMATION ECOLOGY OF AFRICAN AMERICA

Understanding the place of African Americans in the Information Age requires an assessment of the level and extent of black participation in the information economy as producers and consumers of information goods and services. The amount and quality of information available in society depends on the interaction of the forces of supply and demand. This relationship is a core postulate of neoclassical economics and may be held as true as far as it goes. Unfortunately, neoclassical economics has yet to venture very far in trying to understand the nature of the market for information (Mosco and Wasko 1988). Economists have enough difficulty dealing with the mechanism through which tastes and preferences develop and change (Etzioni 1988). They steadfastly refuse to deal with the forces that operate to manage the demand for information. Thus, economists are not much help in explaining why African Americans are such fans of an information source [television] that either ignores or distorts their cultural experience (Gandy and Matabane 1989).

The information environment includes the production subsystem of artists, technicians, and other creative workers; the distribution system, which includes publishers, theater owners, and the owners and managers of broadcast, cable, and telecommunications; and the retail outlets, which dispense books, magazines, compact discs, videotapes, and other information media. Because they influence what is produced and made available for distribution, the formal and informal regulators are also considered part of the environment. While we traditionally think of the formal regulators of the information environment such as the Federal Communications Commission (FCC) and the Federal Trade Commission (FTC), professional groups such as the National Association of Broadcasters (NAB), the Directors Guild, and even public interest pressure groups such as People for the American Way, also act to regulate the flow of information. The financial subsystem, which includes the advertisers, the advertising agencies, and the audience assessment firms such as Nielsen, are perhaps the most important forces guiding the production system. While the audience is necessary for the operation of the system, their lack of organization makes them relatively powerless. Indeed, their definition as an audience is an imposed one, rather than a case of self-identification (Anderson 1989). Some viewers, readers, and listeners are simply ignored, as if they did not exist. Prior to the time when the numbers of African Americans in television audiences grew to the point where they could make the difference between success and failure for a given series, blacks were systematically ignored. However, beyond the occasional self-serving reports of a particular medium's "reach" into the black middle class, very little effort has been expended to describe the nature of African American demand for information. Information about the supply side is even more rare.

Creators, Consumers, and Information Workers

Traditional studies of ownership, management, and employment in the broadcasting industry have to be expanded to include analysis of the participation of African Americans in advertising, insurance, financial services, and telecommunications, as well as the growing number of businesses dependent on the marriage of computers and telecommunications. Current assessments and projections of future trends will have to take into account the likelihood that automation will eliminate jobs in these industries. Dramatic reductions in the workforce in the U.S. Post Office, AT&T, and the local Bell operating companies have followed substantial and continuing automation of these businesses. African Americans have suffered severe losses in employment as these industries have modernized their operations.

The special character of telecommunications means that many information processing jobs no longer need to be located in proximity to main offices. Rosenbluth Travel, a Philadelphia-based giant in the travel services industry, recently established a remote processing center in the agricultural west of the United States because the company found a well-educated but economically depressed population willing to be trained for remote data entry. The same rationale finds other American firms shipping their information processing tasks to the Caribbean,

India, South Asia, and the British Isles. The economics of the new telecommunications mean that it is increasingly profitable for industry to bypass or ignore the economically depressed center cities where the bulk of the African American poor reside (Hepworth and Robins 1988; Kasarda 1989).

Annual surveys of news directors provide evidence of either stagnation or decline in the numbers of African Americans in broadcast newsrooms (Stone 1988). Stone notes (p. 289) that "erosion is a gradual process. Whereas blacks and other minorities entered broadcast news with publicized wholesale hirings in the late 1960s and early 1970s, their exit, if there is such, may be so gradual as to go unnoticed." The rapid and widely generalized success enjoyed by white women who have sought entry into journalism appears to have displaced the black male in almost equal proportion. The expansion of news channels has not, apparently, provided any greater opportunity for African Americans. The willingness of broadcasters to make room for African Americans at the bottom has not been matched by any such willingness to make room at higher levels of management. In Stone's view, "The closed doors to managerial offices may be making broadcast news unattractive to minorities" (p. 293).

Mainstream, Midstream, and Crossing Over

At the same time that the evidence reveals stagnation or decline in the black presence behind the scenes in the mass media, African Americans are becoming much more visible downstage center. The *World Almanac*'s ninth annual poll of American high school students sought to identify the "Heroes of Young America." Eddie Murphy, Michael Jordan, Bill Cosby, and Oprah Winfrey took the top four slots. African Americans were selected as six out of the ten top people that American youngsters admired most in 1988 (*World Almanac* 1989). Out of eight categories of "heroes," African Americans were in first or second place in all but the "news and sports media" and "artists and writers" categories. What are we to make of this? Mainstream commercialization of black superstars makes them household names. Indeed, social scientists even use the Cosby "family" as an index of relative wealth, asking respondents to indicate how similar their household is to that of the Cosbys.

The penetration of the MTV wall of exclusion, the graduation of rap music to the status of musical award category, and Arsenio Hall's spectacular success in late night syndication, all reinforce the impression that African Americans have been awarded an honored place in mainstream American commercial culture. "Bad boy" Spike Lee even seems destined to join Eddie Murphy and Richard Pryor as a reliable source of mass appeal cinema. Rather than criticize the images these visible minorities present, I suggest that we give some thought as to how their position may be put to good use. But before we move to that task, we must consider additional attributes of the information environment.

Information Utilities

The Information Age heralds the introduction of an array of communications systems and services designed to increase the rate at which individuals can gain access to information in usable form. The linkage between computers and telecommunications systems, guided by sophisticated software, has revolutionized access to knowledge (Peled 1987; Kahn 1987). Galernter (1987; 1989) describes advances in parallel programming that turn computers into "information refineries" capable of monitoring complex, rapidly changing systems, searching massive databases, and presenting the analysis in high-resolution full-color graphics. Networking reduces the need to duplicate databases, parallel processors, or even the software that drives the systems. Users with access to such systems may only need the displays presented in answer to their inquiries.

Technologies such as these are designed primarily for utilization by business and government. Adaptation for the consumer market may be projected far into the future, and the distribution will follow along the predictable lines of education and social class (Baer 1985; Dizard 1985; Shoemaker, Reese, and Danielson 1985). Because information utilities are telecommunication network dependent, the fact that poor African Americans in the urban core do not yet enjoy the benefits of "universal service" (Aufderheide 1987; Mosco 1988; Pepper 1988) suggests that they will not soon be able to make use of these commercial databases. The "lifeline" services that were introduced to soften the blow of deregulation (Mosco 1988) will in no way guarantee access to high-capacity information utilities.

However, the show must go on, bills must be paid, and progress must be achieved. Thus, as part of its promotional efforts to develop support for its "intelligent network," Pacific Bell organized a task force of experts conversant with a variety of public interest perspectives. That there would, indeed, *must*, be some kind of intelligent network was never questioned. The task force served its legitimation function by helping Pacific Bell articulate its position on the particular forms the network, public access, and rate-payer finance should take. In response to a recommendation that Pacific Bell design intelligence *into* the network, as a way of avoiding the development of an elitist system of differentiated user capacities, Pacific Bell (1988, 13) almost grinned:

> Clearly the promise of the Information Age lies not only in the deployment of new technology, but in the participation of customers. Information services need to attract a critical mass of users to be successful. Pacific Bell—and other local telephone companies—are ideally positioned to play the role of facilitating Information Age services by providing economics of scope and scale to make them successful and widely available to both service providers and users.

Permission for the telephone companies to provide video dial tones, full cable services, or a host of competitive ISDN services (Pepper 1988), will hasten the arrival of a very different information environment from the one we presently observe. As more of these services are added, the disparity between the technical elites and the technopeasants is bound to grow (Mulgan 1991).

THE END OF MASS MEDIA

Wilson and Gutiérrez (1985) discuss changes in the nature of the mass media in the United States that they suggest point to the end of mass communications as we know it today. While some observers (Meehan 1988) resist labeling program channels with audiences of several million as anything other than mass, it is clear that there is a movement toward greater diversity among channels and greater homogeneity within each in terms of the primary attributes of the program content

(Baldwin and Wirth 1989). The concern of theorists is the implication that these changes will have for their social theories, which depend upon the assumption of broad, simultaneous exposure to common content. The dominant theoretical position, which was expressed by the Cultural Indicators team headed by George Gerbner (Signorielli and Morgan, in press), argues that audiences are exposed to homogeneous content through their relatively nonselective use of television. The growth in specialized mass-oriented channels, such as music, sports, news, and health and fitness, suggests that individuals will be able to substantially increase their intake of more homogeneous fare. The question remains as to whether at some important social level the difference between program genres actually supports the development of isolated subcultures.

Cable penetration, with subscribers estimated at over 56 percent of American households in July 1989, is expected to grow to at least 70 percent by the turn of the century. Cable networks provide specialized channels for sports, news, health and exercise, business, and children's programs. Numerous studies demonstrate that the availability of greater diversity in program content is associated with increased concentration in viewer's attention to favored channels (Barwise and Ehrenberg 1989; Webster 1986). The provision of specialized channels allows individuals to consume more of what they prefer. VCRs and the network of video stores have dramatically increased public access to theatrical film. Video distribution has provided an economic base supporting the production of specialized "genre" films, including unrated and unreleased (to theaters) horror and softcore and hardcore pornography. The impact of this increased diversity on the broadcast networks is clear (Blumler 1988). Continually declining shares of the video audience have led to frantic churning in program schedules as producers look for some magic formula for generating mass-appeal television (Kneale 1989).

The relationship between video programmers and their audience is one of successive approximations, what Gitlin (1985) might characterize as "ready, shoot, aim." Greater awareness of measurably distinct tastes and preferences among groups defined in demographic, psychographic, or behavioral terms leads programmers increasingly to produce programming that responds to the apparent interests of these narrow audience groups or to the interests of advertisers who would like to reach them. Tracking the performance of these programs requires developing improved audience research technologies. The people meters, soon to be improved with passive monitoring technology, cannot perform their function well if particular interest communities are not well represented in the national sampling frames. Because of this, such major research firms as Nielsen and Arbitron have established specialized black and Hispanic samples.

Segmentation of mass audiences into specialized channels generates what system theorists refer to as a *deviation amplifying loop*. As program research and development demonstrates value in pursuing narrower audience segments, there are rewards for developing still narrower segments. In each successive wave of adjustments, which includes the introduction of new channels of distribution, greater segmentation emerges. At the same time, organizations committed to the capture and sale of mass audiences must expend greater resources in creating a visual display that will attract a crowd. These increased budgets have two immediate effects on the production system. The cost of production and the price of talent escalates, raising minimal costs for successful programming, increasing the riskiness of programming, and extending the time horizon beyond which profits might be realized for mass appeal video (Gulback 1987; Owen and Wildman 1992; Wildman and Siwek 1988.) It is only the megafirm with deep pockets that can provide the venture capital for the development of such programs. Thus, we witness the growing trend towards mergers and acquisitions, such as the Time/Warner merger and the acquisitive binge of Rupert Murdoch's News Corporation.

PERSONAL INFORMATION AND THE NEW DISCRIMINATIONS

The development of segmented media and targeted promotions is dependent upon growth and integration of the technologies of mass surveillance (Flaherty 1988; Gandy 1993; Marx 1988; Wilson 1988). *Addressability* and *verifiability* (Gandy and Simmons 1986) refer to the ability of new information systems to send program material to a single individual, or to a specified subset of the audience pool, and to determine that the message was received. This feature not only allows precision in targeting messages, but it facilitates transforming the household information utility into a remote laboratory for testing promotional appeals (Gandy and Simmons 1986). Different promotional messages sent to different homes, in different editorial contexts, allow marketing analysts to estimate the synergistic potential of a given program format for maximizing the effectiveness of novel approaches to particular audience segments.

Consumer Profiles

The continual improvements in telecommunications networks that facilitate the remote processing of a variety of commercial transactions charged to credit or debit cards increase the amount of information available about consumers. High-speed digital networks and parallel processing routines (Galernter 1989) facilitate the rapid searching of remote databases to match and compare information in discrete files. The information is used to build profiles, or models of consumer behavior, which guide corporate decisions about whether to extend credit, offer insurance, or deny access to a variety of goods and services. The same sort of models inform the judicial systems about which of the accused should be offered the option of a plea bargain (Jaynes and Williams 1989) and which convicts are to be offered early release or given indefinite sentences (Morris and Miller 1987). Similar models inform politicians which neighborhoods to eliminate from their mailing lists or phone bank schedules when running for office or developing support for a referendum issue (Armstrong 1988; Weiss 1988).

Consumer profiles are used to include or exclude individuals or groups from the flow of communication and information based on the predictions of an analytical model derived from the past behavior of individuals in the database. With continued reductions in the cost of collecting, processing, and sharing information, the databases upon which such models are built continue to grow. In the rational pursuit of profits, corporate actors seek those targets that these profiles reveal to have the potential for generating the greatest profit with the minimal risk.

Government decision makers utilize the same intellectual technology to "avoid waste, fraud, and abuse" in the provision of government services (U.S. Office of Technology Assessment 1986), including the massive transfer payments upon which many Africans Americans have come to depend. Politicians, or would-be politicians, utilize these methods to develop political campaigns, to manipulate grassroots public opinion, and to reduce the clamor of open public debate to the level of hushed whispers between a small circle of friends (Armstrong 1988). The use of these analytical models and delivery systems has the potential to introduce novel forms of discrimination that bypass many of the legislative and judicial protections that have been won through civil rights struggles over the years.

Redlining and Exclusion

Armstrong (1988) describes several political campaigns, including the defeat of Tom Bradley in his run for the governor's seat in California, that have utilized voter profiles and targeted messages to subvert the political process by effectively bypassing segments of the electorate and targeting others for special attention and support. Rule and At- tewell (1989) describe new computer applications that suggest how the experience of African American males, unable to flag down a taxi to take them across town, is likely to become automated when such attempts are made by telephone. Commercial firms provide service as dispatchers for city cab companies and classify customers in terms of the probability that they will produce large fares and substantial tips. Callers who do not fit the preferred profile find themselves in a long queue. With the spread of the service known as "Caller ID," busi- nesses will be able to utilize even more data to construct profiles that support electronic redlining of incoming calls for information or serv- ice.

Caller ID is a seemingly innocuous service that displays the number of the incoming call before any connection is made. While such a fa- cility might facilitate the delivery of service by calling up a customer's records before the first voice contact is established, its use as a screen- ing device is particularly troublesome. Calls from particular neighborhoods, which have been identified by a geodemographic clus- tering analysis (Weiss 1988) as having a large proportion of low-income marginal consumers or in some other way seen as being unproductive, can be greeted with a busy signal or routed to a digital message designed to eliminate further interest in the service. While clustering is not an exact science, information suggesting that the caller is likely to be both black and poor has been demonstrated to have substantial value to firms in the real estate and insurance businesses. The fact that African Americans, more than any other ethnic minority in the United States, tend to be restricted to same-race communities (Wacquant and Wilson 1989) suggests that geodemographic clustering will be seen as a reliable indicator for these firms.

There is also every reason to expect that the industry that sells the names, addresses, and telephone numbers of people who pay their bills on time, read fishing magazines, buy expensive chocolates, or are at risk of bankruptcy, will not hesitate to offer screening services to firms with Caller ID (Gandy 1990). African Americans are therefore increasingly subject to exclusion from markets that their tastes, preferences, and resources suggest they might enter, but where racist marketing profiles identify them as avoidable risks. At the same time, information channels serving the cultural interests of impoverished African Americans will become increasingly dependent upon that small cluster of advertisers who have targeted this community for the sale of those poisons that the middle class has begun to reject and to eliminate from their lives (Davis 1987).

Information Dependence and Independence

While there has been dramatic progress in increasing the numbers of media outlets owned or managed by African Americans, these businesses have become almost entirely dependent upon cigarette and alcohol advertising for their survival. The tobacco industry has begun to develop a range of specialized marketing approaches to match their ads with the perceived interests and orientations of their target audiences (Altman, Slater, Albright, and Maccoby 1987). A growing literature has also established the linkage between the amount of advertising for these products and the absence of critical editorial content in media dependent upon those ads (Tankard and Pierce 1982; Weis and Burke 1986). Magazine publishing, an area where African Americans have made significant progress in recent years, is heavily dependent upon tobacco advertising, and these publishers are therefore most susceptible to editorial pressure. Activist pressures from Mothers Against Drunk Driving (MADD), the American Medical Association (AMA), and other groups to reduce or eliminate the

470 MEDIA, COMMUNICATIONS, AND CULTURE

promotion of cigarettes and alcohol from mainstream media will unquestionably increase efforts to market to the dependent black press.

POLICY OPTIONS

The question, "What is to be done?" has been asked before. The kinds of answers we have been offered vary in part according to our belief that theory provides guidance and that social pressure carries weight within the social system. Giddens (1984) has suggested that we tend to underestimate the influence of social theory because the most influential theories have become incorporated into the ways in which we understand the world. What we now take as common sense denies its historical origins in ideological struggle. The present "gospel" of the competitive marketplace is a fairly recent phenomenon in American social thought. The behavioral revolution in the social and policy sciences did not spring forth unaided from the depths of human consciousness, but was the result of a well-coordinated campaign supported by the Ford Foundation (Seybold 1987). The transformation of regulatory logic from one based on values and a sense of justice to one driven by a concern for economic efficiency finds its roots in foundation-supported research centers, institutes, and special programs in this nation's research universities (Alpert and Markusen 1980; Brown 1988; Domhoff 1979).

This suggests that it is possible to change how the United States comes to understand the plight of the African American. The long-awaited report by the Committee on the Status of Black Americans (Jaynes and Williams 1989) moves in such a direction by its selection of a title—*A Common Destiny: Blacks and American Society.* The title implies and its content supports the conclusion that African Americans are an integral and growing part of the American society, and the growing disparity between blacks and whites and between the poor and relatively well off, spells disaster for an economy already in decline. While this report is not radical, it is clear that a radical *change* in our approach to social policy must be developed and then brought to dominance in the political sphere.

Access

Part of this radical approach must directly and creatively address problems in the political economy of communication and information.

Movement toward a pay-per society guarantees the disenfranchisement and isolation of the poor. The commoditization of information, combined with privitization of libraries and public information services, threatens to accelerate the decay in educational attainments that begins when youngsters leave school. We must insure ready access to information. The ability to pay cannot be the ultimate determinant; access to information must be negotiated as a right, as important as the rights to housing and medical care.

But access to a book you cannot read, a film you cannot understand, or even a news program that goes over your head (Gunter 1987; Gandy and El Waylly 1985; Gandy and Matabane 1989; Kozol 1985; Matabane and Gandy 1988) is no access at all. The goal of access is understanding. Thus, a radical perspective must argue that we do not need equality of access to whatever the market provides, but equality of access to whatever individuals need to be able to construct accurate and useful images of their environment. Current debates over the nature of democracy and the importance of equality for its survival generally conclude that information inequality must not be allowed to continue, unless conditions set by Rawls (1971) are obtained (Guttman 1980; Lakoff 1984). Rawls's *difference principle* argues that inequalities can be maintained only if they benefit those with the least privileges. That is, "When information gaps actually exist, we can only approve of them (as fair) if those in a weaker position are better off than they would have been if others were not communicationally stronger" (Sauerberg 1986). The claim that all benefits ultimately trickle down (Compaine 1988) cannot be allowed to stand. We must demonstrate that the present and increasing inequality of access to useful information in no way advantages the underclass and therefore cannot be tolerated if this democracy is to survive and prosper in the Information Age.

Participation

African Americans will have to participate more actively in the production and distribution of information in the United States. Participation cannot be limited to the assignment of African Americans to the writing of stories for or about African Americans. Participation means sitting in on story conferences, reading and discussing scripts, sorting through wire service reports, press releases, and public relations kits. Participation also means serving as the representative or spokesperson for organizations, even when the issue at hand is not specifically related to African Americans. While membership in a racial or ethnic group is no guarantee that a particular perspective will be developed, the common experience of blackness does guarantee a special awareness and sensitivity to parts of the environment that may be ignored by others. The mere presence of an African American changes the chemistry of any working group, especially those for which integration is a novel experience. But simple ethnic self-identification will not do. We need the participation of specialists. Just as organizations seek journalists who have specialized knowledge in economics or the health sciences to improve their coverage of health policy debates, we must begin to cultivate the demand for communicators who are specialists in the coverage of black America, specialists who participate actively in revealing the linkages between the status of African Americans and the health of the U.S. economy.

Ownership

African American ownership of media outlets does not guarantee that information inequality is reduced. Some have argued that expecting minority owners to provide special services to their communities is to guarantee their failure as broadcasters. "That is, by inadvertently placing expectations of greater social responsibility on minority station owners than on other owners, the FCC may make minority station owners appear to have failed in the public eye by merely performing up to present industry standards" (Schement and Singleton 1981, 82). Fife (1986) suggests that there are at least three different strategies that minority broadcasters take that reflect the nature of the communities they have chosen to serve: *targeting*, or direct service to the African American community; *mainstreaming*, where minority service is integrated into a general interest program schedule; and *nonrepresentative service*, where the media outlet serves a community in which African Americans are not a significant presence. This third circumstance describes ownership where the private goals of profit and growth are dominant and any reduction in information inequality is an unintended side benefit.

While there may be spillover benefits from the growth in the number of African American information entrepreneurs, unless that growth is accompanied by a commitment to improve the quality of life for African Americans in general, it is no more useful than, say, the growth in the number of theater screens owned by Canadian multinationals. Black owners of information businesses that serve largely nonblack clients can still make an impact on African America. Black people can be trained and put to work, even if that means recruiting, transporting, and subsidizing the housing of employees brought to Bangor, Maine. Our efforts to change public policy must be willing to take the stand that minority ownership, per se, is not enough. The black middle class is "doing very well, thank you" (Landry 1987). It has begun to close the gap with whites in terms of unearned income in recent years, making important gains in the amount of revenue received from property (Jaynes and Williams 1989). But, at the same time, the black middle class has become increasingly isolated from those African Americans who remain trapped in the inner-city ghetto. Bridging this communications gap remains a critical problem.

Control

Murdock (1982) discusses the distinction between ownership and control in mass media industries. Two kinds of control are important: (a) allocative control, which determines the overall goals and policies of the organization; and (b) operational control, which is confined to decisions about "the effective use of resources already allocated and the implementation of policies already decided at the allocative level" (p. 122). Murdock's concern with the distinction was offered in response to the claim that changes in the nature of media organizations had removed control from the hands of individual capitalists and located it within the realm of a managerial elite no longer driven by the same goals and motives of capitalism.

African Americans are poorly represented among the owners of communications firms. Many entrepreneurs have seen their ownership positions diluted as they sought financing for expansion of their business. Allocative control is elusive, and once gained, is hard to maintain in the face of historic tendencies toward concentration and consolidation. It is not at all clear that operational control, exercised by midlevel managers, is sufficient to make a measurable difference in business practices as they apply to African Americans. Cantor (1987) continues to ask the question, "Will more women make a difference?" She suggests that despite the increase in women's employment, including their visibility in management, researchers have not provided sufficient data to conclude that presence influences performance. The same questions must be asked of the African American experience in management. Does the process of selection and socialization that takes place as individuals move up the corporate ladder diminish their commitment and capacity to respond to the crisis in black America? Or is the nature of the modern organization such that one or two individuals have only a limited possibility of influencing the corporate culture and its commitment to social goals?

FINANCIAL OPTIONS

It is clear that a sense of commitment, obligation, and duty to the organization and the consumer provides a spur to productivity that dollars alone cannot provide. Even though American workers are among the best paid in the world, they have lost a sense of pride and personal investment in the products of their labor. The declining quality of American goods and services reflects that loss. However, until such time as we are able to increase our sense of community we will have to continue to use economic incentives to insure that individuals "do the right thing." Vigilance will have to be maintained to see that greed and corruption do not continue to distort programs established for positive social purposes. Resource controllers within the public and private sectors will need to develop programs of grants, subsidies, and loans that reinforce the investment of time and energy in generating solutions to the problems of black America. The following suggestions are examples of federal policies that ultimately represent increases in the budget, or the budget deficit, and thus must be justified in terms of expected long-term contribution to the economy.

Grants

Recent controversies over the provision of federal grants to artists who have produced "blasphemous" or distasteful works suggest that political and ideological struggles over the assignment of grants to support a New America's (Taylor 1989) project may be difficult to avoid. Although we may not read about them in the press, there are also bound to be similar struggles within corporations and private foundations. But grants provide an explicit affirmative response to initiatives directed at the survival of African Americans. The mere announcement that such a program exists provides legitimation for the concern. A program of grants validates scholarly pursuit of areas that might have previously been viewed as unproductive and unlikely to contribute to the careers of academics. Such a program could support the creation of institutes, research centers, special seminars, and graduate programs focused on aspects of the problem of national integration. Grants may also be offered in the form of prizes for work contributing to the national effort.

Hall and Preston (1988) have written convincingly on the place of innovation in the stimulation of economic growth. Innovation differs from simple invention in that it involves the identification and demonstration of applications of new technologies. While small business will increasingly be barred from playing a significant role in the development of high technology systems, the capital requirements for the development of applications within the information and service sectors of the economy are less constraining. Thus, there should be a willingness to subsidize the pursuit of social applications for existing knowledge rather than focusing on the development of expensive high technology systems in areas with only minimal evidence of consumer demand. Decisions to invest in the information sector must be based on full understanding of the reasons why venture capitalists have not already provided a basis for development of the industry.

Subsidies

Subsidies reduce the cost of research and development efforts in areas that do not seem to be immediately profitable, or even to have immediate commercial application. Subsidies to a single organization frequently distribute benefits throughout the economy because the industry in question is central to the rest of the economy. The housing industry, for example, is closely linked to other domestic sources of supply, but nowhere near as much as is the automobile industry in the United States. The Congressional Task Force on the Future of African Americans (1988) suggested that the U.S. "bail-out" of Chrysler was extremely important to African Americans because of the number of black people who were employed by this single firm. The French experiment with Minitel has led some to believe that an initial investment in the development of a technical infrastructure could provide an important stimulus for the development of an information services industry (Aronson and Cowhey 1988; Voge 1986).

It should be possible to develop an input-output analysis of national and local communications and information-intensive industries to evaluate the consequences of subsidizing their location in the nation's urban centers. Proposals might be evaluated on the basis of their backward linkages to the resources that are or might easily become available in our urban centers.

Subsidies should not become dependencies. While there is always a danger that social programs, like network television series, might be killed before they are given a chance to succeed, it will be necessary to avoid pressures to continue providing support to projects that show little promise of reaching their goals or even of generating secondary benefits throughout the local economy.

Discounts

Discounts are like subsidies, but are tied more closely to the logic of the business world. We have accepted as legitimate the idea of providing discounts to large-volume buyers. The transaction costs of supplying a few large lots are frequently lower, and the discount reflects a sharing of the economies of scale. Discounts may also be used as instruments of social policy. Discounts may be treated as earned benefits. Students may earn discounts for school supplies through good performance or even regular attendance in school. The discount used in this way reinforces behavior, distributes resources, and targets sales of particular products, brands, or vendors. Vendors may qualify to participate in a discount program through commitment to locate their operation in a targeted community, to train and employ residents, and to buy resources from other participating suppliers. Clearly, this kind of program becomes a visible target for complaints by any vendors who believe they are disadvantaged by the program. It is important, therefore, that all have an "equal opportunity" to qualify.

Credits

Tax credits are familiar and quite "legitimate" instruments of public policy. Tax credits are also subsidies in the sense that they lower the cost of acquiring the goods and services favored as qualifying. Tax credits have been successful in generating sales of broadcasting facilities to minorities (Wimmer 1988). The record in this area is clearly one of success, with the only cautions being the potential of inflating the price of facilities, or of creating incentives to form organizations with fictitious minority ownership or control. Sensitivity analyses should be performed to determine the extent of the credit necessary to elicit the desired behavior.

Wimmer (1988, 26) has suggested the possibility of establishing a category of "public interest" tax credits: "Public interest tax incentives could be devised in a parallel manner to the tax certificate policy in the Internal Revenue Code, and could provide deductions or credits to broadcast licensees in direct proportion to the amount of minority-oriented programming produced or the amount of access granted to minority groups."

Tax credits might be especially useful in inducing advertisers to purchase time or space in minority media. As with credits for investing in capital equipment, enjoyed in addition to the normal tax deductions for business expenses, such credits could be seen as rewards for investment in the independence of African American editors no longer solely dependent upon alcohol or tobacco ads. The credits should not be large enough to cause firms to buy time indiscriminately. There should be a rational expectation that the ads would increase their sales in the targeted community.

TRANSITIONAL PHASES—GETTING THERE FROM HERE

We all desire to live in an America where each person has the opportunity and the desire to participate fully and effectively in the economic, social, and political life of their community. That is clearly not the America we live in today. Movement toward a new America will require radical change in the way we organize our lives. This change will, of necessity, involve a transformation in our values and in the ways in which we apprehend the world and our place in it. As Marx wrote, through our actions we change the world, even if the world we create is not the one we designed. We create our futures out of the residue of our pasts. We must act, even though we cannot be sure that we will reach our goals as we understand them today. The recommendations we make must be based on a vision of a better future. We cannot be sure of our plans because we cannot predict how others with different visions will react, and we may not have the power to help them see it our way. But we can be sure that the idea of the new America we share will reflect the changes we must make in our systems of education, in our systems of public communication, and in the organization of our productive resources.

Education

With regard to education, it is clear that the population of educationally disadvantaged individuals is growing rapidly both in number and in the extent of their deficiencies. At the same time, the labor market is demanding increasingly high levels of interpretative, expressive, and computational skill. Levin (1985) suggests that policies that seek to increase the time in school and the number of requirements for graduation without at the same time changing the nature of the educational experience will only exacerbate the problem, providing increasing pressures on students to drop out. The returns on investments in education are quite high, yet under times of economic stress, American society has refused to make those investments in its black citizens. Pipelines previously opened have begun to close, and African Americans have turned away from higher education (Jaynes and Williams 1989).

Education is a communications function. It depends upon information technology for its success. Technology is not merely the hardware of computers and the software of drill and practice programs. Technology involves the reliable integration of the components of success into a reproducible format for sharing. We know how to teach. The educational literature is filled with individual examples of success in reaching the hard to reach. In every success story, we find evidence that communication has taken place within the context of a community of interest. Teachers and students felt a common bond and a mutual benefit in the advancement of every member of that community.

Educational attainment is more than test scores. A truly functional educational experience produces a greater array of necessary competencies than just literacy and numeracy. Cooperation, rather than individualistic competition, produces more than elevated test scores. It produces a sense of identity, commitment, and community hard to find outside the youth gangs that roam the halls and the streets around our city schools. The movement toward individualized instruction, each student with his or her own microterminal, might be a source of demand for the output of our faltering electronics industry, but it cannot serve the complex educational needs of African American youth. Students need to learn as part of a team. They need to learn to care, and they need to learn from, and contribute to, the learning of others for whom they care.

The one-room classrooms of rural America generated fine basic education at the same time that they cemented community ties. We might consider creating contemporary analogues of the one-room school, extended one step further. Integrating learning with economically productive activities has tremendous potential for individual and community benefit. If we are to succeed in attracting communications-related industries to the central cities, education and employment must be combined. Periods of intensive formal instruction may be scheduled in between cycles of work for members of production teams. Scheduling cycles would facilitate the sharing of teacher-specialists who would move throughout the day to different work sites around the city. The possibility that students would work side by side with their older siblings or parents in a publishing, editing, or data processing facility would increase the likelihood that any progress would be rewarded and encouraged. While such facilities might not match the production rates of highly automated processing centers, the educational and social learning benefits would far exceed the net costs of their production.

Public Relations

In the absence of a cultural revolution led by Jesse Jackson or some equally charismatic leader, achieving our goals will require a massive, well-financed, tightly coordinated public relations campaign. We are seeking to create a mass mobilization of this nation's collective economic and human resources in a movement to transform the national malaise into a spirit of optimism, shared vision, and commitment to the survival of the nation. The knowledge, the skill, and the resources necessary to develop such a campaign already exist in good measure. They have been mobilized repeatedly on behalf of particular corporate and government interests, often to set aside what we have come to understand as the *public* interest (Adams and Brock 1986; Domhoff 1979; Gandy, 1982, 1992; Levitan and Cooper 1984; Steinberg 1975). For example, in Great Britain, the Thatcher government had gone further than most in utilizing marketing and public relations to effect a transformation in British social consciousness while the administration worked to dismantle much of the infrastructure of the British welfare state. Recent reports (Lohr 1989) indicate that the British government is the world's third largest advertiser, behind Unilever and Procter & Gamble. The largest campaigns have been developed to support a massive privitization effort that has witnessed the sale of government-run public utilities, such as telecommunications, air travel, and gas.

Part of the goal of the public relations effort will be to bring about a change in the way that citizens frame policy questions. This goal legitimizes taxation to finance investments in black America. Khaneman and Tversky (1986) have demonstrated that framing changes peoples' preferences for objectively equal policy outcomes. Where a tax is objectionable, a fee is a reasonable and just charge for individual or collective benefits received.

A massive public relations campaign might involve African American and other youngsters at all levels of the pipeline in working on a common project (Trayes 1990). Just as youngsters are involved in producing posters for a variety of health and public safety campaigns, a "New America" campaign could involve them in writing stories, songs, plays, advertisements, press releases, and radio scripts. This experience may well turn out to be important in some youngsters' decisions to pursue a career in communications.

Such African Americans as Oprah Winfrey and Eddie Murphy, who have achieved visibility in mainstream American culture, must be induced to offer testimonials for the goals and projects of a "New America" campaign in the same way they lend their fame and features to the marketing of shoes, cereals, and soft drinks. Just as a "spiral of silence" (Noelle-Neumann, cited in McQuail 1983, 201–2) may have served to quiet the voices of responsible liberalism in the wake of the Reagan revolution (Paletz and Entman 1981, ch. 12), in the times of President Clinton's calls for change a swelling chorus of voices must rise to express support for this movement toward a new America. The mass media must come to depend upon a pool of "experts" who are knowledgeable of and competent to speak about his new groundswell of progressive ideas.

Gerbner (1988, 1990) has identified television as the dominant source for the cultivation of social perceptions. Television's coherent system of messages teaches its audiences about what exists in the world, whether it is good or bad, and how it is related to other things that matter. Others who share Gerbner's belief in the power of television have also noted that organized interests have the power to influence the kinds of stories that television tells (Gandy 1982, 1992) and the kinds of impressions its images form. Just as the American Medical Association (AMA) has influenced how doctors were presented on television (Turow 1989), we must begin to find ways, beyond the threats of boycotts and demonstrations, to shape television's window on our world. Turow (p. 275) suggests that the efforts of the AMA "involved encouraging fictional images along lines that hyped high-tech, specialty-oriented, high-cost care." Our efforts must encourage images that promote responsible, cooperative, generous, and above all, optimistic perspectives on the future role of African Americans.

Organization

Clearly we must become organized. We do not need, and should not support, the development of a top-heavy, centralized panel of experts. This must be a grassroots movement for it to work. While there is a role for leadership and support, the participation of every American must eventually be won and welcomed. While this revolution might be televised, it cannot be a Hollywood, New York, or Washington, DC, production. Task forces must be developed in every identifiable community. Existing organizations are a good place to start. This cannot and should not be a clandestine movement. The hidden media may work well in achieving short term goals (Armstrong 1988), but the price we pay in alienation and mistrust is too high. Our goals are honorable. There is nothing to hide.

This does not mean there will not be opposition. When scarce resources are redirected, someone must suffer a loss. Powerful interests will resist with all the power and creativity that money can buy. But this *is* a time of change. As the 1992 presidential election demonstrated, the desire for change is strong, and we must believe that at some level, and one well within the reach of our voices, the hearts and minds of the American people are still open. And if there is strong, credible leadership able to point the way, I believe they are more than ready to "do the right thing."

REFERENCES

Adams, W., and J. Brock. 1986. *The bigness complex*. New York: Pantheon.

Alpert, I., and A. Markusen. 1980. Think tanks and capitalist policy. In *Power structure research*, ed. G. Domhoff. Beverly Hills, CA: Sage.

Altman, D., M. Slater, C. Albright, and N. Maccoby. 1989. How an unhealthy product is sold: Cigarette advertising in magazines, 1960–1985. *Journal of Communication* 37 (4): 95–106.

Anderson, J. 1989. Some preliminary thoughts on the elaboration of audiences. Paper delivered at the conference of the Association for the Education of Journalism and Mass Communication, August, Washington, DC. Photocopy.

Armstrong, R. 1988. *The last hurrah: The communications revolution in American politics*. New York: William Morrow.

Aronson, J., and P. Cowhey. 1988. *When countries talk: International trade in telecommunications services*. Washington, DC: American Enterprise Institute.

Aufderheide, P. 1987. Universal service: Telephone policy in the public interest. *Journal of Communication,* 3 (1): 81–96.

Baer, W. 1985. Information technology comes home. *Telecommunications policy* (March): 3–22.

Baldwin, T., and M. Wirth. 1989. Public policy implications of the transition to a subscription-based economic structure for the television industry. Paper presented at the conference of the Association for Education in Journalism and Mass Communication, August, Washington, DC.

Barwise, P., and A. Ehrenberg. 1989. *Television and its audience*. Newbury Park, CA: Sage.

Bates, B. 1988. Information as an economic good: Sources of individual and social value. In *The political economy of information,* ed. V. Mosco and J. Wasko. Madison: University of Wisconsin Press.

Bell, D. 1973. *The coming of post-industrial society*. New York: Basic Books.

Beniger, J. 1986. *The control revolution: Technological and economic origins of the information society*. Cambridge, MA: Harvard University Press.

Blumler, J. 1988. *The role of public policy in the new television marketplace*. Washington, DC: Benton Foundation.

Boswell, T., and A. Bergeson, eds. 1987. *America's changing role in the world-system*. New York: Praeger.

Born, R., ed. 1987. *Artificial intelligence: The case against*. New York: St. Martin's Press.

Brown, D. 1988. Reshaping the debate over broadcast regulation in the United States. Paper presented to the Working Group on Communication Policy at the 16th Conference and General Assembly of the International Association for Mass Communication Research July, Barcelona, Spain. Photocopy.

Cantor, M. 1987. Women and diversity. Report to the Benton Foundation, May, Washington, DC. Photocopy.

Clayton, C. 1989. *We can* educate all our children. *The Nation* (24/31 July): 132–35.

Compaine, B. 1988. Information gaps: Myth or reality? In *Issues in new information technology,* ed. B. Compaine. Norwood, NJ: Ablex.

Congressional Task Force on the Future of African-Americans. 1988. *The future of African-Americans to the year 2000*. Washington, DC.

Davidson, W. 1984. *The amazing race. Winning the technorivalry with Japan*. New York: John Wiley.

Davis, R. 1987. Television commercials and the management of spoiled identity. *The Western Journal of Black Studies* 11 (2): 59–63.

Dizard, W. 1985. *The coming information age*. New York: Longman.

Domhoff, G. 1979. *The powers that be: Processes of ruling class domination in America*. New York: Vintage.

Donner, F. 1980. *The age of surveillance: The aims and methods of America's political intelligence*. New York: Alfred A. Knopf.

Etzioni, A. 1988. *The moral dimension: Toward a new economics*. New York: Free Press.

Fife, M. 1986. The impact of minority ownership on minority images in local news. In *Communications: A key to economic and political change*, ed. O. Gandy. Washington, DC: Howard University, Center for Communications Research.

Flaherty, D. 1988. The emergence of surveillance societies in the western world: Toward the year 2000. *Government Information Quarterly* 5 (4): 377–87.

Galernter D. 1987. Programming for advanced computing. *Scientific American,* 257 (October): 90–115.

————. 1989. The metamorphosis of information management. *Scientific American* 261 (August): 66–73.

Gandy, O. 1982. *Beyond agenda setting: Information subsidies and public policy*. Norwood, NJ: Ablex.

————. 1989. The surveillance society: Information technology and bureaucratic social control. *Journal of Communication* 39 (Summer): 61–76.

————. 1990. Caller identification: The two-edged sword. In *Pacific telecommunications: Weaving the technological and social fabric,* ed. D. Wedemeyer and M. Lofstrom. Honolulu, HI: Pacific Telecommunications Council.

————. 1992. Public relations and public policy: The Structuration of dominance in the information age. In *Rhetorical and critical approaches to public relations,* ed. E. Toth and R. Heath. Hillsdale, NJ: Lawrence Erlbaum.

————. 1993. *The panoptic sort: A political economy of personal information*. Bouldar, CO: Westview.

Gandy, O., and M. El Waylly. 1985. The knowledge gap and foreign affairs: The Palestinian-Israeli conflict. *Journalism Quarterly* 62 (4): 777–83.

Gandy, O., and P. Matabane. 1989. Television and social perceptions among African-Americans and Hispanics. In *Handbook of interna-*

tional and intercultural communication, eds. M. Asante and W. Gudykunst. Newbury Park, CA: Sage.

Gandy, O., and C. Simmons. 1986. Technology, privacy, and the democratic process. *Critical Studies in Mass Communication* 3:155–68.

Gerbner, G. 1988. *Violence and terror in the mass media*. Reports and Papers in Mass Communication No. 102. Paris: Unesco.

———. 1990. Epilogue: Advancing on the path of righteousness (maybe). In *Cultivation analysis: New directions in media effects research*, eds. N. Signorielli and M. Morgan. Beverly Hills, CA: Sage.

Giddens, A. 1984. *The constitution of society: Outline of a theory of structuration*. Cambridge, UK: Polity Press.

Gitlin, T. 1985. *Inside prime time*. New York: Pantheon.

Guback, T. 1987. The evolution of the motion picture theatre business in the 1980s. *Journal of Communication* 37 (2): 60–77.

Guttman, A. 1980. *Liberal equality*. Cambridge: Cambridge University Press.

Gunter, B. 1987. *Poor reception: Misunderstanding and forgetting broadcast news*. Hillsdale, NJ: Lawrence Erlbaum.

Hall, P., and P. Preston. 1988. *The carrier wave: New information technology and the geography of innovation, 1846–2003*. London: Unwin Hyman.

Hamelink, C. 1988. *The technology gamble: Informatics and public policy; A study of technology choice*. Norwood, NJ: Ablex.

Hepworth, M., and K. Robins. 1988. Whose information society? A view from the periphery. *Media, Culture and Society* 10:323–43.

Hollist, W., and J. Rosenau, eds. 1981. *World system structure: Continuity and change*. Beverly Hills, CA: Sage.

Jaynes, G., and R. Williams, eds. 1989. *A common destiny: Blacks and American society*. Washington, DC: National Academy Press.

Jonscher, C. 1983. Information resources and economic productivity. *Information Economics and Policy* 1:13–35.

Kahn, R. 1987. Networking for advanced computing. *Scientific American* 257 (4): 136–43.

Kahneman, D., and A. Tversky. 1986. Choices, values and frames. In *Behavioral and social science: Fifty years of discovery*, eds. N. Smelser and D. Gerstein. Washington, DC: National Academy Press.

Kasarda, J. 1989. Urban industrial transition and the underclass. *The Annals of the American Academy of Political and Social Science* 501:26–47.

Katz, R. 1987. Measurement and cross-national comparisons of the information workforce. *The Information Society* 4 (4): 231–77.

Kneale, D. 1989. Reshaping the irrational tv-pilot game. *The Wall Street Journal*, 14 April: B1.

Kozol, J. 1985. *Illiterate America*. Garden City, NY: Doubleday.

Landry, B. 1987. The new black middle class (part I). *Focus* (September): 5–7.

Lakoff, S. 1964. *Equality in political philosophy*. Boston: Beacon.

Levin, H. 1985. The educationally disadvantaged: A national crisis. Report No. 85-B1. Standford, CA: Institute for Research on Educational Finance and Governance.

Levitan, S., and M. Cooper. 1984. *Business lobbies: The public good and the bottom line*. Baltimore: Johns Hopkins University Press.

Lohr, S. 1989. Major British advertiser: Government. *New York Times,* May 23: D1.

Machlup, F. 1962. *The production and distribution of knowledge in the United States*. Princeton, NJ: Princeton University Press.

Marx, G. 1988. *Undercover: Police surveillance in America*. Berkeley: University of California Press.

Marx. K. 1906. *Capital: A critique of political economy*. Ed. F. Engels. New York: Modern Library.

———. 1973. *Grundrisse*. New York: Vintage.

Matabane, P., and O. Gandy. 1988. Through the prism of race and controversy: Did viewers learn anything from *"The Africans"*? *Journal of Black Studies* 19 (September): 3–16.

McQuail, D. 1983. *Mass communication theory: An introduction*. London: Sage.

Meehan, E. 1988. Technical capacity versus corporate imperatives: Toward a political economy of cable television and information diversity. In *The political economy of information*, eds. V. Mosco and J. Wasko. Madison: University of Wisconsin Press.

Morris, N., and M. Miller. 1987. Prediction of dangerousness in the criminal law. *National Institute of Justice, Research in Brief*.

Mosco, V. 1988. Telecommunications and social policy: Deja vu all over again? Paper presented at the Conference Commemorating the

150th Anniversary of the Telegraph, June, Princeton, NJ. Photocopy.

———. 1989. *The pay-per society*. Norwood, NJ: Ablex.

Mosco, V., and J. Wasko, eds. 1988. *The political economy of information*. Madison: University of Wisconsin Press.

Mulgan, G. J. 1991. *Communication and control: Networks and the new economies of communication*. New York: Guilford.

Murdock, G. 1982. Large corporations and the control of communications industries. In *Culture, society and the media*, eds. M. Gurevitch et al. London: Metheun.

Novek, E., N. Sinha, and O. Gandy. 1990. The value of your name. *Media, Culture and Society* 12: 525–43.

Owen, B., and S. Wildman. 1992. *Video economics*. Cambridge, MA: Harvard University Press.

Pacific Bell. 1988. *Pacific Bell's response to the Intelligent Network Taskforce report*. Sacramento, CA: Author.

Paletz, D., and D. Entman. 1981. *Media power politics*. New York: Free Press.

Peled, A. 1987. The next computer revolution. *Scientific American* 257 (4): 56–65.

Pepper, R. 1988. *Through the looking glass: Integrated broadband networks, regulatory policy and institutional change*. OPP Working Paper Series No. 24. Washington, DC: Federal Communications Commission, November.

Porat, M. 1976. *The information economy*. Stanford, CA: Stanford University.

Rawls, J. 1971. *A theory of justice*. Oxford: Oxford University Press.

Robins, K., and F. Webster. 1988. Cybernetic capitalism: Information technology and everyday life. In *The political economy of information*, eds. V. Mosco and J. Wasko. Madison: University of Wisconsin Press.

Roszak, T., 1986. *The cult of information*. New York: Pantheon.

Rule, J., and P. Attewell. 1989. What do computers do? *Social Problems* 36 (3): 225–41.

Salvaggio, J. 1987. Projecting a positive image of the information society. In *The ideology of the information age*, eds. J. Slack and F. Fejes. Norwood, NJ: Ablex.

Sauerberg, S. 1986. Democracy and information gaps. Paper

presented to the conference of the International Association for Mass Communications Research, August, New Delhi. Mimeograph.

Schement, J., and L. Singleton. 1981. The onus of minority ownership: FCC policy and Spanish-language radio. *Journal of Communication* 31 (2): 78–83.

Schiller, D. 1988. How to think about information. In *The political economy of information,* eds. V. Mosco and J. Wasko. Madison: University of Wisconsin Press.

Schiller, A., and H. Schiller. 1986. Commercializing information. *The Nation* (4 October): 306–9.

Schiller, H., and A. Schiller. 1988. Libraries, public access to information and commerce. In *The political economy of information,* eds. V. Mosco and J. Wasko. Madison: University of Wisconsin Press.

Schoppers, M. 1986. A perspective on artificial intelligence in society. *Communication* 9:195–227.

Seybold, P. 1987. The Ford Foundation and the transformation of political science. In *The structure of power in America,* ed. M. Schwartz. News York: Holmes and Meier.

Shoemaker, P., S. Reese, and W. Danielsen. 1985. *Media in ethnic context: Communications and language in Texas.* Austin: University of Texas.

Signorielli, N., and M. Morgan, eds. 1990. *Cultivation analysis: New directions in media effects research.* Newbury Park, CA: Sage.

Steinberg, C. 1975. *The creation of consent.* New York: Hastings House.

Stone, V. 1988. Trends in the status of minorities and women in broadcast news. *Journalism Quarterly* 65 (2): 288–93.

Tankard, J., and K. Pierce. 1982. Alcohol advertising and magazine editorial content. *Journalism Quarterly* 59 (2): 302–5.

Taylor, O. 1989. The education of journalists and mass communicators for the 21st century: A cultural perspective. Keynote speech, teaching standards plenary, Association for Educational in Journalism and Mass Communications, August, Washington, DC. Photocopy.

Trayes, E. 1990. Minorities and mass media careers: Pipeline problems of the 1980s. In *Minorities and Communications,* eds. C.

Stroman and M. Williams. Washington, DC: Howard University Center for Communications Research.

Turow, J. 1989. *Playing doctor: Television, storytelling, and medical power*. New York: Oxford University Press.

U.S. Congress, Office of Technology Assessment. 1986. *Electronic records systems and individual privacy* (OTA-CIT-296). Washington, DC: U.S. Government Printing Office, June.

————. 1990. *Critical connections: Communication for the future* (OTA-CIT-407). Washington, DC: U.S. Government Printing Office.

Voge, J. 1986. A survey of French regulatory policy. In *Marketplace for Telecommunications*, ed. M. Snow. New York: Longman.

Wacquant, L., and W. Wilson. 1989. The cost of racial and class exclusion in the inner city. *The Annals of the American Academy of Political and Social Science* 501:8–25.

Webster, J. 1986. Audience behavior in the new media environment. *Journal of Communication* 36 (3): 77–91.

Weis, W., and C. Burke. 1986. Media content and tobacco advertising: An unhealthy addiction. *Journal of Communication* 36 (4): 59–69.

Wildman, S., and S. Siwek. 1988. *International trade in films and television programs*. Washington, DC: American Enterprise Institute.

Wilson, C., and F. Gutiérrez. 1985. *Minorities and media: Diversity and the end of mass communication*. Beverly Hills: Sage.

Wilson, K. 1988. *Technologies of control: The new interactive media for the home*. Madison: University of Wisconsin Press.

Wimmer, K. 1988. Deregulation and the future of pluralism in the mass media: The prospects for positive policy reform. *Mass Comm Review* 15: 20–31.

World Almanac. 1989. *The world almanac and book of facts, 1989*. New York: Author.

Yearly, S. 1988. *Science, technology and social change*. London: Unwin Hyman.

24 Independent African American Cinema: The Creation of an Alternative Cultural Infrastructure

HAILE GERIMA

U p to the present, most mainstream, Hollywood producers have rejected those truly serious motion picture ideas proposed to them by African Americans. By and large, if an African American script is outside of the comedic, buffoonish expectations of dominant society, it will be rejected by the Hollywood film industry. As a result, African Americans throughout the history of cinema have attempted, as independent producers operating outside of the establishment, to organize a film movement capable of responding to the cultural demands of their people.

I posit that, instead of spending our money, time, and energy trying to correct other people's conceptions of us, we should instead spend it taking charge of our own notions of ourselves. It is through such a self-participatory process, engaging all aspects of society, that internal transformation of a culture takes place. People of African descent in America, in Africa, and throughout the diaspora have diverse cultures, each with its own subjective and objective reality. Each people must invent, out of its own reality, a culturally appropriate cinema visionary to respond to that people's need for self-defined images. For each people, cultural and countercultural movements will then emerge.

INDEPENDENT CINEMA

When we look at the history of cinema in the United States, we search for independent traditions of African

American people that contemporary filmmakers may draw lessons from. However imperfect, the most significant manifestation of independent African American cinema took place in the 1920s, 1930s, and 1940s, during the time of the early independent film pioneers. George Foster, Oscar Micheaux, Noble Johnson, and others all made magnificent sacrifices to engrave into history universal, enduring aspects of the African race and its notion of its own humanity. Their work will continue to be studied throughout the world because buried in the celluloid and emulsion is the testimony of a people. The dramatized psychological scarification and sociological, economic, and cultural alienation will be seen as the forerunners in the continual struggle for the redemption of cinema, for the true democratization of the screen for and by all people.

True, their films were imperfect. They were entitled to that perfection as a logical consequence of their reality. It emanated from the absence of finance, their distance from the banks that controlled film production capital. When compared to those who abandoned the historic task of inventing a people's own image, these early relentless pioneers stand forth as giants. In the end, they may be seen as grappling with universal issues of human community. They attempted to define the shape of the African American within the cinematic landscape. In their themes of love and loneliness, in their adopted reality of miscegenation, of light skin and dark skin, they reflected the human dimensions of their era. We have much to learn from them. We must study their experience as we attempt today to establish our own independent system of film production, distribution, and exhibition.

As we enter the twenty-first century, independent, low- and medium-budget cinematic expression will be our best hope. From past independent filmmakers we may learn a great deal for the future. Most especially, we will learn that the struggle to make our own image must be fiercely fought, without compromise. African Americans must today declare, as in the past, our right to make our own image, to set our own lights, to invent and tell our own story. We must put our own resources at the disposal of this declaration.

As African Americans, we must integrate our notion of culture into our everyday activity. We should never separate our biological needs for food and shelter from our need for culture. These needs are in fact inseparable, and as our best artists (filmmakers, writers, poets, and others) explore them, their work nurtures our consciousness and tells us who we are and where we wish to be. We cannot achieve the promise of the twenty-first century without attempting to fully integrate our culture with the rest of our needs. When we look back to Africa, what makes us proud? It is the culture and literature of the precolonial nations in every part of Africa, north to south, east to west, from Zimbabwe to Ethiopia to Benin. Our cultural heritage has been the source of our strength for survival throughout the world. For, deep down, the Greco-Roman cultural descendants, from Aristotle, Caesar, and Napoleon all the way to Stanley and Livingstone, knew that our people are the descendants of many higher, proud cultures. This knowledge has lived coded in our marrow and has fueled our resistance and preserved our humanity under the most awful, obscene circumstances.

Since the coming of Europe into Africa, Europeans erected statues of their kings and queens and built roads only to exploit African resources. They transplanted and scattered our people throughout the Americas. But, whatever else they did, they did not build the pyramids. They did not erect the Axumit kingdom in Ethiopia or the kingdom of Zimbabwe. Our culture is the testimony of our people, speaking loud and clear. This is why it is crucial that we teach the importance of culture throughout the African American community. It is the footprint of a people, showing where they were, who they are, and where they are going. If we do not inculcate this understanding into the minds of our people, the fullness of our cultural heritage will be unknown, all but nonexistent, not only in motion picture history, but in the larger human history as well.

FILM CULTURE

The countercultural activity of the African and the African American onscreen will be one of the most important activities in the process of giving African cultures their rightful place in world history. It is crucial that we weave our human tapestry into the motion picture fabric of twenty-first century global culture. The battle for control of our image will be waged more fiercely with the continuing growth and domination of television and video technology. We must win this battle and control the multifaceted aspects of our image. We can continue in our day-to-day human lives to be doctors and lawyers, lovers and haters, but if we fail to establish our image through the mass media our cultural identity will perish, a victim of this very media.

It follows that we must create a holistic cinematic approach that will make the masses of our people fully aware of the seriousness of motion pictures and television and their impact on people worldwide. We must struggle for a higher cultural standard. We must respect our people, and through the power of our control over our own image, win the ungrudging respect of all other peoples.

This holistic approach must analyze the way we perceive and express ourselves, the way we conceive content and form. Such understanding must provide the foundation for our cinematic ideas, themes, and scripts. We must promote pride and avoid paternalism. We have a profound, longstanding cultural tradition as storytellers and listeners; we have a theatre of mutual exchange of intellectual and emotional magnitude. The spiritual depth of our music equals or exceeds that of any other culture in the world. We must use this tradition and this theatre to tell our own story in our own way. It will be revolutionary to confront our people—to challenge them to see, to hear in silence and respect, to react and reflect, to cry and laugh, and, if necessary, to act.

Culture is constantly built and transformed through the accountability of both storyteller and listener. We must destroy the current theatre of tension, created because we are intimidated and apprehensive. We enter the cinema today with a deeper subtext of anxiety and nervousness, for we have been more loyal to motion pictures than has any other race. We have lined up in the cold, in the snow (the worst weather), to give our money loyally, knowing deep down that we will not see ourselves or our humanity. As a result, we have developed defensive psychological responses that hide our true human responses. We hide, we grunt, we shout, we nervously laugh; for more than anyone, we are scared of the true, ignored part of us contained within our bodies. Like many Third World people, in the dark we close our eyes and role play. In the theater, we fantasize the illusion of white, European America's notion of life and human standards (love, life, sex, violence, war, and the rest) propagated by the gamut of this entertainment world. This abnormal relationship creates a theatre of tension and interdependency. This neurotic tension continues to alienate and deform our sense of reality and, consciously or unconsciously, its manifestations are apparent in our daily social interactions.

This deeply rooted psychological crisis, manifested in hatred and violence toward each other, is provoked by mirroring, contradictory human images: one real and one false. The false, devalued image of our people from the screen wins in the end and lives to disfigure our real selves.

Our countercultural cinematic expression has within it the power to break these barriers and restore the rightful place of the true African image on the screen. When movies actually reflect the multiple human dimensions of the African people, as a very few do now, our cinema will normalize and present for public consumption true, fully dimensional portraits. This, in turn, will invoke logical human responses to our onscreen image that will consequently forge a cinematic language that is dynamic, harmonious, and unique, and at the same time, universally accessible.

African American cinema must go beyond the superficial depiction of physical traits with the intention of explaining a given behavior to other people. I call this the cinema of the tour guide. We must not simply show ourselves in terms of how we walk, talk, and curse; that is just recording. It is important to be accurate, but this basic level of representation is a tool, not a goal. Showing superficial aspects of ourselves, regardless of the level and accuracy of detail, is a minute part of the whole language through which we convey the images of our culture and our identity. As individuals, we must prepare for years, mastering scriptwriting, directing, cinematography, and the other cinematic creative processes to arm ourselves with the utmost professional skill so that we may magnify and reveal the soul and essence of our people. Whatever the subject matter, we must develop our characters extensively and refine our command of the manipulation of sight and sound. It requires years of work, as filmmakers and as audiences, to learn to avoid the hasty superficial representation. We must challenge ourselves to push beyond the known limits of the motion picture medium.

I must note here that it is crucial for us to invent a cinematic code that corresponds to the aesthetic and technical standards that Africans and African Americans have developed in the global music industry—

standards that are second to none. However, this code, this language, cannot be invented by filmmakers alone. It requires collaboration from filmmakers, audiences, historians, and critics to create a common cinematic language. This association forces all parties to be involved in and to be accountable to each other at all stages of the endeavor. Such a relationship would transform film, filmmakers, audiences, and critics alike. Masters of their craft would create masterworks; audiences would perceptively view and respond to them; critics would evaluate them with intelligence and compassion. This obviously subverts the existing, conventional relationships of active filmmaker, passive audience, and mercenary critic, all at the disposal of the profit orientation of the merchant class.

As a people, African Americans apply vast energy to many social activities and art forms. We must turn this energy toward mastering, as a people, the basic tools of mass communication and toward establishing our ownership of the system within which we work. We must be willing to place both individual wealth and corporate finances at the service of making and controlling public images of ourselves. We must take full responsibility for creating and maintaining institutions to enable us to own, organize, create, produce, distribute, and exhibit feature films and television programming in the twenty-first century.

CREATING AN INSTITUTION

Individual communities must develop multipurpose media centers capable of catering to the particular local culture. These centers must then link up with each other so that they may exchange information, ideas, tools, financing, and personnel as desired. Such a network may be created and sustained by entrepreneurs working in concert with local artistic, business, and social communities. Those who create it must use vigorously the tools of interpersonal communication—telephones, personal computers, video conferencing, and the rest—to empower their ownership of the means of mass communication. To finance these centers, we must induce local and regional corporations and individuals to invest large amounts of start-up capital. Initial expenses will be high, and the centers will be expensive to run, but they will ultimately more than repay their investors both by operating economically and by becoming local institutions whose worth cannot be measured in dollars.

A truly functional national network of multimedia centers will take time to develop. Each center will start small, and start slowly, and will add components as it becomes a viable, valuable part of its community. Each multimedia center should ultimately include resource, training, preproduction, production, postproduction, and exhibition facilities as basic components. Distribution should be handled as a network service, taking advantage of economies of scale. Centers may allow individuals, businesses, and civic organizations to become charter members, and may develop other alliances as opportunity permits. The following sections elaborate on this concept, describing an idealized individual center.

The Multimedia Center Building

The building(s) housing the multimedia center must meet certain criteria. In addition to the production and exhibition space discussed, it must accommodate administrative offices, classrooms, workshop areas, and equipment storage. While the facilities may initially be small, it must be possible to expand as necessary to accommodate increasing use.

The building must be located as centrally as possible within the community it serves and must be reached easily by both public and private transportation. Parking must be sufficient. The building must be accessible to people with disabilities. It must be well lit and secure. All members of the community should feel comfortable coming to the building day or evening.

Resource Facilities

The resource facilities will provide information and referral services and will include a library. The library will contain works in two primary categories: a) material relating generally to film and television production and b) material relating specifically to African Americans and, by extension, to visual media production by citizens of other cultures who are of African descent. Materials in both categories will include bibliographies, filmographies, periodicals, textbooks, product catalogs, and other practical and theoretical information regarding all aspects of visual media creation and distribution. Publications will be solicited from local, national, and international sources.

When sufficient library resources have been acquired, educators on staff will develop and disseminate needed materials, including teaching notes, publications designed to help audiences develop visual literacy, and operating guidelines for those wishing to use the center. These educators will also create a locally oriented media arts services periodical designed to make the region's resources known and available to all segments of the community. The specific purpose of this handbook will be to enable private, corporate, and government organizations and individuals to have information about and access to all of the region's media services, whether African American-owned or otherwise. Such a work will also, of course, serve the reverse purpose: African American media entrepreneurs will have accurate, timely information concerning potential markets.

Training Facilities

The center will be funded and equipped to provide state-of-the art training to aspiring local filmmakers, teaching everything from backlighting a closeup to managing a cinema multiplex. Training will encompass (a) literacy training and general use information for media consumers and secondary users; (b) production and theory courses providing academic credit to students from area high schools, colleges, and universities; and (c) ongoing, career-oriented professional training. While the first two aspects are indispensable, the third will form the core purpose of the center, bringing aspiring filmmakers together with working professionals, giving these aspirants invaluable experience on actual productions, and making a pool of talent available to the industry. African Americans and members of other American minority groups will have the opportunity to capitalize on their collective knowledge and will acquire the means with which to disseminate their products to wider audiences.

The center will also present to students, professionals, and the public an evolving series of seminars and workshops on all visual media-related subjects. Industry executives, equipment manufacturers, technical researchers, theatre owners, writers, producers, directors, actors, agents, and others will deliver lectures, offer encouragement and advice, and help create invaluable networks of contacts for those working at the local level.

The training facilities themselves will be used simultaneously for education and to produce professional artistic and commercial work. The center will be staffed by talented, experienced professionals committed to bringing their knowledge to all members of the community. Everyone interested will be encouraged to participate and learn. Local professionals and aspirants will be able to rent, for a nominal charge, up-to-date equipment, with which to produce work of exacting standards.

Production Facilities

The center will hire working professionals to serve as resident artists and technicians. These individuals will coordinate the operations of the various departments and will give seminars and teach classes. In addition to pursuing and completing their own projects, they will serve to attract students and other professionals, thus imbuing the center with a vital, enriching versatility.

Production facilities will be funded and maintained by (a) soliciting community investment, (b) adjusting tuition costs for classes and workshops to cover material expenses, and (c) charging users nominal fees for services and equipment. The center will sell film, video- and audiotape, and other production materials at a small markup. Professionals who use the center may receive discounts by training student interns and by patronizing local businesses and media-related services. Available facilities will include complete preproduction, production, and postproduction work areas.

Preproduction

The center will be equipped with computers featuring a complete selection of scripting and production management software. The information resources library will include comprehensive equipment and service price catalogs. The center will rent conference, audition, and rehearsal areas, as well as private office space. In addition, individual and group members may "audition" any of the available production and postproduction services for the purposes of determining budgets and schedules.

Production

The center will provide facilities for both studio and location film and television production. Film, videotape, lighting, sound recording, and other equipment will be of the highest available grade. Sufficient equipment will be purchased to enable teaching all scheduled classes, while outfitting at least one complete feature film production team.

Postproduction

Postproduction facilities primarily involve film, tape, and sound editing, but also include special effects and various technical services. These services can be the most expensive of the entire filmmaking process. The postproduction phase is critically important to independent filmmakers, who often have enough capital to shoot a film but not enough to produce the final viewing print. The center will provide such individuals or groups with editing and other equipment at discount rates in exchange for training interns in editing, special effects, and other postproduction processes. Available equipment will include film, videotape, and audiotape editing tables; a dialogue and sound effects loop recording studio with Foley stage; an animation camera; and a videotape-to-film/film-to-tape transfer system. Users will be able to process their films at discount rates through arrangements the center will make with independent services.

Exhibition Facilities

The multimedia center's system for exhibiting films and video programs will directly affect its ability to achieve its overall goals of raising the local African American community's standards of visual literacy and cultural opportunity. Comfortable, accessible exhibition space will entice community members to participate in the center's activities. Ideally, exhibitions will be designed to engage viewers in reviewing and analyzing video and film, educating them while enhancing their capacity to appreciate the visual arts. The two primary functions of the center's exhibition facility will be to hold public screenings on site and to provide outreach services to the community and region served by the center.

The absence of permanent locations throughout the country for screening independent film had been the primary obstacle in audience development. Whenever artists and entrepreneurs hold public screenings, African American filmmakers find themselves confronted with the public's seemingly insatiable thirst for high-quality, thought-provoking, independent cinema. Families especially appreciate such occasions, which allow them to see and respond to films together. Audiences become very involved when exposed to images and experiences that touch them significantly. Regular exhibitions held by the multimedia center will rapidly become an integral part of the community's cultural life.

Screenings will be held both at the center itself and on location throughout the region. The center will contain at least one 35 mm and one 16 mm film theater, each with a minimum of one hundred seats. Facilities will also include at least two portable 16 mm film theaters, each with a minimum of one hundred seats. In addition, facilities will feature at least two portable 16 mm film projectors and screens and four VCR/monitor systems. Showings will be heavily advertised in local media, with emphasis on African American-owned outlets.

Each center will develop its own series of film and video screenings. Suggested basic formats include the following:

1. Ongoing inhouse screenings that alternate classic and recent African American film and video productions.
2. Children's programs—screenings of internationally produced films designed to expose children to the lives and cultures of people throughout the world.
3. A traveling film screening van (the Cinemobile) able to screen programs to small audiences at any location.
4. Outreach exhibition services to churches, schools, community organizations, businesses, and residences (when practical) designed to ensure that worthwhile films and videos reach wide audiences.
5. Outreach screenings specifically for the elderly at nursing homes and community centers, designed to overcome the mobility limitations of this important segment of the population.

COLLECTIVE AND COLLABORATIVE PRODUCTION AND DISTRIBUTION

Among the primary long-term functions of our proposed multimedia center network would be (a) to pool financial resources so that more individuals and groups would be able to make low-budget films and (b) to operate as distributor for these films, sharing them among all centers and extending their reach into surrounding communities.

Low-Budget Cinema

The cost of making feature films in the United States has skyrocketed in recent decades. Mainstream Hollywood films today commonly cost more than $10 million to produce and distribute. It is almost impossible to make a feature film for less than $2–5 million (apart from distribution costs). However, many filmmakers are able to create short films and video productions for $1 million or less, and some have made "low-budget" feature films for similar costs. The public has proved itself willing to pay to see these films, especially when a body of diverse work is grouped under a common theme and presented as a festival or film series.

Low-budget films made by university students, aspiring professionals, and daring entrepreneurs have over the years proven to be fertile ground for new ideas and social commentary and have launched the careers of many well-known filmmakers and performers. The quality of a low-budget film is entirely up to the skills of the filmmaker, the storyteller. Many artists find themselves to be unexpectedly inventive when faced with budget constraints. The story becomes all, not the tricks used to tell it. African American filmmakers and those belonging to other minority groups in the United States and elsewhere have many important stories to tell. As many of these stories are in some way about hardship and deprivation, low-budget cinema truthfully reflects reality. Moreover, since many of the stories are about transcending externally imposed limitations, a story well told in a low-budget film is, in the cinematic sense, its own best argument.

We must learn to efficiently produce low-budget films. It takes perhaps more skill and preparation to creatively use the low-budget format than to spend the seemingly limitless cash available to a Hollywood film. Of course, filmmakers who can get the money, and who can use it to make truly worthwhile films, should certainly do so. My point is not to discourage African Americans from attempting high budget projects. Rather, my goal is to introduce the following idea: African Americans and people of African descent throughout the world must create a true alternative network through which we may extend our own ideas, images, and stories. Individuals and groups in each country or region (such as the Afro-Caribbean/Brazilian basin) should pool their resources to allow as many people to make films as possible. Collaborative financing of many projects will ultimately reward us more than selective financing of a few. This international network should then take on the task of distribution, ensuring the largest possible audiences at the greatest possible number of screening locations.

Distribution

It is imperative that we establish a truly alternative worldwide distribution system for work that emphasizes our common histories and our current sensibilities. Only by understanding what is common to all of us will we come to perceptively view those unique stories told by individual filmmakers from different Africa-descended cultures.

Our multimedia centers will be ideally placed to manage national and international film distribution. A fully functioning network of centers in the United States will be able to fulfill the following tasks:

1. Individual centers will (a) produce their own work and (b) enable independent entrepreneurs to produce low-budget films and videos. The centers will copy and share this work throughout the network. Centers will exploit to the fullest the low cost and availability of video as a distribution medium.
2. Centers will combine resources to produce and distribute worthwhile high-budget films and videos.
3. Centers acting in concert will have the financial capability to acquire and distribute selected mainstream films from both Hollywood and major international studios.
4. The network of centers will import and distribute the work of filmmakers of African descent from throughout the world and will export the product of African American filmmakers.

5. As a network, the centers will encourage groups in other countries to form similar organizations for like purposes.

The market for African and African American-created images and stories is open both within the United States and throughout the world. Here in this country, the media center network can encourage partnership among producers, distributors, and theater owners. African American individuals have always made films that would be commercially successful if screenings were targeted to the larger African American community. However, due to the lack of organized, committed distributors and exhibitors, many important and artistically valuable films and videos have been denied community-wide distribution. African Americans, unaware of these films, continue to consume largely alien cultural manifestations and distorted images of themselves—consumption that will ultimately deform our very human sensibility.

Production, distribution, and exhibition institutions have always played significant complementary roles, and the infrastructure has long been in place for them to collaborate efficiently. What we require is for individuals to act on the basis of our common cultural origin and collective economic necessity. African peoples have historically valued community and willingly put collective interests ahead of those of the individual. While we cannot hope to reverse the tide of purely individualistic, capitalistic action, we can act intelligently and compassionately within it, placing individual and corporate profit at the service of the betterment of the worldwide community of peoples of African descent.

International distribution of films and videos involves the inevitable recognition of our global economic interdependency. While economics will form the basis for any business partnerships, truly collaborative enterprises will, of necessity, forge themselves on the basis of common cultural origin and common current need. The media center network will help identify and nurture individuals with the vision, commitment, and professional skills to operate such enterprises and will attract aspirants from around the world.

CONCLUSION

We of African descent must challenge our own societies to see the importance of culture as a tool for the spiritual and material advancement of us all. This is equally true in Africa, where we are in the majority, and in the United States, where we will soon make up one-third of the nation. We must create institutions and encourage activities that raise our consciousness. Whatever our class, education, pigmentation, or sexual orientation, African peoples must each contribute to our living culture. We cannot continue to neglect our dynamic, inclusive, shared cultural heritage. We must empower ourselves and our art, celebrating both our common origins and our different experiences.

Individual intellectuals, doctors, lawyers, students, parents, politicians, storekeepers, and laborers as well as academic, social, and political organizations must sanction and encourage all forms of art that teach us about our heritage. If African Americans, as a people, choose to fail to see connections among the social and psychological problems of violence, teenage suicide and pregnancy, economic deprivation, illiteracy, and alienation, and if we fail to relate these problems to our fragmented heritage, then we neglect our own cultural imperative, and as a people we will disappear.

In traditional African societies, cultural institutions were held in the highest esteem. In some societies, they were represented by gods and goddesses. Domination from without replaced the power of our culture with the power of politics, replaced tradition with expediency. I strongly believe that all negative, demented, and self-destructive feelings shared by African peoples worldwide are subconscious reactions to the erosion of our cultural identity. We have long understood Eurocentric domination as essentially a war of cultural aggression. Its battlegrounds are those institutions wherein we acquire our individual sense of our collective identity. Future generations will understand and interpret our efforts in terms of whether we successfully express *artistically* our perceptions both of alienation and community.

Present conditions will never truly be transformed for African Americans as long as we are systematically closed out of those mainstream cultural institutions that put forth those images by which we define ourselves. In this regard, as I have stated, our best hope lies in simply circumventing those institutions by creating and supporting our own alternative networks. This is especially important with regard to the visual media industries of the twenty-first century. Without control of our own images, we will remain stereotypes, both to others and to ourselves. Without control, such powerlessness will only exacerbate our rage and intensify our inwardly and outwardly directed violence. The end results of Eurocentric domination of Afrocentric images will be horrible psychological scarring for *all* people and the polarization and regression of those few aspects of Western culture that have evolved toward true community.

Motion pictures, video, and other visual media comprise the most powerful tools for cultural enrichment currently available to humanity. Visual media technologies enhance the music and literature of a people, simultaneously coalescing communal identity and engendering social transformation. Through such experiences we may individually and collectively understand and transcend our fears, may grow in spirit and in health, and may attain states of compassion and human empathy undreamed of in past ages. Conversely, the power of images may be used to suppress knowledge, to indoctrinate people to false ideas, and to incite hatred and bigotry. We have the power to choose which of these we accept and which we allow others to promote.

African Americans must truly be owners, inventors, producers, distributors, and exhibitors of the images that define the African American cultural heritage. We *must not* imitatively reproduce deformed, substandard images. Rather, we must express imaginatively our highest senses of ourselves, both our collective strengths and our individual understandings. If we clearly comprehend this, we may then create, out of the visual arts, a true global cultural institution. We may then teach each other, and the rest of the world, those parts of our heritage that will benefit all peoples. As African Americans, and as people of African descent everywhere, we may then know that we have fulfilled our historical task of reawakening, reincarnating, and revitalizing the images of our ancestors, transforming our sense of ourselves and transcending the sins of history.

25 | *One-Third of a Nation: One Hundred Percent Ourselves*

Edmond Barry Gaither

N ear the end of the twentieth century, African Americans find themselves battling the tragic but enduring effects of pervasive racism, colonialism, and slavery. Racism, with its corrosive and bitter social perversions, remains alive as a malignant force, sometimes hidden behind apparent benevolence. European colonialism, having passed the apex of its global dominance, has left behind an aftermath of seriously distorted values, self-alienation, cultural debasement, and confused identity. Slavery, its formal institutionalization in this hemisphere having ended by the late nineteenth century, also left behind a lingering impact on the descendants of its victims. Many African Americans still suffer aborted initiative, ruptured lineage both literal and figurative, generalized cultural bastardization, and destroyed self-image. Like other peoples, especially those of the Third World, African Americans share the desperate need in this last decade of the century to regain control over the presentation, discussion, and interpretation of their own experiences, cultural imperatives, and lives.

Reflecting upon these concerns, we are able to distinguish clearly a series of problems that must be surmounted if African Americans are to recover the sense of positive identity necessary for psychological wholeness and for genuine, cogent, and authentic cultural expression.

Foremost among the problems African Americans face is the waning of identity as a distinct *community* and the resulting loss of a clear appreciation for our common interests. Although the most salient observation that can be made pertaining to black people in the

Americas is that the vast majority of them do live—and always have lived—in communities that are overwhelmingly African American. Still, we too often and too completely confuse *our* interests with those of the surrounding Eurocentric culture. Like Phillis Wheatley's testament in, "On Being Brought from Africa to America," we sometimes see ourselves through the eyes of others, although that view is contradicted by our objective condition. We undermine—perhaps even destroy—the development of our youth by our failure to foster cohesive social values that reward those who direct their energy toward collective growth. Our sense of mission often has no higher ambition than the acquisition of luxury goods as individual markers of prestige and privilege. We have prized individual success over collective advancement and thereby underdeveloped our communities.

At the international level, black people in young nations often relate themselves more closely to their former colonizers than to their fellow blacks who have shared experiences comparable to their own. In an era of internationalism, black people are still prone to cling to national identities without fully grasping the need to adopt a larger, global identity derived not just from common historical and cultural roots but also from the similar economic and political yokes we have borne. We must learn to see ourselves as an aggregate of vital communities with particular national experiences subsumed within a unified global African population.

It is important that African Americans remember that all peoples have lineages that give them a sense of place, a grounding in geography, and a body of shared experiences over time. From this fact comes the abiding need to acknowledge and extend both our direct and our symbolic legacies. Our heritage, no matter how we regard it, is constituted of a complex set of factors and experiences which we—and we alone—own. These cultural features are self-validating, requiring no external sanctions or acceptance. Culture is therefore our most essential source of identity, our garment against the wind, our core testament of our own humanity. Cultural heritage is an inseparable aspect of the matrix in which we are socialized. It is the source of our fundamental knowledge of language, values, social behavior, and the like. It is also the context in which both group and personal identities are formed and confirmed.

One of the consequences of slavery was the loss of a sense of ownership of one's self; a tendency to default on fully accepting the existential obligation of and responsibility for "being" as such. The question of manhood—a frequent theme in black literature and history—is profoundly related to this issue as it often evidences itself through assertive, sometimes violent reactions to oppressive confrontations, belittling encounters, and humiliating invisibility. Accepting the existential challenge of *being*, of owning one's self, empowers men and women to refuse to cower in the face of threats and assaults and to dare to use their own voices to interpret their own experiences from their own perspectives. Was this not the ultimate meaning of the life of Malcolm X? He dared "to be" without apology or retreat. His "being" itself intimidated those accustomed to self-effacement and deference in the behavior of blacks. In spite of Malcolm X's dramatic example, many African Americans still continually seek justification in relation to Eurocentric standards, as if their "value" is directly proportionate to the degree to which they adhere to Eurocentric standards.

Among the manifestations of our alienation from "self" are cultural forms that, instead of heralding our uniqueness and creativity, conform with perverse images that degenerate into mere commercial vehicles devoid of profound sentiment. African Americans' extraordinary musical gifts, for example, pander to immature sexuality even though black music has influenced virtually all other music of the modern era.

Across the nation, African American urban experiences are characterized by perceptions of pervasive welfare dependency. Self-destructive drug economics prevail because many African Americans refuse to assume responsibility for their own children, parents, and grandparents. We seem determined to remain supplicants and petitioners, rather than defining ourselves by our own positive actions. Self-respect eludes us because we are accustomed to cowardice, disguised as expediency. We discuss, pontificate, declare, and gesticulate regarding the abuses heaped upon us, but these actions are rhetorical devices that substitute for the braver action of simply "being," of accepting responsibility for ourselves, of exercising our own voices to celebrate our own realities in our own interests, and of creating our own art—for ourselves.

When African Americans become whole, our art will not only attain a new level of originality, it will also attain new truthfulness. Such growth and development, however, is impossible without institutional support. American society is an advocacy-driven society. Every successful initiative requires active supporters, advocates, marketers, and investors. These elements are given enduring direction and thrust by their incorporation into institutional forms.

Conversely, a major weakness in the cultural life of African Americans is the relative lack of strong cultural institutions. The African American community is certainly large enough, rich enough, and diverse enough to support a spectrum of cultural institutions, ranging from the casually informal to the exceedingly formal. Until a spectrum of such cultural institutions is forged and supported by African Americans, there can be no genuine flourishing of authentic black cultural expression, nor will the creation of a salient and sharp criticism and analysis of creative production thrive. Control over the meaning of black cultural life is inseparable from the establishment and support of strong institutions charged with the responsibility of fostering our heritage and *legacy* in the mix of competing cultural traditions that constitute America's artistic fabric. Of course, all institutions serving Americans and receiving direct or indirect public sector support have the obligation to serve black Americans well. Yet, it is abundantly clear that the unique history of black Americans also merits institutions dedicated to exploring the implications and meaning of black culture. These institutions should play a primary role in supporting scholarship, criticism, and communication pertaining to the direct and symbolic legacy of African people worldwide. Only such institutions can provide platforms from which appropriate criticism and scholarship—unsuspected of the taint of racism—can radiate.

What does appropriate criticism mean? Cultural criticism should have at least three qualities in order to be appropriate for the culture and art under scrutiny. First, it should be sympathetic to its subject matter. There should not be antipathy between the forms/traditions to be examined and the interests of the critic. Second, criticisms should derive, in a fundamental way, from the cultural matrix that spawned and sponsored the art under analysis. In this way, the aesthetic and other assumptions informing the creation of the art also inform the criticism of it. Third, critics should know the history and potential of the medium in which the art has been rendered.

Obviously, critics in general contribute significantly to the discussion of works of art, yet it is equally obvious that critics often espouse a point of view consistent with their institutional sponsors. It follows that black cultural institutions would offer more opportunity for scholars and critics sympathetic to the artistic life of the historic black world to generate a criticism that leads toward gaining control over the meaning of that creative production. Black cultural institutions therefore have a mandate to assure the continuation, expansion, and interpretation of black creative expression, with emphasis on the development of its proper criticism.

There is a close and parallel relationship between the preceding cultural concerns and the conditions characterizing the field of the visual arts. For example, the assumptions undergirding the launching of African American fine arts traditions in the eighteenth and nineteenth centuries align closely with the embracing of colonial values and directions. Early black American painters, for example, accepted Eurocentric aesthetic and technical painting models. They wanted to demonstrate that African Americans could match the same prevailing standards as white painters. Although they were occasionally interested in subjects related to the abolition movement, most preferred to work with neutral subject matter and to sidestep undue association—in their artwork—with the racial issues of the day. In the early twentieth century, with the emergence of large urban black communities, came an enhanced self-awareness expressed in the formation of what Alain L. Locke called the *New Negro*. Fundamentally, the New Negro was characterized by the declaration of a new and more aggressive identity—an identity that merged southern folk roots, African heritage, West Indian presence, and old northern communities in a fresh urban personality. The casting aside of earlier parochial identities for larger, more dynamic ones released the energy that was to fuel the Negro Renaissance era.

Directly expressive of the declaration of this new self-identity was the appearance of African and African American themes as the dominant subject matter for black artists. Desire to encounter African art firsthand, for instance, abounded. Some African American artists went to Haiti instead of France in pursuit of their artistic fulfillment. Later, in the 1960s, African American artists emphatically embraced and assimilated both technical and aesthetic influences from all parts of Africa and the African diaspora. It was clear that the more deeply African Americans sought to know themselves, the more distinctive and distinguished their artistic product was. An ancient and inexhaustible source had been found and successfully tapped, and it was changing the art of the black world.

The consolidation of these changes was secured by important, if not fully complete, institutional developments. Historically, black colleges had become, and remain, the largest repositories of the visual arts heritage of African Americans. These institutions, in spite of themselves, had also provided the bases for the earliest historians to address critically the black visual arts heritage. Alain L. Locke and James A. Porter both were professors at Howard University when they published their books on African American art. There was little evidence of sustained interest outside of the black colleges, where not only the historians were to be found but also many of the artists.

Recent decades have witnessed the birth and growth of museums dedicated to African American art, including the Museum of the National Center of Afro-American Artists in Boston, the Studio Museum in Harlem, the African-American Art Museum in Los Angeles, and others. In addition, many cultural and historical museums, such as the National Afro-American Museum and Cultural Center in Wilberforce, Ohio, have acquired or expanded permanent art collections. These museums, in combination with black-owned galleries and a growing body of scholars and critics, are authoritatively moving the discussion of African American art into new prominence.

These observations lead us to realize that the work of African Americans over the next decade consists of not only repossessing ourselves by reclaiming our collective heritage and accepting the existential freedom that comes with the donning of true selfhood; it also consists of advancing the discussion of African American art history from a defensive dialogue to a declarative one. We must gain new appreciation for the inner integrity of African American art and for the dynamic interplay through which it has taken shape. We must evolve an appropriate criticism and body of interpretations rooted in the experience from which the art springs. The African American visual arts heritage must be studied, not because it testifies to black humanity and not only because it highlights the many contributions of black artists to American art, but rather, because the art, like its makers, has its own value and vitality.

Contributors*

WALTER R. ALLEN is a Professor of Sociology at UCLA. He was formerly an Assistant Professor at the University of Michigan and the University of North Carolina. In 1987, he won the Distinguished Scholar Award from the American Educational Psychological Association. Dr. Allen is the author of *The Colorline and the Quality of Life in America* and numerous other publications.

URA JEAN OYEMADE BAILEY is the Executive Director of the Center for Drug Abuse Research, College of Medicine, Howard University and an Associate Professor in the School of Education at Howard University. She is the former Associate Director for Research of Howard University's Institute for Child Development and Family Life. Among her publications are *Project Head Start: Models for the 21st Century* (with Valora Washington) and "Prenatal Correlates of Neonatal and Infant Development." She received her B.S. from Southern University and her M.S. and Ph.D. from Tulane University.

WILLIAM ARTHUR BLAKEY is a Partner in the law firm of Dean, Blakey, and Moskowitz. He is the former Staff Director and Chief Counsel for the Subcommittee on Employment and Productivity of the Committee on Labor and Human Resources in the U.S. Senate. He is also former Staff Director for the Subcommittee on Post-Secondary Education of the Committee on Education and Labor in the U.S. House of Representatives. He is the author of "Public School Desegregation: Education, Equal Protection, and Equality of Opportunity" and "Legal Aspects of Access in Higher Education: History and Prospects for the Twenty-First Century."

*This listing reflects contributors' affiliations at the time of the conference or as updated by editors Bailey and Morris during the production process.

ANNIE BROWN is a Doctor of Social Work (DSW) student in the School of Social Work at Howard University. Her interests include African American adolescent mental health, social welfare history, and children and families.

JAMES EDWARD CHEEK is President Emeritus of Howard University (1969-1989). He is the former Commissioner of Education of the Virgin Islands. In 1970, he served as Special Consultant to President Richard Nixon on Black Colleges and Universities and on President Nixon's Commission on Campus Unrest. He is the recipient of the 1983 Presidential Medal of Freedom. He received his B.A. from Shaw University, his Master of Divinity from Colgate-Rochester Divinity School, and his Ph.D. from Drew University.

JAMES E. CRAIGEN is an Associate Professor in the School of Social Work at Howard University. He is also the President of Human Services Systems Associates and a consultant to Macro International. He is the former Policy Analyst for United Neighborhood Centers of America. He has been a Supervisor for the Church Association of Community Services. He received his B.A. from Morris Brown College, his M.S.W. from Atlanta University, and his Ph.D. from the University of Maryland.

ROBERT MICHAEL FRANKLIN is Program Officer at the Ford Foundation in the Rights and Social Justice Program responsible for grants to African American churches. His research focus is social ethics, psychology, and African American religion. He is a former Associate Professor of Ethics and Society, and Director of the Program of Black Church Studies at Candler School of Theology, Emory University. He is the author of *Liberating Visions*. He received his B.A. from Morehouse College, his Master of Divinity from Harvard Divinity School, and his Ph.D. from the University of Chicago Divinity School.

EDMOND BARRY GAITHER is the Director of the National Center of Afro-American Artists, Inc., located in Boston, Massachusetts.

OSCAR H. GANDY, JR. is an Associate Professor at the Annenberg School at the University of Pennsylvania. A former Associate Professor at Howard University, Gandy also previously served as Director of Howard University's Center for Communications Research. Among his published works are "Beyond Agenda Setting" and "Telecommunications and Privacy." He received his M.A. from the University of Pennsylvania and his Ph.D. from Stanford University.

LAWRENCE EDWARD GARY is a Professor in the School of Social Work at Howard University. He has acted as Director of Howard University's Institutes for Urban Affairs and Research, and has been a Samuel Wurtzel Professor at Virginia Commonwealth University. His research focus is on mental health and depression, African American men, and the African American family. His recent publications include "Major Depression in a Community Sample of African Americans," and "African American Males' Perception of Racial Discrimination: A Sociocultural Analysis Social Work Research."

HAILE GERIMA is an Associate Professor in the School of Communications at Howard University. He is also the President of Mypheduh Films. His films have received worldwide acclaim and distribution. His awards include a Guggenheim Fellowship, a Rockefeller Fellowship, and the Fipresci Film Critics Award. Among his publications are "Triangular Cinema, Breaking Toys and Dinkenesh vs. Lucy" and "Around the Fire." He received his B.A. and M.F.A. from UCLA.

CHERYL TOWNSEND GILKES is an Associate Professor of Sociology and African American Studies at Colby College. She was previously an Assistant Professor of Sociology at Boston University and an Instructor/Lecturer at Northeastern University. She was the recipient of the Service to Eastern Sociological Society award. Her areas of research include the empowerment of African American women. She received her M.A. and her Ph.D. from Northeastern University.

ROBERT BERNARD HILL is Director of the Institute for Urban Research at Morgan State University. He served as a Visiting Professor at the University of Pennsylvania, and was a Senior Research Associate at the Bureau of Social Science Research. Hill is also a former Director of Research for the National Urban League. His publications include *Research on the African American Family: A Holistic Perspective* and "Breaking the Cycle of Disadvantage: Toward a Comprehensive National Policy for Social Intervention." He received his B.A. from City College of New York and his Ph.D. from Columbia University.

SYLVIA T. JOHNSON is a Professor of Research Methodology at the Department of Psychoeducational Studies in the School of Education at Howard University. She is a former Special Research Assistant with the Iowa Testing Programs. She has also served as Assistant Professor at Western Illinois University. Her publications include "Test Fairness and Bias: Measuring Academic Achievement Among Black Youth." She received her B.S. from Howard University, her M.S. from Southern Illinois University, and her Ph.D. from the University of Iowa.

LAWRENCE N. JONES is the Dean of the Howard University School of Divinity. He was previously a Professor and the Dean of the Seminary at Union Theological Seminary. He was also the former Dean of the Chapel at Fisk University. He is a recipient of the Julius Rosenwald Fellowship and the Rockefeller Doctoral Fellowship. Among his published works are "Organized Religion Among Blacks" and "The Black Pentecostals: The Charismatic Movement." He received his B.S. from West Virginia State University and his Ph.D. from Yale University.

FAUSTINE C. JONES-WILSON is a Professor of Education in the School of Education at Howard University. She is also the Editor of the *Journal of Negro Education*. She is a former Associate Professor of Adult Education at Federal City College and a former Assistant Professor of Education at the University of Illinois-Chicago. She is the author of "The Changing Mood in America: Eroding Commitment?" and "A Traditional Model of Educational Excellence: Dunbar High School of Little Rock, Arkansas." She received her Ed.D. from the University of Illinois-Urbana.

LORENZO MORRIS is an Associate Professor of Political Science at Howard University. He has taught at the University of Chicago and MIT. His areas of research include black political behavior, education policy, and international affairs. He has conducted studies on black delegate participation at the Democratic and Republican national conventions and a study of the participants at the 1995 Million Man March. He is the author of several books and numerous scholarly articles.

CLARENCE G. NEWSOME is an Associate Dean at the Howard University School of Divinity. He was previously an Assistant Professor at the Duke Divinity School and Assistant Vice Provost and Dean of Minority Affairs at Duke University. His areas of research include the role and history of the Baptist Church and the religious life of Mary McLeod Bethune. Among his articles are "Black Baptists in America: Historical Overview" and "Mary McLeod Bethune: Missionary to America." He received his B.A., Masters of Divinity, and Ph.D. from Duke University.

WILLIE PEARSON, JR., is a Professor of Sociology and an Associate in Medical Education at the Bowman Gray School of Medicine at Wake Forest University.

ANNE REYNOLDS is an independent researcher and consultant with the Fairfax County Public Schools and the Office of Teacher Education at George Mason University. From 1988-1993, Dr. Reynolds worked as a Research Scientist in the Division of Cognitive and Instructional Science at the Educational Testing Service in Princeton, NJ. She received her Ph.D. from the School of Education at Stanford University. Dr. Reynolds' research interests center around teacher education and assessment.

CAROLYN STROMAN is an Associate Dean of the School of Communications at Howard University. A former Associate Professor in the School of Communications, Stroman has also served as Director of its Center for Communications Research. Among her publications are "Black Family Interactions and Imagery," "African American Women and AIDS," and "Television's Role in the Socialization of African American Children and Adolescents." She received her B.A. from Howard University, her M.S. from Syracuse University, her M.A. from Atlanta University, and her Ph.D. from Syracuse University.

BILLY J. TIDWELL is President and Chief Executive Officer of Data Deeds. He is the former Director of Research for the National Urban League and former Senior Researcher at Mathematics Policy Research. Among his publications are *The Black Report* and *The State of Black America 1995* (editor). He received both his B.A. in Social Welfare and his M.S.W. from the University of California – Berkeley, and his Ph.D. from the University of Wisconsin.

JOHN WALLACE is a Postdoctoral Scholar in the Institute for Social Research at the University of Michigan.

VALORA WASHINGTON is at the W. K. Kellogg Foundation. She is former Vice President for Research and Grants Administration and was previously a Professor of Education at Atioch College. She also served as the Associate Dean of Undergraduate Studies and an Associate Professor of Education at the American University. Among her publications is (with William Harvey) *Affirmative Rhetoric, Negative Action: The Status of Black and Hispanic Faculty in Higher Education.* She received her B.A. from Michigan State University and her Ph.D. from Indiana University.

STEPHEN J. WRIGHT is the former President of the United Negro College Fund and former President of Fisk University. He is retired as Vice President of the College Entrance Examination Board. He has received 12 honorary degrees from universities, including Howard University, Michigan State University, Notre Dame, and New York University. Among his articles are "The Black Colleges and Universities: Historical Background and Future Prospects" and "The Black Educational Policy Researcher: An Untapped National Resource." He received his B.A. from Hampton University, his M.A. from Howard University, and his Ph.D. from New York University.

INDEX